SPORT DIVING

BS·AC

SPORT DIVING

BS·AC

The British Sub-Aqua Club Diving Manual

Stanley Paul

London Sydney Auckland Johannesburg

Stanley Paul & Co Ltd
An imprint of the Random Century Group
Random Century House, 20 Vauxhall Bridge Road,
London SW1V 2SA

Random Century Australia (Pty) Ltd
20 Alfred Street, Milsons Point,
Sydney, NSW 2061

Random Century New Zealand Limited
191 Archers Road, PO Box 40-086
Auckland 10

Century Hutchinson South Africa (Pty) Ltd
PO Box 337, Bergvlei 2012, South Africa

First published 1959
Revised editions 1960, 1962, 1964, 1966, 1968, 1972,
    1975, 1976, 1977
Reprinted 1978, 1979, 1980, 1982, 1983
Revised editions 1985, 1987, 1988, 1990, 1991
Copyright © The British Sub Aqua Club 1959, 1960,
    1962, 1964, 1966, 1968, 1972, 1975, 1976, 1977, 1985,
    1987, 1988, 1990, 1991

Set in 9 on 10 Rockwell Light

Printed and bound in Great Britain by
    Butler & Tanner Ltd, Frome and London

British Library Cataloguing in Publication Data
Sport diving: the British Sub-Aqua club diving manual.
    1. Diving Sub-marine
    I. British Sub-Aqua Club
    797.2'3   GV840.S78

ISBN 0 09 163831 3

Also available
Safety and Rescue for Divers
Seamanship for Divers
Advanced Sport Diving

Contents

Figure 1

Foreword

The British Sub-Aqua Club is the governing body for sport diving in the United Kingdom and a leading member of the World Underwater Federation. From its inception, it has actively set out to promote underwater sport and related activities. By setting and maintaining the highest standards of education and training it has encouraged hundreds of thousands of people to take up sport diving in both United Kingdom and overseas waters with safety.

The British Sub-Aqua Club's diving manual has been the world's bible of safe sports diving practices for over twenty-five years. The eleventh edition carries on this influence. The manual has been written not only for current divers but also for those who would like to experience another and greater world. It is a practical introduction to the technique of the sport and all aspects of diving. It is easy to study and understand and the aim is to give the reader the basic knowledge to enjoy the undersea environment in a safe but enjoyable manner. The principles of safe diving are easily understood, the practice of safe diving requires proper training, constant attention to prevailing circumstances in the water and the modification of acquired techniques through the advance of knowledge and the introduction of new equipment. The British Sub-Aqua Club provides this training, our manual gives the essential background.

Many members have contributed to this manual through the sharing of their experiences, skills and the donation of significant time to what is a major publishing effort. We should all be grateful for their dedication to our sport and their desire to encourage more people to enjoy one of the most adventurous and exciting sports of our time.

I.A.N. Irvine
Chairman
BSAC

For many years The British Sub-Aqua Club's diving manual has been one of the world's recognized authorities on sports diving.

The BSAC is to be congratulated on the production of this fully updated edition.

It is a great pleasure for me to be asked to introduce this manual for what is a growing number of diving enthusiasts. I am sure it will continue to influence significantly the growth of this adventurous activity, and I am sure it will also provide me with extremely useful information on how to improve my own diving technique!

Charles.

Introduction

This book contains a wealth of information for the would-be sport diver, provided by distinguished contributors, each of whom backs his theoretical knowledge with an active, practical and successful expertise in the field of sport diving.

Learning to dive is but the beginning of years of fun. However, as no book can be a substitute for experience itself, the reader is advised to use this book in conjunction with the appropriate practical instruction provided by the British Sub-Aqua Club, BSAC schools and other recognized sport diver training agencies.

The authors' vast accumulation of experience and knowledge of sport diving cannot, of course, be compressed into a single book. Nevertheless, the authors believe that the information presented here will give the reader, in clear and exciting form, the essentials for safe and enjoyable diving. Further specialist publications on, for example, advanced diving, diver rescue, seamanship, equipment, underwater photography, underwater archaeology and marine biology are planned to complement this, the first in the series.

On almost every page a topic is presented in both words and pictures, and very often a single picture suffices to explain a particular technique or skill. The many hundreds of illustrations which form the basis of this book are often self-explanatory and convey information both vividly and simply. We hope that readers of all ages, even those to whom sport diving is quite new, will find the subject matter interesting and easy to understand.

Mike Holbrook
National Diving Officer

Acknowledgements

This eleventh edition of the British Sub-Aqua Club's Diving Manual is the product of many authors, all of whom are specialists in their particular section of the sport.

The British Sub-Aqua Club gratefully acknowledges the efforts of the following persons who have contributed to this publication:

Editors:
Mike Busuttili
Mike Holbrook
Gordon Ridley
Mike Todd

Contributors:
Mike Busuttili
Trevor Davies
Peter Edmead
Deric Ellerby
Jerry Hazzard
Mike Holbrook
Gordon Longworth
Peter Moir
Alistair Reynolds

Gordon Ridley
Dave Shaw
Nick Tapp
Dr Eric Thompson
Mike Todd
Reg Vallintine
Stuart Ward
Alan Watkinson
Dr Peter Wilmshurst
Barry Winfield

The Lure of Diving

People dive for different reasons. For some, the opportunity to enjoy a contrast to their everyday life is sufficient attraction. The undersea world is quiet; it allows movement in three dimensions; it supports a totally different range of plant and animal life; and it enables the diver to enter, for a brief period, another medium.

Many people are amazed at the profusion of life and colour found in the seas, not just in tropical waters but also around temperate coasts. Colours will often be muted by the filtering effect of water but can be instantly restored by an underwater lamp or a photographer's flashgun. The range of life which the diver can study underwater extends from the microscopic to the largest mammals on earth.

For other divers the fascination may be the search for evidence of man's passing, for much remains to be discovered in this least-explored part of our planet. The remains of ancient civilizations have been discovered and brought to the surface by divers in many parts of the world, filling in gaps in our knowledge of the ancient world and opening up many new avenues of research. Old ships hold a unique fascination for the exploring diver and also attract a wide variety of undersea life, making them perhaps the most enjoyable of dives.

Diving is not restricted to coastal sites or the seas; any appropriate body of water can be explored by the inquiring diver. Inland fresh-water locations have a quite different nature and often allow valuable experience to be gained closer to home before visiting the sea. Rivers can be rich in archaeological finds and some truly unique discoveries have been made in old wells.

For most of us in the civilized world the need to take a break, to get away for a while and experience new things, is very strong. Diving adds purpose to your travel and can bring new wonder and adventure to a holiday which other, less fortunate people may spend just lying on a beach. Diving can involve the whole family, a group of friends, the members of a club or new friends acquired during a stay at a diving centre.

For some, diving will become more than just a pastime. The world's increasing need to exploit the resources of the seas will involve more and more people in research and work under the surface in a wide range of occupations. Some will study the cycle of life in the sea and the part each organism plays within the system, while others will play a role in extracting the energy and mineral resources which lie below the seabed.

For all who dive, the sea will soon become a familiar place and their understanding of the world will become a little greater.

Figure 2 While diving a wreck in Scapa Flow, divers take time to feed a friendly wrasse

The Undersea Challenge

There are those who see diving as a recreation to be enjoyed in its own right. The sensation of travelling without weight through water is undoubtedly pleasurable and it will be a long time before this novelty wears off for the novice diver. However, the moment arrives when the diver's interests develop in one direction or another and diving becomes a means toward a more specialized approach to the underwater world.

An awakening interest in underwater life will often lead the inquiring diver to learn more about the creatures which he can observe so easily. This will lead to a better understanding of the order of life on the seabed and may even result in our developing diver finding a need to improve his photographic skills so that the creatures observed can be recorded and studied at leisure. An interest in a specialized area of marine life will sometimes involve study of a species over a period of time, involving diving in many different weather and tidal conditions. It will very often require travel to other locations to compare development of the species under study.

Thus an increased interest in a particular field will almost always increase the demands made on the diver. He will need to develop his skill and experience to match the situations and conditions in which he finds himself. A good grasp of the basic skills and an understanding of

Figure 3 Snorkelling down to explore a wreck in Canadian waters

the forces affecting the diver are essential.

The exploration of new areas and the search for the unknown is a main activity of many experienced divers. As you move farther from the swimming pool or the sheltered beach the need for a more fully developed ability in the water becomes clear. The better informed diver will be capable of planning dives in a wide variety of conditions. Experience will pay off when he has a purpose to follow during the dive and his basic skills have become virtually automatic.

The real challenge comes when you know there really is the chance of discovering something never before seen or perhaps lost beneath the waves for many years. Amateur divers have been responsible for many extremely significant discoveries in the fields of archaeology and biology. Some of the world's most prestigious underwater photographic awards have been won by dedicated amateur photographers. And many divers will tell you that they have never had so much fun, excitement, adventure and a sense of real achievement until they took up diving.

Diving offers a fascinating challenge; in return it asks that you respect the sea, ensure that you are properly trained for the diving you plan to do, that you equip yourself properly and maintain a level of fitness which will allow you to enjoy your diving with confidence.

Figure 4 Fish lose all their fear of divers, particularly if they feel there's a chance of food

Is Diving for You?

Sport diving is an activity that can be undertaken and enjoyed by practically anybody. The important qualification to this is that you will enjoy it more if you are aware of your own limitations, learn to recognize them and stay within them.

Diving can certainly offer you fun and adventure, and in return will ask that you learn to respect the safety rules and accept a degree of responsibility towards your companion divers. Diving is not a solitary pursuit; it is safer and more enjoyable when shared with others. There is an element of risk inherent in diving as in other adventure sports, but this risk is reduced to acceptable limits by the observation of basic safety disciplines and the acceptance of the need for sound training.

Diving will make certain physical demands on you, so it is important to maintain a good level of physical fitness. This does not mean athletic prowess or superhuman physical strength. The sort of fitness most useful to the diver is the ability to expend energy in a slow, controlled way, usually leaving some stamina in reserve for the unplanned emergency. The fit diver will also suffer less from the effects of cold or exposure to the weather. Although diving requires fitness, you will not improve your fitness if you treat it as an occasional pursuit; some additional form of exercise, even normal swimming, will usually prove beneficial.

Most of us do not live near to the most interesting diving locations, so we will need to travel in search of good diving. If you are the sort of person who soon gets bored with a traditional beach holiday, then diving is the answer to your prayer. Diving can add a new dimension to your holidays and will soon send you off around the coasts of your own country and abroad as you look for new underwater experiences.

Although you can enjoy escorted dives after a relatively short period of instruction, it will take more commitment if your aim is to become a competent diver. There is much to learn about the physics and physiology of diving, the technical aspects of diving equipment and the environment in which we dive. Once you are hooked on diving you will find yourself acquiring more knowledge while your confidence increases with further experience.

Most normally healthy people will be capable of meeting the demands of diving, but there are a few medical conditions that make diving inadvisable. The most important of these include epilepsy, mental illness, diabetes and a history of heart disease. Any doubts as to your medical suitability are answered by the medical examination required before commencing dive training.

If you are seeking true adventure, then there is unlimited potential in diving. However, true exploratory diving in little-known sites in unfamiliar areas is best undertaken by well-experienced, qualified divers. If you should choose to expose yourself to a higher degree of risk, then this must be balanced by greater competence and experience. In sport diving risk must be reduced to the minimum and this is achieved by staying within your capabilities.

Perhaps the most significant qualification for new divers is the combination of enthusiasm and curiosity that makes them want to find out more about the undersea world. Those who find comfort in the familiar and the everyday will find little to please them underwater, but those who are looking for a totally new experience will certainly find everything they seek in sport diving.

Figure 5 Jumping in at the start of a Scapa Flow wreck dive

Figure 6 Preparing to dive at a freshwater granite quarry

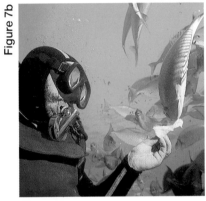

Figure 7a   Tropical waters offer a wealth of colour

Figure 7b   Fish feeding

Figure 7c   A giant basket sponge

Figure 7d   Diving a wreck in UK waters

Figure 7e   The Prince of Wales dives under polar ice

14

Figure 8a

Figure 8b

Figure 8c

Figure 8d

Figure 8a Pike *(Esox lucius)*

Figure 8b Angler fish

Figure 8c Sea anemone surrounded by brittle stars

Figure 8d Cuckoo wrasse

Figure 8e Anemone in Scottish waters

Figure 8f Plaice in mid-water

Figure 8g Mediterranean jellyfish

Figure 8e

Figure 8f

Figure 8g

Figure 9a

Figure 9b

Figure 9a French angel fish

Figure 9b Shoaling fish on an eel-grass bottom

Figure 9c Mediterranean red coral

Figure 9d

17

Figure 9c

Figure 9d A corner of a coral reef

Figure 9e Surgeon fish in Mexican waters

Figure 9e

Learning to Dive

Figure 10a

Figure 10b

Figure 10c

If we wish to enjoy the pleasures that diving can offer then we must first prepare ourselves for the adventure. There are skills that we must acquire and knowledge that we must gain before we can dive with confidence in open water. Sport diving is not a 'teach yourself' sport; you will need the help of qualified instructors.

Instruction

You can learn to dive in three main ways.

1. By joining a diving club, probably in your own locality, and attending its regular training meetings.
2. By going to a diving school which runs courses at a convenient centre at times which suit your requirements.
3. By visiting a diving centre which runs residential or holiday courses which allow you to combine learning to dive with a holiday.

In all cases the training will progress from initial lessons in the basic skills, which are carried out in a swimming pool or other sheltered water, through to training dives in suitable open water or in the sea. The training will be progressive in that you will learn important skills and become familiar with your equipment step by step until you are ready to bring your new skills together for the early dives.

Along with the practical lessons in the water, you will also learn about the effect that diving has on your body and how to avoid problems, together with how your equipment works and how to select the right equipment for your needs. The basic knowledge required in a diving course will be that contained in this book, which is designed to cover all the essential information needed up to the level of Advanced Diver.

The early lessons will introduce you to the basic equipment – fins, mask and snorkel – and to the aqualung and weight belt. Familiarity with these items is essential and this will include being able to clear any water which may leak into the mask or into the aqualung's mouthpiece. The ability to achieve neutral buoyancy, the desired weightless state, will be taught, and later this will be adjusted by means of a buoyancy compensator/lifejacket.

Figure 10a   New divers start by learning correct finning technique

Figure 10b   Further information is absorbed in classroom lessons

Figure 10c   The group learns to use the aqualung

The course will then teach you how to handle an aqualung and how to remove it in the water and refit it, together with the important maintenance and dismantling procedures. You will learn about the 'buddy system' and gain specialized life-saving skills which will allow you to bring assistance to your partner in an emergency. Soon you will be ready to continue your training in open water with full equipment and to gain an appreciation of how diving is organized.

The Early Dives

The diving course will start in shallow protected areas where you can become familiar with the full equipment and learn the essential safety procedures which allow us to enjoy diving. With the experience of a few dives you will soon be enjoying the sensation and exhilaration of diving in open water. Your awareness of marine life will grow as you become more familiar with nature's tricks of camouflage and colouring. Under the supervision of qualified divers and instructors, you will broaden your experience and ability and progress first through the Novice Diver grade, and then to Sports Diver.

Further Training

As your experience grows and you receive more instruction you can gain the Dive Leader qualification, which allows you to take novices for dives. Your next aim would be the Advanced Diver grade, which indicates that the holder is capable of organizing groups of divers and ensuring the safe and successful conduct of diving expeditions. This is a sound base for gaining more specialized knowledge and experience in related fields. Other courses are available in subjects like boat handling, navigation, life saving and rescue, compressor operation, VHF radio use, and many others. Many divers aim to improve their ability as instructors and enjoy the satisfaction of teaching others. Three grades of instructor qualification are available following the appropriate special training and experience.

Figure 11a

Figure 11b

Figure 11c

Figure 11a   Training moves to open water

Figure 11b   Briefing the diving group

Figure 11c   The first dive

The Oceans

The oceans are where most diving takes place and a simple understanding of their characteristics should be of interest to all divers.

The oceans cover 71 per cent of the earth's surface, or 355 million square kilometres (139 million square miles), so perhaps our planet should be called 'Ocean' rather than 'Earth'! The major oceans comprise the Pacific, the Atlantic, the Indian and the Arctic; the large seas such as the North Sea, the Mediterranean, the Baltic and the Bering Sea are also included in this category.

Figure 12a   Oceans of the world
Figure 12b   Seabed features

Origins

The solar system condensed out of interstellar gas and the primitive earth became a ball of molten rock, which solidified as it gradually cooled. Over a long period of time, numerous volcanoes and hot rocks discharged many gases, including water vapour, into the atmosphere. With further cooling, this changed to liquid water and built up into the primitive ocean.

Being lighter, the continents floated on the molten rock of the earth's mantle. Circulation currents in the mantle caused the continental plates to move very slowly around the earth's surface. When they collided, major mountain chains were thrown up. The plates were (and still are)

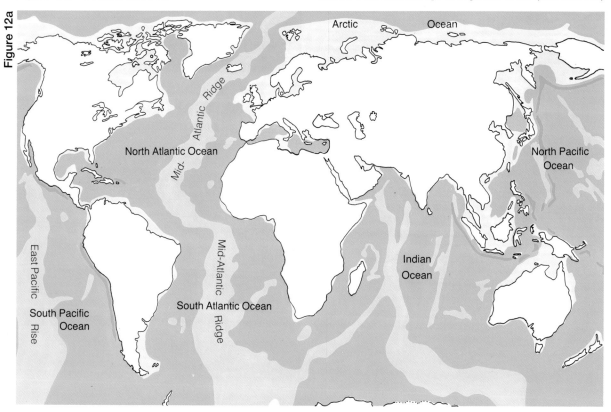

Figure 12a

Arctic Ocean

Mid-Atlantic Ridge

North Atlantic Ocean

North Pacific Ocean

East Pacific Rise

Mid-Atlantic Ridge

Indian Ocean

South Pacific Rise

South Pacific Ocean

South Atlantic Ocean

Continental Shelf

Abyssal Plains

Mid-ocean Ridges

Deep Trenches

pushed apart by new material from the mantle upwelling along the midoceanic ridges.

Seabed Features

The average depth of the oceans is about 4000 metres, but this is far from uniform. Where plates are pushed under one another beneath the ocean, usually near the continental edges or island arcs, an oceanic trench is formed which can be almost three times as deep as the 3000–4000 metres of the abyssal plain. These abyssal plains stretch under the oceans for huge distances, until either a midocean ridge or a continent is reached. The plain then rises at an angle of about 5 degrees up the continental slope to the edge of the continental shelf (at a depth of about 200 metres). It is the shallower portions of this shelf, of course, that are of interest to divers.

The Midocean Ridge, with a length of 65,000 kilometres, is the biggest geological feature on the surface of the earth. Its general depth ranges between 2000 and 9000 metres. Associated with it are many smaller areas of rugged seabed and much geological faulting. There are also isolated sea mountains (called guyots) and oceanic islands formed by previous volcanic and tectonic activity.

The abyssal plains are largely covered with fine sediments, which blanket many smaller underlying features.

Figure 12b

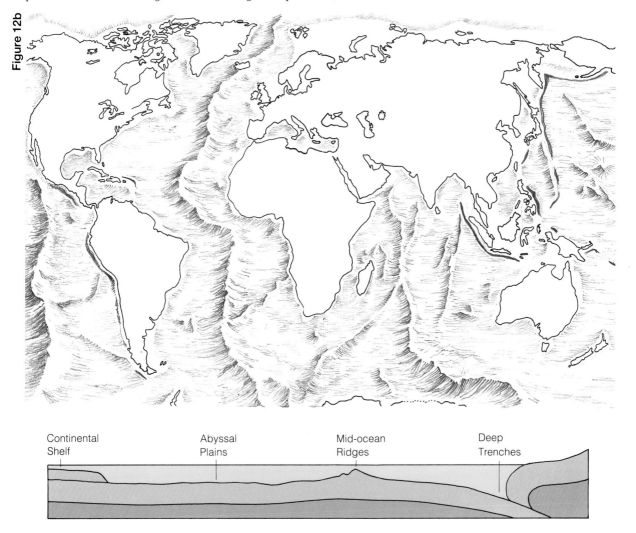

| Continental Shelf | Abyssal Plains | Mid-ocean Ridges | Deep Trenches |

We have seen a little of how the oceans of the world were formed and also something of their present structure. As divers, we should also take an interest in the ocean water in which we mostly dive.

What makes the sea behave in the way it does? Why do the tides rise and fall? What are the mechanisms of the currents? Why do waves have their characteristic shape?

Sea water Composition

Simply stated, sea water is a dilute solution of common salt or sodium chloride. The concentration in midocean is about 3.5 per cent (usually stated as 35 parts per thousand), although this can drop much lower in almost land-locked seas where fresh-water run-off can lead to the formation of *haloclines*. Other factors can affect salinity, e.g. evaporation, freezing, melting, and precipitation.

In addition to sodium chloride, sea water contains small amounts or traces of eighty other elements.

Temperature

Surface temperatures in the oceans range from −2 degrees C in polar waters to about 30 degrees C in tropical waters.

Geographical and seasonal differences in sea temperature determine to some extent when and where diving is most enjoyable. Superimposed upon these broad climatological features are rapid fluctuations caused by weather changes, such as wind speed, humidity, air temperature and cloud cover.

The most striking feature of the temperature structure of the surface layer of the sea is the *thermocline*. This marks the interface between waters of markedly different temperatures. A diver can detect the presence of a thermocline by feeling the sharp temperature difference, by seeing changes in the refractive index or by observing mixing eddies. The different water layers can have varying plankton or suspended-particle concentrations, thus visibility can vary markedly between the layers.

Waves

The decision as to whether to dive or not is frequently reduced to an assessment of whether it is too rough for the diving boat to put to sea.

Waves are created by the wind, and stronger winds give longer and higher waves. After a storm in the Atlantic Ocean, for instance, waves travel out from the storm centre. The longer waves travel fastest across the ocean surface and arrive at eastern Atlantic shorelines to herald the coming of rough seas and stormy weather.

Wave structure

A deep-water wave travels by virtue of a circular motion of the water near the surface and its speed decreases with depth. This explains why a diver at 30 metres, say, can be quite unaware of the development of a rough sea.

The energy of a wave is spread through a layer of water whose depth is comparable with the wavelength. When waves approach shallow water, this energy is concentrated into the available depth, making the height increase and the speed decrease, both of which increase the steepness of the wave. This increase in wave height is known as *groundswell*. In the end, the wave becomes so steep that it breaks, either by plunging over in a graceful arc or in a less spectacular spill down the leading edge. The deceleration of the water bends the waves so that they tend to run up a beach square on, regardless of their original direction.

Ocean Circulation

The oceans of the world are in continual motion and this circulation strongly follows the prevailing winds. This is to be expected, as the wind provides the motive force for the major surface currents, although water temperature, atmospheric conditions and the rotation of the earth also have considerable effects. Equatorwards flows are generally slow and broad, while polewards flows are rapid and concentrated near the western margins of ocean basins.

Figure 13 A wave accumulates energy as it travels across the ocean

Under sea ice, water becomes so dense by cooling and the addition of salt drained from the ice above that it sinks to the bottom of the ocean. Where this occurs beneath the Antarctic ice shelves the cold bottom water spreads northwards and eastwards along the ocean floor. Arctic bottom water flows south out of the Arctic basin.

Tides and Tidal Streams

In addition to this ocean circulation, there is a 'bulge' of water, caused by the gravitational pulls of the sun and moon, through which the earth continually rotates. This causes tides and tidal-stream patterns, which are explained on page 168.

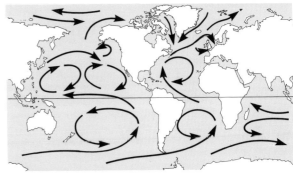

Figure 14 Direction of main currents

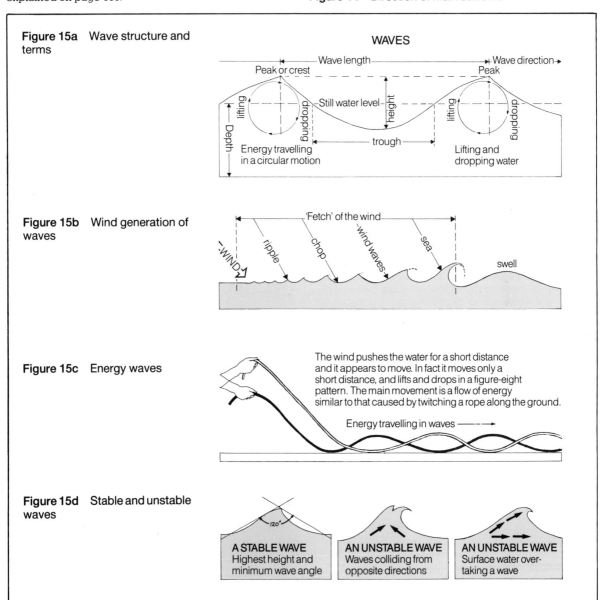

Figure 15a Wave structure and terms

WAVES

Figure 15b Wind generation of waves

Figure 15c Energy waves

The wind pushes the water for a short distance and it appears to move. In fact it moves only a short distance, and lifts and drops in a figure-eight pattern. The main movement is a flow of energy similar to that caused by twitching a rope along the ground.

Energy travelling in waves ──→

Figure 15d Stable and unstable waves

A STABLE WAVE
Highest height and minimum wave angle

AN UNSTABLE WAVE
Waves colliding from opposite directions

AN UNSTABLE WAVE
Surface water overtaking a wave

The History of Diving

Human beings have been diving since primitive man was forced to forage for food in the sea. In the past the recovery of valuables from shipwrecks provided the impetus for a number of experimental diving devices, culminating in two successful forms: the diving bell, in which workers could spend periods submerged, and the diving helmet, invented by John Deane of Whitstable in 1820.

The history of sport diving can be traced more directly to the invention of the first autonomous diving apparatus which did not require lines and air hoses to the surface. This new concept was pioneered by William James, an Englishman, who, in 1825, produced a workable design in which compressed air was carried in a circular iron reservoir around the diver's waist. We have no record of James diving and so the credit for the first independent apparatus that was actually used must go to an American, Charles Condert, who built and used a horseshoe-shaped waist-mounted air reservoir which provided a continuous flow of air to a flexible helmet. Condert dived with this equipment many times in New York's East River before suffering a broken air tube and a quick death in 1832.

The next breakthrough was made by two Frenchmen, Rouquayrol and Denayrouze, in 1865 whose lightweight design included a metal canister charged to a pressure of 40 bars and carried on the diver's back. Their most important invention was a demand regulator which enabled the diver to valve his air at the same pressure as the surrounding water. The apparatus was marketed for sponge and wreck diving.

With the development of high-pressure cylinders, more experiments using compressed air took place. Louis Boutan, a French pioneer underwater photographer, produced an air-breathing set with a cylinder charged to nearly 200 bars, but it fell to those ingenious entrepreneurs, the Japanese, to market 'Ohgushi's Peerless Respirator', patented in Britain in 1918.

Another important pioneer was Commandant Yves Le Prieur of the French Navy, who was the first to consider amateur sport diving in the sea. He produced a lightweight compressed-air apparatus with a regulator that was not quite fully automatic. He initially used the equipment with goggles and later with a full face mask. In 1935 he founded the first diving club to train with his apparatus in Paris.

The development of modern masks, fins and snorkel tubes was due to the breath-holding underwater fishermen who operated in the South of France in the 1920s and 1930s. The first of these was an American, Guy Gilpatrick, who inspired both Hans Hass and Jacques Cousteau. Gilpatrick used a pair of old flying goggles, plugged with putty and painted over. His Russian friend, Karamarenko, produced the first rubber mask with a single-pane window. Fins were patented by de Corlieu in France in 1929. The first successful snorkel tube was used by Steve Butler, an Englishman. The development of the basic equipment was therefore a joint effort by Americans, Russians, Frenchmen and Englishmen.

The first fully automatic aqualung was developed by a young Frenchman, Georges Commeinhes. The twin cylinders were used with a full face mask and air escaped from a special valve instead of around the edges of the mask. The demand valve was mounted between the shoulderblades and the set had a pressure gauge. The cylinder pressure was 150 bars. The equipment was approved by the French Navy in 1937, but Commeinhes was killed in the war in 1944. Hans Hass, who had met Gilpatrick in 1937, decided to photograph and film underwater and led his first expedition in 1938 using homemade helmets. His books and films, finally shown after the war, were the first to inspire amateur divers in Britain. Jacques Cousteau, another French Navy officer, had also been working to develop an efficient aqualung after being introduced to the sport by his compatriots Philippe Tailles and Frédéric Dumas. In 1942 he combined with engineer, Emile Gagnan, to produce a new regulator with an inlet and exhaust tube that was fully automatic. The modern aqualung was born.

British Diving and the British Sub-Aqua Club

A British sportsman, Colin McLeod, had used mask, fins and snorkel tube in the South of France while recuperating from wartime flying operations. After the war he became a director of Lillywhites in London and in 1947 imported the first frogman's fins into England. The aqualung had become available in 1950 and a number of

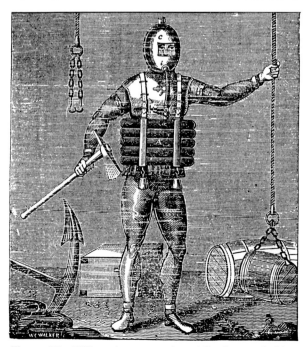

Figure 16 William James produced the first workable design for an autonomous diving apparatus

clubs and schools were formed, the first being the British Underwater Centre run by another RAF officer, Trevor Hampton. By 1953 there were two clubs in London, the Underwater Explorers Club and the British Sub-Aqua Club. The BSAC had been formed by Oscar Gugen, a farsighted businessman, helped by Peter Small, an enterprising journalist. The Underwater Explorers Club collapsed, but the BSAC continued to grow.

The first issue of the club's magazine, *Neptune,* appeared in 1954 and described the diving centres run by Trevor Hampton at Dartmouth and Brud Martin in Kent. The BSAC also ran a diving holiday supervised by its first training officer, Jack Atkinson. Soon after the BSAC had been formed under the chairmanship of Oscar Gugen, Peter Small suggested that the club should form branches. The idea was approved and a national committee was formed, the original members in London becoming the London (No. 1) Branch. The second branch soon formed in East Lancashire and the third and fourth at Bristol and Blackpool. Peter Small became the first national secretary and editor of *Neptune* (later to become *Triton* and *Diver*). The club grew steadily. Members received the new diving manual and the magazine in return for the portion of the subscription that went to the general committee. The BSAC was recognized as the governing body of the sport by the Central Council of Physical Recreation in 1955 and by 1956 had 2000 members. The training programme was established, branches qualifying members as Third or Second Class divers and First Class being awarded by national examination. In 1957 local enthusiasts formed the club's first overseas branch in Jamaica. In 1958 Oscar Gugen gave up the chairmanship to concentrate on helping to form the World Underwater Federation (CMAS). By the end of 1958 the club had 3000 members in sixty-five branches. They helped local authorities and police by recovering bodies and surveying reservoirs. In 1959 Alan Broadhurst, who followed Jack Atkinson as Club Diving Officer, helped Douglas Balaam to form the first BSAC federation – Norfed.

In 1962 Colin McLeod, who followed George Brookes as chairman, organized a highly successful world congress for the new World Federation. Sadly, Peter Small lost his life in a deep-diving experiment using new gas mixtures. From 1963 to 1969 the club was led by Harry Gould, who persuaded the Sports Council to finance a full-time national coach, Brian Booth. By this time the administration of the club was handled by an administrative agent and diver, Major Hume Wallace. In 1968 the Sports Council financed a full-time club director, Reg Vallintine, with an office in London, and nine part-time regional coaches led by the national coach, John Towse, who was followed by Jeremy Hazzard. During these years the membership rose sharply from 9000 in 1968 to 35,000 in 1986. The BSAC had become the biggest diving club in the world.

Figure 17 The Rouquayrol and Denayrouze

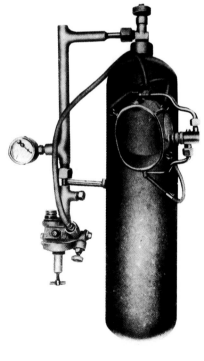

Figure 18 The Ohgushi breathing apparatus was connected to an air cylinder charged to 150 bars pressure

Basic Physics

Air

Atmospheric Pressure

The earth is surrounded by a layer of air which we call the atmosphere. Air is a mixture of gases and, like all matter, has mass. A mass exerts a force on those things which lie beneath it and at sea level the atmosphere presses down with a force of approximately 1 kilogramme for every square centimetre of the earth's surface.

Atmospheric pressure = 1 kgf/cm^2 (approx.)

In diving, it is customary to use the simple measure of '1 bar' to describe the earth's atmospheric pressure at sea level. This is an approximate figure.

Atmospheric pressure = 1 bar or 1 kgf/cm^2 (approx.)

Atmospheric pressure varies slightly with changes in weather and decreases with altitude, until it reaches zero at the extreme outer limits of the atmosphere. At about 45,000 metres above sea level, for example, the atmospheric pressure is about 0.05 bar.

Our bodies do not suffer in any way from this pressure, which is applied to every square centimetre of their surface – we are born to it!

Gauge and Absolute Pressure

When pressure is to be measured it is normal practice to relate it to atmospheric pressure. Thus a simple gauge would read zero when in fact the atmospheric pressure is 1 bar. An aqualung cylinder pressure gauge might read 200 bar, but this really means 200 bar above the normal atmospheric pressure of 1 bar. Such a reading is known as 'gauge pressure'. If the gauge were calibrated to true zero as found in space or in a vacuum, it would read 201 bar – the extra bar being atmospheric pressure. Such a gauge reading is termed 'absolute pressure'.

Absolute pressure = gauge pressure + atmospheric pressure

In diving physics, it is normal to work in terms of absolute pressure.

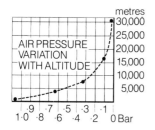

Figure 19a

Figure 19b

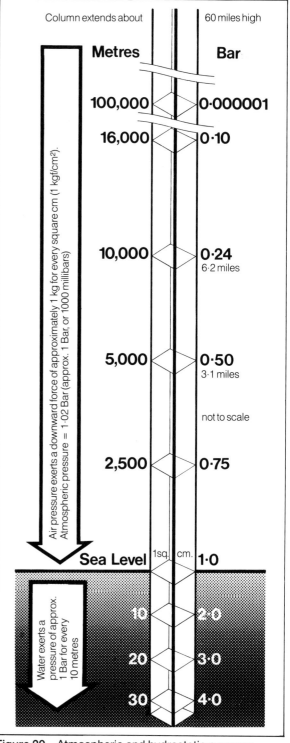

Figure 20 Atmospheric and hydrostatic pressure

Composition of Air

The air which makes up the atmosphere, and which we breathe, comprises:

> nitrogen (N_2) 79 per cent (say, 80 per cent or 4/5)
> oxygen (O_2) 21 per cent (say, 20 per cent or 1/5)

There are traces of carbon dioxide (CO_2) and other gases, but these occur in such small quantities that they can be safely ignored.

The body uses oxygen in its metabolism (see p. 78). Nitrogen is an inert gas which serves no useful purpose in the body. However, as it constitutes almost four-fifths of the air we breathe, it is present in all body tissues and under certain conditions has noticeable effects on the diver (see p. 100).

Compressibility

All gases, including air, are compressible, having neither shape nor volume. On the other hand, liquids have a definite volume and mass and may be regarded as incompressible at the pressures we are considering.

Air Density

Air becomes denser (thicker) at depth and a diver using breathing apparatus encounters a slight increase in breathing effort when deep. Modern aqualungs are designed to minimize the effects of increased air density, but it can be a problem if a diver is expecting to undertake hard work at depth.

Water

Water Density

Water is a very dense medium compared with air. Sea water is slightly more dense than fresh water. Because of water's great density, its resistance to body movement is considerable. Movements should be slow and deliberate, and the diver should swim through the water so as to present the minimum frontal area and resistance.

Hydrostatic Pressure

Being a dense medium, water exerts a noticeable pressure upon anything immersed in it. Water pressure increases rapidly with depth and a cubic metre of water (1000 litres) has a mass of 1000 kg or 1 tonne. Some fairly simple arithmetic will reveal that, if our cubic metre is divided up into 1-metre-high columns, each of 1 square centimetre cross-section, the mass of water in each centimetre column is 0·1 kg. If each 1-centimetre-square column were extended to 10 metres in height, the mass of water would be 1 kg and the pressure exerted by it would be 1 kg force per square centimetre (1 kgf/cm^2).

It has already been explained that atmospheric pressure presses down with a force of 1 kg for every square centimetre of the earth's surface. So at 10 metres beneath the surface, the water pressure or hydrostatic pressure is equivalent to the atmospheric pressure at the surface. At 10 metres the water exerts the same force as 1 bar gauge pressure or 2 bar absolute, and for every further descent of 10 metres beneath the surface the hydrostatic pressure increases by another bar. Thus at 30 metres the absolute pressure is 4 bar, at 50 metres 6 bar, and so on.

In air and water – especially in water – pressure has the property of acting in all directions. Thus, 30 metres down, a body is subjected evenly to 4 bar absolute pressure over its whole surface and from all directions. For example, the pressure in an underwater cave at 30 metres is still 4 bar, the pressure being transmitted horizontally through the water.

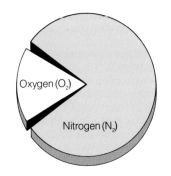

Figure 21
Composition of air

Since the human body consists largely of fluids, an increase in the hydrostatic pressure does not result in a decrease in volume. Problems occur, however, in body airspaces when a diver descends and is subjected to increasing water pressure.

It is necessary to study the behaviour of airspaces underwater, whether they are within the diver's body or part of his equipment, and to see how they behave as pressure changes.

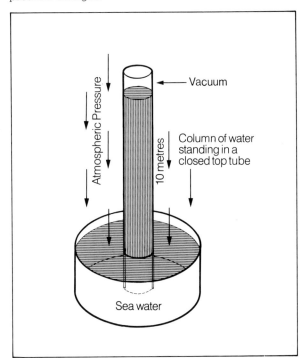

Figure 22   10m water column supported by atmospheric pressure

Gases under Pressure

Pressure/Volume Changes

Since gases are compressible, the space (volume) they occupy will be reduced if the pressure is increased and enlarged when the pressure is decreased. If changes in pressure are the result of descent or ascent while diving, the air pressure within an airspace will always seek to remain equal to ambient pressure. The volume will change while the pressure remains equal to ambient pressure.

Thus, an inverted open-ended container full of air at the surface, where the pressure is 1 bar absolute, will appear half full of air at a depth of 10 metres, where the total pressure is 2 bar absolute, and only one-quarter full at 30 metres, where the total pressure is 4 bar absolute.

During ascent, the air will expand in volume as the ambient pressure falls and, on reaching the surface, it will have expanded to fill the container once again. Note that the greatest pressure and volume changes occur between the surface and 10 metres. On descent to 10 metres, pressure doubles and volume is halved. For every further 10 metres thereafter, the pressure and volume changes are smaller. On ascent, the reverse applies.

If the container were filled with air at depth, the air would expand on ascent and the surplus would escape from the inverted mouth of the container. If a closed but flexible air container were used rather than an open inverted one, it would start off full at the surface, but it would progressively collapse as it was taken deeper.

If it were filled with air at depth, sealed and returned to the surface, volume would increase as pressure fell. It would expand to the limits of the material and then rupture, as the internal pressure tried to remain equal to ambient water pressure. This pressure/volume relationship is Boyle's Law, a relationship first recorded by the physicist of that name. In diving, it is a fundamental physical relationship which cannot be ignored. Divers encounter the effects during training and diving, whether snorkelling or using an aqualung. Any compressible airspace, whether in the diver's body or equipment, will change its volume in proportion to pressure during descent and ascent; and if pressures in the body's rigid airspaces are not kept equal to ambient pressure, injury or damage of some sort will occur.

Partial Pressure

It has been explained that air comprises approximately 80 per cent nitrogen and that atmospheric pressure is 1 bar. It is correct to assume, therefore, that nitrogen is responsible for 80 per cent of atmospheric pressure and oxygen for the remaining 20 per cent. In a mixture of gases the total pressure is equal to the sum of partial pressures which each gas would have if it alone occupied the available space. The physicist Dalton discovered this state of affairs, and Dalton's Law of Partial Pressure was established to describe it.

It is normal to use the prefix 'pp' to indicate partial pressure, thus:

> pp N_2 = 80 per cent of 1 bar = 0·8 bar
> pp O_2 = 20 per cent of 1 bar = 0·2 bar
> Total pressure of air = 1·0 bar

Partial pressure increases in direct proportion to absolute pressure. For example, at 30 metres (4 bar absolute) the pp nitrogen is 3·2 bar and the pp oxygen is 0·8 bar.

The significance of partial pressure in diving concerns the toxic effects which various gases can have on the body at elevated pressures. Even oxygen, essential for life, can have adverse effects if breathed at a partial pressure in excess of 2 bar absolute.

One hundred per cent oxygen breathed at depths in

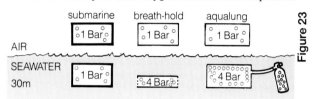

Figure 23

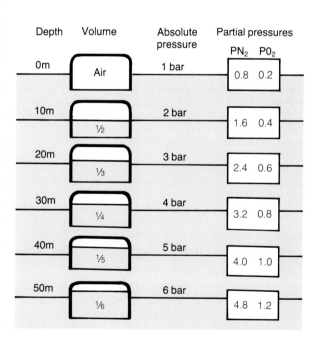

Figure 24   Boyle's Law

Figure 25   Water pressure will collapse a sealed container

excess of 10 metres (2 bar absolute) can lead to oxygen poisoning. When breathing air, the pp oxygen can reach 2 bar absolute at a depth of 90 metres (10 bar absolute). Carbon monoxide (CO) is a contaminant sometimes found in air. It is highly toxic (see p. 99). At atmospheric level the body can safely withstand 10 parts per million (p.p.m.) of CO, but if the same air were breathed at 50 metres (6 bar absolute) the effect on the body would be the same as breathing 60 p.p.m. at the surface – a dangerous level of poisoning.

Solubility of Gases

Wherever there is an interface between gases and a liquid, gas will dissolve in the liquid. The amount which dissolves is dependent on various factors, the main one being the partial pressure of the gas. As pressure increases so more gas will dissolve. When pressure falls, the situation is reversed and gas will be released from the liquid, appearing as bubbles. This relationship is governed by Henry's Law of gas solubility.

Everyday examples of gas dissolved in a liquid and the effects of its sudden release can be found in aerated drinks. Bottled or canned drinks have carbon dioxide dissolved in them. If the drink is opened rapidly the release of gas can be violent enough to cause aerated liquid to rush from the container.

The significance of this gas law to the diver is that it explains two important functions: first, the uptake of oxygen by the blood and the release of carbon dioxide from it – an exchange which happens virtually instantly and continuously; second, the absorption/release of nitrogen by/from the blood and tissues on descent/ascent, when the ambient pressure of air in the lungs is increasing/decreasing. Descent is not the problem – it is on ascent that absorbed nitrogen can cause trouble to the diver, especially if its rate of release from body tissues is rapid. Nitrogen bubbles can actually form in certain tissues, giving rise to the various problems of decompression sickness (see p. 104).

Effects of Temperature

While temperature underwater may be considered relatively constant, air temperature can vary considerably throughout the course of a day. If a gas is heated, it will either increase its volume or its pressure will increase if the volume is constrained. This relationship is known as Charles' Law.

Charged aqualung cylinders should not be left in the hot

Figure 28   Archimedes' principle

sun, where their pressure will steadily increase until it possibly exceeds the safe working pressure of the cylinder. Inflatable boats should be slightly deflated if they are to be left in strong sunshine.

Buoyancy

Any object immersed in water will receive an upthrust equal to the weight of water it displaces (i.e., whose volume it occupies). This is the basis of Archimedes' Principle.

If the weight of the immersed object is less than the weight of water it displaces, it will float (positive buoyancy). If the weight is greater, it will sink (negative buoyancy). An object whose weight is the same – or is capable of being adjusted until it is the same – will neither float nor sink. It will have neutral buoyancy.

Since the body contains a lot of water, the weight of the average unclad human body almost exactly matches the weight of water it displaces when immersed. Slight differences can usually be accommodated by varying the depth of breathing – exhale, reduce lung volume, displace less, sink, and vice versa. By varying the volume of the body, its buoyancy will also vary.

A diver is able to vary his volume (by adjusting his depth of breathing or the equipment he uses) and therefore the amount of water displaced, so that it matches his own total weight, leaving him in a state of neutral buoyancy (weightlessness) while underwater.

Air is an easily packaged and very buoyant gas, and is regularly used to adjust or achieve buoyancy underwater.

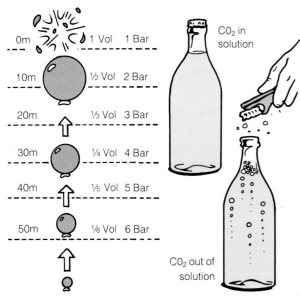

Figure 26   Relationship between pressure and volume

Figure 27   Solubility of gases in liquids

Vision/Light

Magnification

A diver's mask allows the eyes to operate in their normal medium of air. Without an airspace, eyes cannot focus and vision will be blurred. Light rays, passing from water into air, are bent, causing objects to appear about 33 per cent larger and 25 per cent closer to the viewer. Until he gets used to a slightly magnified outlook on the underwater world, the beginner may find this a little confusing.

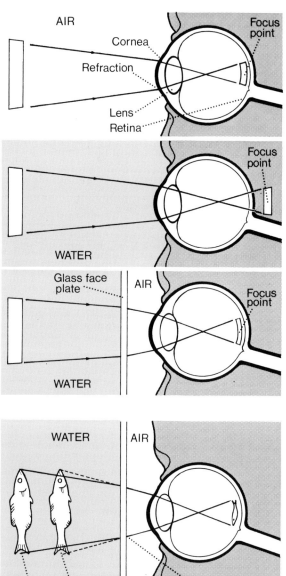

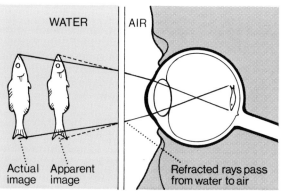

Figure 29   Focusing of the eye in air and underwater

Light Absorption

Light is both absorbed and scattered by water. Daylight is made up of different colours, each of which is absorbed at a different depth. Since each colour is part of the total light entering the water, as depth increases, less light remains to penetrate. Reds are the first to go, with only blue light reaching great depths. Colour can be restored by use of artificial light.

Light Scattering/Diffusion

Light will also be blocked and scattered by particles suspended in the water, which prevent it penetrating to great depths.

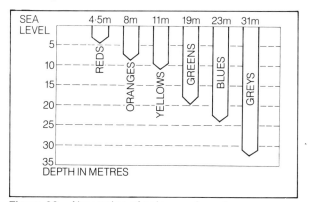

Figure 30   Absorption of colour underwater

Sound

In air and at normal temperatures, sound travels at approximately 350 metres/second. Underwater, it travels much faster – approximately 1400 metres/second. The human ear is confused by the high speed of sound underwater and cannot accurately focus on the source of the sound, which becomes all-enveloping. The underwater world is far from silent. A diver can clearly hear not only the sound of his buddy's exhaust bubbles, but also the throb of a distant ship's propellers, the swirl of wave-washed shingle or the sound of prawns as they feed!

Sound can be a useful means of attracting attention underwater, but the diver being signalled will have to look up and around to locate the sound source. Sounds made above the water's surface will not penetrate into the water, and vice versa.

Conduction

Water has a colossal capacity to conduct heat away from the body – some twenty-five times more effectively than air. An unclad diver in waters of less that 21° C will lose heat faster than his body can generate it, and will become chilled. In extreme cases, hypothermia can follow. Diving suits are necessary to maintain body temperature in all waters other than in the high tropics.

Body Airspaces

The Ear

In addition to being the organ of hearing, the ear is also concerned with the senses of balance and position. The visible outer ear consists of the ear and the external auditory canal, which is closed off at its inner end by the eardrum. The outer ear is open to air and its purpose is to collect sound waves and direct them to the eardrum, which will vibrate as a result.

The middle ear is a rigid air-filled space, mostly surrounded by the bone of the skull. The eardrum forms an outer wall and the airspace is connected to the rear of the throat by the Eustachian tube. The centre of the middle ear is a series of bones which transmit vibrations from the eardrum to the inner ear.

The inner ear is filled with fluid and is embedded in the bone of the skull. Vibrations picked up at the eardrum and transmitted to the inner ear are converted into nerve impulses that are sent to the brain and perceived as sounds.

The semicircular canals are considered to be part of the inner ear but play no part in hearing. They are of major importance for a sense of balance and position and their function can be upset by certain conditions affecting the middle ear (see p. 32).

The Sinuses

Sinuses are rigid filled airspaces within the bone of the skull and are mostly connected to the upper nasal passages. The largest are the frontal sinuses in the bone over the eyes, and the maxillary sinuses in the cheekbones. There are other smaller sinuses elsewhere within the skull. Sinuses appear to serve no useful purpose other than to reduce the total weight of the skull.

The Respiratory Airways

The entire network of respiratory airways, from the mouth and the nose to the bronchi and the bronchioles within the lungs, may be considered to behave as a rigid airspace.

The Lungs

There are two separate lung sacs within the chest cage. They are airspaces containing millions of flexible alveoli through which gas exchange takes place with the blood. The lungs are regarded as flexible airspaces and will reduce in volume in order to maintain ambient air pressure within the lungs and airways. The part played by the lungs in respiration is explained on p. 80.

Stomach and Gut

Air may be ingested into the stomach and the normal digestive process generates gases in the gut. Any air/gas pockets which exist will behave as flexible airspaces.

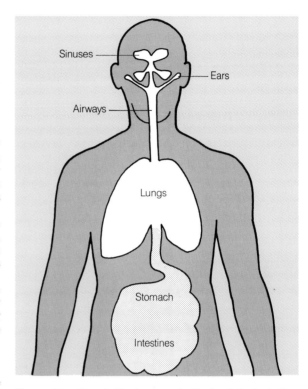

Figure 31 The air filled spaces in the body include the sinuses, the ears, the bronchial airways, the lungs, the stomach and the intestines

The Effects of Pressure

If not already familiar with pressure/volume relationships, the reader is advised to gain an understanding of that subject before considering the effects of pressure on body airspaces. The latter will not be clear without an appreciation of the former.

The Effects of Pressure on Body Airspaces

Any compressible airspace in the diver's body will change its volume in proportion to ambient pressure during descent and ascent; and if pressure within the body's rigid airspace is not kept equal to ambient pressure, injury or damage of some sort will occur. During descent, when pressure increases and volume reduces, the problems that arise are the result of compression. On ascent, when pressure falls and volume increases, problems are caused through expansion.

Compression Problems

Ears and Sinuses

The ears are very sensitive to changes in pressure and will be affected within 2 metres of leaving the surface. Increasing external water pressure will depress the eardrum inwards in an effort to reduce the volume of the near-rigid middle-ear cavity. Pain is felt, increasing as pressure increases. If the imbalance of pressure is not relieved, the eardrum will rupture, allowing cold water to enter the middle-ear cavity, where it will upset the organs of balance and hearing. Vertigo is likely to follow rapidly. Deafness and risk of middle-ear infection are longer-term risks.

The effects of pressure on the ears can be avoided by allowing air from the nasal passages to pass through the Eustachian tubes into the middle-ear cavity, where it balances external pressure. For reasons which are explained shortly the pressure in the respiratory airways will always be effectively equivalent to ambient pressure. In their normal state, the Eustachian tubes are closed, but by swallowing or by closing the nostrils and blowing into the nose, they can be opened and air admitted to the middle-ear cavity.

The process of blowing against closed nostrils to force air up the Eustachian tubes is known as the 'Valsalva manoeuvre' or, more commonly amongst divers, 'ear clearing'. A diver's face mask must include the nose and will usually have pockets built into it which allow the nose to be pinched so that the ear-clearing action can be made. The ears should then be cleared regularly during descent before any discomfort is felt.

If a normal healthy person finds it difficult to clear his ears, it is a good idea to ascend a little to relieve the discomfort and then try ear clearing once again.

External ear plugs which seal the outer-ear passage may appear to prevent compression of the eardrum but can damage it in another way. Increasing air pressure within the middle-ear cavity will push the eardrum outwards and, in some cases, it can rupture. However, the tissues surrounding the outer-ear passage are likely to bleed and fill the space with blood, thereby relieving the pressure but nevertheless rendering the diver unfit to dive. This condition is known as 'reversed ear'. Sometimes a very tight-fitting diving suit hood can block off the outer-ear passage. Air or water at ambient pressure must be encouraged to enter the hood and outer-ear passages.

Sinuses

Like the middle-ear cavity, the sinus spaces are connected to the respiratory airway by fine passages. If the air passages within the sinuses do not balance automatically, they will almost certainly do so as a result of ear-clearing efforts.

If the connecting passages are blocked for any reason, an imbalance of pressure will cause acute pain. If the pressure is not relieved by equalizing or by reducing the

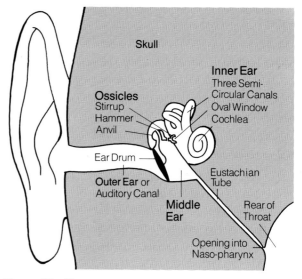

Figure 32   The ear

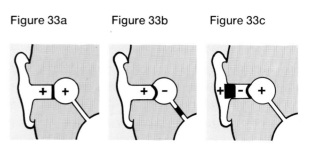

Figure 33a   **Figure 33b**   **Figure 33c**

Figure 33a   Ear in normal state

Figure 33b   External pressure due to blocked tube

Figure 33c   Reversed ear due to blocked outer ear

ambient pressure, the linings of the sinus cavity will bleed, flooding the cavity to balance the pressure. A slight nosebleed during or after a dive is a common sign of a mild sinus blockage.

Diving with a Cold or Nasal Infection

A cold, heavy catarrh or hay fever will cause inflammation and swelling of the tissues making up the nasal tract, Eustachian tubes, sinus cavities and airways, and the secretion of mucus, all of which lead to blockages of the airways and inability to clear ears and sinuses.

> **DO NOT DIVE WITH SEVERE NASAL CONGESTION OR INFECTION.**

Ears and sinuses are unlikely to clear; eardrums may be damaged and infection may be forced into the ear and sinus cavities.

Decongestant medication should only be used under medical guidance. Seek medical advice if you suffer persistent difficulty with ears and sinuses.

Lungs and Respiratory Airways

Being flexible, the lungs of a breath-holding diver will reduce in volume on descent, while the air pressure within them, and also within the rigid respiratory airways which are directly connected to the lungs, will maintain a pressure equal to ambient.

The breath-holding diver will also lose buoyancy as he descends because of the reduction in lung volume.

The reduction in lung volume is in direct proportion to the increasing ambient pressure, and if a breath-holding diver commences a descent with full lungs (total lung volume = 6 litres), at 4 bar absolute pressure the total lung capacity will be compressed to 1·5 litres – a figure equal to residual volume in normal full exhalation. In practice, it appears that the lungs can withstand further compression, but the limits have not been quantified. The fact that the world record for breath-holding diving stands in excess of 100 metres (more than 10 bar absolute) says much for the versatility of the human body. This type of diving is ill-advised for sports divers and the BSAC strongly recommends against any attempts at depth or endurance records.

A slightly different form of lung squeeze, but with similar theoretical results, can occur when a diver attempts to breathe surface air through a long snorkel tube. The air pressure within the lungs remains equal to atmospheric pressure, while the outside of the chest is exposed to water pressure. At as little as 0·5 metre depth (1·05 bar absolute), pressure on the outside of the chest is sufficient to inhibit the muscular action of inhalation. A further increase in depth will expose the diver to the risk of lung squeeze.

The diver using aqualung breathing apparatus breathes normally throughout the dive and therefore maintains normal lung volumes (and normal buoyancy). There is no risk of compression injury unless the diver breathes out hard to commence a descent and fails to resume normal breathing within a few metres. Under these circumstances there is a possibility of thoracic squeeze. It is easily avoided by resuming normal breathing once the descent has begun.

It should be remembered that the diver's mask represents an extension of the nasal airways and the airspace between will be compressed on descent. This could lead to the condition of 'mask squeeze', which can damage the delicate tissues of the eyes and the eye sockets. Mask squeeze can be prevented by deliberate efforts to exhale a small amount of air through the nose into the mask during descent. This will return the lower pressure mask space to ambient pressure.

There is a remote chance that air under pressure will enter minute cavities within dental fillings and this can lead to pain on ascent. It is a very rare condition which can be put right with fresh dental filling.

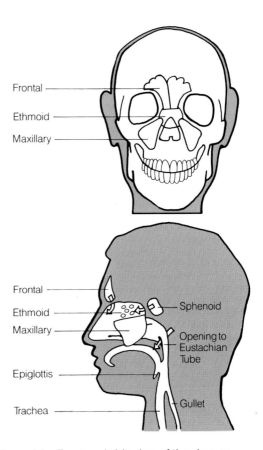

Figure 34   Front and side view of the sinuses

Basic Equipment

Masks
To see clearly underwater, the diver needs a diving mask. A typical mask will consist of four main parts:

The Frame
This secures the body to the lens.

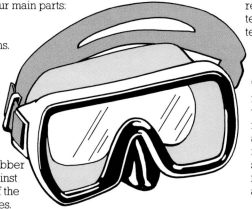

The Strap
This is either a split or single rubber strap which holds the mask against the wearer's face. The length of the strap can be adjusted by buckles.

The Lens
This must be scratch- and shatter-resistant and is usually made from tempered glass. Avoid plastic, which tends to scratch and fog easily.

The Body
This is usually made from a soft rubber compound to form a waterproof seal against the diver's face. It encloses the eyes and nose and allows the wearer to pinch his nose in order to clear his ears while submerged. Drain valves may be fitted to aid mask clearing, but these are unnecessary.

standard

low volume

silicone

Many different types and styles of mask are available. Take advice from an experienced diver or instructor.

People who have eyesight problems should have corrective lenses fitted to their masks. The advice of the diving shop should be sought.

Silicone rubber is often used for the body of the mask. This material is non-allergenic to body tissue and very long-lasting. The translucent type of silicone also allows light to enter the body of the mask. Silicone rubber maintains its flexibility over a wide temperature range.

Since faces differ in shape, you should select a mask which will seal against your face and yet be comfortable. Test a new mask for correct fit by putting it on your face without using the strap and inhaling. A correctly fitting mask will stay in place until you exhale through your nose. Look for a mask with a good angle of vision, both vertically and horizontally.

Avoid full face masks and/or masks which have attached snorkels.

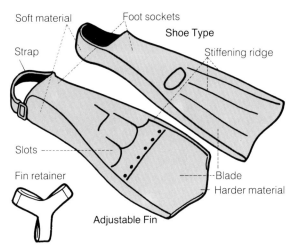

Soft material

Foot sockets

Shoe Type

Strap

Stiffening ridge

Slots

Fin retainer

Blade

Harder material

Adjustable Fin

Fins
Fins are worn to propel the diver through the water by leg action alone, thereby leaving his hands free.

The fin is made up of two main parts – the shoe and the blade. The shoe needs to be made from a soft rubber compound to ensure maximum comfort and freedom from chafing during prolonged use. The blade should have a graduated stiffness in order to transmit the power of the finning action of the legs and feet.

A harder material is used for the blade section and the stiffening ridges. Various rubber, plastic or fibreglass compounds are used in the blade.

Many designs incorporate slots or apertures in the area in front of the toes to reduce the effort required to move the fin through the water on the recovery stroke.

Since the fin which satisfies all the criteria for swimming pool use may not be the best fin for use in open water, and vice versa, many divers keep two pairs of fins – one for pools and one for open water. Remember that when you are in open water you will probably be wearing boots or bootees and the fins must fit comfortably over them.

Fins fit in one of two ways: either the foot fits into a close-fitting shoe which retains the fin; or the fin is open at the back to take the foot and is retained by a strong rubber strap. The advantage of the second system is that it gives a wider range of adjustment for different sizes of feet and for use with different thicknesses of boots or bootees. It is also possible to obtain fins which use a combination of the two systems. Additional security can be obtained by the use of rubber fin retainers. These are Y-shaped rubber straps that fit around the ankle and over the fin-clad foot.

Snorkels

A snorkel allows the user to breathe while lying on the surface with his face in the water. This makes finning on the surface much easier than if he has continually to lift his head in order to breathe. It also permits continuous observation of the underwater scene from the surface.

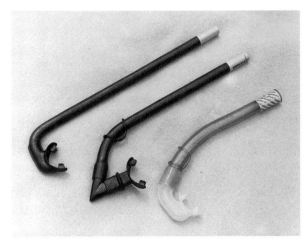

In its simplest form, the snorkel consists of two parts: a soft rubber mouthpiece which is gripped by the teeth and forms a seal under the lips, and a rigid, or semi-rigid, tube which points upwards over the submerged head. The top of this tube is open and allows the user to draw in air without risk of inhaling water.

The most common shape for the snorkel is a simple J or L, although there are various curved shapes available. A typical length will be 40-45 cm. If the tube is too long it will require too much effort to clear it of water, and if it is too short it may allow water to splash into the open end. The bore of the tube should be about 20 mm. If it is too wide it will be difficult to clear, and if it is too narrow it can restrict breathing.

Avoid snorkels which have complicated bends or valves at the open end. Some snorkels have valves at the lower end of the tube to assist clearing.

Most snorkels are supplied with a retaining ring for attaching them to the mask strap. With the snorkel attached to the strap it is ready for use. For normal diving many divers prefer to carry their snorkel elsewhere – tucked under their knife strap, on a lanyard around their neck or attached to a lifejacket – and remove and fit it as and when needed.

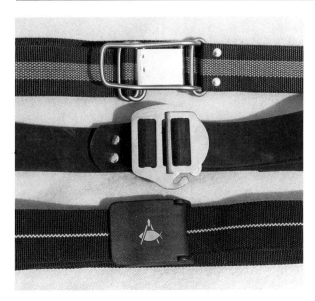

Weight Belts

A wetsuit or a drysuit will increase the diver's buoyancy, making it necessary for him to weight himself so that he can become neutrally buoyant. This is achieved by wearing lead weights on a suitable weight belt.

A vital part of any weight belt is the quick-release buckle. It ensures that positive buoyancy can be achieved quickly in an emergency by the rapid jettisoning of the weight belt. It also makes it easy to remove the belt before climbing into a boat after a dive.

Many types of quick-release buckles exist, so look out for one which is simple, easy to operate (even with cold, gloved hands!) and which contrasts strongly with the buckle of the aqualung harness. It should allow the belt to come away easily and without snagging. Avoid spare webbing, which might foul at just the wrong moment. If necessary, cut the belt so that it is a neat fit.

Remember to put on your weight belt in such a way that it will *always* come away freely and easily when the quick release is operated. This is usually achieved by fitting the weight belt after all the other equipment has been put on.

The Aqualung

Components

The components which go to make up the aqualung are the air cylinders, the regulator and the harness.

The diver's air supply is contained in one or more high-pressure cylinders mounted on his back. The pressure of the air in a full cylinder will be about 200 bars, or about a hundred times the pressure in a conventional car tyre! The cylinder will give many years of trouble-free service if treated sensibly and tested regularly. Cylinders are made from either steel or aluminium alloy and come in many different sizes.

The air in the cylinder, being at such a high pressure, needs to be reduced in pressure before the diver can breathe it. To facilitate this, a regulator is attached to the cylinder valve by means of a simple A-clamp. In countries where high pressures are more common (300 bars), screw fittings (DIN fittings) are used.

The regulator, or demand valve, is a truly remarkable piece of engineering design. It takes the very high-pressure air from the cylinder and reduces it exactly to the same pressure as the surrounding water (ambient pressure). It supplies this air on demand and shuts off the air when the diver breathes out. Since the diver is able to breathe into his lungs and into the body's airspaces air which is at ambient pressure, he is not subjected to any feeling of great pressure.

Basically there are two main types of regulator, the twin-hose regulator and the single-hose regulator. The twin-hose version was the first type to be developed, but has now been largely superseded by the single-hose type.

The single-hose regulator has a robust first-stage housing which fastens onto the cylinder valve and is connected to the second stage by a hose. The second stage is held in the diver's mouth by a soft rubber mouthpiece, not unlike the one used on a snorkel tube.

The final part of the system which, in total, is called the 'aqualung' is the harness. This is the means by which the aqualung is carried on the diver's back.

If larger capacity is required, for longer dives, then two cylinders may be carried. This is normally referred to as a twin set and consists of two cylinders connected together by a manifold and braced rigidly together by a suitable harness. For sport diving use it is normal to open both cylinders and to treat them as a single supply of air.

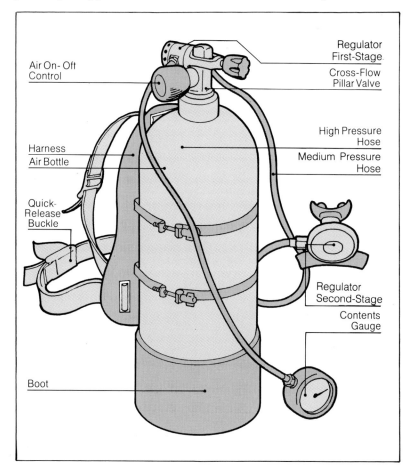

Air On-Oft Control

Regulator First-Stage

Cross-Flow Pillar Valve

High Pressure Hose

Medium Pressure Hose

Harness Air Bottle

Quick-Release Buckle

Regulator Second-Stage

Contents Gauge

Boot

Figure 35a The aqualung

Figure 35b Aqualung cylinders may be made from steel *(left)* or aluminium *(right)*

The Regulator

Principle of the Regulator

In the simplest, and original, form of the regulator, a flexible diaphragm is connected to a simple push rod and valve. One side of the diaphragm is in contact with the surrounding water while the other side is in contact, via a valve, with the high-pressure air supply. With the pressure equal on both sides of the diaphragm, the valve will be closed and no air can enter the regulator.

As the diver descends, the pressure of the water increases and deflects the diaphragm so that the valve opens and allows air to enter the regulator's air chamber. When the air in the chamber reaches ambient pressure, the diaphragm returns to its normal position and the valve closes.

If the diver takes a breath, it will come from the air chamber of the regulator and this air is already at the same pressure as the surrounding water. However, the act of inhaling causes the air pressure to be reduced, and this causes the diaphragm to deflect once again, allowing air to enter the regulator. When the diver breathes out, the valve closes and the exhaled air escapes through the exhaust valve. Thus the regulator will supply air at the same pressure as the surrounding water on demand.

A regulator working exactly on the principles described is a single-stage device; with two hoses (one for inhalation and one for exhalation) it is called a 'twin-hose, single-stage regulator'. Such regulators are now quite rare, but serve well to explain the principles by which a regulator functions.

Reducing the pressure of the air from cylinder pressure to ambient pressure in one step (i.e. a 'single-stage' regulator) is not nearly as efficient as doing the operation in two stages (i.e. a 'two-stage' regulator). In this latter type of regulator, the air from the cylinder is first reduced to an intermediate pressure, usually about 8-10 bars above ambient, and this pressure is fed into a regulator system such as has been described above. Nowadays, the most common type of two-stage regulator is the single-hose variety. In this type, the first-stage (the reducing valve) is attached to the valve of the diving cylinder and the second stage (the demand valve) is held in the diver's mouth.

There are many variations in the construction and design of diving regulators. The first stage diaphragm can be replaced by a robust metal piston. The piston or diaphragm can be 'balanced', which means that the force at each end of the valve head is the same, or nearly the same. There are also very high-performance regulators which incorporate servo assistance for reducing the effort needed for inhalation.

At the front of most second stages there is a 'purge' button. The function of this button is to allow the diver manually to depress the second-stage diaphragm thereby allowing the air to be forced into the mouthpiece. This can be used to flush water from a flooded second stage, and also to check that the regulator is working correctly before entering the water.

Figure 36a

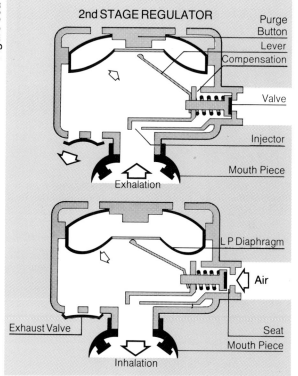

Figure 36b A two-stage regulator

Regulator Types

Figure 37

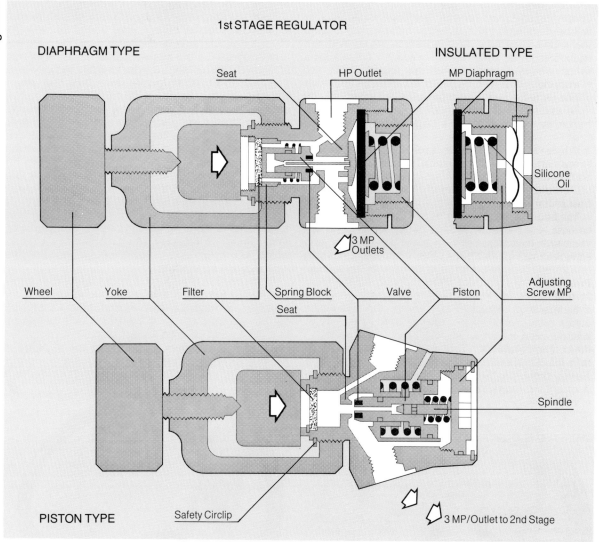

1st STAGE REGULATOR

DIAPHRAGM TYPE

INSULATED TYPE

Seat — HP Outlet — MP Diaphragm

3 MP Outlets

Silicone Oil

Wheel — Yoke — Filter — Spring Block — Valve — Piston — Adjusting Screw MP

Seat

Spindle

PISTON TYPE — Safety Circlip — 3 MP/Outlet to 2nd Stage

Figure 37 The diaphragm type of regulator is operated by water pressure acting on a diaphragm, supplemented by force exerted by the main spring. With the insulated type, no water enters the main body

The piston type is operated by a main piston which incorporates the valve seat. Water enters the main body

Figure 38 A twin-hose single-stage regulator

Harnesses

The harness is needed to mount the heavy air cylinders comfortably on the diver's back. The very simplest will have two shoulder straps and a waist strap – all adjustable. Usually the straps will be nylon webbing and the buckles will be stainless metal or strong plastic. One variation of the standard harness uses the weight belt as the waist strap. This requires a jock strap, which is attached to the cylinder, passes between the diver's legs and is fastened to a specially designed buckle on the weight belt.

Widely used, also, is the back pack. Made from high-impact plastic, it sits comfortably on the diver's back and has the harness straps and the cylinder bands connected to it.

Whichever type of harness is selected, ensure that the straps can be easily and quickly adjusted and that any buckles are of the quick-release type, so that the aqualung can be ditched if an emergency dictates that this is the best course of action.

The beginner should practise adjusting the straps of his harness, and removing it. Remember, what is easy in a warm swimming pool may be quite difficult in the cold sea, especially with gloved hands.

Pressure Gauge

In order to monitor the pressure of air in the diving cylinders, most regulators have a pressure gauge fitted onto a high-pressure tube and connected to the high-pressure side of the regulator. This is often referred to as the 'contents gauge', although it measures pressure rather than volume. This device allows the diver to plan his dive. He can check that he has enough air to start the dive and decide when the air is reduced sufficiently for the dive to be terminated.

Figure 39 A back-pack

Figure 40a The gauge indicates pressure in the cylinder

Additional Medium Pressure Outlets

Modern regulators have extra medium-pressure tappings to enable the diver to use his air supply to feed a lifejacket or a drysuit. Such devices are usually referred to as 'direct feeds'. These tappings can also be used to connect an extra second-stage regulator for use by a fellow diver who has run out of air. This is known as an 'octopus rig' and is favoured by many instructors.

Figure 40b Additional M.P. outlet

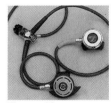
Figure 40c Regulator with octopus rig

Reserve Valve

Some sets, particularly those of continental origin, use a reserve valve which warns the diver, by restricting airflow, when the cylinder pressure reaches a pre-set level. It is overriden by a diver-operated pull rod.

Figure 40d A reserve valve

Cylinders

Cylinder Types

A charged diving cylinder contains air at a pressure of 200–300 bars. With such great pressure, safety can only be guaranteed if the cylinder is manufactured by a specialist working to very stringent specifications. Only cylinders that have been manufactured for diving should be used for diving.

Diving cylinders are made from steel or from aluminium alloy. Steel cylinders are usually made by a combination of drawing and spinning, and since steel is relatively strong, cylinders made from it will have a fairly thin wall of 4–5 mm.

Aluminium-alloy cylinders are made by extrusion and forming, and since the alloy is not as strong as steel, the walls will be quite thick, possibly as much as 11 mm. The result is that, although aluminium alloy is about one third the weight of steel, steel cylinders will usually be lighter than aluminium ones of the same internal capacity.

Cylinders are described in terms of the material (steel or aluminium), their working pressure (e.g. 200 bars) and their capacity. The capacity in litres should be stamped on the shoulder of the cylinder.

Steel cylinders are usually galvanized on the outside prior to painting in order to improve their corrosion resistance. Aluminium cylinders may be anodized prior to painting for the same reason. Aluminium cylinders do not corrode to the same extent as unprotected steel, but they are by no means free from corrosion.

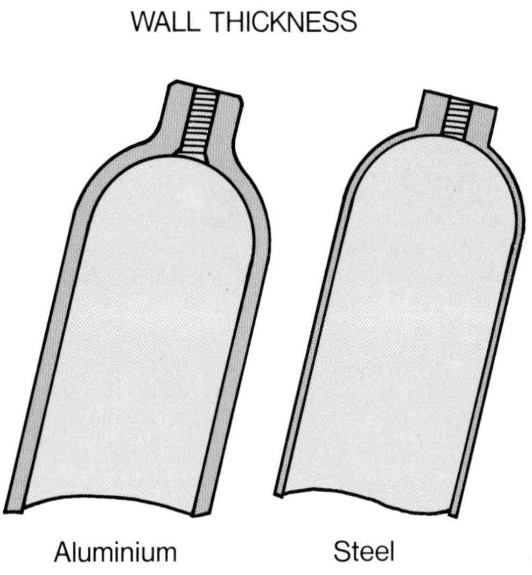

WALL THICKNESS

Aluminium   Steel

Figure 41 Aluminium cylinders have a thicker wall than steel cylinders due to the properties of the metal

Cylinders for diving should be painted for maximum visibility and contrast – yellow, white and orange are very popular. The words 'BREATHING AIR' should clearly appear on the cylinder in a colour that contrasts with the main colour.

Take good care of your cylinder. Fill it only with pure, dry air. Keep it clean, dry and well painted. Corrosion inside or outside will then be a minor problem or no problem at all.

It is common to refer to cylinders by their total air capacity. However, this capacity is only achieved if the cylinder is charged to its full working pressure. It is misleading to call a cylinder, for example, 'an 85 cubic foot cylinder' when this is only the case when it is charged to 232 bars. Learn to consider the water capacity, say 10 litres, and practise calculating your total air supply (see 'The Air Supply' page 114).

Cylinder Regulations

Most countries have regulations governing the design, manufacture and testing of high-pressure cylinders. In the UK it is the responsibility of the Health and Safety Executive (HSE), and the relevant regulations are the Gas Cylinder (Conveyance) Regulations Nos. 679 (1931), 1594 (1947) and 1919 (1959). In a nutshell, these regulations prevent the conveyance of any cylinder that has not been manufactured and tested to the accepted specifications.

The only current specification relevant to diving cylinders is BS5045 Part 1 (Steel) and Part 3 (Aluminium). There are cylinders to obsolete specifications still in use and these specifications are:

> HSE Spec. EX401, HOT and HOS (Steel)
> HSE Spec. HOAL1, HOAL2, HOAL3, and HOAL4 (Aluminium)

Prior to the full introduction of BS5045 Part 3, the current lightest aluminium-alloy specification is HOAL3.

The specification covers all aspects of design and manufacture including the composition of the alloy and the wall thickness for any cylinder. All cylinders carry markings on their shoulders or on a brass ring around the neck. Typical markings are likely to be:

> manufacturer's mark and serial number
> specification
> date of manufacture/test
> water capacity (WC) or volume
> cylinder weight
> working pressure (WP)
> test pressure (TP)

All cylinders must be regularly tested by a competent test house. The relevant standard for testing cylinders is BS5430 and no other is acceptable.

The test covers visual inspection and hydraulic testing and should be carried out three years from new and

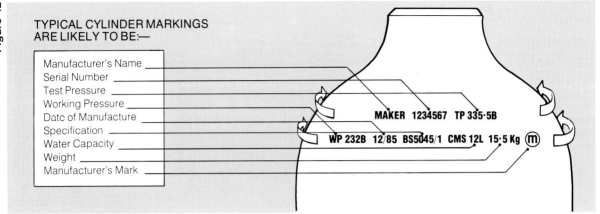

Figure 42

TYPICAL CYLINDER MARKINGS
ARE LIKELY TO BE:—

Manufacturer's Name
Serial Number
Test Pressure
Working Pressure
Date of Manufacture
Specification
Water Capacity
Weight
Manufacturer's Mark

MAKER 1234567 TP 335·5B
WP 232B 12/85 BS5045/1 CMS 12L 15·5 Kg ⓜ

every two years thereafter, but the visual inspection should be carried out every year.

The visual inspection covers both the external and internal surfaces of the cylinder. The tester looks for damage, scores, deep scratches, pitting, corrosion and thread damage, all of which may cause the cylinder to fail the test. Corrosion and/or coating may need to be removed in order that the tester can investigate the true extent of any damage.

The hydraulic test consists of filling the cylinder with water before hydraulically pumping up the cylinder to its test pressure. The expansion of the cylinder is measured. When the pressure is released, that expansion should return to normal. If the permanent expansion (permanent 'set') is more than 5 per cent, the cylinder fails the test.

Satisfactory performance in all aspects of the test means that the cylinder is fit for further use and it will be issued with a test certificate. The test house will stamp the shoulder of the cylinder with the date and the test house stamp. BS5430 requires that a test house should destroy any cylinder which is found to be unsatisfactory since such a cylinder is potentially lethal. BS5430 is the *only* acceptable standard of testing.

Figure 44

Taper threads
Valve is fitted with sealing tape

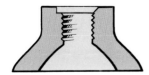

Parallel threads
Sealed with an O-ring, recess may be square *(left)* or angled *(right)*

Figure 43   Cylinder valve

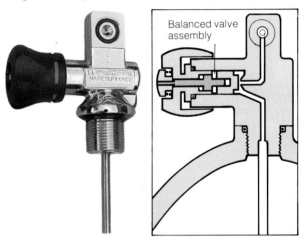

Balanced valve assembly

Cylinder Valve

The cylinder valve is fitted into the neck of the cylinder and is provided with an O-ring seal so that the diving regulator can be connected to it. The valve is screwed into the cylinder neck with either a taper thread sealed with PTFE tape or a parallel thread sealed with an O-ring.

It is not recommended that divers attempt to service their own cylinder valve unless they possess specialist skills and have access to the special tools required. It should be noted that not all taper threads have the same angle of taper and it is potentially lethal to mismatch any thread when cylinder pressures are so great.

Provided that the cylinder valve is washed in fresh water after use and is kept clean, there should be no need for it to be serviced between the intervals of the cylinder test – the obvious time to have the valve serviced, and by the test house experts.

Any stiffness in the operation of the valve or its failure to turn on or off completely is an indication that investigation by a competent person is advisable.

Compressors

Compressor Theory

If you have pumped up a bicycle tyre you will have noticed that the pump tends to get quite hot. The production of heat is a common feature of most compressors and is known as 'adiabatic' compression. If all the heat can be dissipated during compression, we have 'isothermal' compression, which is far more efficient.

The graph shows the relationship between the volume, V, and the pressure, P, for a typical compression stroke. ab1 represents adiabatic compression and ab represents isothermal compression. One can see that the latter is more efficient since it produces a far greater increase in pressure for the single stroke of the piston. Since the amount of work done is equal to the area under the curve, one can also see that isothermal compression needs less strokes than adiabatic compression.

All this means that as much heat as possible should be removed during compression in order to try to make the compressor more efficient. Rather than attempting to increase the pressure in just one stroke, as in a bicycle pump, modern compressors incorporate a number of stages with cooling between the stages.

The most common system is the three-stage compressor. This uses three pistons, each working in its own cylinder. A large piston compresses the air, which then passes into a smaller cylinder for further compression, before being passed into the third, and smallest, cylinder for final compression.

A typical three-stage compressor is shown diagrammatically here. A single crankshaft drives each of the three pistons. Air is allowed into the first cylinder by a valve which closes during compression. Another valve then opens and allows the compressed air to escape, via the cooler, to the next stage. Here the operation is repeated and then on to the third stage. After the third stage the air passes through a chemical filter on its way to the manifold. The manifold usually has a pressure gauge so that the outlet pressure can

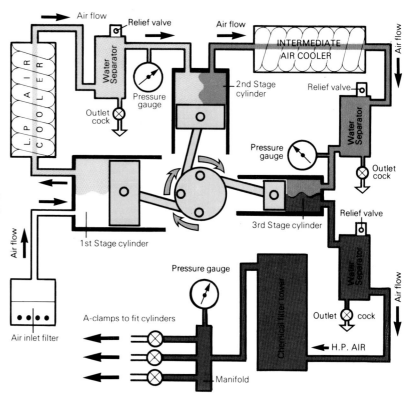

Figure 45 A three-stage air-cooled basic compressor layout

be checked and so that the operator knows when the cylinders are fully charged.

The interstage coolers are usually coiled copper pipes which are cooled by the air from a high-volume fan, driven from the compressor's crankshaft. As well as coolers, after each stage there is usually a water separator.

To prevent damage by overpress-

urization, relief valves are usually fitted to the second and third stages and also to the final supply line, the latter being set to blow off when the working pressure of the cylinders is exceeded.

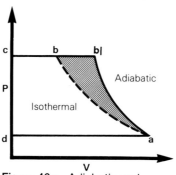

Figure 46a Adiabatic and isothermal compression

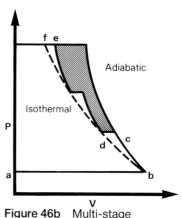

Figure 46b Multi-stage compression

Figure 47   A portable compressor

Figure 48   A large static compressor installation

Figure 49   Using a compressor on site

Compressor Operation

Portable compressors are usually driven by a petrol or a diesel engine and these tend to be quite noisy. You should aim to site the compressor so that it will cause minimal disturbance to other members of the public. At the same time, you should ensure that the air intake is well away from the exhaust fumes and be especially careful if it is a still day with no breeze. Avoid confined spaces, where exhaust levels can build up. Electrically driven motors are usually much quieter and produce no problems due to fumes.

Avoid smoking in the vicinity of the compressor intake.

The following procedure is recommended to anyone who is responsible for running a compressor:

1. Check that there is sufficient oil in both the motor and the compressor. Make sure that there is sufficient fuel in the motor and that it is of the correct type. Open all drain cocks and valves so that there is minimum load on the compressor when it is started up. Check the compressor logbook to see if the filter is due to be changed.

2. Start up the motor, and when this has warmed up close off the drain cocks and valves so that the compressor starts to compress.

3. Connect up the cylinders to be recharged, checking that they are 'in test' as you do so. Do not charge any cylinder which is out of test or which is to a non-approved specification. Open the cylinder valves and keep an eye on the pressure gauge to ensure that all is functioning correctly.

4. After every ten minutes or so of running time, open the drain cocks for a couple of seconds to blow off any condensate. Close the cocks again when no further condensate is emitted. This increases the effectiveness of the filter and also extends its life.

5. When the correct pressure has been achieved, shut off the valve of the cylinder and then the valve on the manifold. Bleed off the air trapped in the charging hose. Unfasten the A-clamps, remove the cylinders, connect new ones and continue until all cylinders are fully charged.

6. When all cylinders are fully charged, allow the compressor to continue running for a few minutes with all the drain cocks open to blow off any traces of condensate. Then shut down the motor but leave the drain cocks open.

7. Log the running times for the compressor, the number of sets filled and any other relevant details.

8. Cylinders become warm during filling. This is quite normal, but they should not be allowed to get hot. Some operators immerse cylinders in a bath of cold water during charging.

9. Make sure that cylinders which have been charged do not get mixed up with those which have not. A strip of adhesive tape around the valve is a useful way of indicating that a cylinder has been fully charged.

Compressed Air

Pure Air Production

It is essential that the air delivered from the compressor to the diving cylinder is pure. Any contamination will cause problems, especially if breathed at depth. Contamination can come from two sources. It can originate from the air that is taken into the compressor or it can be generated by the compressor itself.

Carbon monoxide and/or carbon dioxide can result from exhaust fumes of a petrol or diesel engine or from cigarette smoke being taken in at the air inlet of the compressor, or from the chemical breakdown of the oil used to lubricate the compressor. If the problem is the primary air source, it is a relatively easy task to ensure that the air-inlet hose of the compressor is located well away from the source of any potential contaminant. If the problem is the oil of the compressor, it is a sign that either the compressor is running too hot or it is running with the wrong lubricating oil. In either case, the remedy is to seek expert help. Only oils specially formulated for use in compressors should be used for that purpose.

If the oil used for the compressor starts to undergo chemical breakdown, it can also produce nitrogen compounds which are quite poisonous when breathed at depth. The moral is clear: use only the correct oil and try to prevent the compressor from becoming overheated.

Solid particles, such as dust, can cause irritation and damage to the tissues of the lungs. The source can be either the air taken into the compressor or the substances which are used as filtration media for the air output from the compressor. In each case the remedy is the same and that is to use a filter pad with pores small enough to remove the potentially dangerous particles.

Oil vapour can cause nausea and discomfort if breathed into the lungs. If prolonged inhalation takes place, it can cause pulmonary oedema and consequent lipoid pneumonia. It is essential that all oil vapour be removed from air that is to be breathed. Unless a water-lubricated or a non-lubricated compressor is used, it is inevitable that oil mist will be able to get into the air being compressed. Regular use of the interstage separators will eliminate much of the condensed vapour and any which remains can be removed by a suitable filtering medium.

Water vapour is a contaminant that is not a physiological danger but can give rise to problems with the diver's equipment. The presence of water vapour in the air breathed can give rise to the diving regulator freezing open when diving in cold conditions. Also, air with a high moisture content can cause condensation and the corrosion of the inside walls of a diving cylinder. Besides using the interstage separators regularly to remove oil and water vapour, it can also be removed by use of a suitable filtration medium. A typical compressor will have a filter tower at the outlet end of the airflow. This filter contains layers of selected media to remove contaminants from the air before it is supplied to the diving cylinders.

A typical filter for an average-sized compressor consists of:

> 12·5 mm of felt at top and bottom and separating each layer (solids)
> 100 mm of silica gel or activated alumina (moisture)
> 100 mm of activated charcoal (oil mist and odour)
> 50 mm 13 × molecular sieve (moisture and oil mist)

The filter will have a finite life and this will depend upon the amount of contamination that has to be removed and the volume of air that has been filtered. Regular inspection must be carried out. There are some compressors which use a filter tower similar to the above in the form of a replaceable cartridge. Some of these even have a self-indicating system whereby a change in colour indicates the need for a filter change.

It should be noted that the filter media listed above does not remove carbon monoxide. Should this be necessary, it can be achieved by using a material called Hopcalite. This is quite expensive and, since it also removes most other contaminants as well, these should be removed first in order to preserve maximum life for the Hopcalite.

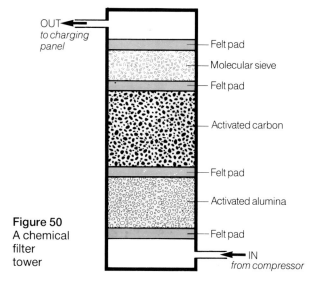

Figure 50
A chemical filter tower

OUT
to charging panel

— Felt pad
— Molecular sieve
— Felt pad
— Activated carbon
— Felt pad
— Activated alumina
— Felt pad

IN
from compressor

Air-Purity Standards

Since the presence of impurities in the breathing air can cause problems, particularly when breathed at depth, it is essential that the air produced by the compressor should be as pure as possible. The following is the BSAC Air-Purity Standard, which is recommended to any supplier of compressed air for diving:

nitrogen	as in atmospheric air
oxygen	21 per cent, ± 0·5 per cent
carbon dioxide	0·03 per cent (300 p.p.m.)
carbon monoxide	5 p.p.m.
oil	1 mg per cubic metre
water	as dry as possible; no condensation above 40 degrees F
solid particles	no residue on Millipore filter* after passing 5 litres of air
odour/taste	none
nitrogen dioxide	less than 1 p.p.m.
nitrous oxide	less than 1 p.p.m.

*Note. This should be a 'fast' Millipore filter of pore size 3·4–5 microns.

Figure 51a Equipment for testing the purity of air. The glass tube contains chemicals which change colour as a measured volume of air is passed through the tube. They check for one impurity at a time

Figure 51b A chemical filter tower with bleed screw and safety valve fitted to a compressor

Air-Purity Testing

Testing is normally carried out by passing a known volume of air through a tube which contains a chemical that changes colour in the presence of the contaminant (similar to the breathalizer for detecting alcohol in the breath).

There are two types of testing apparatus. One consists of a small hand pump which has a set volume. A given number of pumping actions is equal to a known volume and the test tube is connected to the hand pump. This device requires that the air be first taken from the cylinder or the compressor into a plastic bag, since the test is carried out at atmospheric pressure. The second, which is becoming more popular with the larger compressor stations, has a flow meter which can be connected directly onto the cylinder on the compressor outlet. By fixing the flow rate and timing the test, a given volume of air is allowed to pass through the test tube.

Standard test tubes are available for all of the contaminants listed in the table of air purity and the maker's recommendations and instructions should be carefully followed.

Lifejackets

A lifejacket uses the principle of displacing water with air to increase the diver's apparent volume, and therefore his buoyancy, in a controlled fashion. The British Sub-Aqua Club *strongly recommends* that a diver should wear a lifejacket for all normal dives in open water.

The lifejacket is designed to float a diver face upwards on the surface and has an independent means of rapid inflation, usually from a CO_2 cylinder or a separate small air cylinder. Any other inflatable system that a diver might choose to use would come under the heading of 'buoyancy aid' or 'buoyancy compensator' rather than lifejacket.

Surface Lifejacket

This is a frontal vest which is worn over the head and fastened by a waist strap or harness. Being intended for use on the surface only, the emergency inflation is by means of a mechanism firing a small CO_2 cylinder. An oral inflation tube is fitted for non-emergency situations, such as a long surface swim, and also as a simple means of deflating the jacket.

The problems associated with this type of lifejacket are:
1. There is no simple way of checking that the contents of the gas cylinder are intact before making the dive, other than by weighing the cylinder.
2. The size of the cartridge is designed to fill the jacket on the surface, giving about 15 kg of buoyancy. At a depth of 30 metres the buoyancy provided would be under 4 kg.

Depth causes wetsuits to compress and become less buoyant and some means of compensating for this loss of buoyancy is vital.

Figure 52 A surface lifejacket

Oral Inflation

The jacket may be fitted with an oral inflation tube, allowing easy inflation and venting. This is a fairly long tube, corrugated for flexibility, which has an easy-to-operate valve at the open end. Holding the tube above the head and operating the valve will allow air to escape from the jacket should this be necessary, for example when moving into shallower water or surfacing. Most models of lifejacket with oral inflation also provide emergency inflation from a CO_2 cartridge, as in a surface lifejacket.

Since it is now possible to fully inflate the jacket at depth and then come to the surface, causing the air in the jacket to expand, such devices need to have an excess-pressure valve fitted to prevent bursting.

Many experienced divers prefer not to remove their diving regulators from their mouths in order to correct buoyancy. It is also important to be aware of the possible hazard presented by inflating a jacket with CO_2 and then inhaling it via the oral inflation tube.

The Adjustable-Buoyancy Lifejacket

The adjustable-buoyancy lifejacket (ABLJ) is a major contribution to more relaxed and safer diving. It also provides an emergency inflation system that can give full lift even at considerable depth.

The in-built inflation system of the ABLJ is a small air cylinder of about 0·4 litre volume. When this cylinder is filled from a normal diving air supply (usually about 200 bars) it has about 80 litres of air available for inflation for the lifejacket.

To ensure that this supply is always available, the diver refills the small cylinder from his diving cylinder immediately prior to *every* dive. This guarantees that he has a full inflation system at the beginning of the dive. Air is fed into the lifejacket by opening the valve on the small cylinder.

The ABLJ is usually fitted with an oral inflation tube with a valve-operated mouthpiece. This can be used for oral inflation, thereby preserving the contents of the small cylinder for emergency use or for venting. In the latter case the tube is held above the head and the mouthpiece valve operated to allow the air in the jacket to escape.

Most ABLJs are now fitted with cord-operated vent valves (dump valves). These make the procedure of dumping air even easier – just pull the cord and the air escapes. This valve may incorporate the excess-pressure valve (needed to prevent over-inflation).

Since the small cylinder contains an appreciable quantity of breatheable air, in the unfortunate circumstance of running out of air it is possible to breathe the contents. This technique requires considerable practice in order to avoid becoming over-buoyant or breathing in water. Some ABLJs are fitted with an automatic mouthpiece (a sort of basic demand valve) which makes emergency breathing much easier.

Figure 53a Stabilizer jacket

Figure 53b Lifejacket cylinder with integral clamp

The Stabilizer Jacket

This is shaped like a waistcoat and is usually attached to the diving cylinder. It can obviate the need for harness straps and is very comfortable to wear. Many jackets have inflatable areas both at the diver's back and at his front. While swimming horizontally, air for buoyancy adjustment will be located in the small of the back. When fully inflated, air will be in the front of the jacket causing the diver to float face upwards. Stabilizer jackets use CO_2 cartridges and/or small air cylinders for emergency inflation and direct feeds for routine buoyancy adjustment.

Figure 54 An ABLJ

Direct Feeds

The use of a direct-feed inflator removes the need for oral inflation. A tube is connected to the medium-pressure side of the first stage of the diving regulator with its other end connected, via a quick-release connector, to the life-jacket. Whenever the diver needs to put air into the jacket he simply pushes the operating valve of the direct feed. The direct feed is used for routine buoyancy adjustment, saving the contents of the small cylinder for emergency use. Their use is strongly recommended.

Figure 55 A direct feed inflator

The Air-Inflated Drysuit

The drysuit is a potential buoyancy control device and it can be used as such, provided that it is used with extreme care. The volume of air that can be put into a suit and the expansion that can occur on ascent mean that caution must be used. Immediate, rapid venting must be possible if the increase in buoyancy is to be kept under complete control.

The Wetsuit

Need
Water conducts heat twenty-five times more effectively than air. It can hold over three thousand times more heat than air. Water temperature often drops to 4° C or lower in wintertime, so the need for some form of thermal protection is obvious.

The Wetsuit
Probably the most widely used form of thermal protection, the wetsuit is made from synthetic rubber (usually neoprene) that has been foamed or expanded. The gas bubbles which are trapped in the rubber are separated from each other so that the suit does not absorb water as a sponge might. This bubble layer provides effective insulation combined with good elasticity.

Because the suit material stretches, a wetsuit can be reasonably close-fitting. Although water is not prevented from entering between the suit and the body, the close fit restricts the amount to a minimum. This water soon heats up to body temperature and is isolated from the cold surrounding water by the layer of insulating bubbles in the rubber. A loose-fitting suit will allow freer circulation of water and consequently greater chilling.

Suit thicknesses can be as little as 2 mm for use in warmer waters and up to as much as 8 mm for cold-water areas. A standard suit consists of jacket, trousers, hood and boots or bootees. Variations include 'longjohn' trousers which also cover most of the chest and spine area, jackets with attached hoods to prevent seepage of water through the neck opening, spine pads to give extra thickness and warmth to the spinal area and protective pads at the knees and elbows.

Very few wetsuits are now made from plain foam neoprene. The ease with which such material snags and tears has led to the majority of suits being made from neoprene which has one side, or both sides, coated with a flexible fabric, usually nylon. This helps to overcome snagging and tearing, makes dressing easier and the suit more attractive with effective use of colour, which can also be a safety factor if it is bright and conspicuous.

Neoprene is such an inert material that the joints and seams can be made only using a contact adhesive (i.e. it is not possible to vulcanize or weld the material). This makes the joints vulnerable to sunlight, oils and solvents. It also means that repairs are easily made by using a suitable adhesive. When fabric reinforcement is used, extra strength is obtained by stitching through this fabric. This can be done by a needle which goes right through the thickness of neoprene and nylon; protective tape can be attached at the same time. This is called 'Mauser' stitching and has the disadvantage of puncturing the insulating layer and allowing water to penetrate the suit. A better method is to stitch only the reinforcing fabric by means of a loop stitch ('Strobel' stitching). This gives strength to the joint without allowing the ingress of water.

The main disadvantage of the wetsuit is that its insulation and buoyancy vary with depth. The greater the thickness of the material, the greater the thermal insulation and the greater the buoyancy. , As the diver descends, the increase in water pressure causes the insulating bubbles to decrease in volume, causing a loss of insulation and a loss of buoyancy. This means that in deep water the diver is both colder and more negatively buoyant. The latter can be corrected by use of a buoyancy aid, but the lack of insulation cannot be compensated for.

Figure 56 Thermal insulation is achieved by different methods in different types of diving suit

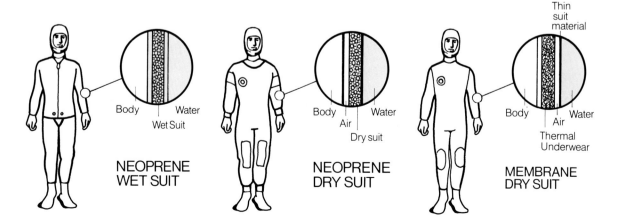

Body | Water
Wet Suit

NEOPRENE
WET SUIT

Body | Water
Air
Dry suit

NEOPRENE
DRY SUIT

Thin
suit
material

Body | Water
Air
Thermal
Underwear

MEMBRANE
DRY SUIT

Figure 57   The wetsuit for men

Figure 59   Wetsuit accessories – boots, gloves and hood

Figure 58   The wetsuit for women

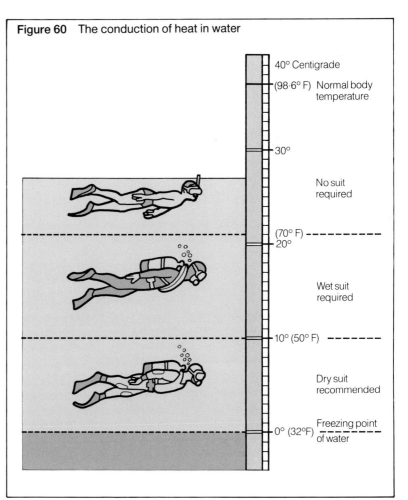

Figure 60   The conduction of heat in water

40° Centigrade

(98·6° F) Normal body temperature

30°

No suit required

(70° F)
20°

Wet suit required

10° (50° F)

Dry suit recommended

0° (32°F) Freezing point of water

The Drysuit

Drysuits were originally made from sheet rubber or rubber-coated fabric with latex-rubber seals for the ankles, wrists and neck. One type had a tunic and trousers, each with a considerable overlap, which were rolled together at the waist. The joint was then secured by a wide rubber cummerbund. The Navy version was a one-piece suit with built-in boots. The diver climbed in through the elastic neck opening. The neck was then sealed with a latex-rubber seal attached to the neck opening by a metal O-ring and clamp.

The main disadvantages of these types of drysuit were the difficulty in dressing and undressing, the ease with which the suit could be torn or punctured and the 'squeeze' that occurred when the suit was used at depth. Since the air inside the suit is at atmospheric pressure when the suit is put on, as the diver descends the increase in water pressure causes the small amount of air trapped in the suit to compress greatly and this squeeze results in discomfort and, possibly, pain. Professional divers solved the problem of squeeze by increasing the amount of air inside the suit to compensate for the decrease in volume and thereby maintaining comfort, buoyancy and warmth.

The emergence of the waterproof zip has helped the rebirth of the drysuit for sport divers. The use of such a zip makes dressing and undressing a much simpler task.

The air-inflated drysuit is widely used by sport divers. This is a drysuit, usually with a waterproof zip, which has an air supply to the inside of the suit. There are two main types of air-inflated drysuits, those made from wetsuit material (foam-neoprene drysuits) and those made from a thin, waterproof fabric (membrane drysuits).

The Foam-Neoprene Drysuit

There are two main versions of this suit. One is relatively loose and is intended to be used with extra underclothes. It usually has a waterproof zip running from the small of the back, under the crutch and up to the chest. It has built-in boots and an attached hood. This type is very much favoured by the professional diver. The other type, favoured by sport divers, is much closer fitting – more like the fit of a wetsuit – and usually has the zip across the shoulders. It is fitted with a neck seal, wrist seals and ankle seals. A separate hood and boots have to be worn.

Both types of suit are made from the same foam neoprene that is used for making wetsuits. Usually, the material is fabric-coated on both sides. All seams are first glued and then the fabric layers are stitched together. The seals for the wrists, etc., are usually also made from expanded neoprene, rendering them both comfortable and relatively easy to alter. If the seals are made from neoprene, which has a smooth skin on both sides, the wearer can elect to turn over the edge of the seal for extra security, since the double thickness gives tightness to the seal. Many divers turn the seals inwards, particularly the neck seal. This makes the seal even more secure against the loss of air, since the turned-in seal tightens when filled with air.

It is possible to get 'dry' gloves and 'dry' boots for this type of suit. These have a neoprene seal similar to that of the suit and the two seals fit on top of each other to keep out the water. However, dry gloves prevent the venting of air via a cuff – a common technique used by drysuited divers.

The suits are quite easy to put on. Body entry is through the zip opening. The legs are inserted into the trouser part of the suit and then the arms are carefully forced into the sleeves (make sure you remove your watch). Finally the head is pushed through the neck seal and the zip can be closed. Make sure that the zip is clear of any protruding clothing (or flesh) and close it with a steady, pulling action to prevent damage – your buddy is the best person to do this job for you. Make sure that the zip is completely closed before you enter the water. If the seals are very tight, a little lubrication can ease them. Depending on the type of seal fitted, French chalk, silicone spray or soap can be quite effective. If you use any form of aerosol, make sure that it does not contain a solvent which might soften the adhesive of the seams. Beeswax is recommended for lubricating the zip.

Air can be fed into the suit by means of a valve which is connected to the first stage of the diving regulator by a direct-feed hose. The valve is usually of the push-button type and is normally situated on the upper or lower chest. Many suits are also fitted with an exhaust valve which can be operated to vent excess air from the suit. This might be situated on the upper chest, the upper arm or the wrist. Some exhaust valves are the push-button type, but pull-cord versions (dump valves) are very popular.

The Membrane Drysuit

The membrane drysuit gets its name from the fact that it is made from a thin material which itself has little or no insulating properties. Warmth is maintained by the use of warm underclothes. The sole function of the suit is to keep the wearer dry.

The suit material is waterproof, usually rubber-coated cloth or coated nylon. Rubber-coated cloth has the advantage that the seams can be vulcanized, which is almost the same as welding the seams together, and this makes them very strong and totally waterproof. If there is a disadvantage to rubber-coated fabric, it is that the cloth used is usually soft and stretchy and the material of the suit is quite easy to puncture; but it is also quite easy to repair.

Strong, puncture-resistant materials such as nylon or polyester can be coated with neoprene or polyurethane. This combination gives a suit material that is both strong and waterproof. The seams may be adhesively bonded and given extra strength and reliability by using tape, again with adhesive bonding. Another solution is to stitch the seams together and then waterproof the joint in some way, usually by fusing a waterproof tape onto the stitched area. An advantage of this type of membrane drysuit is its relatively low price.

The rest of the suit is similar, or identical, to the foam-neoprene suit. There is a waterproof zip, usually across the shoulders. There are neck seals, wrist seals and, often, ankle seals. The main difference in this type of suit is that the seals are usually made from latex rubber. Although very efficient they are vulnerable to puncturing or tearing when pulled by fingers with sharp fingernails or when caught on the corners of watches or other metal objects. The latex-rubber seal is probably the weakest part of the membrane drysuit.

There are versions of this type of suit that have built-in latex socks. These give complete waterproofing without the tightness of ankle seals. The socks are not robust enough to be used alone and it is still necessary to wear wetsuit boots or bootees. Other versions of these suits have built-in boots with hard soles and can be used without any other form of footwear.

Some types have a hood integral with the body of the suit. These reduce the amount of water penetrating the neck seal since much of the water is kept out by the hood.

The membrane drysuit does not have much elasticity and the suits have to be wide enough at the waist to pass over the hips. Some suits incorporate elasticated waists to compensate for this, but overall the membrane drysuit

Figure 61a Neoprene drysuit

Figure 61b Membrane drysuit

tends to be quite baggy. Since body warmth is maintained by the use of underclothing, when squeeze occurs at depth and is relieved by inflation, the flattened underclothing goes back to its natural state and warmth and comfort are maintained. At the same time, since the clothing returns to its normal state, the buoyancy of the diver is also maintained. This is the one big difference between the membrane drysuit and the foam-neoprene drysuit.

Using the Drysuit
Diving with an air-inflated drysuit needs thought and training. Because of the ability to inject large amounts of air into the suit, and because this will expand on ascent unless vented, it is necessary to pay particular attention to how and why air is put into the suit.

It is recommended that the drysuit wearer weights himself correctly for the particular dive. On descent he will start to feel uncomfortable as the suit starts to squeeze. This discomfort is overcome by carefully allowing the minimum amount of air into the suit to restore normal comfort. The foam-neoprene drysuit will show the greatest change in buoyancy as the depth increases since the gas bubbles in the foam will decrease in volume. Compensating for the loss of buoyancy by putting air into a lifejacket means that two separate buoyancy devices have to be controlled. Compensating for loss of buoyancy by putting air into the suit is, probably, the simplest technique, but care must be taken to avoid large volumes of air migrating to the feet and ascent occurring before the diver has remembered to compensate by venting the excess.

The membrane drysuit will show little change in buoyancy with increasing depth, since compensating for squeeze will also compensate for any change in buoyancy. However, the diver should still wear a lifejacket.

Equipment Compatibility
Since the BSAC strongly recommends the wearing of a lifejacket even when diving with an air-inflated drysuit, it makes sense to ensure that the drysuit and the lifejacket are totally compatible. With the ability to adjust buoyancy via the drysuit, the argument for an ABLJ is not quite so great, unless there is a possibility of a massive failure of the neck seal or zip.

In all cases of diving with a drysuit, the position of the inflation and deflation valves needs consideration if the suit is to be completely compatible with other items of normal diving equipment. There have been cases of lifejackets covering the controls of the drysuit and making it difficult to operate them. It is essential that the diver selects gear that is compatible and then any one item of equipment will not prevent the successful operation of another.

Because the lifejacket is more likely to be of use on the surface and is unlikely to be used underwater except in extreme emergencies, a special-purpose ABLJ can be used which is folded in front and, therefore, is well out of the way of the controls to the suit.

Accessories

Depth Gauges

Several types are available:

The capillary gauge consists of a transparent tube, closed at one end, full of air at atmospheric pressure. As the diver descends, the pressure of the water forces the column of air to compress and the interface of water and air can be read against a scale. Because it follows Boyle's Law, the scale is non-linear and the gauge becomes less accurate with increasing depth.

The Bourdon tube uses a curved tube closed at one end. Differences in pressure can be determined by the deflection of the tube.

The open Bourdon tube is open to the water at one end and the casing of the instrument is at atmospheric pressure. Increasing pressure, acting on the open end of the tube, tends to make it straighten and this movement can be transmitted to a moving needle by a simple quadrant and pinion device. Silt and corrosion inside the Bourdon tube can prevent the water from entering and cause malfunction.

The sealed Bourdon tube gauge overcomes the above problem by having a tube that is filled with oil and separated from the water by a rubber diaphragm, the water pressure being transmitted through the diaphragm to the oil inside the tube. Its method of functioning is identical to that of the open Bourdon tube gauge.

In the enclosed Bourdon tube gauge the tube is closed at both ends and filled with air at atmospheric pressure. The instrument casing is pliable and filled with clear oil. On descent, the increase in pressure is transmitted through the pliable casing to the oil which, in turn, causes a deflection of the Bourdon tube and movement of the indicator needle. It is essential that this type of gauge is compensated for changes in temperature which might otherwise cause the liquid in the casing to change in volume and cause a pressure difference other than that due to a change in depth. As it is filled with liquid, this type of gauge is self-lubricating and fairly resistant to knocks.

The diaphragm gauge is probably the most accurate type of gauge but also the most expensive! A metal diaphragm is hermetically sealed to the back of the gauge and the increasing water pressure acts on this and causes it to deflect. The deflection is transmitted through a quadrant system to the needle, which reads depth.

It is important that all gauges have a clear scale with easy-to-read figures and marking. Divisions for every 1 metre enable the gauge to be used with any decompression table, but divisions for every 3 metres will satisfy the BSAC '88 tables.

Electronic depth measurement with digital readout is becoming more readily available with wider use of diving computers. These give far more accurate depth measurement than is possible with Bourdon tube or diaphragm gauges (currently not better than ± 1 metre over a 50-metre scale).

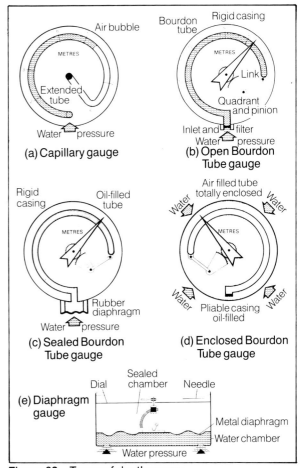

Figure 62   Types of depth gauge

Watches and Dive Timers

The diving watch can be mechanical or electronic and the display can be analogue or digital. The essential requirements are that the watch should be waterproof to at least the maximum depth the diver might expect to dive to and that the watch should be capable of measuring the duration of the dive. The latter can be achieved by means of a stop/start mechanism or a rotating bezel on the outside of the watch casing. Some watches may have both systems and can time the dive and also the surface interval should a second dive be contemplated. If the watch has to fit over a wetsuit or drysuit, it is essential that the retaining strap should be sufficiently adjustable to allow this.

Dive timers can be mechanical or electronic and are usually operated automatically by the pressure of the water acting on the casing. This has the great advantage that the diver does not have to remember to set the device at the beginning and end of each dive. Dive timers may also time the surface interval while still retaining the duration of the previous dive.

Figure 63   A diving watch and a depth gauge

Figure 64   A selection of diving computers

Figure 65   A combined depth gauge and pressure gauge console

Instrument Panel/Console

The essential instruments that a diver will refer to throughout the dive are the depth gauge, the cylinder pressure gauge, the compass and the watch. Some divers prefer to bring these instruments together on a console or instrument panel. It is not difficult to make a panel to which one's instruments can be attached and the panel can then be secured by a cord. If a commercially manufactured console is purchased, it will probably be designed to take the instruments offered by that particular manufacturer and may or may not accept those instruments that the diver already has.

Decompression Meter/Computer

Early decompression meters were calibrated for decompression tables that the BSAC could not recommend and/or were based on the simulated absorption of nitrogen by a single tissue. Before the BSAC can recommend the use of any decompression meter, the instrument should be able to simulate the nitrogen absorption in several tissues and be calibrated to an acceptable decompression table.

With the advent of microelectronics, different types of instruments are possible. Some simply measure the duration and maximum depth of the dive and then look up the appropriate table in their memory store. This, in effect, is exactly what the careful diver should be doing. Another type simulates the absorption and elimination of nitrogen by several tissues and is able to handle variable-profile dives and multiple dives. These are true decompression computers.

Microelectronics can carry out many measurements and calculations very quickly and to great degrees of

accuracy. A dive computer which meets the specification laid down by the BSAC can be used by BSAC members to monitor their dive depth, dive duration and to indicate the decompression required.

Surface Marker Buoy

A useful safety device for most dives is the surface marker buoy. In essence it is an easily seen surface float which is connected to the diver by means of a thin, strong line. Its main function is to allow the surface cover to know where the divers are at all times, and to provide the cover with a means of communicating with the divers should the need arise.

The marker float should be of sufficient buoyancy to ensure that it cannot be inadvertently pulled underwater by the divers. At the same time, it should not be so big that it is difficult to carry or is likely to be caught by the wind and/or surface current. It should have 10–20 kg buoyancy. If the buoy is inflatable, it has the additional advantage of being easy to carry when not being used. The material and colour of the surface buoy should be such that it is visible over a range of at least 200 metres. Several types of surface buoy are pear-shaped or shaped like an upright cylinder and these usually need a small sinker weight to help them float upright – the most visible state.

The line that connects the surface buoy to the divers should be both thin enough to carry sufficient length and strong enough not to break. Soft, plaited nylon cord of about 1–2 mm diameter works well. A suitable means of holding the line is essential. Ideally, there should be a device to keep the length of line to about 1·25 times the depth of the dive at all stages of the dive – paying out more line as the depth increases and taking in line as the dive gets shallower.

A simple device is a winder frame made from wood and, therefore, very cheap and yet easy to use. There are many reeling mechanisms available, usually made from wood, plastic or metal. They consist essentially of a handle, a reel to hold the line and a second handle to operate the reel. The latter is usually supplied with a spring-operated ratchet so that a positive action has to be taken to allow line to run off the reel. Rather than carry the reel throughout the dive, most divers clip the reel to their harness by means of a short length of cord, allowing the reel to float just behind the diver.

A surface marker buoy and line provide a great sense of security for both the divers and the surface cover. For the divers, there is no more comforting sound that that of the boat patrolling above. For the surface cover, it is a relief to be able to see the position of one's divers at all times and to be able to take appropriate action if they appear to be drifting into danger. For night diving, a torch or electronic flasher can be attached to the float for additional visibility and security.

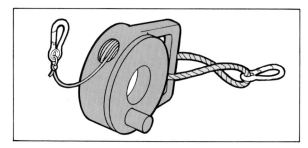

Figure 68   A line and reel for an SMB

Buddy Line

When visibility is poor, or for additional security, it may be advisable to have a pair of divers physically connected together. If they are diving with a surface marker buoy, this can be achieved by one of them holding onto a loop of line that has been let out. An alternative that is suitable for all occasions is the 'buddy line'. This is a length of strong rope, about 1–3 metres in length and with a loop at each end. Each diver puts his arm through one of the loops and he is then able to signal to his partner, and vice versa, and keep in contact even in the worst visibility.

Torch

A diving torch or lantern is an essential item of diving equipment whenever underwater light conditions are poor. For night diving, obviously, it is one of the important items of equipment, but it can also be very useful on other occasions for looking into confined spaces in rocks, wrecks, etc.

A diving torch or lantern can vary considerably in size and power. It may use standard batteries or rechargeable cells. The advantage of rechargeable cells is that operating costs are reduced, but a source of mains or 12-volt (car battery) power is needed for recharging.

With the advent of halogen bulbs and small powerful batteries it is possible to have a quite small underwater torch with remarkable brightness. Whether the torch should have a pinpoint beam or a wide-spread one is usually determined by the use to which it is to be put.

Figure 66   Inflatable surface marker buoys and a reel

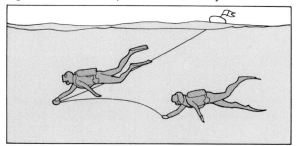

Figure 67   Using an SMB as a buddy line

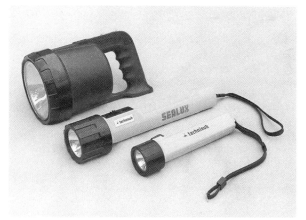

Figure 69   A selection of underwater lamps

Underwater photographers often use a small, pinpoint beam to help aim their cameras and flashguns.

The colours that are filtered out by the water as the diver descends will return as soon as the torch is switched on, and for this reason many divers carry a torch on every dive.

Lifting Bag

A lifting bag is used to lift heavy objects from the seabed. The bag must be strong enough to withstand the demands made on it by the object to which it is attached and also the expansion of the air within the bag as it ascends. The usual design is that of a open-ended bag with the open end attached to the object to be lifted. As a guide to lifting capacity, remember that 1 litre of air displaces 1 kilogramme of water and thereby has a buoyancy of the latter figure. Taken underwater deflated, the bag is attached securely to the object and then air is injected into the open end of the bag – either from the diver's regulator or from a separate supply. Some bags have relief valves fitted to the top which can be operated by the diver if the bag becomes too buoyant and the rate of ascent too rapid.

Knife

Every diver on every dive should carry a knife. You can never be sure when the ability quickly and easily to cut through tangled line, net or rope might become a matter of life or death. Traditionally, the diver's knife is quite large and sturdy and is worn on the calf or thigh. In recent years there has been a tendency for smaller knives to become popular and these are worn on the upper arm or the forearm.

Whichever type of diving knife is selected, there are certain requirements to be satisfied. To minimize corrosion, stainless steel is used for the blade. This type of steel is not as hard as conventional cutting steel and regular sharpening will be necessary. Although its name suggests otherwise, stainless steel can corrode – particularly the grades of stainless steel that are used for making knives – but regular cleaning and oiling will minimize the problem. Besides a plain cutting blade, a saw edge can be quite useful for cutting through thicker ropes. The handle should be comfortable, non-slip and with a means of preventing the hand slipping down onto the blade. Most knives have handles made of hard rubber or plastic, but there are a few one-piece knives with handle and blade all of steel. Wear the knife in its sheath whenever it is not in use and make sure that it can be quickly and easily removed.

Magnetic Compass

In order to navigate while underwater and particularly in poor visibility, the diver needs a magnetic compass. The degree of navigation may vary from simply swimming in the right general direction (e.g. to and from the point of entry) to true navigation as in a search or in underwater orienteering.

The diver's compass must have a waterproof case that can withstand pressure. Most are oil-filled to give good damping of the needle. There is usually a direction-of-

travel arrow on the casing. To allow for swimming on a predetermined heading, most compasses have a rotating bezel around the outside of the casing which is graduated from 0 to 360 degrees and there is often a cursor on the transparent window of the compass, so that if the compass needle is kept within the limits of the cursor line, the direction of travel can be predetermined.

If relatively small, the diving compass is unlikely to allow exact navigation underwater or above it. The accuracy is unlikely to be much better than ±5 degrees. It should be remembered that the diver's compass will be affected by all the factors which affect any compass. Variation is the difference between true north and magnetic north and changes as one moves around the world. Deviation is the difference between magnetic north and compass north and is mainly due to magnetic influences close to the compass – masses of iron or steel, electrical gear, etc. Holding the compass well away from any magnetic material (steel diving cylinders, adjustable-buoyancy lifejacket cylinders, knives, watches, etc.) will minimize the effects of deviation.

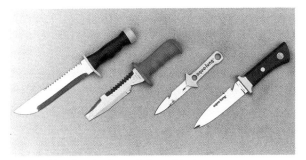

Figure 70   A selection of divers' knives

Figure 71   A magnetic compass

Equipment Care

Basic Equipment

Articles made from rubber may be adversely affected by chlorinated water, sunlight, oil or grease. After use, all such items should be washed in fresh water, allowed to dry and, preferably, stored in a dark place. The straps on masks and fins have a tendency to perish where they are stretched under buckles and you can prolong their life by undoing the buckles when the equipment is not being used. Sun-tan oil can accelerate the deterioration of rubber straps and components, and particular care needs to be taken in sunny climes.

Problems can occur with the face plate of a mask fogging over – particularly when the mask is new. Spitting into the mask followed by vigorous rubbing may not have the desired effect. Persistent misting should yield to rubbing with one, or more, of the following: a slice of raw potato, neat detergent, methylated spirit, French chalk or a proprietary demister.

Most metal components will be made from stainless steel or plated brass and it is sufficient to ensure that these are washed in clean, fresh water and then dried.

Make sure that the weight belt has a buckle that has not been damaged or broken and that still works easily and freely. Watch for frayed webbing and shorten any belt that has excess webbing, since the extra material may cause inadvertent snagging.

Cylinders

The diving cylinder can be expected to have a long life provided that it is well looked after. Do not forget that legislation calls for the cylinder to be visually inspected and hydraulically tested at prescribed intervals.

A steel cylinder will stand up to knocks and scratches better than an aluminium-alloy one, since the latter material is considerably softer. However, an aluminium-alloy cylinder has a much greater wall thickness than a steel cylinder. Because of the tremendous pressure when fully charged, any diving cylinder must be handled with care and not allowed to fall or roll over.

The paint on the outside of the cylinder should be maintained in good condition, since this will minimize the most serious of all cylinder problems, corrosion. Regular inspection of the outside of the cylinder and the making good of any damaged paint areas are good practice. Wash off sea water or swimming-pool water after each and every use. Ensure that metal harness bands do not come into direct contact with the bare metal of the cylinder wall, since this can set up local galvanic corrosion with disastrous results.

The use of a plastic or rubber cylinder boot will protect the base of the cylinder and also allow you to stand it up when needed. Take the boot off from time to time to check that the paintwork under it is still in good condition.

If you decide to repaint your cylinder, remove the old paint with a soft scraper (plastic or soft metal) so that you do not scratch the cylinder itself. The use of most liquid or gel paint removers is not recommended, since many of them can change the mechanical properties of the alloy from which the cylinder has been made. For the same reason, be very careful about any paint process that needs heat for curing it. Aluminium-alloy cylinders should not be subjected to any temperature greater than about 140° C.

Do not be tempted to carry out maintenance on the cylinder valve unless you have the necessary expertise. Removal and insertion of the cylinder valve requires special tools and it is vital that such maintenance is carried out to a high degree of safety. As a cylinder owner, it is sufficient for you to keep the valve clean, dry and free from dust or sand particles, particularly around the O-ring seating for the regulator.

Regulators

The regulator is an important piece of the life-support equipment and it is essential that it be maintained in first-rate condition. To ensure this requires considerable expertise and special equipment and, for that reason, it is recommended that you return your regulator to an expert engineer at regular intervals – probably about once a year for normal usage.

The amount of care and maintenance that is within the scope of the average diver is quite limited. Whenever the regulator is not in use, a plug should be fitted over the first-stage inlet. This is usually supplied with the regulator when it is purchased and it serves to prevent foreign bodies and water from entering the first-stage chamber. At the end of each dive, carefully use high-pressure air from the cylinder to blow away water and debris from the first-stage seating, filter and plug. Then fit the plug and screw it tight. On return to base, the whole regulator and its hoses should be immersed in fresh water, cleaned off and then dried.

If additional hoses for pressure gauge, direct feed, etc., are fitted and removed from time to time, take care to ensure that the threads are not damaged and the O-ring seals are still in good condition. A smear of silicone grease will often help. Avoid the use of any other type of grease on breathing apparatus. Check the hoses for fraying and kinks and replace any that appear doubtful. Hose supports can be fitted at one, or both, ends of the hoses. These are

Figure 72   Blowing the dust cap dry

usually rubber or plastic and serve both to protect the metal unions at the ends and to reduce the amount of kinking of the hoses at these points. When refitting hoses, make sure that you replace them in their correct location, i.e. low pressure to low-pressure ports and high pressure (pressure gauge) to high-pressure ports.

Lifejackets

The whole assembly should be washed in fresh water at the end of every dive and then allowed to dry. Blowing the jacket up fully will usually facilitate drying.

Check all straps for fraying or wear and make sure that the buckles are in good condition and can be adjusted, fixed and released easily.

There have been cases reported of bacteria growing inside the bladder of the lifejacket. It is, therefore, a good idea to wash the inside of the bladder with a suitable disinfectant from time to time. Remember to check the watertightness of the bladder and also to make sure that the excess-pressure valve is fully functional. Failure of the overpressure valve could cause the bladder to rupture on a rapid ascent or if the lifejacket is fully inflated at any time. Ensure that any vent valve is functioning properly and allows air to escape freely when operated.

If the lifejacket is of the two-bag variety, make sure that there are no small, sharp pieces of stone or gravel trapped between the two bags. Make sure that the area between the two bags is thoroughly washed clean.

Make sure that the emergency cylinder is in good condition. There is a statutory requirement that the cylinder be tested at regular intervals, as is the case with diving cylinders. But, in any case, it is good practice to have the valve assembly removed every twelve months so that the inside surface can be checked for corrosion. If much corrosion is present inside the cylinder, play safe and replace it. Obviously, the outside of the cylinder is relatively easy to maintain – it simply needs to be kept clean and well painted. Do not forget to make sure that the valve of the emergency cylinder operates easily, and also the clamp which attaches it to the lifejacket.

Remember that you may need to use your lifejacket in an emergency. Do not wait for that emergency to occur before finding out that routine maintenance of the lifejacket is needed.

Wetsuits

After every dive, wash your wetsuit in fresh water, both inside and out. Occasionally washing the inside of the suit with a solution of disinfectant may help prevent nasty smells developing, particularly in the boots.

Dry the suit completely, both inside and out. Remember that strong sunlight can cause deterioration of the adhesives used in the manufacture of the suit. When dry and not being used, the wetsuit can be conveniently hung from a suitable coathanger. Use one with thick arms or else use a thin one with some foam padding fixed to it. Any metal parts such as press studs or zippers should be kept free from debris or corrosion and a smear of lubrication makes for easy operation. Silicone spray is often used and wax can be effective on metal zippers.

As a regular check, examine the suit carefully for signs of the seams opening up or snags or tears occurring. Correcting such faults early may prevent them from getting worse and also, possibly, avoid an expensive major repair.

Suits made from foam neoprene without fabric reinforcement are very susceptible to tearing during dressing and undressing because fingernails have lethal cutting edges for such material. Take great care. Some divers even wear cotton gloves to avoid damage by fingernails when putting on or removing their suit.

Drysuits

If the drysuit is made from foam neoprene, then all the recommendations given for wetsuits also apply. In addition, take great care to ensure that the seals are not damaged; have them repaired immediately if they show signs of wear. Check that air inflation and deflation valves are free from debris and working properly.

A membrane drysuit usually has seals made from latex rubber. These are very thin, very elastic and very easy to tear or puncture. Wash the suit clean and dry it off completely between dives. Strong sunlight can cause the chemical degradation of rubber, so be careful to avoid allowing the seals to come into contact with strong sunshine for long periods of time. Keeping the seals dusted with a little talc helps to improve their life and also makes the suit easier to put on. Try to prevent oil from coming into contact with the latex seals since this can cause them to perish.

A vital part of all drysuits is the waterproof zipper. To ensure its correct function, keep it clean from debris and lubricate it regularly with wax.

Check all seams for deterioration and aim for immediate repair of suspect areas. Do not wait until diving to discover a leaking seam or seal.

As with wetsuits, hanging the suit from a suitable coathanger is a convenient method of storage when the suit is not in use.

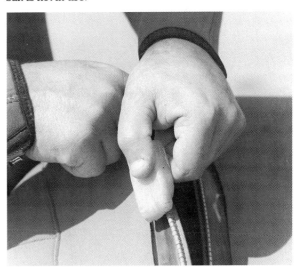

Figure 73   Waxing a drysuit zip

Using Basic Equipment

Fitting and Clearing the Mask

The importance of correct mask-fitting and mask-clearing techniques cannot be over-emphasized. A badly fitting or incorrectly fitted mask can be a major distraction, especially if good mask-clearing techniques have not been mastered.

Having chosen a well-fitting mask, the next stage is to adopt a correct fitting sequence, which you should then habitually follow whenever you put on your mask, above or below the surface.

Step One: Check the mask visually. Is the securing strap fastened and locked at both ends? Is there any damage to face plate or rubber parts?

Step Two: Mist-proof plate. There are a number of suggested methods involving proprietary anti-mist solutions, raw potato, etc., but a coating of saliva well applied with the finger to the inside of the face plate is by far the most common and convenient method. Now rinse the mask, preferably in the water into which you are about to swim.

Step Three: Fit the mask to the face with one hand, pushing back you hair from your forehead with the other.

Step Four: Hold the mask against your face and draw the strap over the crown of your head.

Figure 74   Step Three

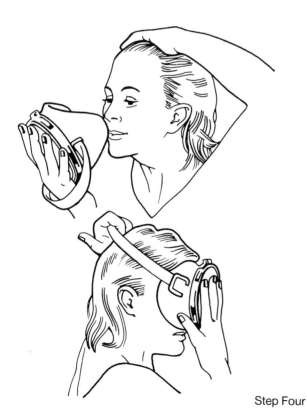

Step Four

Mask Clearing

On the Surface

Should there be any water inside the mask when you are on the surface, simply ease the bottom of the mask away from your face and allow the water to drain out. Nothing more complicated need be attempted.

Below the Surface

Clearing the mask underwater is simply a matter of displacing the water with air. Tilt your head back, trap the top of the mask against your forehead with the fingers of one hand, then gently exhale through your nose. Water will now be displaced by the exhaled air. A second exhalation may be required to complete clearing.

It is recommended that trainee and experienced divers alike should regularly practise mask-clearing techniques.

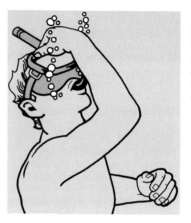

Figure 75   Hold the top of the mask against the face and exhale through the nose to clear any water

Fitting and Clearing the Snorkel

The techniques required for fitting and clearing a snorkel tube are so basic and simple that there is often a tendency to neglect them. However, complete mastery of this essential piece of equipment will ensure comfort and the minimum unwanted water in the diver's mouth. When correctly fitted the snorkel is secure, comfortable and will remain clear of the water surface when you are swimming face down. Therefore it should be secured to the mask strap with a tab or by passing it under the strap, first determining which side of your head the snorkel is designed to fit.

It should be held in your mouth in such a way that the small rubber tabs can be held lightly between the teeth whilst the seal remains in front of the teeth and behind the lips. Test the seal and the angle of your snorkel by submerging your face before commencing swim.

With the mouthpiece gently held in place, move the tube backwards or forwards until it is in a near upright position. Snorkel clearing is achieved by displacing water with air from your lungs.

Method One: On reaching the surface, or when water has entered the tube at the surface, a short explosive breath exhaled through the tube will displace all or most of the water. The next intake of breath should be cautious to

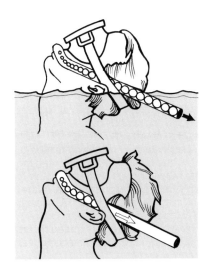

Figure 76
Commence exhaling into the snorkel before reaching the surface and water will be expelled as you break surface

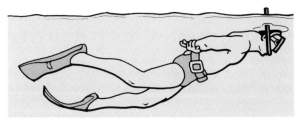

Figure 77 A comfortable surface finning position

avoid inhaling any remaining water; a second blow should complete clearing.

Method Two: Just before reaching the surface, put your head well back so that the open end of the snorkel points downwards; gentle exhalation will displace any water. On reaching the surface, bring your head forward and the tube clear of the water while still exhaling; the tube will be emptied of water.

Fitting and Releasing the Weight Belt

A weight belt will, for comfort's sake, normally be fitted just before the start of the dive and will not be removed until the diver is safely back on the surface or on shore. However, for safety it is essential that this ballast can be discarded at any time, so it must be fitted in such a way that, whatever equipment is worn, the belt with its weights will clear the diver the moment it is released. The belt must therefore be fitted so that no other equipment can obstruct or restrict its immediate release. It should be tight enough to remain comfortable throughout the dive, but remember that if a wetsuit is worn this will compress once you are underwater and this will cause the belt to slacken. The quick-release buckle must be in the most accessible position and unobstructed.

Releasing the Weight Belt

In an emergency the first requirement is cool, quick action. Locate the quick-release buckle on your own or your buddy's weight belt, release the belt but do not let it go until you have cleared it of all other equipment; hold it at arm's length before discarding.

Finning

The diver's fins allow comfortable and easy progress on or under the surface; good technique is essential.

The whole leg should be used to power each fin stroke, keeping the legs as straight as possible with the minimum bending at the knee. Both up and down strokes will effectively propel the diver, with the knees acting as shock absorbers. A 'bicycling' leg action should be avoided as it is a most uneconomical use of energy.

Surface Dives

A well-performed surface dive will take the diver vertically below the surface with the minimum of effort and disturbance of the water.

The dive is best accomplished by three distinct actions, which should blend into one smooth sequence of movement. Start by lying face down on the surface, arms stretched out in front; bend the trunk at the waist, pointing your arms downwards; lift your legs clear of the water so that arms, torso and legs are now straight and vertical. Allow the weight of your legs to push you underwater; at the same time use your arms in a breast-stroke to pull you downwards.

Surfacing Drill

Returning to the surface should be a well-controlled drill, ensuring that after each descent the snorkeller returns safely, ready for the next excursion to the seabed. When making a vertical ascent, fin gently upwards, looking ahead all the way. A hand held above the head will ward off any surface debris and reduce risk of collision with the underside of boats, etc. As an additional safety precaution, turn through 360 degrees as you approach the surface; this will provide visual confirmation of a clear way ahead.

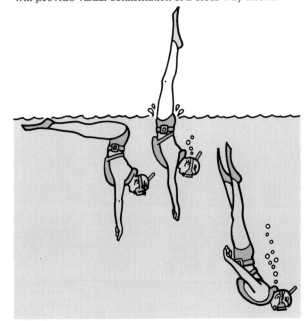

Figure 78 A surface dive

On reaching the surface, clear your snorkel tube while at the same time quickly looking round, making sure that there are no surface craft bearing down on you. At this point you should be prepared to take evasive action by diving back to safety, surfacing again clear of the approaching danger. A distinct OK signal must be exchanged with your companions and cover before you continue to dive. Should the ascent be in an emergency your first action should be to locate the quick-release mechanism of your weight belt; commence swimming upwards, at the same time releasing, removing and jettisoning the weight belt. On reaching the surface, clear your snorkel, inflate your buoyancy compensator or adjustable-buoyancy lifejacket, and indicate an emergency by signalling to your companions and cover.

Breath-Hold Diving in Open Water

Snorkelling activities are not only excellent training for the aqualung diver, but they are, in themselves, a source of much enjoyment. The complete diver will be experienced and competent in breath-hold diving.

Having mastered the use of mask, fins and snorkel in the swimming pool, the transition to open water breath-hold diving involves the use of some additional equipment and new skills. In all but the warmest of waters a diving suit will be required; this will include a hood and possibly gloves or mitts. This protective clothing will, because of its buoyancy, involve the use of a weight belt and weights. With or without a suit, the open-water snorkeller will require a lifejacket, and for additional safety a diver's knife should be carried. This is the minimum equipment required for a snorkelling expedition.

The use of these extra items of equipment involves new skills and techniques. The first of these skills is simply a matter of correct mask fitting, ensuring that the mask is tucked under the hood of the diving suit. This can be a fumbling task and is better completed before you fit your gloves. Familiarity with the use and controls of the lifejacket is essential; inflation and deflation operations should be carried out automatically. While a surface lifejacket will be adequate for snorkelling purposes, an adjustable-buoyancy lifejacket will serve for both aqualung diving and snorkelling, a point worth considering when making a purchase.

Breath-hold diving when using a wetsuit and, to a slightly less extent a drysuit, is all but impossible without the use of ballast in the form of a weight belt. Without this ballast the swimmer will tend to float on top of the surface, making finning difficult, while attempts at surface dives will probably be reduced to comical handstands, the diver rarely getting below waist deep. The belt must have a conventional quick-release system and the diver must be totally familiar with and practised in its use, even when he has cold or gloved hands.

The amount of weight carried should be sufficient to allow the breath-hold diver to go below the surface without expending too much effort. However, a snorkeller must never be overweighted; this is no compensation for good surface-diving technique and is a very dangerous practice, as once below the surface and subject to increased pressure, both the diver's lungs and his suit will rapidly lose buoyancy and the overweighted diver will become dangerously negatively buoyant.

Buoyancy created by the trousers of a diving suit will

Figure 79   Snorkelling is a wonderful way to observe marine life

require the snorkeller to concentrate on his finning action, with particular emphasis on keeping the fins below the surface. Failure to do this will result in noisy, untidy and uneconomical surface swimming. Breath-hold diving is more physically demanding than aqualung diving, therefore snorkelling on the surface should be at a leisurely pace, conserving energy for the dives.

Breath-Hold Diving Techniques

Snorkelling expeditions can take place from shore or boat, but probably most will start from the shore. They must be undertaken by buddy pairs or groups of buddy pairs, who should assist one another to kit up and carry out a pre-dive check before entering the water. During the check they will discuss the safety aspects of the excursion and check their own and each other's equipment with particular emphasis on the location of and operation of the weight-belt release and the lifejacket inflation system. They will decide what the excursion will be, how long, where, for what purpose, and confirm that they understand diver–diver, diver–surface cover signals. It may be some distance from the kitting-up area to the water, therefore the final preparation – fitting mask, fins and snorkel – should be left until the water has been reached. Should there be a need to walk out before starting to swim, walk backwards watching behind you for rocks or anything else which you might fall over. As soon as possible start to swim; there need not be very much depth to accomplish this, but swimming is always safer and more comfortable than walking in fins. Once you have reached an adequate depth, make any final adjustments to your equipment, signal to the shore cover, and off you go.

Having reached a suitable site, diving can commence. Pairs should dive on a 'one diver down, one on the surface' system, with the diver on the surface watching his buddy throughout the dive. Once he is back on the surface and has indicated that he is OK, diver No. 2 may dive while diver No. 1 takes on the role of surface cover. If the first few dives are kept fairly shallow, the depth you can comfortably attain will soon increase. This must be kept within safe limits; the breath-hold diver must not attempt to dive deeper or stay down longer than he can comfortably achieve. The return to shore should start well before cold or tiredness sets in. In this way the party should all reach the shore in comfort.

For additional comfort many snorkellers tow a buoyancy aid with them. This might be a large buoy or an inflated inner tube. It can be used as a support for the diver on the surface, allowing him to relax completely while resting.

The snorkel diver can fulfil a very useful function by giving cover to the submerged diver, either by watching him from the surface or by following his surface marker buoy. This cover can be especially useful when trainees are diving as the snorkeller can offer a safety back-up for the dive leader.

Dangers

Snorkel diving is an enjoyable sport and for the well-prepared and informed snorkeller will be safe and uneventful. However, for the uninformed there are hidden dangers which can, if ignored, be extremely serious. To understand these dangers it is necessary to examine both the physical and the medical aspects of diving.

Effects of Pressure on the Snorkel Diver

It will be clear from an understanding of Boyle's Law that any diver going below the surface will be subjected to an increase in pressure related to the depth to which he dives. It is important that he is skilled in the techniques of ear clearing in order that no pressure damage (barotrauma) occurs (see p. 32). The reduction of volume in the lungs has two main effects. The first is a reduction in the diver's buoyancy (see p. 33), causing him to become apparently heavier the deeper he descends. The snorkel diver's mask and wetsuit will also be subject to increased pressure. The mask will start to squeeze onto the face, but this can easily be overcome by exhaling a little air through the nose.

Hyperventilation

Normally breath-holding will not be dangerous provided the natural desire to breathe created by the build-up of carbon dioxide is obeyed. If the breath-holder attempts to cheat nature by deliberately lowering the normal level of carbon dioxide and increasing that of oxygen by taking a series of very deep breaths before commencing breath-holding, he will deprive the respiratory centre receptors of the stimulus which creates the desire to breathe. This will cause the oxygen to fall to an abnormally low level. This will be picked up by secondary receptors in the heart and brain, which then close down consciousness to hasten recovery. Should this unconsciousness occur in or underwater, drowning will follow. This deliberate deep breathing is known as 'hyperventilation' and should at no time be practised by breath-hold divers. Two medium breaths before each dive are adequate.

Conservation and Spearfishing

Divers and snorkellers alike have a duty to themselves, to those who will follow and to the community at large to conserve the environment they enjoy so much. The simplest way the sports diver can contribute to the conservation of that environment is to follow the maxim: 'Look, but do not touch.' Easier said than done? Well, let's say, look, touch gently, but do not damage or remove.

Snorkelling Activities

Where to Look and What to Look for

If the coast is accessible, this should be your aim. The sea is where marine life will be most prolific and the snorkelling most interesting. Ideally, look for sites with good clear water, with reasonable depth available close to the shore, preferably sheltered, with the minimum of currents and easy access. Sandy beaches rarely fulfil these requirements; they usually produce long swims over a shallow uninteresting seabed. A rocky shoreline will usually provide the type of site you are looking for: a good clean point of entry and exit, with underwater boulders and gullies, deep enough to start your diving close into shore and with a good deal more chance of seeing marine life.

Signals

On the Surface Signals

OK at surface On surfacing, and if all is well, this signal must be given and maintained until it is acknowledged by the surface cover.

Distress at surface – come and get me This signal demands immediate action to assist the distressed diver. Remember also the lack of a signal could mean distress.

Diver to Diver

Stop, stay where you are This is often followed by another signal explaining why, unless the reason is obvious.

OK, all is well This can be either a question from one diver to another or an affirmative reply to this question. Keep the fingers straight.

Go up, I am going up An instruction to ascend. Upward movement of the hand adds emphasis.

You or me The diver points to himself or to another diver, indicating the person referred to in the signal which follows.

Go down, I am going down An instruction to descend, normally made only at the start of a dive.

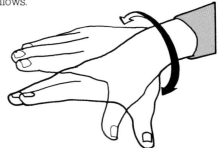

Something wrong This is not a sign of an emergency, but an indication that all is not well. It is usually followed by an indication of the source of trouble.

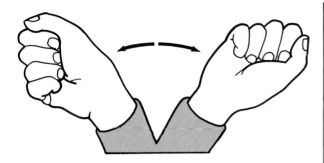

Distress   A signal which elicits immediate action to rescue the diver giving it.

I am on reserve   This signal is used to indicate that the diver's air supply is low and the dive should be terminated. Give the ascend signal in response.

I have no more air   This signal is made by moving the arm with the hand outstretched in and out from the throat. On seeing this signal, close with the diver making it and share air from your regulator.

I cannot pull my reserve   This signal is used in the event of reserve valve failure. Buddy should check the action of the reserve valve and be ready to share air if necessary.

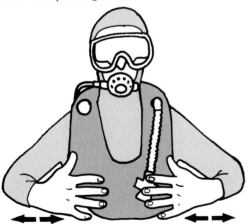

I am out of breath   Your dive buddy indicates his laboured breathing by to-and-fro movements of his hands. Stop, relax and allow your buddy to recover normal breathing.

Signalling

Visual Signalling

The most effective method of diver communication is by the use of hand signals. For this purpose the BSAC have adopted a set of basic hand signals, which are also used by the CMAS and are therefore found in many parts of the diving world. To avoid misunderstandings and confusion, whether at home or abroad, always check that the signals to be used are understood by both divers and surface cover.

Although basic, the BSAC hand signals will cover most normal diving situations and are in the main obvious in their meaning. A pointing finger to indicate direction, a hand held palm to the front, meaning stop, and so on. Those signals which relate to a diver's safety must be learned, remembered and confirmed regularly.

Visual signs are subdivided as follows:

Underwater:	Diver to diver
Surface:	Diver to diver
	Diver on the surface to shore or boat cover
	Boat to boat or boat to shore

Visual Signals Underwater

A regular exchange of signals between divers to pass on instructions, provide information on the dive and a diver's state is desirable but should not be overdone. Each signal is a question, e.g. 'Are you OK?', an instruction or request, e.g. 'Stop', a statement, e.g. 'I am out of breath', or an acknowledgement. Each requires a response and should be repeated until acknowledged by the correct signal or the appropriate action.

When giving signals underwater the diver should first ensure he has the attention of the recipient; he should then make the signal in a clear, accurate and exaggerated gesture and await acknowledgement.

When diving in dark water or at night, divers can use normal hand signals by shining a torch onto the hand, thus illuminating the signal. Great care should be taken to avoid shining the light into a buddy's eyes, thus disrupting his ability to see in the dark for a period of several minutes. A steady torch beam directed by one diver towards another is the signal used to gain the other diver's attention, indicating the wish to close and communicate.

Visual Surface Signals

Diver to Diver

The use of hand signals between divers on the surface, whether in close contact or separated, is preferable to talking or shouting, which requires the removal of the diver's mouthpiece, a practice that is not recommended. Should the surfaced divers be separated, signals should be given as extended arm signals and will probably be restricted to OK or distress. Needless to say, the first priority for these separated divers is for them to come together again.

Diver on the Surface to Boat or Shore Cover

These signals will again be restricted to a few essentials. However, it is important that a diver's cover should be

Figure 80   In dark water illuminate your hand signal

aware of his situation at the surface as this is where he is most vulnerable. A clear OK signal should be exchanged immediately prior to commencing the dive, and again once the diver has returned to the surface. Divers should first check amongst themselves using normal hand signals, then signal to cover by holding a hand straight above the head, fingers in the OK position. Over a distance, only the arm may be visible, therefore a straight arm held high will be read as OK, a waving arm distress. Surface signals in the dark are a steady beam pointed in the direction of boat or shore cover indicating OK. A rapid swinging of the torch beam in a horizontal arc indicates distress. An acknowledged OK signal followed by a controlled horizontal movement of the torch by the diver indicates the diver wishes to be picked up.

Boat to Boat or Boat to Shore

These signals are basically the same as those used by diver to boat and can be used to reassure other cover or summon help.

Rope Signals

The system of communication which has persisted from the earliest days of diving is that of passing signals by means of a rope. Early divers had little choice but to use this system, lacking more sophisticated options. Modern commercial, service and police divers still find the rope signals a useful technique.

Rope signalling is a simple form of communication between a diver and his cover or another diver who is not in visual contact. It consists of a series of long pulls or short tugs on a signal line connecting the two parties, using a code understood by both. Royal Navy and commercial divers use a wide-ranging code of signals made up from pulls – long slow pulls on the signal line – and bells – short tugs. Bells are communicated in pairs; for example, five bells is given by two short tugs followed by a pause, then two more short tugs, a pause, and finally a single short tug.

So that signals are clear and not misunderstood, divers and tenders need to be skilled in the handling of the signal line.

BSAC Rope Signals

The British Sub-Aqua Club has adopted five rope signals considered to be the minimum that should be known and understood by all sport divers. These are for maintaining contact in conditions of low visibility.

Divers engaged in complex projects requiring a more comprehensive range of signals should familiarize themselves with the standardized signals used by commercial and Royal Navy divers. (These are reproduced in full in the *BSAC Advanced Diving Manual.*)

Giving and Receiving Rope Signals

A sequence of signals will, with the exception of the emergency signal, commence with a single pull to call attention. This and all other signals must be acknowledged by the recipient. If, after a short pause, a signal has not been acknowledged, it should be repeated. Should the diver fail to respond after several attempts to make contact, the stand-by diver should be sent down to investigate the diver's situation. A signal which is incorrectly acknowledged should be repeated until correct acknowledgement indicates understanding.

Signalling to Other Surface Craft

All diving activities at sea, and this includes sport diving, are affected by the *International Regulations for Preventing Collisions at Sea, 1972.*

For reasons of safety, special attention should be paid to rule 27(e), which requires that, when diving is taking place, a rigid replica of international code flag A not less than 1 metre in height should be exhibited. Showing the flag indicates: 'I have a diver down, keep well clear and at slow speed.' The flag should be hoisted when divers are about to enter the water and lowered as soon as the divers are back on board.

On small sport diving boats it is permissible to display a flag half the size required by rule 27(e). This flag must be rigid and visible from all directions, with the lowest point at least 1 metre above sea level. In larger boats it should be flown as high as possible.

BSAC ROPED DIVER SIGNALS

Signal	Surface	Diver
One pull	Are you OK?	I am OK
Two pulls	Stay put	I am stationary
Three pulls*	Go on down	Going down
Four pulls*	Come up	Coming up
Continuous pulls	Emergency – bringing you to the surface	Emergency – bring me to the surface

If you wish to stop the diver before he reaches the surface or closes with you if you are using a buddy line, give the two pulls signal.

*When used in conjunction with a buddy line, there is a slight variation in meaning:

Three pulls	Move away from me (to limit of line)
Four pulls	Come to me

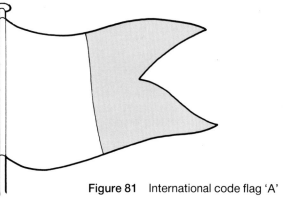

Figure 81   International code flag 'A'

Sound Signalling

With the exception of verbal surface communication, sound signals are the least used among sport divers.

Through-water speech communication and other electronic equipment is expensive and difficult to justify for recreational use. Without such sophisticated equipment, sound signalling becomes very limited as its use is restricted to attracting attention or for the emergency recall of divers.

Diver to Diver

In the comparative silence of the underwater world, any noise is sure to attract attention. A diver wishing to communicate with a buddy who may not be looking in his direction can use sound to attract him. This can be accomplished by tapping a cylinder with the handle of a diving knife. Any metallic clang will carry a reasonable distance; banging rocks or stones together makes a less distinct noise, which probably will not carry so well. Shouting or tooting into the mouthpiece also makes a sound which will be heard by a diver who is reasonably close and is a way to attract attention, after which visual signals can be resumed. Because it is impossible to determine direction of sound underwater, sound signals cannot be relied upon as a method of relocating a buddy who is out of sight.

Surface to Diver

Any prearranged sound signal agreed at the surface can be used as an emergency recall signal. Striking the side of a hard boat below the water line, tapping a metal diving ladder or banging two metal objects together just below the surface produces sounds that will travel a limited distance underwater. A boat engine will be clearly audible to divers and can therefore be used to signal. Revving the engine in short bursts can be used as a signal to return to the surface. A thunderflash exploding below the surface will be clearly heard over a wide area. This method, which is much favoured by service divers, involves the use of a small thunderflash waterproofed with wax. This can be positioned to explode below the surface by adding a small weight. The exploding firework, which produces a loud thud underwater, is comparatively harmless to the submerged divers provided it does not explode in close proximity to them.

Surface Sound Signals

Attempting to communicate across anything but the shortest distance, especially at sea, can be difficult; the wind will carry the sound away or the noise of the sea drown it. The use of a loudhailer will help, while a whistle may be heard where a voice is not, but once again a metallic sound will carry most successfully. A bell will often be heard when other sounds are dulled or carried away by sea and wind.

VHF Radio

Until recent years it was unusual to find radio transmission equipment on board a small diving boat, but, with the introduction of small transistorized VHF sets, more and more diving clubs and boat owners are appreciating the value of this useful piece of emergency equipment. Even small sets will provide the user with a power output of 25 watts, which is the maximum permitted by the GPO in the UK, the mandatory Channel 16, the international calling and distress channel, and Channel 6, the first intership channel. There are also some spare channels which provide the user with any particular wavelength required. The Post Office requires that the set must be of an approved type, that it should be licensed and that the owner or person who will operate the set has a certificate of competency. For such a certificate an inspector of the Department of Trade will ensure that the user understands the correct transmitting procedures and the discipline essential when working at sea. Anyone intending to purchase a VHF set is recommended to consult the *Handbook for Radio Operators* published by Her Majesty's Stationary Office. *VHF Radio Telephony for Yachts* by the Royal Yachting Association and Reed's also contain useful information. In addition the British Sub-Aqua Club coaching scheme runs a marine radio operation course for divers. This course teaches correct techniques for using radio at sea and prepares for the Restricted Certificate of Competence in Radio Telephony examination.

Standard Phraseology

It is important when using a VHF set at sea that correct procedures and phraseology are used. The phonetic alphabet and standard phrases are intended for understanding and economy of words across crowded airwaves. It should also be remembered that a standard phrase will usually be understood even when distorted by poor transmission.

In the UK an initial call is normally made on Channel 16. The coast station will then acknowledge and switch the caller to another frequency.

Signalling Distress at Sea

The signal that takes precedence over all others is 'MAYDAY'. This call should always be made on Channel 16 and repeated three times.

'MAYDAY SEELONCE' from the coast station forbids any other use of the channel. 'MAYDAY PRUDONCE' indicates silence can be relaxed. 'MAYDAY SEELONCE FEENEE' means the incident is over.

Any operator hearing a 'MAYDAY' call has an obligation to take action. If no coast guard or other response is heard, then a 'MAYDAY RELAY' should be transmitted.

Urgency which requires the transmitting of an urgent message in a diving accident for example, but where the safety of the boat is not at risk, is indicated by the words 'PAN-PAN' repeated three times. This message will take priority over everything except 'MAYDAY'.

A safety message which may contain important weather information or something similar will be preceded by the call 'SAY-CURE-E-TAY' repeated three times.

Figure 82   A portable marinized VHF radio

The Phonetic Alphabet

The phonetic alphabet which is used with the English pronunciation is as follows:

Letter	Word	Pronunciation in English
A	Alfa	*AL* FAH
B	Bravo	*BRAH* VOH
C	Charlie	*CHAR* LEE or *SHAR* LEE
D	Delta	*DELL* TAH
E	Echo	*ECK* OH
F	Foxtrot	*FOKS* TROT
G	Golf	GOLF
H	Hotel	HOH *TELL*
I	India	*IN DEE* AH
J	Juliett	*JEW* LEE *ETT*
K	Kilo	*KEY LOH*
L	Lima	*LEE MAH*
M	Mike	*MIKE*
N	November	NO *VEM* BER
O	Oscar	*OSS* CAH
P	Papa	*PAH PAH*
Q	Quebec	*KEH BECK*
R	Romeo	*ROW* ME OH
S	Sierra	SEE *AIR* RAH
T	Tango	*TANG* GO
U	Uniform	*YOU* NEE FORM or *OO* NEE FORM
V	Victor	*VIK* TAH
W	Whisky	*WISS* KEY
X	X-ray	*ECKS* RAY
Y	Yankee	*YANG* KEY
Z	Zulu	*ZOO* LOO

(The syllables to be emphasized are shown in italics.)

The following pronunciation is used when transmitting numerals:

Numeral or Numeral Element	Pronunciation
0	*ZE-RO*
1	*WUN*
2	*TOO*
3	*TREE*
4	*FOW-ER*
5	*FIFE*
6	*SIX*
7	*SEV-EN*
8	*AIT*
9	*NINE-ER*
Decimal	*DAY-SE-MAL*
Thousand	*TOUSAND*

In radiotelephony all numbers are transmitted by pronouncing each digit separately, except that whole thousands are transmitted by pronouncing each digit in the number of thousands followed by the word 'thousand'. For example,

600 is spoken as 'Six zero zero'
1580 is spoken as 'One five eight zero'
12,000 is spoken as 'One two thousand'

Progressive Training Skills

Diving is a sport in which training is never really completed. Even the most experienced diver can learn something new or can practise and improve his skills, in particular, safety skills such as mask clearing, lifesaving and sharing techniques, which require regular practice to maintain optimum levels of safety.

Equipment Assembly

Normally, the backpack or harness will already be attached to your cylinder. Before connecting your regulator to the cylinder valve, check that the O-ring is in place and undamaged. Then stand the cylinder up with the backpack facing away from you and open the cylinder valve momentarily to clear any water or dust from the valve. Connect the first stage by locating the A-clamp screw into the recess on the cylinder valve. Check that the regulator is positioned correctly so that the mouthpiece is not upside-down!

Draw the first stage gently onto the O-ring (O-rings require little pressure to seal). Open the cylinder valve slowly, at the same time ensuring that the submersible pressure gauge is pointing away from you or anybody else. Ensure the cylinder valve is fully open.

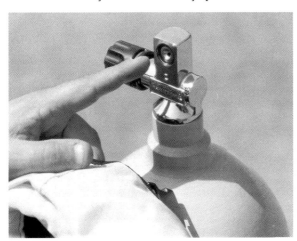

Figure 83   Check the condition of the O-ring

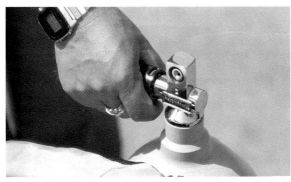

Figure 84   Clear the valve with a quick blast of air

Figure 85   Fit the regulator to the cylinder

Regulator Checks

Open the cylinder valve and take a few breaths from the mouthpiece, at the same time watching the submersible pressure gauge; if the needle swings drastically then it is possible that you have a blocked filter. Turn the air off, while continuing to breathe from the regulator; the needle should drop to zero and no further air will be available. However, should you continue to receive air, the regulator should not be used until it has been checked by an authorized servicing agent.

Figure 86   Test the regulator before kitting up

Checking for Leaks

Open·the cylinder valve and listen for leaks; a slight hissing from the second stage can sometimes be stopped by pressing the purge button. Close the cylinder valve and check the submersible pressure gauge; should the needle drop on its own accord, then there is a leak in the system. An easy way to test for leaks is to submerge the aqualung by holding it just below the surface; any leaks will quickly be identified by the escaping bubbles.

Kitting Up

Before putting your equipment on, the harness straps should be adjusted so that they fit you; use the shoulder adjusters to lengthen or shorten the strap. Ensure that the waist strap is disconnected.

Use your buddy to hold the aqualung while you slip into the harness. Make sure that the straps do not get trapped beneath the aqualung and that your regulator is not accidentally trapped under the waist strap. Pull down on the shoulder adjusters, at the same time leaning slightly forward; this allows easier adjustment. Connect the waist strap to the correct position and adjust the shoulder straps, for comfort.

Fit the weight belt, ensuring that, should you need to release it, it will fall free and not snag on any other piece of equipment.

When the aqualung is in place and secure, check the height of the aqualung by tilting your head back; if your head hits the regulator, then the position is too high and the harness will require adjustment.

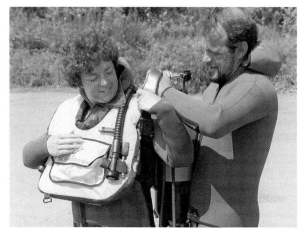

Figure 89   Your buddy should help you put on the aqualung

Figure 87   Check the harness straps

Figure 90   Adjust the straps to position the aqualung

Figure 88   Check the pressure in the cylinder

Figure 91   Check that the aqualung is not positioned too high

Clearing the Mouthpiece and Mask

The Mouthpiece

The mouthpiece of a single-hose regulator is designed in such a way that in normal use water will not enter. However, should the mouthpiece be removed from the diver's mouth for any reason, it will fill with water. It can easily be evacuated via the exhaust valve, requiring only a gentle exhalation of air to displace any water. The position of this valve should be noted, as for efficient clearing it needs to be the lowest point of the regulator.

Should the diver, through poor positioning or insufficient breath, be unable to clear the regulator normally, then the purging facility can be used. The control button for this is usually situated at the front and in the centre of the regulator; when pressed it will allow air to flow freely through the mouthpiece, quickly clearing any water that may be there.

Figure 93   Refitting the regulator mouthpiece

previously described. Next, flood it completely; clear again. Remove your mask, hold it in one hand, making sure that it is the right way up, nose pocket at the bottom. Pass the strap around the front and over the back of the hand holding the mask. With your free hand, push back your hair and hold it clear of your forehead; place mask on your face, pull strap over and onto the back of your head. It should now be clear of water.

This drill should be practised in progressively deeper water until it becomes second nature in any situation.

Descents and Ascents

Descents

Descending when wearing an aqualung should be accomplished smoothly and without disturbance of the surface. The descent can be head first – a surface dive – or feet first. Either way, correct buoyancy is important for a comfortable, safe, neat dive. Too much weight at the surface will result in a rapid, unsafe descent, while the diver who is underweighted will flounder in exhausting attempts to get below the surface.

Before commencing a descent, make sure your snorkel has been exchanged for your aqualung mouthpiece. Check there is no excess air in your adjustable-buoyancy lifejacket or buoyancy compensator and signal your intention to dive.

Surface Dive

This is a head-first dive. Start by lying face down on the surface, bend at the waist, point your arms straight down, lift your legs out of the water so that they are vertical, and allow the weight of your legs and fins to push you down.

Feet-First Descent

Start by finning so as to lift your body high out of the water. Now relax, point fins down to reduce resistance, and sink. When sufficient depth is achieved, turn over into a head-down position and fin. When descending in open water care should be taken to maintain buddy contact throughout.

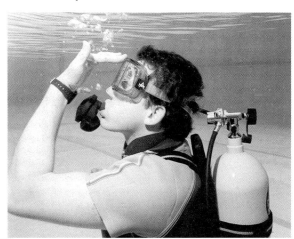

Figure 92   Clearing the face mask

Mask Clearing

Clearing a flooded mask is achieved by displacing any water by air exhaled through the nose. This is done as follows: tilt the head back until the face plate is as near parallel to the surface as possible, gently press the fingers of one hand against the top edge of the mask, steadily exhale through the nose to displace water, which will exit from the bottom edge of the mask. There is always a chance that water will enter or the mask become dislodged during a dive. It is therefore important that every diver is efficient and practised in clearing and replacing a mask in a variety of conditions.

A mask fitted with a drain valve can be cleared without tilting by simply holding the mask in place and exhaling through the nose. However, as drain valves cannot be totally relied on, the owner of such a mask should be proficient in the basic mask-clearing techniques.

Training Drill for Mask Clearing

In shallow water, partly flood your mask by easing the top edge away from your forehead; clear in the manner

Ascending

Normal ascent and surfacing drill is carried out as follows. Exchange 'Go up' signals, face your buddy and make a controlled ascent, looking alternately up to the surface and behind your buddy. On reaching the surface, look all around, exchange aqualung mouthpiece for snorkel, finally give and receive 'OK' signal.

Mobility

The first priority for mobility is correct buoyancy. The aim, as always, should be for neutral buoyancy (see p. 76). The diver who is over- or underweight will be at an immediate disadvantage.

Mobility Exercises

The performance of rolls in the safe confines of a training pool or other sheltered water will develop confidence and overcome the initial feelings of disorientation.

In 2–3 metres depth:

Forward Rolls

Start from a kneeling or standing position. Use breathing control to increase your buoyancy. As your body lifts, bend forward from the waist into a forward roll, pulling water towards you with hands and arms to drive your body round. Return to a kneeling position, exhaling to reduce buoyancy.

Backward Rolls

Begin as above, but bend backwards, use hands and arms to drive your body round by pushing water away from you.

Horizontal Rolls

While finning along 1 metre off the bottom, perform a barrel roll. Twist your body, using your hands to steer you through the roll.

Familiarization with Full Kit

Most diving trainees will have completed initial training in the confines of a swimming pool or other sheltered-water training area. The essential basic diving and life-saving skills will have been mastered and practised and much confidence gained. At this stage and before venturing forth into open water, the trainee needs to put all his skills together while using full open-water diving equipment, including, if conditions outdoors demand, a diving suit.

The familiarization will include preparation and fitting of all equipment, assembly and testing of aqualung and adjustable-buoyancy lifejacket or buoyancy compensator, buddy checks, entry and buoyancy checks, mask and mouthpiece clearing, sharing air with your buddy, simulating an emergency while taking turns to play the static and active roles. There will be buoyancy control and controlled ascents using an adjustable-buoyancy lifejacket or buoyancy compensator inflation and venting systems, and a full lifesaving exercise involving fast underwater swimming, lifting and supporting and expired-air resuscitation in the water, finishing with handing up of weight belt and aqualung and leaving the water.

This familiarization exercise will be completed in a depth of 2–3 metres.

Figure 94   A forward roll

Figure 95   A group under training

Buddy Breathing

In the event of a member of a diving team losing his air supply or suffering a regulator malfunction, sharing air with a buddy may well be the safest solution to the emergency. It is therefore most important that every diver is practised in the techniques of air sharing.

Starting with pool training, buddy breathing drills should be perfected during open-water training and practised on a regular basis, thus ensuring that the techniques can be performed confidently under any conditions.

Buddy breathing involves the sharing by two divers of the air supply carried by one of them. This can be achieved in two basic ways: by the use of an 'octopus rig', which is a supplementary second stage on the donor's regulator, or by taking turns at breathing from one regulator.

Using an Octopus Rig

Should the buddy donating air be equipped with a supplementary mouthpiece, it is comparatively simple for this to be handed to the diver requiring air, who will purge, fit the mouthpiece and start breathing air from his buddy's set.

Training Method

Signal to your buddy 'Out of air'. Buddy approaches face to face, offering the octopus mouthpiece at the receiver's eye level, holding the second stage so that the purge button is visible and accessible. Buddies will hold on to each other while sharing. Once both divers are settled and have established normal breathing, they should practise swimming horizontally.

Sharing Air

The sharing of one mouthpiece requires a little more discipline. As each diver will be without the regulator for half the sharing time, it is important that exchanges are smooth and not fumbled. Firm contact and correct positioning are vital for successful sharing.

Training

The first practice drill should take place in a training pool or other sheltered water. Kneeling on the bottom, buddies will position themselves at right angles to each other. The donor should have the hose of his regulator coming over the shoulder opposite the side where the recipient is positioned. Each diver will take a firm hold of his buddy's cylinder neck so as not to drift away from his companion. The diver requiring air will signal 'Out of air' and remove his mouthpiece. The donor will then pass his mouthpiece, holding it close to the mouth of the recipient, who will guide it by placing his own hand over the donor's. He will then purge the water from the mouthpiece, take two breaths and relax his hold, allowing the donor to recover the mouthpiece. This cycle can be repeated until complete confidence is achieved. As this drill is intended as practice for assisted ascent, both divers should, when not breathing from the mouthpiece, gently exhale to simulate the release of expanding air, essential when doing an assisted ascent. Once a sharing rhythm has been established, training can progress to sharing while swimming horizontally.

Removal of Equipment

The ability to remove and refit equipment underwater has both practical and psychological value. A diver who is able to take off his aqualung and other items of equipment,

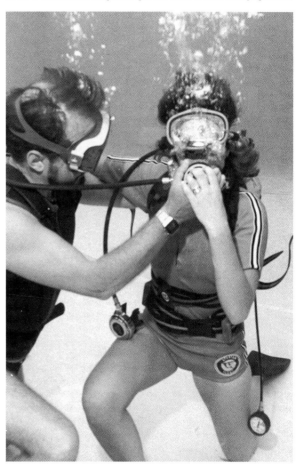

Figure 96 Practising regulator sharing

then refit them in an orderly, unflustered manner, will have gained considerable confidence.

Practice in the Training Pool

Once the diver is competent in removing, refitting and clearing his mask and mouthpiece he may logically progress to removing and refitting the aqualung set. Sitting or kneeling on the pool bottom, disconnect any inflators fitted. Then slacken the shoulder strap opposite the regulator hose, pass your arm through the loosened strap while maintaining a firm hold on the other strap. With your free hand, release the waist strap and slide the aqualung sideways and around to the front. It is important to remember to remove the set on the same side as your regulator hose. Refit in reverse order.

The next step is to practise removing the aqualung at the surface. Release and hand your weight belt to an assistant on the poolside. Turn around so that the assistant can hold your aqualung steady while you remove your equipment in the sequence previously described. Once assistant can lift it clear of the water.

A great deal of sport diving is carried out from small boats and getting back into the boat is easier when your weight belt and aqualung have been removed. Clearly, mastering this technique in a pool will be excellent preparation.

Figure 97 Loosening the shoulder strap . . .

Figure 98 one arm through . . .

Figure 99 releasing the waist belt . . .

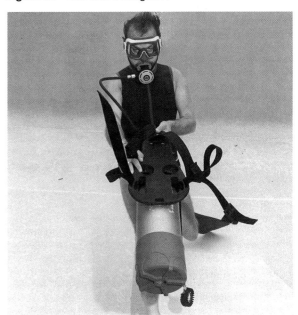

Figure 100 bringing the set forward

Lifejacket Training

The lifejacket is an essential part of your safety equipment. Although lifejackets differ in terms of shape, size and fittings, there are certain elements common to all. The correct techniques for inflating and deflating your lifejacket are among the many skills which are best mastered in a swimming pool or sheltered water before venturing into open water.

One of the primary functions of any lifejacket is to support an unconscious diver on the surface face up, with his head clear of the water. Therefore an inflated lifejacket should provide buoyancy at the front of the diver and around the neck. Most lifejackets specifically made for divers conform to this primary function. However, a diver's lifejacket has other important roles: it enables him to adjust his buoyancy during the dive and, in the event of an emergency, it can quickly be inflated in order to facilitate a controlled buoyant ascent (see p. 131).

The most popular lifejackets are the stabilizer (waistcoat) type and the adjustable-buoyancy lifejacket (front-mounted) type. However, the means by which different types of lifejackets are inflated and deflated vary. Therefore it is essential that you familiarize yourself with your lifejacket controls.

Filling the Emergency Air Cylinder

Lifejackets fitted with an independent compressed-air cylinder should be charged before every dive. This is achieved by decanting air from your aqualung cylinder in the following way:

1. Ensure that your aqualung cylinder is charged to its normal working pressure. Remember that undercharging the emergency cylinder can seriously reduce its capacity to inflate the lifejacket fully at depth. Most lifejackets have a capacity of 18–20 litres of air and the emergency cylinder has a capacity of around 80 litres. Therefore, when charged to capacity, the emergency cylinder will fully inflate the lifejacket approximately four times at the surface, but only once at 30 metres (see Boyle's Law, p. 94).
2. Remove the emergency cylinder from your lifejacket and connect the A-clamp to the cylinder valve in the same way as you would connect your regulator.
3. Open the emergency cylinder valve fully, then slowly open the aqualung cylinder valve, allowing the air to flow slowly to avoid overheating.
4. When the sound of flowing air ceases, close the aqualung cylinder valve, then the emergency cylinder valve.
5. Before trying to disconnect the emergency cylinder you must purge the air remaining in the system by using the purge button.
6. Refit the emergency cylinder to the lifejacket and briefly 'crack' open the valve to test that the lifejacket inflates correctly.

Figure 101   Filling the emergency cylinder

Fitting the Lifejacket

Fitting the stabilizer lifejacket is a fairly simple procedure. Normally the harness and cylinder backpack form an integral part of the lifejacket. Therefore adjustment of the waist strap will usually ensure a good fit. Some stabilizers are fitted with side adjusters and a chest strap. Fit the jacket by putting your arms through the armholes – just like putting on a coat! Then, to ensure correct adjustment, inflate the jacket fully by mouth, checking that it does not restrict your breathing, or movement.

The adjustable-buoyancy lifejacket (front-mounted) is fitted over the head and has two adjustable straps; a waist strap and a crotch strap. By far the most important of these is the crotch strap, as this provides the main support and prevents the jacket being lifted over your head. Unlike the stabilizer, the front-mounted lifejacket is fitted before your aqualung and weight belt. Should you wish to jettison the weight belt or aqualung in an emergency, the lifejacket will remain undisturbed. Adjust the straps so that they are tight with the lifejacket fully inflated. The weight belt should be worn when checking this. Too tight, and it will be uncomfortable; too slack, and it will ride up when inflated. Note that some of the older lifejackets require the crotch strap to be fairly slack; this slackness is taken up when the lifejacket is fully inflated.

Surface Skills

Use of the lifejacket to increase buoyancy at the surface before or after a dive is normal practice and should be encouraged. However, the lifejacket should not be used to compensate for overweighting. A check for neutral buoyancy should be carried out initially with the lifejacket vented.

You should regularly practise inflation at the surface using the emergency cylinder or direct feed. Practise inflation by mouth while treading water in order to conserve air in the emergency cylinder. Only a few breaths are needed to give you that extra buoyancy desirable for a long surface swim.

Practise surface swimming, on your back and face submerged, with the lifejacket fully and partially inflated, both with a snorkel and an aqualung.

Venting the lifejacket at the surface is usually achieved by pulling down on the dump valve or by holding the mouth-inflation hose above the head and depressing the vent button. Water pressure will compress the lifejacket and expel the air. As long as you are not negatively buoyant, full venting of the lifejacket will not send you plummeting to the bottom. You should sink slowly to the bottom, controlling the descent by careful breathing from your regulator.

Compensation

All types of diving dress compress underwater, leaving the diver in a state of negative buoyancy which at depth can be excessive. While drysuits can be inflated to overcome this, the wetsuited diver should use his

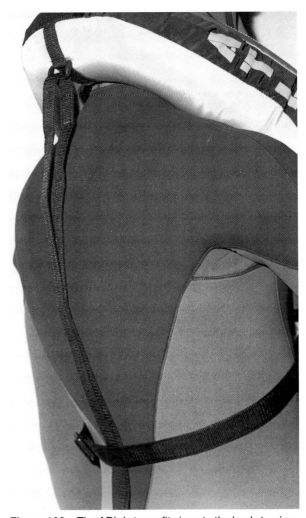

Figure 102 The ABLJ straps fit close to the body to give support to the diver. They must lie underneath all other equipment such as weightbelt and aqualung harness

lifejacket to regain his state of neutral buoyancy. Again, this is normal practice and is one of the prime purposes of this piece of equipment.

Accompanied by your instructor, in shallow water (3 metres maximum) depress the direct-feed button. The transition from negative to positive buoyancy will be felt and, as you start to ascend from the pool floor, air should be vented/dumped. This is a two-handed operation: one hand controls inflation while the other hand is on the dump valve to avoid overinflation. Now try the same exercise using the emergency air cylinder. You will notice that the jacket is filled at a faster rate than with the direct feed. This is because the direct feed is usually fitted to the low-pressure side of your regulator, whereas the air cylinder is at a higher pressure.

Buoyancy Control

The feeling of weightlessness is one of the attractions of diving, but this condition is not achieved by accident. A diver, as any other object, will sink or float in water according to the amount of water he or it displaces. This is Archimedes' Principle and it serves to guide us in our aim to achieve weightlessness, or neutral buoyancy.

If an object floats in water it is said to have 'positive buoyancy'. If it sinks, it has 'negative buoyancy'. As divers, we are interested in being able to control our buoyancy so that we can rise, sink or remain still in the water. It is the ability to adjust our buoyancy easily that has significantly improved safety and diver comfort.

Most humans float in water and many people can demonstrate this easily by floating on their backs or vertically in the water. If you float vertically, you will note that if you take a deep breath you will rise in the water and, conversely, if you breathe out you will sink. This is due to your lungs increasing in volume as you inhale, thus increasing your overall volume and hence the amount of water you displace; at the point at which the weight of the water you displace is greater than your own bodyweight you float.

When you go diving in cold water you add a layer of insulation in the form of a diving suit, either wet or dry. This has the effect of increasing your volume and thus making you more buoyant. You then add an aqualung which is usually negatively buoyant. The combined effect of this is to increase your buoyancy, so, to counteract this, you add weight in the form of a weight belt. The aim is to add sufficient weight to achieve neutral buoyancy. This is the state in which the diver can rise in the water just by inhaling, and sink by exhaling, or hover by holding his breath. The correct weight to carry can easily be determined by trial and error, but there are some further factors to be taken into account.

The Effects of Depth

As the diver descends, the increasing water pressure will tend to compress his suit and, in the case of a thick neoprene suit, the loss in buoyancy will be significant. As a suit is compressed the bubbles in the material become smaller, the suit's volume decreases and so does its buoyancy.

In the case of a drysuit the water pressure will tend to compress the thermal underwater and the airspace it creates, but the diver will restore this airspace by means of inflation and therefore not suffer a loss of buoyancy. (A diver in tropical water who does not need to wear thermal protection will not experience this problem.)

Consumption of Air

The air contained in the diver's air cylinder has weight, typically 2–3 kg for a fully charged cylinder. Weigh your cylinder when it is full and when it is empty to see how significant this amount can be. As the air is consumed by the diver the cylinder becomes correspondingly lighter, thus increasing the diver's buoyancy as the dive progresses.

Other Equipment

Items of heavy equipment carried by the diver add to his overall weight and have just the same effect as the weight belt. These could take the form of a camera, an underwater lamp, surveying equipment, tools for an underwater job, or something being transported to an underwater site. In the latter case the effect of leaving an item on the bottom also needs to be taken into account as the diver will be lighter on his return trip.

Water Density

Salt water is denser than fresh water and thus gives greater support to divers and swimmers. You will therefore require more weight in the sea than you do in fresh water. Remember, if you are diving in fresh water after an excursion to the sea, to lighten your belt, by as much as 2/3 kg.

Lifejackets

The means of gaining neutral buoyancy with all these variables is the adjustable-buoyancy lifejacket, the air-inflated lifejacket or the buoyancy compensator. This essential piece of equipment enables air to be introduced into the bag of the lifejacket until sufficient additional buoyancy is obtained to overcome the increase in weight. The air so introduced can then be released (dumped) by means of a valve if the buoyancy is too great. This is necessary in the case of a wetsuit compressed at depth, since it will regain its buoyancy as the diver returns to the surface. The fine adjustment of buoyancy is usually via an inflator coupled to the regulator which allows the appropriate amount of air to be fed into the lifejacket directly from the diver's main air supply. An additional supply of air to give buoyancy in an emergency can be carried in a small compressed-air cylinder attached to the lifejacket. An alternative to this is a small cartridge of compressed carbon dioxide which gives a fixed amount of gas when fired. There is also the possibility of inflating the jacket by mouth.

Buoyancy During the Dive

The aim is to be neutrally buoyant at all times during the dive. To plan for this you must take into account the extra buoyancy you expect to get as you empty your cylinder, plus the fact that you are more buoyant near the surface.

You need enough weight to allow you to leave the surface comfortably without too much floundering and without having to pull yourself down. As you descend, feed some air into your lifejacket to combat the loss of suit buoyancy. The greatest loss of buoyancy is nearest the surface, so the need to make adjustment will be greatest at the beginning of the dive. As the dive progresses you will need to release some air to compensate for the increasing buoyancy of the cylinder, and as you return to the surface you will need to release any air remaining in your jacket so as not to ascend too fast.

The ability to control buoyancy is important because of the need to either stop at 6m for a decompression stop or assume an ascent rate of 1 minute for the final 6m. Remember that an overfast ascent is a risk to the diver and may provoke the onset of decompresson sickness. Once back on the surface it is useful to be able to inflate the lifejacket to give support while you are waiting to be picked up or for the return to the shore.

Remember that you can gain buoyancy quickly in an emergency in two main ways.

1. By fast inflation of your lifejacket by its small air cylinder or CO_2 cartridge.
2. By dropping your weight belt, making sure that it falls clear and does not catch on any other part of your equipment.

In both cases you should then rise to the surface easily. However, if you have miscalculated your weight badly you may have to use both methods. A torn wetsuit has no effect on buoyancy but a torn drysuit will make the diver heavier due to the loss of air normally trapped in the suit.

Figure 103   Factors influencing the diver's buoyancy

Adjustable buoyancy lifejacket – used to compensate for buoyancy adjustments at depth

Wetsuit – loses buoyancy due to compression at depth

Weightbelt – to give diver neutral buoyancy in the water by compensating for buoyant items

Aqualung cylinder – increases in buoyancy as air is consumed during dive

BC inflator allows fine adjustment of buoyancy by feeding air into BC from cylinder

Surface marker buoy – can provide additional surface buoyancy

The diver – buoyancy will vary with build and weight

Accessories will add to diver's total negative or positive buoyancy according to their characteristics

Respiration

Body Metabolism

The body is composed of a series of organs, for example the brain, the liver, the heart. Each organ is composed of microscopic compartments or cells. Each cell has one or more specialized functions. Some cells transmit electrical impulses. These are nerve cells. Others, muscle cells, produce the mechanical action required for movement. Some, such as the kidney cells, are concerned with removal of waste products.

To carry out its function each cell requires energy. Energy is derived by combining food with oxygen.

```
Food + oxygen → energy + carbon dioxide +
            water + waste products
```

This is called 'metabolism' and the process is similar to combustion, which liberates energy in the form of heat and light.

```
Fuel + oxygen → energy + carbon dioxide + water
```

Without food from our diet or oxygen from the air we breathe, energy cannot be produced and the cells will die. If essential cells are killed, we too will die.

The body is able to store unused nutrients which, when food supplies are scarce, can then be used for energy production. Most unused nutrient is stored as fat. Because of these fat stores, people can go for days without food.

Unfortunately, the body has no way of storing oxygen. After a few minutes without oxygen some cells are irreparably damaged. Those which are most susceptible to lack of oxygen are the ones which have the highest energy requirements, particularly those of the brain.

As a result, an efficient system has been developed for transporting oxygen from the air to the organ which requires it. The system involves the lungs, the blood, the heart and the blood vessels. This transport system is also used to remove waste products from the tissues. Carbon dioxide is a waste gas which dissolves in the blood and is carried to the lungs, where it is liberated when we breathe out. Other waste products of metabolism, including water, are excreted through the kidneys.

The energy requirements of some organs are more or less constant. These organs need the same amounts of food and oxygen at all times. Other organs have periods when the cells are inactive and require only small amounts of food and oxygen to keep them ticking over. At other times these organs do large amounts of work and require lots of food and oxygen.

The brain is an organ which has a relatively constant energy requirement. Even when we sleep the brain's requirement changes little. The only effective way to reduce the brain's energy requirement is to cool it.

Muscles are organs which require little energy when inactive. When we do strenuous work, the energy requirement, or the metabolic rate of the active muscles, may increase over a hundredfold.

Circulation

The circulation is like the central heating system in a building. It consists of a series of pipes, the blood vessels, which contain fluid, blood, and a pump, the heart. A central heating system transports hot water from a boiler to radiators in the rooms. The circulation transports oxygen from the air in the lungs and food from the gut to the tissues. The circulation also removes waste products for excretion.

Blood is a complex fluid which consists of individual cells floating in liquid, the plasma. The average adult contains about 5 litres of blood, of which 55 per cent is plasma and 45 per cent is cells. Plasma consists of a solution of salts, sugars and special proteins, dissolved in water.

There are three types of blood cell. The majority are red cells, which are responsible for carrying oxygen. White cells are responsible for fighting infection. Platelets are the third type of blood cells. These combine with certain blood proteins to form clots and prevent bleeding.

The red colour of the blood is due to a chemical in the red blood cells called haemoglobin. On its own haemoglobin is actually blue, but it combines very readily with oxygen to form oxyhaemoglobin, which is red. Certain chemicals can cause haemoglobin to give up the oxygen which is bound to it. One of these chemicals is produced by working tissues.

The heart consists of four chambers. It has two atria or collecting chambers and two ventricles or pumping chambers. The right atrium and ventricle really form a separate pump from that of the left atrium and ventricle.

The right atrium receives blood returning to the heart from the head and arms via a large vein called the superior vena cava and from the lower trunk and legs via the inferior vena cava. Because the blood flowing to the right atrium comes from working tissues, it has a high carbon dioxide content and a low oxygen content.

After being collected in the right atrium, the blood flows into the right ventricle, which pumps it out to the lungs via the pulmonary arteries (Figure 104). In the lung capillaries the blood releases carbon dioxide and takes up oxygen. It then flows through the pulmonary veins back to the left atrium. It enters the left ventricle, from where it is pumped into the aorta and other arteries and around the body.

The two sides of the heart pump blood at different pressures. The right ventricle develops less pressure than the left because it only has to pump blood for a short distance to the lungs. The left ventricle has to produce more pressure to be able to perfuse more distant structures such as the head and the feet.

The direction of the circulation is maintained by a series of non-return valves in the heart and in the veins, but not in the arteries. The most important valves are those at the entrance to and the exit from the ventricles.

Although arteries do not contain valves, the smaller arteries can contract, so that blood does not flow to organs that are not working. It is similar to turning off the central heating system in unused rooms. At times of great emergency extra blood is diverted to muscles to enable us to act quickly to get out of danger.

When we are exposed to cold, blood is diverted away from the skin to prevent heat loss.

No matter what blood supply other organs may need, the blood supply to the brain must always be maintained. The circulation always tries to maintain the brain's blood and hence its oxygen supply.

Figure 104 The circulatory system

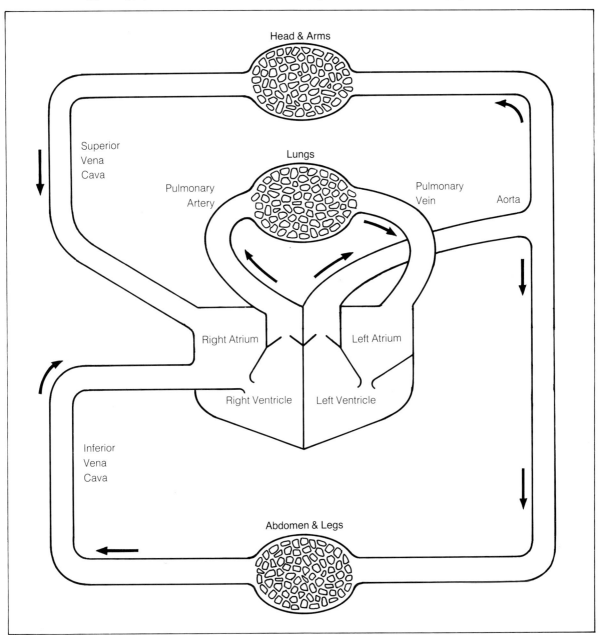

Lung Structure

The lungs are the organs where the exchange of gases between the atmosphere and the blood takes place. They occupy almost the entire chest cavity. In fact, the lungs and the heart are the only major organs within the chest.

The lungs are connected by the trachea (windpipe) to the back of the nose and mouth, the pharynx. The trachea divides in the chest into two bronchi, which supply the left and right lungs. Each bronchus divides many times, like the branches of a tree, to produce millions of tiny passages (bronchioles) (Figure 105).

Each bronchiole ends in many grapelike air sacs called alveoli. Each alveolus is very thin-walled and covered with fine blood vessels called capillaries (Figure 106). Gases readily diffuse across the thin alveolar walls into or out of the blood.

Each lung is enclosed in a double membrane called the pleura. The two layers of the pleura are separated by only a small amount of lubricating fluid. Outside the pleura is the ribcage and below it is a sheet of muscle called the diaphragm. Breathing is performed by movement of the ribcage and diaphragm. To breathe in, or inhale, we contract the muscles between the ribs, which pulls the ribcage upwards and outwards. At the same time the diaphragm contracts downwards. As a result, the volume within the chest is increased and the lungs expand. This produces a negative pressure and air is sucked into the lungs through the mouth and nose.

Exhalation (breathing out) occurs when the diaphragm and the muscles between the ribs relax. The ribcage falls passively and the diaphragm rises, the chest volume is decreased and air is expelled from the lungs (Figure 107).

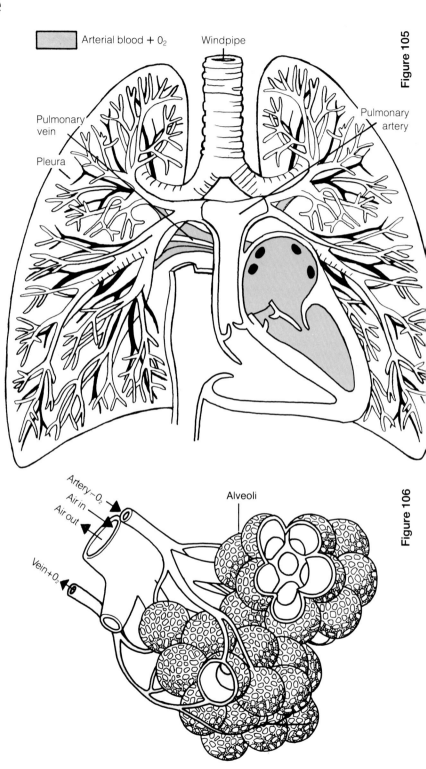

Figure 105

Arterial blood + O_2

Windpipe

Pulmonary vein

Pulmonary artery

Pleura

Figure 106

Artery – O_2

Air in

Air out

Vein + O_2

Alveoli

Figure 105 The structure of the lungs

Figure 106 The alveoli

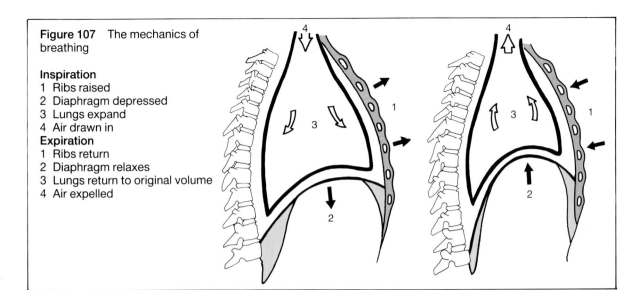

Figure 107 The mechanics of breathing

Inspiration
1 Ribs raised
2 Diaphragm depressed
3 Lungs expand
4 Air drawn in
Expiration
1 Ribs return
2 Diaphragm relaxes
3 Lungs return to original volume
4 Air expelled

Lung Volume

The total volume of gas that the lungs can hold when fully expanded (total lung capacity) varies with the size of the person. In an average man (70 kg) it is about 6 litres. At rest, however, only 0·5 litre is breathed in and out with each breath. This is called the tidal volume (Figure 108). If, after a normal inspiration, we breathe in maximally, the extra volume of air which can be inspired is called the 'inspiratory reserve volume'. After a normal expiration, if we breathe out fully the extra volume expired is called the 'expiratory reserve volume'.

If we breathe out fully, then breathe in fully, the volume of gas we inspire is called the 'vital capacity'. The vital capacity is the maximum volume of air which can be moved into or out of the lungs in one breath. The vital capacity is equal to the expiratory reserve volume, plus the tidal volume, plus the inspiratory reserve volume. In an average man the vital capacity is 4·5 litres.

The difference between the total lung capacity and the vital capacity is called the 'residual volume'. It is the gas that cannot be expelled even by maximal expiration.

The residual volume is of considerable importance to divers. If a snorkel diver fills his lungs (total lung capacity = 6 litres) on the surface (1 bar) and descends to 30 metres (4 bars), his lung volume will be reduced to one-quarter (1·5 litres) (Boyle's Law). His lungs now hold their residual volume. If he descends further, the increased pressure compresses his chest below its residual volume, which can damage the lungs. This type of injury is called a 'lung squeeze'.

When we breathe in, the last portion of air to enter does not reach the alveoli but remains in the larger air passages, where gas exchange cannot occur. The volume occupied by this gas which does not exchange with the blood in pulmonary capillaries is called the dead space. It is usually about 150 ml. When we breathe out, the last 150 ml of gas to leave the alveoli does not reach the atmosphere but remains in the dead space. It is taken back into the alveoli with the next inspiration. If breathing is shallow and the dead space is large, the gas breathed into the alveoli will be similar to that breathed out. Respiration will be inefficient so that the blood's partial pressure of carbon dioxide rises and its partial pressure of oxygen falls. Some types of diving equipment, e.g. long snorkel tubes, will increase the effective length of the air passages and hence the dead space.

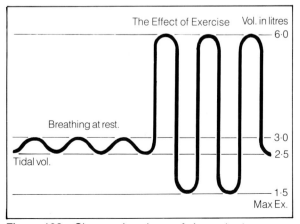

Figure 108 Changes in volume of air required

Pressure Damage

Expansion Problems

The ears and sinuses rarely give problems on ascent. Air within the middle-ear cavity and sinuses will escape back into the nasal passages through the connective airways with no discomfort and no need for assistance by any means. Should there by any obstruction in the connecting passages, there is a risk of reversed ear and sinus pain, the latter being very difficult to relieve. Ultimately the gases will be absorbed into the tissues and metabolized in the usual way.

Gases in the Stomach and Gut

If air has been swallowed during the dive, or if gases have been produced during the normal course of digestion, it is likely to expand on ascent and the feeling of fullness must be relieved by natural methods. Gaseous foods and drinks should be avoided before diving.

Lungs and Respiratory Airways

The lungs of the breath-holding diver will increase in volume on ascent and, assuming no air has been exhaled while underwater, the lung volume on reaching the surface will be the same as it was at the start of the dive. As with normal breathing, the diver will not feel the increase in lung volume but may notice an increase in buoyancy. For the aqualung diver who maintains normal lung volume throughout the dive, overexpansion of the lungs on ascent is a major hazard. It can force air into the blood stream or can cause lung tissue to rupture, trapping pockets of air within the chest cavity. Either way, the results are dramatic and often fatal. Injuries of this sort are collectively referred to as 'burst lung'.

Burst Lung

The lungs of the aqualung diver will be relatively full throughout the dive and, should he ascend without exhaling, lung volume will attempt to increase while pressure falls. Should the chest have *expanded* to the point achieved in normal full *inhalation* and can expand no more, pressure within will increase above ambient. The alveolar membrane will stretch, permitting minute bubbles of air to enter the bloodstream where they will be quickly circulated around the body. These bubbles are known as 'air emboli'. They are likely to block the fine capillaries to essential body organs and, in particular, those within the brain. The condition of air embolism will lead to severe neurological disorders as parts of the brain are starved of oxygen. Should lung tissue continue to be streched, it is likely to tear so that larger bubbles of air are trapped between the lung sacs and chest wall (pneumothorax) or escape inwards between the lung sacs in the vicinity of the heart and major blood vessels (interstitial emphysema).

Such lung damage is only likely to occur when the diver fails to exhale normally on ascent, perhaps as the result of panic. On reaching the surface, breath-holding ceases and the air pressure within the lungs falls to atmospheric. Any air trapped as a result of pneumothorax or interstitial emphysema will now have serious effects on the normal respiratory process.

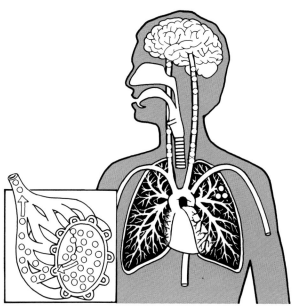

Figure 109   Air Embolism
Excessive stretching of the alveolar membrane can allow minute bubbles of air to enter the capillaries and thus the bloodstream. The circulation would carry these bubbles – which unite into larger bubbles – to the brain, heart and other vital organs where they could lodge, blocking further blood flow and thus oxygen supply. All manner of neurological disorders will follow, and in severe cases, death can occur within seconds.

A pneumothorax can cause a lung sac to collapse, drastically reducing the distressed diver's ability to breathe normally. Air trapped around the heart and the major arteries between the heart and lungs will apply abnormal pressure to them, interfering with blood flow and heart function. Add to these conditions the possibility of severe neurological disorders caused by air embolism, and it will be clear that the diver is fighting for survival.

Remember that the greatest pressure/volume change, and therefore the risk of burst lung injuries, occurs in the last 10 metres of ascent to the surface. It is possible to suffer burst lung conditions during an emergency ascent in a training pool. A golden rule to avoid burst lung injuries is *never hold your breath on any ascent if using breathing apparatus.*

In this case, an ascent does not necessarily mean a return to the surface, but simply any reduction in depth.

Effects and Symptoms of Burst Lung

Any abnormality after an abnormal ascent

Air embolism   Very wide ranging, affecting respiratory, circulatory, nervous and muscular systems. Giddiness, numbness, paralysis, visual disturbances, respiratory difficulty, heart failure, death. Symptoms usually appear rapidly after surfacing.

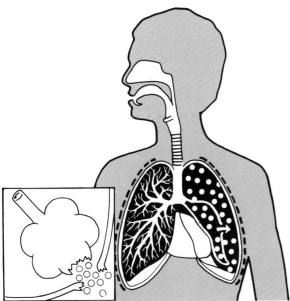

Figure 110   Spontaneous Pneumothorax
In some cases, the alveolar tissue may suffer a major tear, allowing considerable quantities of air to escape outwards and become trapped between the lung sac and chest wall. As the ascent continues, the pressure of the trapped air will be greater than that of the air in the lungs, and this will cause the lung sacs to collapse. The lung will then be unable to perform its function, and the subject will be starved of oxygen

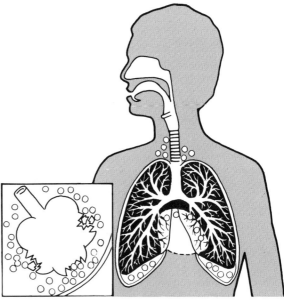

Figure 111   Interstitial Emphysema
On the other hand, the air may escape inwards and become trapped among the tissues and organs between and above the lungs. It can apply abnormal pressures on airways, blood vessels, heart and lung sacs, with consequent difficulties.

Lung tissue will normally stretch before it tears and therefore it should be remembered that air embolism may also be present in cases of pneumothorax and emphysema

Figure 112   Remember the importance of a controlled ascent

Pneumothorax   Shortness of breath, coughing of blood, pain on breathing, swollen appearance of chest cage: cyanosis – plus those for air embolism.
Emphysema   Shortness of breath, difficulty in swallowing, swollen appearance of skin at base of neck – plus those for air embolism.

Burst lung conditions can also induce effects and symptoms of hypoxia (see p. 86) if normal respiration is upset. Note that decompression sickness can reveal similar symptoms, although they do not usually appear so rapidly. Always consider the nature of the ascent. If it was an abnormal ascent suspect a burst lung condition and treat accordingly.

Treatment of Burst Lung
The only successful treatment for air embolism is immediate recompression in a recompression chamber. Pneumothorax and emphysema may require minor surgical treatment.

First aid: keep the casualty in a head down position on a 30-degree slope. If the casualty is having difficulty in breathing, give expired-air resuscitation and administer pure oxygen if available. See 'use of oxygen' on page 109.

Man Underwater

We are adapted for walking on land. Swimming underwater is not natural for us. Engineering advances such as the fin, the face mask and the aqualung enable us to swim, see and breathe underwater, but these alone are not enough for continued survival in this foreign environment. The underwater environment produces alterations which affect bodily functions. Some of these alterations can produce physiological or psychological problems if we are not aware of them or fail to adapt adequately to them.

The Senses

On land, vision is our most important sense. Even in clear water refractive changes require the diver to make mental adjustments for size and distance and also reduce the area of the diver's field of vision. As depth increases, the colour of objects is distorted. Most divers will at some time dive in murky water and this is when other senses become more important.

Hearing, smell and taste are important senses on land, but usually have little value to the diver. The altered conduction of sound waves that occurs underwater means that sounds are distorted and we cannot easily judge the direction or the distance of the object producing the sound. The only value of smell and taste is that they may enable the diver to detect impurities in the air he is breathing.

Underwater, touch is of great importance. Special nerves send information to the brain about objects that are in contact with the skin. Without touch the diver would be unable to interpret rope signals or to locate equipment he cannot see. It is essential that divers learn to locate and operate their equipment by touch alone.

On land, we are able to perform actions because we can co-ordinate movements and orientate our body positions correctly. Vision plays a part in this, but, even with eyes closed, we are able to perform movements and stand up and walk. We can do this because the brain knows exactly what the rest of the body is doing because of the position-sensing nerves in muscles and joints.

The position-sensing nerves alone cannot keep us upright. The inner ear contains an organ called the vestibular apparatus, which is important for our perception of orientation and movement.

To know exactly our position and posture we rely on a number of sensory organs. The vestibular apparatus, position-sensing nerves and skin-pressure receptors tell us in which direction gravity is acting and the eyes give us a visual horizon.

Underwater there will be no horizon as visibility decreases. Also the pressure sensed by the skin's pressure receptors will be equal all over the body. The diver is then dependent on his vestibular apparatus to know which way is up. If cold water suddenly enters the ear, the function of the vestibular apparatus can be disturbed. The effect is the same as when someone is spun around very fast. The diver will be totally disorientated.

Weightlessness

Out of the water, a diver and all his equipment may weigh over 100 kg. Once he enters the sea, the effect of gravity on his body and his equipment is countered by the buoyancy he derives by displacement of water. He is weightless.

Weightlessness gives us the ability to move freely in three dimensions. It may also make it more difficult for us to distinguish which way is up. Weightlessness means that the effects of gravity cannot be used to anchor the body. Underwater, if we push an object away from us, we move in the opposite direction, unless we hold onto something. For divers working underwater, weightlessness may be a disadvantage. Professional divers frequently dive heavily overweighted, so that they can remain firmly anchored to the seabed. For safety, these divers operate on a rope from the surface. Free-swimming divers should not be overweighted.

Weightlessness also affects our circulation. When standing on land, some blood collects in veins in the lower parts of the body because of gravity. When we are weightless this does not happen. Therefore, when we are in the water, less blood is in our legs and more blood is in the chest. When there is an increased volume of blood in the chest, our bodies think we have 'too much blood'. The immediate effect is that the kidneys start to produce more urine in an attempt to reduce blood volume!

Exercise

Diving involves physical activity. Usually the exertion of carrying the equipment to the sea exceeds that expended underwater, but occasionally diving can involve considerable exercise.

During exercise, the working muscles require more oxygen and produce more carbon dioxide. In response to the increased metabolic rate of the working muscles, circulatory and respiratory adjustments are made.

The rate of the flow of blood around the body is the cardiac output. It can be calculated by multiplying the volume of blood ejected on each contraction of the heart (stroke volume) by the number of contractions per minute (heart rate). The cardiac output is about 5 litres/minute. During heavy exercise the heart rate can increase from 70 beats/minute to 200 beats/minute and the stroke volume will increase slightly. As a result cardiac output will increase to 20–25 litres/minute.

The total volume of air breathed in and out in a minute is the respiratory minute volume. In a person at rest it is 6 litres/minute. It is calculated by multiplying the tidal volume (0·5 litre) by the respiratory rate (12 breaths per minute). During exercise, both the respiratory rate and the tidal volume increase. The respiratory rate may rise to 30–35 breaths per minute and the tidal volume to 3 litres during maximum exercise. This produces respiratory minute volume of about 100 litres.

The increases in cardiac output and respiratory minute volume occur immediately the exercise begins, because of nerve signals from active muscles and joints. As exercise progresses and more carbon dioxide is produced, the partial pressure of carbon dioxide in the blood increases, causing further stimulation. In particular, a raised partial pressure of carbon dioxide stimulates the respiratory centre in the brain to increase respiration.

Oxygen consumption is the amount of oxygen used in metabolism per minute. At rest this is 0·25 litre/minute, but it rises on maximum exercise to 4–5 litres/minute. The amount of carbon dioxide produced is about 0·8 times the oxygen consumption, i.e. 0·20 litre/minute at rest.

If work is done at a constant rate, the depth at which the work is done does not affect the number of molecules of oxygen consumed or of carbon dioxide produced. Thus, if work done at the surface requires a number of oxygen molecules which occupy 1 litre at 1 bar, at 10 metres (2 bars) the volume occupied by the number of molecules of oxygen required will be 0·5 litre.

Unfortunately this does not mean that the respiratory minute volume can also be halved. Although carbon dioxide production will be unaltered and the volume it occupies at 10 metres will be half that on the surface, elimination of carbon dioxide is dependent on the volume of gas moved in and out of the lungs during each breath. Thus, if the metabolic rate requires a respiratory minute volume of 20 litres/minute on the surface to eliminate the carbon dioxide produced, it will also require a respiratory minute volume of 20 litres/minute at 2 bars.

Pressure and Cold

Some of the responses of the diver to pressure have been described earlier (pp. 32–33).

As pressure increases, the density of gas also increases. Therefore, to have the same respiratory minute volume at depth requires more work from the respiratory muscles. The maximum breathing capacity at 30 metres is about half that at the surface. This is one of the reasons why professional deep divers use a breathing mixture with a lower density than air (e.g. oxygen–helium). The responses to cold exposure are discussed later.

Psychological

Little is known about the psychological effects of diving. There is, however, some evidence to suggest that psychological factors play an important part in many serious diving incidents.

Diving is an exciting sport, but it can be hazardous. It is natural to feel some degree of apprehension before a dive, especially when conditions are not ideal. Divers who are never apprehensive may fail to cancel a dive when conditions are too severe.

Appreciation of the potential hazards of diving should lead to adequate preparation of the diver and of his equipment.

Unless a diver is confident of himself, his training and his equipment, when under stress anxiety can turn to panic. Panic is when the diver loses control.

Panic may be recognized by an increase in the respiratory rate, reduced awareness of surroundings with the diver concentrating on a single solution to a problem and repetition of actions which do not lead to a solution. Under similar stress, a diver who is coping tries a number of different actions until the problem is solved. In the most extreme form of panic the diver just gives up and freezes, rather than looking for any solution.

The only way to prevent panic is by training. This produces competence and self-confidence in the diver's ability to cope with the underwater environment.

Figure 113 The diver truly moves in three dimensions, orientating himself with the surface, the bottom and the anchor line

Hypoxia

Anoxia means that there is no oxygen. However, even a reduced amount of oxygen can have serious consequences or can cause death. A reduction in the amount of oxygen is called 'hypoxia'.

Whether or not the cells are hypoxic depends upon the composition of the gas we breathe and the function of the lungs, circulation and blood.

Hypoxia will occur when:

1. The gas breathed contains a reduced amount of oxygen.
2. The movement of air in and out of the lungs is reduced (e.g. obstruction to the air passages or paralysis of the muscles of respiration).
3. The lungs are diseased, so that alveolar gas transfer is reduced.
4. When the blood is unable to take up enough oxygen because it has a reduced haemoglobin content (i.e. when a person is anaemic or has bled) or when poisons combine with haemoglobin to prevent it taking up oxygen (see carbon monoxide poisoning, p. 98).
5. The heart is unable to pump with enough force to ensure that all tissues receive enough blood.

If any of these conditions are present, the cells use up oxygen more quickly than it can be delivered to them. They use up all the available oxygen. As a result, there is little red oxyhaemoglobin. The subject will appear progressively less pink and more blue. This blue colour is called cyanosis. It is most noticeable at the lips, earlobes and fingernail beds.

If the hypoxia is not relieved at this stage, cells begin to malfunction. The brain will cease to work and the subject will initially develop poor co-ordination and fatigue, and then convulsions and unconsciousness. The heart may also stop.

If hypoxia is not relieved immediately, serious damage will be done. The brain will be damaged irrevocably after about four minutes of severe hypoxia. Muscle cells can survive over 30 minutes of severe hypoxia. It is not much use if a hypoxic casualty regains normal muscle power but little brain function. Therefore four minutes of hypoxia is usually considered the limit of time we have for relieving hypoxia.

There is one important exception to this. Brain cells can survive more than four minutes of hypoxia when they are cold. In fact, people in very cold conditions have been resuscitated successfully without brain damage after more than forty minutes of hypoxia.

The Snorkel Diver

Anyone who leaves the surface of the earth, where he can breathe air freely, and dives underwater is placing himself at the risk of developing hypoxia. This is particularly true for a snorkel diver. He holds his breath while carrying out physical exertion. He uses up oxygen in his body and, unlike the aqualung diver, has no source from which to replenish it.

Whilst the snorkel diver's oxygen is being consumed, he is also producing carbon dioxide. A raised partial pressure of carbon dioxide in the bloodstream is the main stimulus the body has to increase respiration. When the respiratory centre in the brain detects the raised partial pressure of carbon dioxide in the blood, a desire to

Figure 114   The snorkel diver must heed the body's message to breathe

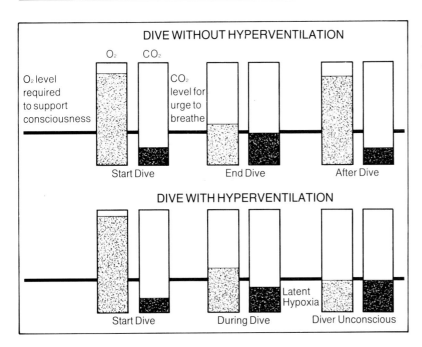

DIVE WITHOUT HYPERVENTILATION

O₂ level required to support consciousness

CO₂ level for urge to breathe

Start Dive   End Dive   After Dive

DIVE WITH HYPERVENTILATION

Start Dive   During Dive   Diver Unconscious

Latent Hypoxia

Figure 115 In a normal breath-hold dive the increase in CO_2 level triggers the response to breathe.
After hyperventilation the build-up of CO_2 is supressed, delaying the response to breathe

breathe is stimulated and the diver returns to the surface. In normal circumstances the raised partial pressure of carbon dioxide will cause a desire to breathe before the partial pressure of oxygen is dangerously low. Occasionally, in an effort to achieve a particular goal, the diver may choose to override this stimulus to breathe out and, as a result, an abnormally low partial pressure of oxygen occurs. This may cause unconsciousness with the attendant risk of drowning.

In snorkel divers two additional factors aggravate the dangers of hypoxia. One is hyperventilation before a breath-holding dive and the other is the depth of the dive.

The object of hyperventilation before a breath-holding dive is to increase the length of time the diver can remain underwater. By hyperventilating, the partial pressure of carbon dioxide in the blood is considerably reduced. Unfortunately, the chemical reaction between oxygen and haemoglobin is such that hyperventilation has little or no effect on the amount of oxygen in the blood. When the diver is finning hard underwater, oxygen is rapidly consumed, but it takes longer for the amount of carbon dioxide in the blood to reach a level at which it stimulates the desire to breathe. The oxygen content of the blood may be reduced to dangerous levels and unconsciousness may occur before the carbon dioxide content is sufficient to stimulate the respiratory centre.

The problem is exacerbated by an increase in depth. If a breath-holding diver descends to a considerable depth, say 30 metres, he will be subject to a pressure of 4 bars absolute. The partial pressure of oxygen in the air in his lungs and in his blood will be increased fourfold. Since the partial pressure of carbon dioxide in the lungs is minimal at the surface, considerable quantities of carbon dioxide can duffuse from the blood into the lungs at depth. The partial pressure of carbon dioxide in the blood and the

respiratory centre will be insufficient to stimulate the desire to breathe.

During his ascent, the partial pressure of carbon dioxide will fall as the surrounding water pressure is reduced. This produces a false sense of relief from the urge to breathe. At the same time the partial pressure of oxygen will fall rapidly and may drop below the level required to maintain consciousness. If this happens, the diver will become unconscious while still at depth. His lung volumes and buoyancy are reduced and he will sink, drowning as he does.

Occasionally breath-holding divers become unconscious, as a result of hypoxia, a few seconds after surfacing and despite having taken a breath. This is because there is a lag of a few seconds between the blood picking up oxygen in the lungs and delivering it to the brain.

Hypoxia in breath-holding divers is most common in competitive spearfishermen. In some, the desire to win overcomes common sense and sound practice, and a number of deaths have occurred in such individuals.

The Aqualung Diver

The Aqualung diver may also develop hypoxia. This can occur if the aqualung has been filled with a gas containing insufficient oxygen (e.g. pure nitrogen). It can also occur if he exhausts his air supply, if his equipment fails to deliver sufficient air or if the mouthpiece of his regulator is dislodged from his mouth.

Hypoxia should be considered as a possibility in all snorkel or aqualung divers who become unconscious underwater or shortly after surfacing from a long, deep snorkel dive or, possibly, after a free ascent. It is suggested by strong breathing efforts and the presence of cyanosis.

Drowning

Drowning is a condition produced by the inhalation of fluid. Strictly, the term drowning should only be applied if death occurs. People who inhale water but who are successfully resuscitated should, technically, have the term 'near drowning' applied.

Drowning and hypoxia are related conditions. We have discussed above how hypoxia can lead to unconsciousness in the water and drowning. In addition, if water is inhaled because, for example, the regulator mouthpiece malfunctions, the water in the air passages will prevent gas exchange and will cause hypoxia.

Drowning is the ultimate cause of death in most diving fatalities. It must be remembered that drowning is not the primary event. Some other condition causes the diver to inhale water. It may be that the diver has become unconscious because of hypoxia, exhaustion, cold or a coincidental medical condition. He may, however, be conscious but his diving equipment has failed.

A lot of the things that people commonly believe about drowning are entirely untrue. It is a myth that people who drown on the surface come up three times before going under for a final time. Once someone takes a breath of water, his buoyancy is reduced and he is unlikely to surface again.

We are able to eat, drink and breathe through our mouths. Sensors at the back of the mouth (in the pharynx) detect the nature of substances passing through. Control of pharyngeal and laryngeal muscles directs gases into the trachea and diverts solids and liquids down the gullet. If solids or liquids go down the wrong way, this produces laryngeal spasm and we cough.

The spasm prevents the solids or liquids passing all the way down into the lungs and the coughing helps us push them back up into the pharynx, so that they can be redirected into the gullet. If a diver inhales water, laryngeal spasm and coughing also occur. The laryngeal spasm directs the inhaled water into the stomach. Coughing prevents his maintaining an adequate breathing pattern and hypoxia is worsened.

In 20–25 per cent of the people who drown, the laryngeal spasm is so powerful that little or no water enters the lungs themselves. This condition is known as dry drowning.

In the remaining 75–80 per cent of drowned people, water is found in the lungs. This is because, when most people become unconscious, the laryngeal spasm relaxes and allows water to enter the lungs. It is often said that if people drown in fresh water they die in a much shorter time than they do if they drown in sea water. The reason for this is supposed to be that fresh water is absorbed across the alveolar walls into the blood, where it damages the blood cells and the heart.

Although this has been shown to be true for experimental animals, studies in hundreds of cases of drowning and near drowning in humans show that there is little or no difference between salt- and fresh-water drowning.

From a practical point of view, drowning or near drowning have only one important immediate effect. They produce hypoxia. They do this by filling the air passages with water or by producing laryngeal spasm. In either case air cannot enter the lungs. A near drowning casualty will have a similar appearance to other hypoxic subjects. He will be cyanosed. In milder cases he may be trying to breathe or cough. In more severe cases he will make no respiratory effort and he may be pulseless. Frequently froth issues from the mouth and nose and this may be bloodstained.

The way we resuscitate the casualty by getting oxygen into his lungs and bloodstream and around his body is discussed later (p. 152).

If we successfully resuscitate a near drowning casualty we must not start to congratulate ourselves too soon. Fresh or salt water inhaled into the lungs can damage the alveolar membrane. Fluid enters the alveoli from the blood very slowly. Although the casualty has been resuscitated, over a period of time the lungs will start to fill up with fluid again. This may take a few minutes or as long as twelve hours. It is called 'secondary drowning'.

There have been a number of instances where people have been successfully resuscitated from near drowning, only to die some hours later as a result of secondary drowning. Secondary drowning can only be adequately treated in hospital. All people who have survived a near drowning incident must immediately be taken to hospital.

It is a common misconception that the majority of people who drown are non-swimmers. In fact, the majority are competent swimmers who have misjudged the conditions or who are inadequately prepared for the conditions they meet.

About one-third of people who drown have a significant amount of alcohol in their blood.

Figure 116 Practising diver rescue

Avoidance and Treatment of Hypoxia

To avoid hypoxia a snorkel diver should never hyperventilate before a dive and should not overwork or linger at depth. He should stay at depth no longer than the time he would be able to hold his breath on the surface while performing similar exertion.

Because unconsciousness from hypoxia usually occurs in snorkel divers during the ascent or shortly after surfacing, he should arrange to be buoyant from 10 metres upwards.

Snorkel divers should always operate in pairs. One person remains on the surface keeping watch while his buddy dives.

For an aqualung diver to avoid hypoxia, he should ensure that his equipment is working correctly and his cylinder is filled with compressed air. During the dive he should check that he has sufficient air left for his ascent. He should always dive with a buddy who can supply him with air if his own air supply fails. Both divers should return to the surface before either has run out of air.

Drowning

The risk of a diver drowning will be considerably reduced if he has attained a level of knowledge and skills which enables him to understand the hazards of the conditions in which he intends to dive, so that he can anticipate, prepare for and overcome any problem he is likely to meet.

If a diver has any doubts about his ability to cope with a planned dive, he should not dive. The ability of divers to make rational choices about their actions is impaired by alcohol and certain other drugs. These also increase the risk of hypothermia and nitrogen narcosis. Divers should never drink alcohol in the period immediately before diving.

Treatment

The treatment of drowning and other causes of hypoxia are basically the same. There are, however, a few differences.

The commonest cause of hypoxia on land is heart disease. The heart stops beating and blood flow to the brain ceases. Respiration usually ceases shortly afterwards.

When someone drowns, hypoxia is caused by obstruction of the air passages and failure of gas to enter the lungs. In this case, breathing usually stops some minutes before the heart ceases to beat. Therefore, someone who drowns may still have a heart beat and a circulation, although it will be weak.

Whether a heart beat is present or not, it is essential to ensure that a gas containing as much oxygen as possible is pushed into the lungs and that this is pumped around the body. Precise details of how this is done are provided in the section on rescue and resuscitation (pp. 152–3). However, some points should be emphasized. In all cases of drowning, some degree of obstruction to air entry to the lungs will be present. In dry drowning, the laryngeal spasm will relax when the casualty becomes unconscious.

If the casualty is removed from the water at this stage, ventilation of the casualty's lungs should be relatively easy.

When wet drowning has occurred, the air passages contain a significant amount of water. There is no point in trying to remove this water. Attempts to hang up the subject by the feet to let the water drain out only increase the amount of fluid which runs out of the casualty's stomach into the back of his throat. This may then go down into the casualty's lungs. Instead, it is recommended that after clearing foreign material from the mouth and back of the throat, the rescuer ventilates the casualty's lungs without attempting to drain them. In hospital, a casualty who is not breathing and who is hypoxic is treated by passing a special tube through the mouth into the trachea. The tube allows the lungs to be inflated with pure oxygen. It also prevents fluid from the stomach being regurgitated into the lungs. In addition, it prevents the stomach being filled with gas as the patient is ventilated.

In an emergency, we do not have such equipment. The best way we have of filling the casualty's lungs is by blowing our own expired air into them. Our expired air contains about 16 per cent oxygen.

It is a common but very serious mistake to think that by placing an oxygen mask over the face of someone who is not breathing you are doing more good than by giving expired-air resuscitation. Delivering 16 per cent oxygen to the alveoli does much more good than delivering 100 per cent oxygen to the face of someone who is not breathing.

Systems which deliver 100 per cent oxygen but which do not inflate the casualty's lungs are only of value if the casualty is able to breathe (see p. 163). Quite frequently an hypoxic casualty will not be breathing, but when the rescuer clears his airway and extends his neck, the casualty will start to breathe again.

In cases of drowning, breathing may stop before the heart has ceased to beat. Nevertheless, the pulse may be weak and this is likely to be exacerbated if the casualty is also hypothermic. It may be that the diver's heart is beating, although he is unconscious, blue and not breathing.

If you are unable to detect a pulse in the carotid artery, it is best to assume that there is no heart beat and apply external cardiac compression as well as expired-air resuscitation.

It is important that all rescuers are aware that although severe hypoxia usually causes brain damage after about four minutes, drowning is usually accompanied by hypothermia. Cold reduces the brain's oxygen requirements and hence increases its resistance to hypoxia. There are cases where people have been successfully resuscitated after being underwater without air for over forty minutes. Therefore, it is essential that resuscitation measures on drowning and other hypoxic casualties are not stopped until the rescuers are advised to do so by a doctor or other competent authority.

Effects of Cold and Hypothermia

Man is adapted in such a way that his bodily functions work best at an optimal temperature of 37° C. If the temperature of his vital organs (e.g. brain and heart) rises above this, he has developed mechanisms which intervene to bring it back to 37° C. The temperature of the vital organs is called the 'core temperature'. Man can reduce his core temperature by reducing his energy production (metabolic rate) at the same time as he increases his heat loss.

The seas of the world all have temperatures below 37° C, so the diver is unlikely to suffer from overheating. He is more likely to experience excessive cooling or hypothermia. (Technically, hypothermia occurs when the core temperature falls below 35° C.)

People immersed in water are more likely to experience hypothermia than any other group. This is because water is an excellent conductor of heat. It conducts heat twenty-five times better than air. Water can also hold three thousand times more heat than air. It is no surprise that people who fall into very cold water without adequate protective clothing may die within seconds or minutes.

Normally, if we are cooled to a little below 37° C, we start to produce more heat. We do this by increased voluntary activity, as well as by increased involuntary muscular activity – shivering. These activities increase our metabolic rate. We burn up more nutrients and, as a consequence, may feel hungry and breathe more rapidly.

At the same time we try to reduce heat loss. Blood flow to the skin and peripheries is reduced, so that less heat is lost from the skin capillaries to our surroundings. Our fingers and toes become cold, blue and numb. The blue colour of the extremities is caused by slow blood flow in these tissues and hence local hypoxia.

A reduction in blood flow to the skin and peripheries means that the amount of blood in the core is increased. A large increase in the core, or central blood volume, increases the blood pressure and this means the heart must pump harder. This will put a strain on the heart and is the reason that heart attacks are more common in cold weather than in warm conditions.

The body is able to sense the increase in blood pressure and central blood volume. It tries to get rid of some of the blood. The only way we can do this is by passing more water through our kidneys. Everyone notices that in cold weather they need to go to the toilet more frequently.

The effects on central blood volume, blood pressure and urine production are exaggerated if the reason we are cold is because of immerson in cold water. Immersion itself causes an increase in central blood volume, blood pressure and urine production because of weightlessness and the hydrostatic effects of the surrounding water.

The increase in metabolic rate which occurs as we are cooled begins to disappear as we become hypothermic. Below 35° C our metabolic rate decreases progressively. At the same time the respiratory rate, heart rate and blood pressure begin to fall.

As the core temperature is reduced further, difficulty in concentration and muscle stiffness progress to unconsciousness and convulsion. The breathing pattern and cardiac rhythm become irregular and eventually cease at temperatures between 25–30° C. At these core temperatures the casualty will appear to be dead.

Cooling to even lower temperatures is, however, quite compatible with successful resuscitation without any permanent damage. This is particularly true if cooling has occurred rapidly, for example, if someone falls through ice into very cold water. Successful resuscitation from severe hypothermia is possible because the metabolic rate of all organs, particularly the brain, is slowed by cooling. Hypoxic damage takes a long time to occur in the cold. This fact has been successfully used by surgeons for many years when operating on the heart or brain.

Hypothermia may occur in anyone who is exposed to cold. Whether the casualty is an Arctic explorer or an elderly person with inadequate heating, the effects are similar. Only the rate of heat loss differs. People immersed in water are particularly susceptible to hypothermia because, as we have seen, water is such a good conductor of heat and the rate of heat loss is very rapid.

Divers and others immersed in cold water are also susceptible to a number of other forms of cold injury.

Someone who jumps or falls into very cold water may experience a very severe shock, sufficient to stop the heart immediately. The effect is so instantaneous that it has been likened to electrocution, and is called 'hydrocution'. It is found in people who fall overboard in Arctic seas and those swimmers who jump into icy lakes.

If a person survives the initial impact of falling into cold water, he will gradually cool down. If he has no buoyancy aid and no thermal protection, after about ten to fifteen minutes in very cold water he will be unable to remain afloat. He will sink and drown.

If he has a means of remaining afloat, he will not sink but will become hypothermic and unconscious. He will eventually die from hypothermia if he is not rescued in time.

Even after his rescue, the problems are not over. It is quite common for people suffering from hypothermia to die at the moment of rescue or soon afterwards. It is not uncommon for people to be alive in the water when a helicopter starts to winch them up and dead thirty seconds later when they are in the helicopter. Alternatively, they may die during transit to hospital.

These deaths at the time of rescue occur because, as the casualty cools down, his central blood volume increases and he passes urine to prevent his blood pressure rising too high. As we have seen, immersion exaggerates this effect. As soon as the casualty is lifted out of the water, the hydrostatic effect of the water is removed. Blood returns to the peripheries, particularly the legs. The central blood volume is suddenly reduced. As a result the blood pressure drops and the casualty becomes shocked.

The effect is identical to having a massive haemorrhage.

The treatment for this is to lay the casualty down immediately and to raise the legs. This will increase blood return from the legs to the core, which will improve the blood pressure. If the casualty is completely conscious and able to drink, giving warm fluids by mouth will help to return the central blood volume to normal. The casualty should not be given anything to drink if he has injuries and there is a possibility he may require an operation. If medical help is available, the best and safest way of returning the central blood volume to normal is by giving intravenous fluids. Some deaths could probably be prevented if the casualty were lifted in a horizontal position (i.e. legs at the same level as head), rather than with legs hanging down.

Deaths in hypothermic casualties on the way to hospital are called 'rewarming deaths', although some may be due to secondary drowning (see p. 88). Rewarming deaths occur for two reasons. As the casualty warms up, his skin and peripheral blood vessels dilate. This has two effects. It allows warm central blood to pass through the periphery where the blood is cooled. This cooled blood on returning to the central pool causes a reduction in core temperature. This is called the 'afterdrop'. This sudden surge of cold blood through the heart may be enough to stop it.

However, there is disagreement about the importance of the afterdrop. The other effect of dilating peripheral blood vessels, by warming, is that the central blood volume is again reduced and may produce a fatal reduction in blood pressure. Whichever of these mechanisms is responsible for the rewarming deaths that occur in hypothermic casualties, care must be taken when rewarming someone (see p. 93).

In addition, cold has a number of other serious effects. As mentioned above, the increase in central blood volume which occurs in cold and on immersion causes an increase in blood pressure. Breathing a gas with a raised partial pressure of oxygen also slightly increases a person's blood pressure. Divers are exposed to all three of these conditions – cold, immersion and a raised partial pressure of oxygen. If the diver is already predisposed to high blood pressure or has heart disease, a further rise in blood pressure may cause the heart to fail. The result is that a back pressure builds up on the heart and consequently in the lungs. Fluid passes out of the capillaries into the alveoli, which fill up. The effect is identical to drowning.

Cold may also produce spasm in the arteries of the heart itself (coronary arteries). This spasm will reduce the blood flow to the heart and cause a heart attack.

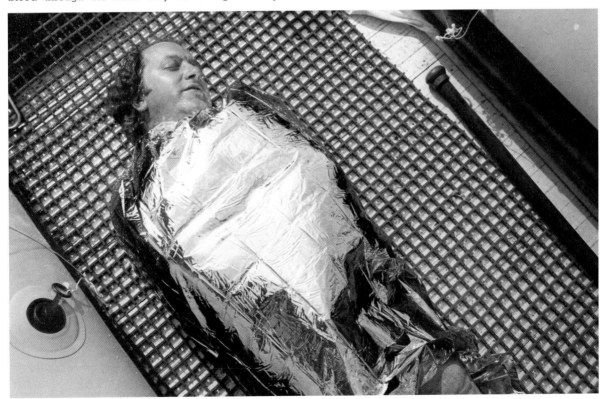

Figure 117   To reduce the effects of exposure a 'space blanket' can be used to limit the loss of body heat; additionally steps should be taken to limit loss of heat from the head

Avoidance and Treatment of Hypothermia

The seas around the British Isles vary from 4–16° C throughout the year. In fresh water, the temperature may be as low as 0° C. In such conditions the maximum survival time of an unprotected (naked) swimmer varies from a few minutes to a few hours (see Figure 118).

The rate of heat loss is related to body surface area, while the rate of heat production is related to body volume. Therefore, people such as children, with large surface area to volume ratio, will cool more quickly.

The best way to prevent heat loss is by insulation. We all have some natural insulation in the form of subcutaneous fat, which helps prevent heat loss. There is evidence that, during exposure to cold, the core temperature of fat people falls more slowly than that of thin people. However, it is not wise to sacrifice fitness for fatness.

Insulation can also be provided by a layer of water around the body which has been warmed up by the subject's body heat. Clothing worn by someone who falls into cold water should not be discarded. It will help to maintain this insulating layer of warm water.

Movement of the water, produced by swimming, will disrupt the insulating layer. Generally it is not advisable to swim if one falls into cold water, unless safety is very close. It is better to bring the knees up and arms into the side to stay afloat and wait for help to arrive. Curling up helps to turn the body into a sphere. A sphere has the smallest surface area to volume ratio of any shape and loses heat most slowly.

A good way of maintaining a layer of insulating warm water around the swimmer is by use of a wetsuit. The thermal protection offered by the wetsuit has been described earlier (p. 48). It must be remembered that the foam neoprene of a wetsuit is compressed at depth, so that it not only loses buoyancy but also some of its insulating properties.

Since air has a much lower thermal conductivity than water, a more efficient way of supplying insulation is by trapping a layer of warm air around the diver. This is the principle used in drysuits (see p. 50).

Whether the diver uses a wetsuit or a drysuit, it is essential to remember that a large amount of the body's heat loss occurs from the head. The head always has a

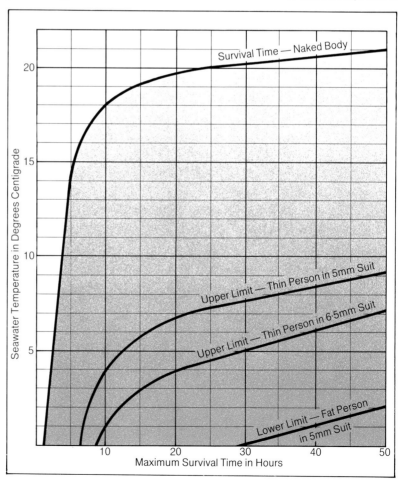

Figure 118 The human body's ability to survive in water varies dramatically with the temperature of the water, the effectiveness of the diver's protective clothing and the diver's build

high blood flow and has little insulation. An insulated hood should be worn except in the warmest seas. Indeed, in the coldest conditions it is essential to leave none of the body uncovered.

For divers the problem of heat loss is not confined to the time spent in the water. Significant heat loss can occur on the way to or from the dive. While foam neoprene offers good insulation against heat loss underwater, it is not such a good insulation material on the surface. Evaporation of water from a wet neoprene suit can produce rapid cooling. The wind-chill effect will increase this cooling. It should be remembered that even when there is no wind, if you are sitting in a boat travelling at about 10 knots, then the wind-chill effect is the same as in a 10-knot wind. It is a good idea to wear a waterproof and windproof garment in the boat to and from the dive site. There is no value, and obvious dangers, in arriving at the dive site blue with cold and shivering even before the dive starts.

The dive should be stopped if a diver starts to feel cold. By the time shivering has started, significant body cooling has already occurred. After the dive, a diver should get himself as warm as possible. He should get out of the wind into a warm environment and change into dry clothing. A hot, high-energy drink will help warm him up. People who are cold, or likely to become cold, should not drink alcohol. Alcohol increases heat loss by dilating the blood vessels of the skin and reduces heat production by lowering the amount of sugar in the blood.

It is said that people who are often exposed to cold become acclimatized to it. This does not mean that they are less likely to become hypothermic. In fact, the opposite is true. People who are frequently exposed to cold seem to be less aware of the fact that they are becoming hypothermic than are people who are rarely exposed to cold. This type of silent hypothermia may be a cause of death amongst experienced and professional divers.

Treatment

Despite taking precautions, a diver will still risk becoming hypothermic. This may be because he becomes separated from his support vessel and by the time he is rescued hypothermia has set in. It is important that we should know how to initiate treatment in such casualties.

The treatment of hypothermia requires urgent admission to hospital. About 20 per cent of those people rescued alive from the sea die on the way to hospital. We have a duty to try to prevent this happening.

The most important measure that we can take is to prevent any further heat loss. The casualty should be removed from the water and protected from wind, rain and spray.

Other measures will depend on the condition of the casualty. If he is not breathing and has no pulse, expired-air resuscitation and external cardiac compression take priority. If he is breathing but is unconscious, he should be placed in the recovery position. Some people who are conscious are so exhausted that they are unable to protect their airway. These casualties should also be in the recovery position (see p. 150).

Even if the casualty is conscious he must be made to lie down, preferably with his legs slightly raised. This will reduce the possibility of a reduction in blood pressure and shock.

The casualty should be kept still. Muscular activity will increase the risk of an afterdrop in temperature.

Handling of the casualty should be reduced to a minimum. Rough handling may cause cardiac rhythm problems. This must not stop expired-air resuscitation and external cardiac compression if these are necessary.

At the same time as these measures are being taken, the casualty should be slowly rewarmed. How this is done will depend on the facilities available. In an open boat the only way possible may be for the rescuers to surround the casualty and warm him with the heat of their own bodies. It is a sensible idea for all diving boats to carry an exposure bag or space blanket in which to place hypothermic subjects. This ensures that their own body heat loss will be prevented and they will warm themselves slowly.

In an open boat it is not advisable to remove the casualty's wet clothing. If a warm cabin is available, removal of the wet clothing is advisable.

Ideally, the casualty's core temperature should be corrected before the arms, legs and skin are warmed. This reduces the risk of an afterdrop in temperature and shock.

There are many ways of doing this. These include warming the gases the casualty breathes, putting the trunk in a warm bath but leaving the arms and legs out, hot compresses to the chest, washing out the stomach with hot water and giving hot intravenous fluid.

None are really practical as first-aid measures. With all of these there are dangers that the heat applied will be either too hot or not hot enough. It is essential that heat of friction is not applied to arms and legs. This will cause an afterdrop.

If the casualty is suffering from mild hypothermia and is fully conscious, it is permissible to give him a hot, high-energy drink. He must never be given alcohol.

Gas Laws

First we should be certain that we understand what property distinguishes a gas from a solid or a liquid. A gas is a substance that will expand to fill all the space available to it. A gas can also be compressed into a smaller volume.

A gas is composed of millions of small particles, called 'molecules'. The molecules move about freely and randomly. There is nothing in between the molecules.

Boyle's Law

This states that 'for a fixed mass of gas at constant temperature (T), the pressure (P) is inversely proportional to the volume (V)' $(P \propto 1/V)$. Stated more simply, if the amount of gas and the temperature do not change, pressure multiplied by the volume is constant.

If a fixed quantity of gas is placed in a rigid container, say an aqualung cylinder, the pressure will be determined by the volume of the container. Alternatively, we can pump the gas into a flexible container, say a balloon. The pressure inside the container is determined by the pressure in the gas or liquid outside the balloon. In this case the volume inside the container is determined by the pressure.

Constant-Volume Law

This states that 'if the volume of a fixed mass of gas is held constant, the pressure is directly proportional to the temperature' $(P \propto T)$ (in degrees absolute). This means that if the temperature of a gas is increased so is the pressure. Similarly, if the pressure is increased so is the temperature.

Charles' Law

Charles' Law is less relevant to divers than Boyle's Law or the Constant-Volume Law. It states that 'for a fixed mass of gas at constant pressure, the volume is directly proportional to the temperature' (in degrees absolute): $(V \propto T)$.

Boyle's Law, Charles' Law and the Constant-Volume Law can be combined to give an equation relating pressure, volume and temperature: $PV = RT$ where R is a constant.

It is important to remember that, although in theory pressure and volume may be altered while temperature remains unchanged, in practice it is difficult not to alter all three parameters together. For example, when we pump air into a cylinder using a compressor, the cylinder and the air it contains always become warm.

Dalton's Law of Partial Pressures

This states that 'in a mixture of gases, the pressure exerted by one of the gases is the same as it would exert if it alone occupied the same volume'.

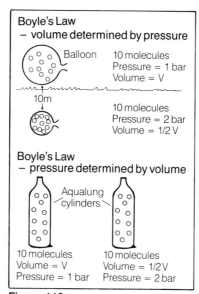

Figure 119

Henry's Law

Figure 120

Henry's Law

This is one of the laws governing absorption of gases by fluids. It states that 'at constant temperature, the amount of gas which dissolves in a liquid with which it is in contact is proportional to the partial pressure of that gas'. It will be seen in Figure 120 that 10 molecules of gas (1 bar) have been placed in contact with a set volume of liquid.

Three molecules have dissolved in the liquid. Anything which dissolves in a liquid is said to be in solution.

If we double the pressure to 2 bar, the number of molecules of gas will be doubled (Boyle's Law) and twice as many molecules will be dissolved in the liquid (Henry's Law).

It should be noted that the proportion of

the molecules still in the gaseous phase to those in the liquid phase remains constant (in this case 7:3). This ratio is called the coefficient of solubility of the gas in the liquid. Different gases have different coefficients of solubility in the same liquid. The same gas will have different coefficients of solubility in different liquids.

Absorption and Release

The absorption and release of gases by the tissues determine whether a diver develops such problems as decompression sickness, nitrogen narcosis and toxic effects.

We learned in the previous section that Henry's Law is one of the rules governing absorption of gases by liquids. The human body cells are composed largely of water and a small amount of fat. At body temperature water and fat both behave as liquids. Different tissues have different amounts of water and fat in them, so they behave like different liquids.

Therefore, different tissues have different coefficients of solubility for the same gas. In Figure 121a it can be seen that when both liquid X and liquid Y are exposed to an atmosphere containing 10 molecules of nitrogen per unit volume, liquid X will dissolve twice as many molecules of nitrogen as liquid Y.

In addition, a tissue will have different coefficients of solubility for different gases. We can use a bowl of water as a model of our tissue (Figure 121b). The water is in contact with gas containing 20 molecules/unit volume. When the gas in contact with the water is 100 per cent nitrogen, a fixed number of molecules of nitrogen will dissolve in it. In this case, let us assume 5 molecules dissolve for every 20 molecules in contact. When the water is exposed to 100 per cent oxygen at the same temperature and ambient pressure, approximately twice as many molecules of oxygen will dissolve in the water (i.e. 10 molecules of oxygen in the water when exposed to 20 molecules of oxygen/unit volume).

Air contains four times as much nitrogen as oxygen (i.e. 80 per cent v. 20 per cent). The same volume of air will contain the same number of molecules in total (20), but 80 per cent (16) will be nitrogen and 20 per cent (4) will be oxygen.

We learned from Henry's Law that the amount of gases dissolved also depends on their partial pressure.

When the nitrogen was 100 per cent, 5 molecules of nitrogen dissolved in the water. Thus, when the nitrogen is 80 per cent, 4 molecules of nitrogen will dissolve in the water.

When the oxygen was 100 per cent, 10 molecules of oxygen dissolved in the water. Thus, when the oxygen is 20 per cent, 2 molecules of oxygen will dissolve

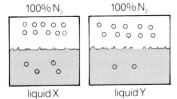

Figure 121a

100% N₂   100% N₂

liquid X   liquid Y

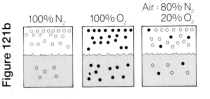

Figure 121b

100% N₂   100% O₂   Air : 80% N₂ 20% O₂

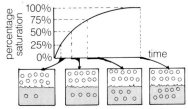

Figure 121c

amount of gas in solution

in the water.

Henry's Law has one important qualifier. The law only applies if temperature is kept constant. Changes in temperature also affect the solubility of gases.

It must also be remembered that if we bring a gas suddenly into contact with a liquid, it takes time before the equilibrium state is reached in which all the gas which is going to dissolve in the liquid is, in fact, in solution. This equilibrium state is known as saturation.

Figure 121c shows that, after a liquid is exposed to a gas, initially the gas starts to enter the liquid rapidly. The rate of entry of the gas into solution then becomes slower.

In the example in Figure 121c it will be observed that it takes little time for the first 2 molecules of gas to enter the water, and progressively longer for the next and subsequent pairs of molecules to enter. The time taken for the final pair of molecules to enter is longer still.

This type of graph is called an exponential curve. When no more gas will enter the liquid, it is said to be saturated.

There are different types of exponential curves for different liquids and different gases. In Figure 121d you will see that liquid B takes longer to become saturated

with gas than liquid A. Each of the tissues of the body has a different rate at which it becomes saturated.

If a liquid has been exposed to a gas, and the gas is removed, the molecules of the gas will come out of solution. The rate at which the molecules of gas come out of solution is also exponential (Figure 121e).

These exponential changes not only apply when a gas is suddenly added to liquid, or suddenly removed; they also apply when the partial pressure of gas is altered, for example, when we dive to different depths.

Figure 121f shows what happens to the amount of nitrogen in the body of a diver. He starts out at 1 bar and at this point his body is already saturated with nitrogen at the partial pressure found in atmospheric air (partial pressure of nitrogen = 0·8 bar). He dives to 20 metres (3 bar) while breathing air (A). Although he goes straight down to 20 metres, it takes some time before his body is saturated with nitrogen at the new partial pressure of nitrogen (2·4 bar) (B).

Once he is saturated, no matter how long he stops at 20 metres, no more nitrogen will dissolve in his tissues. He then surfaces back to 1 bar pressure (C). It takes some time before the nitrogen in his body comes out of the tissues and he is

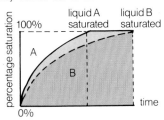

Figure 121d

liquid A saturated   liquid B saturated

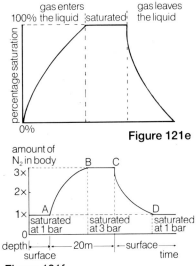

Figure 121e

gas enters the liquid | saturated | gas leaves the liquid

amount of N₂ in body

Figure 121f

again in equilibrium with nitrogen at 1 bar pressure (D).

During the period immediately after the diver has returned to the surface, his body contains more nitrogen than can properly dissolve in it at 1 bar pressure. At this time he is supersaturated with nitrogen.

When someone is supersaturated with a gas, bubbles may form in the tissues, producing decompression sickness. The diver in the example shown would almost certainly develop decompression sickness.

There are additional factors which affect the absorption and releases of gases by the tissues of the body.

The farther a cell is from a blood vessel, the farther the gases have to diffuse to get from the blood to the cells and vice versa.

Tissues with poor perfusion, or at a long distance for gases to diffuse, take up gases more slowly than other tissues, but also release them more slowly.

It can been seen that two divers who dive to the same depth for the same length of time may take up and release gases from their tissues at different rates. These rates will depend on a number of factors. The diver's build will affect the ratio of fat to lean in his body and these take up and release gases at different rates. The amount of work a diver does at depth and whether he gets cold will also affect blood flow and hence gas transfer.

Oxygen

We learned earlier how oxygen is essential for metabolism and life (see p. 78). It is perhaps surprising to learn that oxygen can also be toxic or poisonous.

We normally breathe air at 1 bar which contains 21 per cent oxygen (partial pressure of oxygen of 0·21 bar). The body will tolerate slight reductions in the partial pressure of oxygen and quite large increases.

Increases in the partial pressure of oxygen may occur if the concentration of oxygen in the air breathed is increased, if the ambient pressure is increased or a combination of both.

A large increase in the partial pressure of oxygen can produce significant changes in the metabolism of many tissues. How and why this happens is not entirely clear, but, for a diver, only the acute effects on the central nervous system (the brain) and the chronic effects on the lungs are important.

Acute Oxygen Toxicity

Acute oxygen toxicity occurs when a person is exposed to a partial pressure of oxygen of 1·8 bars or greater. The effects do not occur immediately but usually within minutes of exposure to oxygen at this partial pressure. If a diver is breathing 100 per cent oxygen, this will occur at depths greater than 8 metres. If a diver is breathing air (21 per cent oxygen), it will occur at depths of 80 metres and deeper.

The most important effects of acute oxygen toxicity are unconsciousness and convulsion. With a diver, these would probably lead to drowning. Acute oxygen toxicity is, therefore, a very important consideration for divers.

Prior to becoming unconscious, the diver commonly notices twitching of the lips or face. He may also become dizzy and feel nauseated. Less commonly, the breathing pattern will alter and breathing may become rapid, slow or simply difficult. Difficulty in concentration, disorientation, drowsiness, numbness, tingling or inability to focus may occur.

The diver's buddy may notice him acting strangely or may be aware of his altered breathing pattern. He may also notice facial pallor in the casualty, due to the peripheral vasoconstriction of hyperoxia. If he sees the casualty's face or lips twitching, this is a sure sign of an impending convulsion.

Usually, the buddy notices nothing until the diver starts to convulse. Initially there is a phase during which all of the muscles become rigid. This is the tonic phase. The casualty holds his breath and is stiff. After some seconds or minutes, the casualty enters the clonic phase in which he jerks violently. After this the casualty becomes relaxed. This sequence will be repeated unless the casualty can be removed to safety.

Ideally, it is suggested that the casualty should not be brought to the surface during the tonic phase, because he will be holding his breath and will be in danger of sustaining a burst lung. In the practical situation it may be difficult to follow this advice.

On returning to the surface, the affected diver may have further fits. Indeed, a diver who is developing acute oxygen toxicity may not start to convulse until he starts to ascend or has actually reached the surface. However, if a diver is developing acute oxygen toxicity, there is no alternative to surfacing. It is better to have a convulsion on the surface than underwater. After the diver has had a fit, it may be some time before he is fully recovered. He may be unconscious or sleepy and may have no recollection of events. He should be nursed in the recovery position and his airway should be kept open.

During a convulsion, care should be taken that the casualty does not injure himself or inhale vomit. Do not put your fingers in his mouth; he might bite them!

Acute oxygen toxicity should not happen to divers who breathe compressed air unless they go beyond a depth of 80 metres. Before a diver could reach this depth, nitrogen narcosis would preclude safe diving anyway.

Acute oxygen toxicity should only be a problem for amateur divers if their aqualung is accidentally filled with a gas containing more than 21 per cent oxygen, in which case acute toxicity will occur at shallower depths. Acute oxygen toxicity presents serious problems for naval divers, who use oxygen rebreathing systems for underwater sabotage and mine disposal. The BSAC does not allow its members to use this type of equipment.

Finally, it should be noted that individual susceptibility to acute oxygen toxicity varies. Indeed, susceptibility can vary in the same individual from day to day.

Fatigue, stress, exertion, a high partial pressure of carbon dioxide, cold, immersion, poor physical fitness or a hangover can all increase susceptibility to acute oxygen toxicity. These will reduce the depth at which acute oxygen toxicity occurs and increase the speed at which it comes on at any given depth.

Chronic Oxygen Toxicity

Chronic oxygen toxicity occurs at a partial pressure of oxygen greater than 0·6 bar. It will occur in someone on the surface breathing a gas containing over 60 per cent oxygen if they breathe it for long enough.

The effects take some hours and sometimes a number of days to develop. Chronic oxygen toxicity is unlikely to affect amateur divers. It can be a problem for professional divers in a high-pressure habitat for a long time or for amateur divers undergoing treatment for decompression sickness.

Chronic oxygen toxicity affects the lungs and the air passages. The effects are rather like a chest infection, with a sore throat, soreness behind the breastbone, cough, wheeze and shortness of breath. Blood-stained sputum may be produced. If the subject is not removed from the effects of the raised partial pressure of oxygen, permanent lung damage and death may occur.

Figure 122 A Royal Navy diver wearing oxygen rebreathing equipment

Toxic Gas Effects

Carbon Dioxide

Carbon dioxide is the gaseous waste produce of metabolism. If it cannot be eliminated by the lungs, it will accumulate in the body and its concentration in the blood will increase. A raised partial pressure of carbon dioxide in the blood is called 'hypercapnia'.

Most of the carbon dioxide in the blood is carried in chemical combination with water as carbonic acid, a weak acid. The presence of carbonic acid is detected by the respiratory centre in the brain. If the level of carbonic acid in the blood increases, the respiratory centre increases the rate and depth of respiration so that the carbon dioxide content of the blood is reduced and the amount of carbonic acid returns to normal.

Thus, if we start to exercise, metabolic rate and carbon dioxide production increase, the carbonic acid concentration in the blood increases and the respiratory centre stimulates an increase in respiration.

In the atmosphere, the concentration of carbon dioxide is only about 0·04 per cent. Normally, any carbon dioxide in our lungs is the result of our own metabolism. Air in our alveoli contains about 5 per cent carbon dioxide – partial pressure = 0·05 bar. It has a partial pressure identical to that of carbon dioxide in arterial blood, but slightly lower than in the venous blood (0·06 bar). The partial pressure of carbon dioxide in arterial blood and alveoli are in equilibrium and the respiratory centre acts to ensure that the partial pressure of carbon dioxide in the blood is about 0·05 bar.

During diving, although the ambient pressure is increased, the arterial and hence alveolar partial pressures of carbon dioxide are maintained at 0·05 bar.

If the same amount of work is done at depth as on the surface, the same number of molecules of carbon dioxide will be produced whatever the depth. Alveolar partial pressure of carbon dioxide is therefore independent of depth, although the alveolar partial pressures of oxygen and of nitrogen increase with depth. The percentage of carbon dioxide in the alveoli will decrease with depth. Whereas a partial pressure of carbon dioxide of 0·05 bar represents 5 per cent of the alveolar gas at the surface, it is only 1 per cent of the alveolar gas at 40 metres.

If the diver at 40 metres is supplied with a gas contaminated with only 1 per cent carbon dioxide, it will double his alveolar and blood partial pressures of carbon dioxide, with very serious consequences. Supplying the same gas at the surface would only raise his partial pressure of carbon dioxide by 20 per cent, which would have little effect.

Hypercapnia occurs when breathing ceases. So all casualties of asphyxia and near drowning will suffer from hypercapnia as well as hypoxia.

We have learned that the last portion of gas breathed out of the lungs goes only as far as the large airways, i.e. into the dead space. It is breathed back in on the next breath. Some types of diving equipment, such as full face masks or long snorkel tubes, increase the volume of the dead space. Equipment which allows carbon dioxide to accumulate should not be used by amateur divers.

During very deep dives, gases become denser. More work is required from the diver to move the denser gases into and out of the lungs. This can lead to the diver taking shallow breaths, allowing carbon dioxide to build up. Some divers deliberately underventilate in an attempt to conserve air. This can also lead to hypercapnia.

Finally, the diver's air supply may be contaminated with carbon dioxide. In this case the carbon dioxide has usually entered the compressed air from the exhaust of an engine. Other impurities such as carbon monoxide may also be present.

Carbon dioxide build-up is also more likely to occur when a diver is exercising and producing large amounts of carbon dioxide himself. Unfortunately, exercise may also mask the symptoms of the carbon dioxide build-up, because some of the symptoms may be mistaken for the effects of exercise.

Initially, an increase in partial pressure of carbon dioxide causes an increase in the depth and frequency of respiration. Throbbing headaches and confusion follow. Dizziness, disorientation and flushing may also occur.

A further increase in the partial pressure of carbon dioxide produces depression of the nervous system, with a reduction in pulse rate, blood pressure and respiration, leading to convulsions and death.

It will be clear from the description of the effects of carbon dioxide toxicity that it may be difficult to distinguish the effects from those of oxygen toxicity. Similarly, it may be difficult to distinguish these from carbon monoxide toxicity. Checks of the purity of the air produced by compressors and used for diving should ensure that the diver's air supply does not contain excessive amounts of carbon dioxide.

If, despite these measures, a diver develops symptoms which suggest that he has carbon dioxide toxicity, he should immediately cease activity and relax. He should take deep regular breaths. At the same time he should abandon his dive and return to the surface. To do this he should use as little energy as possible. If necessary he should put some air into his lifejacket in order to perform a controlled buoyant ascent to avoid hard finning.

The only other point of note is that hypercapnia increases the risk of nitrogen narcosis.

Carbon Monoxide

Carbon monoxide is a deadly poison. It is the product of incomplete combustion of fuels which results when burning occurs in the presence of insufficient oxygen.

Carbon monoxide is often produced by petrol and diesel engines and significant amounts are produced by burning cigarettes. Carbon monoxide is never produced by the body itself during metabolism.

Carbon monoxide is colourless and odourless and people who breathe it may not realize anything is the matter until too late.

The danger from carbon monoxide arises because it has a high affinity for haemoglobin. Carbon monoxide binds to haemoglobin 300 times more powerfully than oxygen itself.

If a person breathes gas contaminated with carbon monoxide, much of his haemoglobin will be bound to carbon monoxide to form carboxyhaemoglobin, and so it will be unable to carry oxygen. The effect will be that the tissues become hypoxic.

There is one important difference from other causes of hypoxia. Carboxyhaemoglobin is cherry red and people with carbon monoxide poisoning do not appear cyanosed but have flushed lips and cheeks.

If someone breathes a gas mixture containing carbon monoxide, the level of carboxyhaemoglobin in his blood will increase the longer he breathes the gas. Initially he develops headache, dizziness and breathlessness. Exhaustion and confusion follow, progressing to unconsciousness and death.

If someone is breathing air contaminated with 1000 parts per million (0·1 per cent) of carbon monoxide on the surface, he would develop severe symptoms of carbon monoxide poisoning in about an hour. The severity and speed of onset of the symptoms vary from individual to individual. If a diver, breathing the same gas, descends to 40 metres, he would probably be dead before he reached the bottom. This is because the increase in partial pressure of carbon monoxide with depth considerably increases the severity and speed of onset of carbon monoxide toxicity.

For this reason, although 100 parts per million of carbon monoxide is considered by many to be a safe limit for industrial workers on the surface, the BSAC states that breathing air for divers should contain no more than 5 parts per million. Air used by divers should be checked periodically to ensure that this and other standards of air purity are met.

These checks should also be made if a diver develops symptoms suggestive of carbon monoxide toxicity. The most sensitive symptom seems to be a headache.

The only way to treat carbon monoxide toxicity is to remove the casualty from contact with the gas to allow its elimination. If the casualty breathes pure air, this will occur slowly. It occurs more rapidly if he breathes a gas with a raised partial pressure of oxygen, e.g. 100 per cent oxygen on the surface or, better still, in a recompression chamber.

Finally, it should be remembered that smoking prior to a dive leaves an abnormally high level of carbon monoxide in the lungs and blood, which can predispose to carbon monoxide toxicity. This habit should be discouraged.

Others

A number of other impurities may find their way into the breathing air of divers. Most of these impurities originate from the compressor used to fill the diver's cylinder, although some could be present in the air drawn into the compressor air inlet. For example, some impurities could come from the chimneys of nearby factories.

Oil, if inhaled in sufficient quantities by a diver, will damage his lungs and produce an effect like pneumonia.

Solid particles in the diver's air may produce lung problems, resulting in coughing. They may also block filters and cause equipment to malfunction.

Small amounts of water in the inhaled air would not be harmful to the diver. In fact, many divers find that the air they use causes an unpleasant dry throat.

Oxides of nitrogen (nitrous oxide and nitrogen dioxide) may be generated in a compressor by the breakdown of the lubricant. These oxides are acid and very irritant. Small amounts can produce lung damage and therefore they must not be present.

Figure 123 Avoid charging cylinders where pollution from boat engines or vehicles may contaminate air fed to the compressor

Nitrogen Narcosis

Introduction

One hundred and fifty years ago it was first observed that men exposed to hyperbaric air behaved as if intoxicated by alcohol. Since then it has become clear that this condition, which is called 'nitrogen narcosis', will occur in anyone exposed to a raised partial pressure of nitrogen.

As soon as he leaves the surface and descends, a diver is exposed to an increasing partial pressure of nitrogen. At the same time the effects of nitrogen narcosis begin. At shallow depths the effects are mild, but, as he descends, the effects increase, altering his awareness of events and of his own behaviour.

The danger from nitrogen narcosis lies mainly in the effect it has on the diver's awareness. Like a drunk who refuses to believe he has had too much to drink, a diver with nitrogen narcosis may not accept that there is anything the matter with him.

The analogy between alcohol and nitrogen narcosis is very pertinent. Alcohol, if taken in very large amounts, can prove fatal purely because it poisons the brain cells and the person who takes it passes into a coma, stops breathing and dies. Most deaths from alcohol occur when people have much less alcohol than this in their blood. At these lower levels of blood alcohol, people make irrational decisions about their ability. They may decide that they can safely drive home when they are really incapable and have an accident in the attempt.

Nitrogen narcosis may prove fatal in its own right, but this is very rare. It has, for example, happened to divers who have attempted to set new depth records (at about 100 metres). Much more frequently, nitrogen narcosis causes the death of divers at shallower depths and in indirect ways.

Nitrogen narcosis may cause divers to misread their gauges or to make inaccurate calculations of depths or times. There have been cases in which divers could not decide in which direction to go to reach the surface. Hallucinations and bizarre beliefs and behaviour may occur. Any of these can result in the diver drowning.

Nitrogen narcosis is a significant danger to the diver because it increases the risk of an accident and, at the same time, decreases his ability to cope with the emergency.

Nitrogen narcosis differs from alcohol intoxication in a number of ways. Unlike alcohol, which takes time to be absorbed from the stomach into the blood, during a dive the partial pressure of nitrogen in the blood changes quickly with depth. The effects of nitrogen narcosis occur as the partial pressure of nitrogen changes, with little delay.

Symptoms

The table opposite shows the main symptoms experienced by a diver with nitrogen narcosis. These findings were obtained from observations made during compression in a chamber under dry conditions. Underwater, the effects of nitrogen narcosis are apparent

Figure 124 When diving deeper watch for signs of the onset of nitrogen narcosis

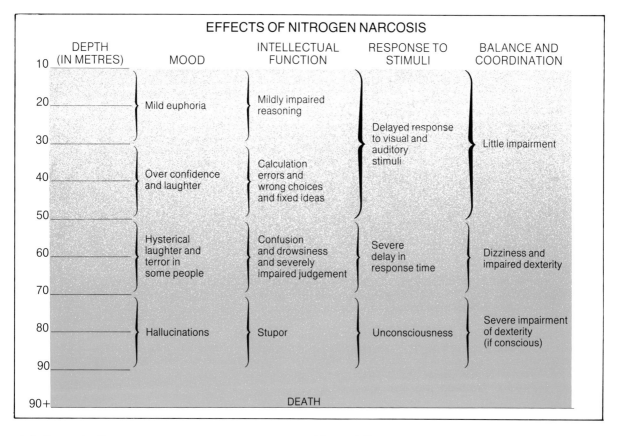

EFFECTS OF NITROGEN NARCOSIS				
DEPTH (IN METRES)	MOOD	INTELLECTUAL FUNCTION	RESPONSE TO STIMULI	BALANCE AND COORDINATION
10				
20	Mild euphoria	Mildly impaired reasoning		
30			Delayed response to visual and auditory stimuli	Little impairment
40	Over confidence and laughter	Calculation errors and wrong choices and fixed ideas		
50				
60	Hysterical laughter and terror in some people	Confusion and drowsiness and severely impaired judgement	Severe delay in response time	Dizziness and impaired dexterity
70				
80	Hallucinations	Stupor	Unconsciousness	Severe impairment of dexterity (if conscious)
90				
90+		DEATH		

Figure 125

at shallower depths.

There is individual variation in susceptibility to nitrogen narcosis. In addition, the same individual may be susceptible to the effects of nitrogen narcosis on some occasions more than on others. There is no doubt that, if measurements are made, everyone shows some evidence of nitrogen narcosis at quite shallow depths.

Some divers claim that they never get nitrogen narcosis, even on dives beyond 30 metres. These divers are either not telling the truth or they do not remember that they were affected. If tests are performed on any diver at 30 metres or deeper, it is possible to demonstrate some slowing of thought and impairment of concentration.

It is extremely common for divers who have had nitrogen narcosis to be unable to recall the fact after surfacing. The mental problems that they had or the odd acts they performed at depth are forgotten. This type of amnesia is rather like getting so drunk that the next day you cannot remember what happened.

At shallow depth, nitrogen narcosis causes mild impairment of concentration and the ability to reason, some delay in response to stimuli and mild euphoria. As the diver goes deeper he makes more serious errors of judgement and at the same time becomes overconfident. Confusion and hallucinations follow, leading to unconsciousness and death.

Underwater, the diver would probably have lost his regulator mouthpiece and drowned long before unconsciousness occurred.

If the diver reaches depths in excess of 80 metres, the effects of nitrogen narcosis will be added to those of oxygen toxicity. In addition, at great depths the increased density of air will make the work of breathing more difficult. The risk of the diver inadequately ventilating his lungs and developing hypercapnia will also occur. Hypercapnia has been demonstrated to increase the severity of nitrogen narcosis.

There are a number of other factors which increase an individual's susceptibility to nitrogen narcosis. Sedative drugs, particularly alcohol, fatigue, heavy exertion, ill health, apprehension, poor visibility and cold all increase the severity of nitrogen narcosis.

The effects of nitrogen narcosis increase progressively with depth, but do not increase over time at the same depth.

Repeated exposure to depth allows some degree of tolerance to develop. How this occurs is unclear. It may be that repeated exposure enables some divers to function with a high level of nitrogen narcosis in the way chronic alcoholics can function with blood alcohol levels which would put most people to sleep.

Effects on the Body

Since the first observations of men breathing hyperbaric air, scientists have been investigating the causes of nitrogen narcosis. This condition, which has been termed 'the narks' and 'rapture of the deep', has also been given a variety of other names by scientists. Some call it 'inert gas narcosis', others 'air intoxication' and yet others 'depth intoxication'.

The reason for the different names used by scientists to describe this condition is that none of the experts has yet produced an adequate explanation of its cause. There are a number of theories, but none adequately explains everything observed in divers suffering from nitrogen narcosis.

There is, however, general agreement that in people breathing air at a raised ambient pressure the presence of nitrogen is important for the development of the condition.

It is known that the effects of nitrogen narcosis are similar to the effects of some anaesthetic agents used during surgery (e.g. nitrous oxide or 'laughing gas'). The effects are also similar to those of sedative drugs such as alcohol. These agents and nitrogen all have one thing in common. They are more soluble in fats than they are in water.

Nerve cells contain a lot of special fats. These fats are important in enabling nerves to conduct electrical impulses. Anything that dissolves in the fats of nerve cells will reduce the speed at which these cells conduct nerve impulses. Eventually the cells will stop conducting impulses altogether.

One particular group of nerve cells in the brain appears particularly sensitive to nitrogen and other narcotic agents. They are in the reticular centre, which is really the brain's telephone exchange. The reticular centre receives messages from one part of the brain and transmits them to other parts to act upon. If the reticular centre is not working properly, all brain function becomes disrupted and, eventually, the subject becomes unconscious or narcotized.

If a second agent is dissolved in the fat of nerve cells, it will increase the effect that the other exerts. In some cases, the combination will exert a greater effect than would be expected from adding together the effects produced by each agent alone. This is what happens with alcohol and a raised partial pressure of nitrogen. A small amount of alcohol in the body can make the effects of nitrogen narcosis much worse.

Nitrogen is not used by the body in metabolism. It is said to be metabolically inert. Other metabolically inert gases also produce narcosis, but the depth at which the symptoms occur varies. The gases with smaller molecules (e.g. helium) do not produce narcosis until at considerable depths.

The reason gases with bigger molecular weights produce narcosis at shallower depths is not entirely clear. It may partly be because the bigger the molecular weight of a gas, the denser it is and the more likely it is to cause underventilation of the lungs and hypercapnia. This certainly increases the severity of narcosis.

With increasing depth, the partial pressures of other gases also alter. At great depths, say 80–90 metres, for a diver breathing air the effects of nitrogen narcosis and oxygen toxicity will be additive and produce even more severe problems.

Prevention and Treatment

Any diver breathing air underwater will be subject to the effects of nitrogen narcosis. There is no way of eliminating these effects, unless a gas mixture is used which has less of a narcotic effect than the nitrogen in air has.

Professional deep divers use gas mixtures such as helium plus oxygen to prevent nitrogen narcosis. These gas mixtures and the equipment required for their use are expensive.

Amateur divers have neither the resources nor the appropriate training to use such equipment. At the present time amateur divers must confine themselves to breathing air from basic aqualung equipment.

The diver must appreciate that this type of diving will impose limits on the depths to which he can safely dive. There will always be people who dive deep because they enjoy the thrill of unnecessary danger or feel they must prove themselves in this way. Sensible divers, on the other hand, may be prepared to accept the increased risk associated with depth in order to perform a dive with a particular objective, but they will prepare themselves adequately for the task and not take any unnecessary risks.

The main limits imposed by breathing air underwater are those of depth and time. The effects of nitrogen narcosis become significant at depths greater than 30 metres and are of great importance below 50 metres.

It is impossible to lay down precise limits of acceptable depth. This must depend on the objective of the dive and the experience of the divers in the prevailing conditions. The term 'limit' itself implies that at a particular depth things are safe, while at a metre deeper they are unsafe. Clearly, danger increases progressively with depth and safe cut-offs are never precise.

Few experts would disagree with the statement that at depths approaching 80 metres the risk of sudden unconsciousness and death make these depths inappropriate for air-breathing divers.

Few amateur divers can accept the risks that diving deeper than 50 metres involves and accordingly the RNPL/BSAC Decompression Table does not allow for dives below 50 metres.

The risks of nitrogen narcosis are considerably reduced if dives below 30 metres are only performed with specific objectives in mind, by suitably experienced divers after adequate work-up dives.

The effects of nitrogen narcosis can also be reduced if divers ensure that they leave a sufficient time after taking alcohol or sedative drugs for these to be eliminated from the body.

Should a diver experience symptoms suggestive of nitrogen narcosis he should immediately ascend to a shallower depth. The symptoms will improve almost immediately. If a diver behaves in an unusual manner and fails to respond to the signal to ascend, his buddy should

assist him upwards. Care must be taken, because in severe cases people with nitrogen narcosis might behave violently, although this is not usual.

Figure 126 The effects of nitrogen narcosis will add to apprehension caused by darkness, poor visibility and cold

Decompression Sickness – Causes

Decompression means a reduction in ambient pressure, such as that which occurs when a diver ascends to the surface. Decompression sickness is one of the two groups of illnesses that can result from decompression.

The other group of conditions is called 'barotrauma' and includes burst lung. Barotrauma can also occur during compression (when the ambient pressure increases), but this is less common. Barotrauma is injuries brought about by changes in the volume of gas-containing spaces in the body as a result of changes in pressure (see p. 82).

Decompression sickness, often referred to as the 'bends', is due to the liberation of gas bubbles from a soluble substance into the tissues or the blood. For divers breathing air, the gas bubbles which are liberated and which produce decompression sickness are composed predominantly of nitrogen. (For simplicity, only nitrogen will be considered.) Changes in ambient pressure cause corresponding changes in the partial pressure of nitrogen in the air in our lungs. The blood in the capillaries, which are in contact with the alveoli, changes its partial pressure of nitrogen very rapidly when the alveolar partial pressure of nitrogen alters. This blood is carried around the body, so that alterations in ambient pressure also bring about changes in the partial pressure of nitrogen in the tissues.

As we learned in the section on absorption and release of gases (p. 94), the amount of a gas that can dissolve in a tissue is predominantly dependent on physical laws (Dalton's and Henry's Laws) and upon the solubility of that gas in the tissue.

Nitrogen is much more soluble in fat than it is in water. Therefore, tissues containing a lot of fat will take up a much greater total amount of nitrogen than those tissues containing little fat. We also learned that the rate at which a gas will dissolve in the tissues is affected by the perfusion of the tissue (rate of blood flow) and by diffusion.

If a diver descends from the surface (1 bar) to, say, 20 metres (3 bars), the increase in partial pressure of nitrogen will cause three times more nitrogen to dissolve in his tissues than was dissolved at the surface, provided he stays long enough to saturate the tissues. Some tissues are well perfused by a large blood flow (e.g. the brain, the heart, the kidneys) and these will saturate with nitrogen quickly. Other tissues have poor blood flow (e.g. the cartilage in joints, the tendons and fat stores), so they will take a longer time to become saturated with nitrogen.

Tissues which become saturated rapidly are called 'fast tissues' and those which become saturated slowly are called 'slow tissues'.

When the diver starts to ascend, the reverse of these processes occurs. The ambient pressure is reduced and the partial pressure of nitrogen in the lungs decreases. The blood now has a higher partial pressure of nitrogen than the alveolar air, so nitrogen passes out of the blood and into the lungs. The partial pressure of nitrogen in the blood is thereby reduced. When the blood next passes through the tissues, they now have a higher partial pressure of nitrogen than the blood and nitrogen passes from them into the blood and will eventually get back to the lungs.

It is clear that, after decompression, some tissues may contain more dissolved gas than they are able to retain in solution and bubbles will form. A few small bubbles probably do no harm and it can be demonstrated that they are produced after all decompressions.

Occasionally, larger bubbles occur which produce the serious problems of decompression sickness. The difference between having a few small bubbles and many large ones can be compared to what happens when we take the top off a bottle of fizzy drink. If we unscrew the top slowly, only a few bubbles are produced. If we take the top off very quickly a lot of froth results.

If the bubbles occur in the blood of an ascending diver as he performs his ascent, the ambient pressure will be reduced and the bubbles will get larger (Boyle's Law). In addition, bubbles in the blood tend to clump together and attract platelets and blood proteins. A large foreign object, or embolus, is now present in the blood stream. This gas embolus can wedge in a blood vessel and prevent blood flow to a tissue, which will soon become hypoxic and may be permanently damaged.

If the bubble is produced in a tissue and not in the blood, it will still expand as the ambient pressure is reduced. This can damage surrounding structures by pressure and by preventing the blood flow by external compression of vessels.

The symptoms of decompression sickness depend on just where the bubbles form, how large they are, how many there are and where they eventually lodge.

The dive profile influences the site of the nitrogen bubble formation. A short, deep dive (say, ten minutes at 50 metres) produces a high nitrogen load in the fast tissues, but does not allow much nitrogen to dissolve in the slow tissues. If the diver fails to perform the appropriate decompression on his ascent from this dive, bubbles will form in the fast tissues (e.g. the blood itself and the brain). A rapid ascent (e.g. an emergency ascent) will make it even more probable that many bubbles will form in the blood, because the lungs might have insufficient time to eliminate the nitrogen.

A long dive to a shallow depth will cause more nitrogen to dissolve in the slow tissues. Incorrect decompression in this case is likely to produce bubbles in the slow tissues. From a shallow depth, the change in pressure is unlikely to occur sufficiently rapidly for bubble formation in the blood to occur.

Exercise during or after decompression increases the rate of bubble formation. Decompression sickness is also more common in the old, the unfit and the obese – possibly because increased body fat allows greater nitrogen absorption. Exposure to cold, dehydration, hypercapnia or recent overindulgence of alcohol predisposes to decompression sickness. A physical injury or a previous episode of decompression sickness predisposes to decompression sickness at the site of the injury. Most of these effects are thought to be due to alterations in tissue perfusion.

Repeated exposure to depth appears to reduce the probability of decompression sickness and, therefore, work-up dives for anyone planning deep dives are advisable.

Symptoms of Decompression Sickness

Symptoms of decompression sickness may start during the ascent, but this is unusual. Symptoms more usually begin after the diver has surfaced. In 50 per cent of cases symptoms begin less than one hour after surfacing and in 90 per cent of all cases start within six hours. A small proportion of divers do not develop symptoms until more than twenty-four hours after their dive, but problems beginning more than forty-eight hours after a dive are unlikely to be due to decompression sickness.

For the reasons we have discussed in the last section, decompression sickness occurring within minutes of a dive is more likely to follow a deep, short dive, while symptoms occurring hours after a dive more usually follow longer, shallower dives.

There is a system of classifying decompression sickness which attempts to differentiate non-serious (type I) from more serious (type II). Type I symptoms include pain in and around the joints, itching of the skin and rashes. Type II symptoms involve the nervous system, lungs and heart and, rarely, the gut.

This classification has major disadvantages and it is probably better to classify the condition according to the part of the body which is involved, e.g. spinal decompression sickness.

The Joints

The commonest site for decompression sickness is in and around a joint. The commonest joints involved are the large joints, particularly the shoulders and the knees. The symptoms rarely start immediately after surfacing. In mild cases there may only be an ache lasting a few hours – sometimes called 'niggles'. In other cases the pain may increase in severity over twelve to twenty-four hours. Frequently the pain is eased by keeping the joint flexed and immobile, and this is how decompression sickness came to be called the 'bends'. If left untreated, the joint pain will normally improve over a week, but the only really effective treatment is recompression.

The Skin

Itchiness and irritation, rashes and mottling of the skin are less serious consequences of decompression sickness and these will not normally require recompression. However, they should be regarded as warning signs of a more serious manifestation.

The Nervous System

Numbness and tingling are not a form of skin decompression sickness. If these occur, it means that the nervous system is involved. Other signs of nervous system involvement are weakness or paralysis of the limbs (particularly the legs), difficulty with vision, problems with balance (the 'staggers'), confusion, convulsions and unconsciousness. When the spinal cord is involved, paralysis of both legs and inability to pass urine may occur. This is the commonest form of neurological decompression sickness.

Because neurological involvement may also impair judgement, there have been cases in which a diver severely paralysed by decompression sickness has refused to be taken for treatment because he did not believe that anything was the matter with him. In such cases, the diver's companions have a responsibility to ensure that he gets adequate treatment.

Heart and Lungs

After every decompression, bubbles are formed in the veins. These bubbles return in the blood through the right side of the heart to the lungs, where they are trapped in the lung capillaries. In the capillaries the gas in the bubbles slowly passes into the alveoli.

A small number of bubbles which are formed after short, shallow dives can do no harm, unless the diver has a hole in his heart, in which case the bubbles can pass from the right side of the heart to the left side without going through the lungs. Any bubbles in the blood on the left side of the heart can cause problems by affecting the blood supply to the brain or the heart itself. (Hence people with a hole in the heart are not permitted to dive.)

After longer, deeper dives more bubbles are formed. If a diver performs a dive outside the safe limits (see decompression tables, pp. 110–113), so many bubbles may be formed that they form a froth in the lungs and the right side of the heart. These bubbles block the circulation to the lungs, causing low blood pressure and shock. They also prevent effective breathing, which may cause cyanosis.

This problem usually occurs soon after a dive. The diver suddenly feels short of breath and has a tight feeling across his chest. The condition is called the 'chokes' by divers and 'gas embolism' by doctors. (Some people call it 'air embolism', but strictly this is not correct – the bubbles are mainly nitrogen.) The chokes is an extremely serious condition and can cause death.

Occasionally, when there are lots of gas bubbles in the lungs of a diver with the chokes, some of the bubbles pass through the lung capillaries to the left side of the heart. These bubbles then travel with the blood and become lodged in essential organs (e.g. the brain), where they can cause further problems.

The effects of these gas bubbles are identical to those of air embolism due to burst lung (see pp. 82–3). Distinguishing them is particularly difficult because both can occur after rapid ascents from depth. The difficulty in distinguishing them may not matter too much because they are treated in a similar manner, i.e. by recompression, although the actual recompression tables to be used may differ.

The Gut

Decompression sickness involving the gut is very uncommon, but it can cause pain in the abdomen, vomiting, diarrhoea or bleeding. Abdominal or back pain can also be due to spinal decompression sickness.

Bone Necrosis

The precise cause of this condition is unknown, but it is thought to be a delayed effect of decompression sickness.

It is believed that during decompression the blood supply to an area of bone is interrupted, either by a bubble of nitrogen or by swelling of the fat cells in the bone marrow. This causes the affected area of bone to die.

Dead bone does not cause any symptoms, unless a joint is involved, when arthritis will occur. The commonest joints involved are the shoulders, hips and knees.

Bone necrosis rarely occurs in amateur divers. It most frequently occurs in tunnel workers and professional divers exposed to hyperbaric conditions for long periods of time and with frequent decompressions.

It may occur in amateur divers, particularly those who perform inadequate decompression and those who have suffered from decompression sickness.

Figure 127 Layout of a recompression chamber

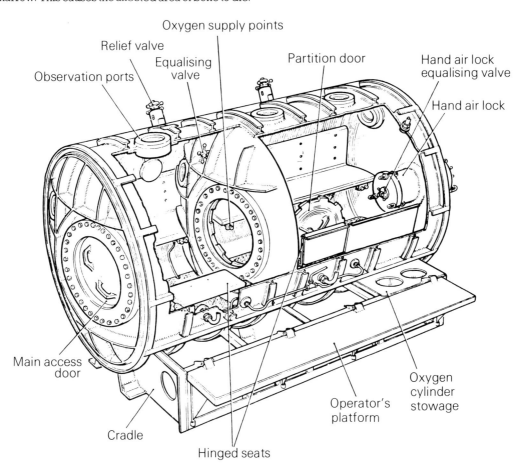

Decompression Sickness – Treatment

The aim of the treatment of decompression sickness is to prevent further gas bubbles forming in the body, to remove those which have already formed and to relieve the secondary effects which have occurred as a result of bubble formation.

The treatment involves immediate recompression, followed by gradual decompression. This prevents new bubbles forming and shrinks the bubbles which have already formed (Boyle's Law). The secondary effects are dealt with by appropriate supportive medical measures.

The only safe way to undertake this treatment is in a medical centre which is equipped with an appropriate recompression chamber (Figure 127) and staffed by qualified personnel.

The form of treatment used will depend on the depth required for the therapy, the gas mixtures used and the rate of decompression. These factors are all interrelated.

There are three basic approaches to therapeutic recompression.

1. Recompression to a pressure (depth) dependent upon the depth and duration of the original dive. This technique will cause the gas bubbles to return to solution (provided that the diver is honest about the depth to which he dived). It has the disadvantage that a further load of nitrogen enters the tissues and means that decompression to atmospheric pressure may take a long time. This technique is most useful when the diver develops symptoms soon after surfacing and is used if gas emboli are suspected.
2. Recompression to a fixed depth, using standard tables of recompression and known gas mixtures. Usually air or oxygen is used. Air is used to 50 metres. Beyond this depth the benefit gained by further decreasing the bubble size is countered by the prohibitive increase in tissue nitrogen absorption. Also, beyond 50 metres the medical attendant who enters the recompression chamber with the casualty may be unable to function because of nitrogen narcosis.
   Oxygen toxicity restricts the use of oxygen to shallower chamber depths, usually 18 metres. Immediate bubble shrinkage is not very great, because at 18 metres the bubble volume will still be about one third its surface volume (Boyle's Law). However, the partial pressure of nitrogen in the inspired gas is reduced and bubbles dissolve rapidly as a result. In addition, the oxygen supply to the tissues is quickly improved. The use of standard recompression tables produces relief in 90 per cent of cases if treatment is started within thirty minutes of the onset of symptoms, but a delay in seeking treatment will decrease the efficiency.
3. Recompression to a depth which produces a clinically acceptable result. This allows greater flexibility, with the casualty being compressed to a depth which relieves his symptoms by an acceptable amount and the gas mixture administered being determined according to the depth.

A medical attendant will be required to enter the recompression chamber with the casualty. He may need to administer drugs (to reduce blood clotting and inflammation) and to give intravenous fluids. At the present time, in the United Kingdom the professional treatment of decompression sickness as outlined above is performed by the Royal Navy and a number of commercial diving companies. These organizations will treat amateur divers, provided that their recompression facilities are not being used for their own personnel. Amateur divers who develop decompression sickness are entirely dependent on the goodwill of these organizations. This goodwill must not be eroded by abuse of diving procedures which might place excessive demands upon these organizations.

It should be recognized that decompression sickness is more frequent and more severe after dives to below 50 metres, and treatment of such decompression sickness may require equipment and gases which are not available in all recompression facilities.

The methods by which divers can obtain advice about diving emergencies is outlined in the next section.

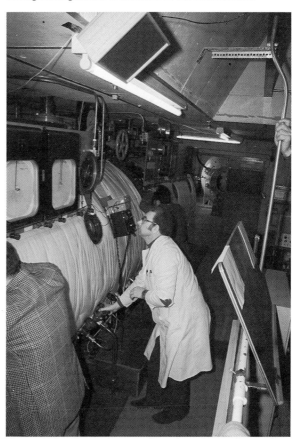

Figure 128 Operating a well equipped experimental recompression chamber

Decompression Sickness – First-Aid

It is important that all divers are aware of the possibility that they or another diver may develop decompression sickness.

Since decompression sickness is a serious, potentially fatal emergency, it is appropriate that amateur divers should receive help from experts on how to manage the problem.

In order to obtain expert medical advice about a diving emergency in the United Kingdom, the BSAC recommends that divers initially contact the coastguard. This can be done at sea by ship's radio, or on land by dialling 999 and asking for the coastguard.

The coastguard will want to know your position, the name of the patient, the symptoms exhibited and the precise details of the dives performed. It is essential to give honest information otherwise inappropriate treatment might be given.

The coastguard will alert specialists to provide treatment and can arrange transport for the casualty to the nearest available facility.

If symptoms develop after the diving party has left the coast, it may be more convenient to contact the Navy on Portsmouth (0705) 818888 and ask for the Duty Diving Medical Specialist or the Duty Lieutenant Commander.

When diving outside the UK, divers should establish in advance the location of the nearest operational recompression chamber and the procedure for getting help.

Until the care of the casualty can be passed to the experts, the amateur diver has a duty to perform basic first-aid measures. These must never be considered a substitute for recompression therapy, even if the symptoms appear to be subsiding. This is because the symptoms of decompression sickness may recur after the first aid is stopped. In addition, first-aid measures should not be allowed to delay the institution of definitive treatment in a recompression chamber. Any delay will reduce the chance of recovery.

It should also be appreciated that, compared with other diseases (e.g. heart attacks), decompression sickness is rare. Most doctors will have received no training in its management and will probably never have seen a case. Doctors without an interest in diving medicine may not even appreciate the urgency of the situation. It will be up to the diver's companions to explain tactfully to the hospital casualty officer or to the general practitioner who sees the casualty the need for urgency in the transfer of the casualty to a recompression chamber.

There are a number of first-aid measures that have been suggested for treating casualties with decompression sickness. Some of these are controversial and some highly dangerous. In severe cases of decompression sickness involving the heart and lungs, the heart may stop and breathing may cease. Clearly, in this situation expired-air resuscitation and external cardiac compression take precedence over all other measures. If the diver is able to breathe unaided but gas embolism is suspected, he should be laid down with his feet slightly raised. This will improve blood flow. He should be turned on his side to maintain his airway. If possible, oxygen should be given.

In other cases a diver may have developed less serious symptoms following a dive. The diver should resist any advice to re-enter the water to perform in-water recompression while breathing air. This procedure requires the diver to descend to the depth of his dive to relieve his symptoms. The re-entry causes a further increase in the amount of nitrogen in his blood. To return safely to the surface requires a very slow and continuous ascent over many hours or even days. If the diver comes up more rapidly than this, it could cause more severe decompression sickness than he originally suffered.

It is difficult to supply a diver performing in-water recompression with enough air for effective treatment; and other divers bringing him the air might also be at risk from decompression sickness. In British waters he might die from hypothermia before the decompression was completed and, in warmer waters, exhaustion might cause him to drown.

Similar problems also apply to the use of in-water recompression for missed decompression stops, due, for example, to the diver running out of air and rushing to the surface. Decompression sickness can occur after the re-entry, and if this produces unconsciousness, drowning can follow. Divers should never re-enter the water in an attempt to make up for missed stops. It will only conceal symptoms, delay proper treatment and make appropriate treatment more difficult.

Another measure suggested for first-aid treatment of decompression sickness is in-water recompression treatment using oxygen. With this technique a diver breathes 100 per cent oxygen in water at 9 metres using specially designed equipment. This technique has been successfully employed by some divers in the Pacific Ocean. The BSAC is not prepared to allow this technique to be used by branches in the UK, where adequate alternatives and safer recompression facilities are available and where the risk of the affected diver becoming hypothermic during treatment is appreciable.

Mild symptoms of decompression sickness (e.g. joint pains or skin rash) mean that some bubbles have formed. First-aid measures can be taken to prevent a worsening of the symptoms.

Exercise, after decompression, has been shown to increase the number of bubbles formed and their speed of development. It is considered that exercise increases agitation and turbulence in the tissues in the same way that shaking up a fizzy drink increases the number of bubbles produced. Divers with decompression sickness should be kept still, preferably lying down.

Cold, dehydration and hypercapnia also increase the risk of decompression sickness. It is, therefore, wise for divers with symptoms to keep warm. They should only be given fluids by mouth if they are fully conscious, have no abdominal pain and there is no risk that associated injuries may require them to have surgery. They should not be given oral fluids if they can be transported quickly to a recompression facility. Oral fluids may cause vomiting, which will make oxygen administration difficult in the recompression chamber.

Pain arising from a joint can often be improved by applying pressure around the joint. It is believed that the local pressure makes the bubbles which are causing the pain shrink. Bind the joint tightly but take care to ease the binding periodically, otherwise the blood supply to the limb beyond the joint will be obstructed. Divers should never be given Entonox (50:50 nitrous oxide/oxygen mixture). This will increase bubble size and make the bend worse.

As divers dive in pairs, if one diver has decompression sickness his buddy will also be at risk of developing symptoms. If possible, the buddy should also be kept warm and still. He should drink fluids and, if possible, accompany the affected diver to the recompression chamber. He may not need recompression but should have expert advice on hand if he does get problems.

Finally, it cannot be emphasized strongly enough that first-aid measures can never replace, and should never delay, appropriate expert treatment of decompression sickness by recompression.

Use of Oxygen

The use of oxygen for the treatment of diving-related problems can, like all other medical treatments, have considerable advantages when used appropriately, but may be dangerous when used inappropriately.

Who Should Get Oxygen

There are good theoretical reasons to believe that normobaric oxygen (100 per cent oxygen at 1 bar) will improve the symptoms and reduce the mortality for a number of diving-related illnesses. In some, but not all, cases there is also practical proof that this is so.

Decompression sickness is the illness for which normobaric oxygen is most frequently recommended.

In this condition normobaric oxygen may have a number of beneficial actions. It is believed to increase the rate of nitrogen bubble resolution and to improve the oxygen supply to hypoxic tissues. In fact, if a diver with decompression sickness starts to breathe 100 per cent oxygen, there may even be an initial small increase in bubble size as oxygen enters the bubbles, prior to the decrease in size as nitrogen is reabsorbed into the blood. This may be the reason for the transient worsening of symptoms which sometimes occurs with this therapy. In addition, oxygen is a powerful constrictor of blood vessels. The benefit to hypoxic tissues of an increase in partial pressure of oxygen, thus allowing a greater diffusion of oxygen into the tissues, may be offset by the reduced perfusion resulting from vasoconstriction.

However, on balance, the evidence suggests that, in decompression sickness, normobaric oxygen improves the prognosis for recovery and reduces residual damage. The same arguments also apply to air embolism occurring as a result of burst lung. Other results of burst lung (e.g. surgical emphysema and pneumothorax) resolve more rapidly if normobaric oxygen is administered during transportation to an appropriate medical centre. This treatment is particularly useful to divers with pneumothorax, in which lung collapse causes difficulty in gas exchange and severe breathlessness.

Normobaric oxygen is also valuable for the treatment of all cases of hypoxia arising from diving, e.g. near drowning. It can only be administered to casualties that have recovered sufficiently to be able to breathe for themselves. If the casualty is not breathing, expired-air resuscitation must be performed instead.

Normobaric oxygen is most valuable in cases of carbon monoxide poisoning. Oxygen is the only substance that will stop carbon monoxide binding with haemoglobin, but it does so very slowly.

Who Should Not Get Oxygen

High partial pressures of oxygen are toxic. Normobaric oxygen, if given continuously over some hours, can cause permanent lung damage to normal people. This is not usually a problem during transfer of diving casualties.

Normobaric oxygen given for short periods can cause blindness and brain damage in very young children.

Some people with severe chronic lung disease are always cyanosed and have a very low arterial partial pressure of oxygen. They also have a very high arterial partial pressure of carbon dioxide and, unlike in normal people, the respiratory centre no longer responds to an increase in partial pressure of carbon dioxide by increasing depth of breathing. These people only respond to changes in their partial pressure of oxygen and if they are given a gas containing even a slightly raised partial pressure of oxygen, say 0·3 bar, they may stop breathing altogether. Because a diver knows that normobaric oxygen is good for cyanosed, hypoxic divers, who should have no underlying lung disease, he should not assume that it will also be beneficial for a person with chronic cyanosis and hypoxia due to lung disease. It could kill that person in twenty to thirty minutes.

Normobaric oxygen may also cause problems for people with high blood pressure by raising their blood pressure further.

Because young children, people with chronic lung disease and those with very high blood pressure do not dive, normobaric oxygen therapy may safely be given to divers.

> **Divers in possession of the equipment for administering oxygen should not give it to a non-diver unless directed to do so by a doctor.**

Decompression Tables

The object of a decompression table is to present the diver with a selection of dive profiles and ascent procedures which, if properly followed, should minimise the risk of decompression sickness. This is not a simple aim to achieve due to the many variables at work, especially where sport diving is concerned. Tables are based on mathematical hypotheses which in turn use various experimental test data, and are then used by military, commercial and sport divers. Experimental data is often obtained from very carefully controlled test dives performed using compression chambers, sometimes further validated by carefully controlled wet dives. In sport diving this degree of control of the dive profile is rarely achievable and in many cases not even desirable. This means the sport diver must understand the principles of decompression sickness avoidance as well as the mechanics of reading dives from a table. These same principles will also assist divers using decompression computers towards safer diving.

Table Terminology

Decompression tables present a selection of possible dives with a set of rules to enable this selection to encompass as wide a range of diving situations as possible. Sometimes, to enable a small and compact layout, only a few dives are shown. To broaden the applicability of such tables, rather complex rules or methodology are then needed (together with a degree in mathematics!). The BSAC '88 Tables employ the opposite approach, the rules and operational procedures are kept simple and straightforward, and the penalty of a multi-table layout accepted. In practice this should mean less chance of error in dive planning and conduct.

It is important to understand the correct interpretation of the various terms used in decompression tables. Some are fairly obvious, others may need explanation.

Depth
The deepest depth reached during the dive, measured in metres.

Ascent Check Depth
A depth reached on the ascent where a pause is made to verify the dive has been conducted according to the plan. A decision is then made on the remaining ascent procedure, either to continue to the surface or make appropriate in-water decompression stops. The *Ascent Check Depth* may be 9, 7, 6 or 5 metres, depending on the dive planned and the table used.

Descent Rate
The speed at which the diver descends from the surface to any deeper depth. The maximum descent rate allowed for is 30 metres per minute.

Ascent Rate
The speed at which the diver ascends through the water. The maximum permissible rate is 15 metres per minute;

up to the *Ascent Check Depth*. On all dives, one minute should be taken to ascend from 6 metres to the surface, and this 6 metres per minute speed is appropriate from deeper *Ascent Check Depths*.

Dive Time
The time elapsed from leaving the surface to reaching the *Ascent Check Depth* on the return to the surface. Not the total time immersed!

Ascent Time
A guideline time shown to assist in dive planning, being the minimum time to be allowed for ascent from the maximum depth of the dive to arrival at 6 metres. It is calculated at a rate of 15 metres per minute and rounded up to the nearest minute.

Surfacing Code
The code describing the diver's tissue saturation state on surfacing from a dive, a code using the letters A to G.

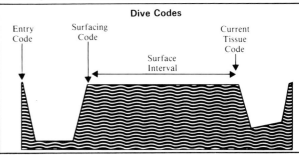

Dive Codes

Entry Code   Surfacing Code   Surface Interval   Current Tissue Code

When a diver finishes a dive, the dive has a **SURFACING CODE**. During the course of the surface interval the diver's **CURRENT TISSUE CODE** changes. This is shown in the **SURFACE INTERVAL TABLE** for the appropriate **SURFACING CODE**. The diver's **CURRENT TISSUE CODE** at any time indicates the table which can now be used for diving.

Surface Interval
The time elapsed from leaving the water at the end of one dive to leaving the surface at the beginning of the following dive, or some other time interval following a dive when a current tissue saturation state is required.

Current Tissue Code
The code produced by applying a *Surface Interval* to the *Last Dive Code*. It indicates the diver's current tissue saturation state and the table on which the diver can now dive.

No-Stop Dive
A dive for which the table indicates no need for an in-water decompression stop or stops.

Decompression Stop
The time to be actually spent at the decompression stop depth indicated.

Decompression Stop Dive
A dive for which the table indicates the need for an in-water stop or stops to be carried out. Usually a dive with a *Surfacing Code* of G, although a few G code dives do not require an in-water stop.

Decompression Sickness Avoidance
Because of the wide variations in human physiology and the large number of factors that can affect your susceptibility to decompression sickness, no table can guarantee to protect you against all risk. On all dives your tissues will absorb gas due to the higher surrounding pressures, and this gas must later be released. Some of the gas will be released during the ascent but on the majority of dives most of the excess gas is released on the surface after the dive. The quantity of gas absorbed and the manner and rate at which it is released are the main factors in influencing the onset of decompression sickness. Always remember that most of your time underwater is spent absorbing gas, with only a very short ascent time devoted to releasing sufficient gas to safely return to the surface. Your ascent rate is obviously an important feature of the dive!

Time and depth are crucial in deciding how much gas is taken up by the body; the maximum recommended depth for sport diving is 50 metres. As there is a faster rate of gas uptake on deeper dives, the time that can be spent underwater is severely curtailed, and eventually is so short that the dive is pointless for the risk involved. It is also important that deep dives are commenced with as low a gas tissue loading as possible. This means that in any series of dives, the deepest should be done first.

If a series of dives is being undertaken there is likely to be a build up of excess gas in the body tissues. This is because the post-dive gas elimination phase can be very lengthy. Depending on the dive performed, gas off-loading can take many hours, and lengthy repetitive diving can cause a potentially dangerous build-up of gas levels. For this reason it is recommended that no more than three dives be performed in any 24 hours and any dive series involving consecutive days diving to 30 metres (or greater) should be limited to four days, followed by a 24 hour break. As an example, on a week long expedition, this could mean halting diving at lunch time on the fourth day and starting again after lunch on the fifth day.

Bearing in mind that sport diving is a leisure activity, performed for enjoyment, it is always advisable to keep the risks within sensible bounds. The greater the gas absorption, the more complex the ascent procedure becomes. Very large tissue gas loads mean the diver can no longer ascend directly to the surface, but must 'stage' the ascent, stopping at various depths to wait for some of the excess gas to off-load. For sport diving it is recommended that dives carried out should not require more than 20 minutes total of such decompression stops in any 24 hour period.

As mentioned earlier, the rate of ascent is very important and traditionally has been a weak skill amongst sport divers. Whilst the ascent is not usually the most interesting part of the dive, it is vital to your safety. Fortunately de-velopments in equipment and measuring devices are making ascent rate control simpler, but it is up to the individual diver to make sure buoyancy is always under control, especially as the surface is approached. The maximum ascent rate from depth should be 15 metres per minute, until the Ascent Check Depth is reached. From 6 metres to the surface should take at least one minute, the maximum ascent rate being 6 metres per minute in this potentially hazardous ascent range.

The BSAC '88 tables have been designed to encourage slow ascents and incorporate the idea of maximum ascent rates, rather than fixed ascent rates. This means 'V' shaped dive profiles or other profile shapes such as a staged ascent up a reef face are easily planned and executed. Profiles involving a descent then an ascent followed by a re-descent, possibly repeatedly (a 'yo-yo' or 'sawtooth' profile) are not advisable. This is because each ascent can provoke bubble formation, which will then modify further gas uptake by the tissues in a way no table (or computer) can predict. It is also possible that bubbles formed in the venous blood, believed to be trapped normally by the lung capillary bed, may be compressed enough on the re-descent to break through to the arterial system and present a potential embolism problem.

> Traditionally, decompression tables were constructed by the navies of various nations and therefore have their basis in military diving. As sport divers we are not prepared to accept the same incidence of bends as may be acceptable to those diving for military purposes. Usually the military diver has excellent surface support, in the form of recompression chambers, rapidly available together with experienced and qualified attendants and medical personnel. Sport divers don't, and must therefore use a table which, as far as possible, avoids the risk of getting the bends. However, due to the differences in personal physiology, health, fitness and other factors, no decompression table can guarantee to remove this risk completely.

Following any dive or series of dives, the diver's tissues will be saturated with higher than normal gas levels for the duration of the surface decompression stop. These gas levels may mean that any further reduction in ambient pressure could provoke decompression sickness. Ambient pressure may be reduced by either ascending to altitude or by weather related air pressure changes, though the normal range and time scale of the latter mean they are unlikely to be a real problem to divers remaining at one level. If ascent to altitude is made by climbing hills or flying, even in a pressurised aircraft, then problems may occur if a safe surface decompression time has not elapsed. Detailed information may be obtained from the full edition of the BSAC '88 Tables, Levels 1 to 4, but generally ascents to altitude should not be made until a current tissue code of B is established. A current tissue code of A, normal saturation, is better still.

In addition, because of the rapid pressure drop experienced when an aircraft takes off and climbs to cruising altitude, such ascents are now believed to cause micro-bubbles to form frequently in the occupant's bloodstream. For a diver this is not only a possible risk after a dive, but also before a dive. If the flight is short, less than 90 minutes, there may be insufficient time for all the micro-bubbles to disappear before a dive is undertaken. Our advice is to use Table B for any dives made within 10 hours of landing, following short flights.

There are a number of physiological factors believed to increase the risk of decompression sickness. Some can be avoided by suitable abstention, such as reducing smoking and alcohol intake. Others, such as increasing age or excessive body fat, medical conditions affecting respiration or circulation, can mean extra precautions should be employed. The most significant precautions should be careful selection of suitable conservative dive plans, accurate dive profile monitoring and good control of safe ascent rates. Another useful precaution with the BSAC '88 Tables is to move to a more conservative Tissue Code. This gives a consistent method of increasing the safety margin without involving any calculations where errors can be made. A similar procedure can be adopted with the full set of all four air pressure bands, by choosing to dive on the next more conservative level set than the dive site air pressure would indicate – for example Level 2 instead of Level 1.

There is no doubt that many sport diving decompression sickness cases could be avoided if the advice in this section was followed – too many incidents feature deep or repetitive dives which are badly planned or executed.

TABLE B

Figure 130b

SURFACE INTERVAL TABLE

LAST DIVE CODE	Minutes 15 30 60 90	Hours 2 3 4 6 10 12 14 15 16
B	B	A

DEPTH (metres)	ASCENT TIME (mins)	DIVE TIME (minutes) No-Stop Dives					Decompression Stop Dives							
3	(1)	–	∞											
6	(1)	–	80	504	∞									
9	1	–	27	113	148	188	255	272	284	292	300	307	314	321
12	1	–	14	52	67	84	116	129	137	143	148	152	156	160
15	1	–	8	31	40	48	69	79	86	90	94	98	101	105
18	1	–	21	27	32		47	55	61	64	68	71	74	76
DECOMPRESSION STOP (minutes) at 6 metres							1	3	6	9	12	15	18	21
SURFACING CODE		B	C	D	E	F	G	G	G	G	G	G	G	G

DEPTH	ASCENT	No-Stop					Decompression Stop Dives							
21	1	–	15	19	23		35	42	47	50	52	55	57	
24	2	–	12	15	19		28	35	39	41	43	45	47	
27	2	–	10	12	15		23	29	33	35	36	38	40	
30	2	–	8	10	12		20	25	28	30	32	33	35	
33	2	–		8	10		17	22	25	26	28	29	31	
36	2	–		7	8		15	20	22	24	25	26	28	
39	3	–			8		14	19	21	23	24	25	26	
DECOMPRESSION STOPS (minutes) at 9 metres										1	1	1	2	
at 6 metres							1	3	6	9	12	15	18	
SURFACING CODE		B	C	D	E	F	G	G	G	G	G	G	G	

DEPTH	ASCENT	No-Stop	Decompression Stop Dives							
42	3	–	15	17	20	21	22	23	24
45	3	–	14	17	18	19	20	21	22
48	3	–	13	16	17	18	19	20	21
51	3	–	12	15	16	17	18	19	
DECOMPRESSION STOPS (minutes) at 9 metres			1	1	1	2	2	3	
at 6 metres			2	3	6	9	12	15	18
SURFACING CODE		B C D E F	G	G	G	G	G	G	G

TABLE A

Figure 130a

SURFACE INTERVAL TABLE

LAST DIVE CODE	Minutes 15 30 60 90	Hours 2 3 4 6 10 12 14 15 16
A		A

DEPTH (metres)	ASCENT TIME (mins)	DIVE TIME (minutes) No-Stop Dives					Decompression Stop Dives							
3	(1)	–	166	∞										
6	(1)	–	36	166	593	∞								
9	1	–	17	67	167	203 243	311	328	336	348	356	363	370	376
12	1	–	10	37	87	104 122	156	169	177	183	188	192	197	201
15	1	–	6	24	54	64 74	98	109	116	121	125	129	133	136
18	1	–	17	37	44	51	68	78	84	88	92	95	98	101
DECOMPRESSION STOP (minutes) at 6 metres							1	3	6	9	12	15	18	21
SURFACING CODE		B	C	D	E	F	G	G	G	G	G	G	G	G

DEPTH	ASCENT	No-Stop				Decompression Stop Dives							
21	1	–	13	28	32 37	51	59	65	68	72	75	77	
24	2	–	11	22	26 30	41	49	53	56	59	62	64	
27	2	–	8	18	21 24	34	41	45	47	50	52	55	
30	2	–	7	15	17 20	29	35	39	41	43	45	47	
33	2	–		13	15 17	25	30	34	36	38	40	42	
36	2	–		11	12 14	22	27	30	32	34	36	37	
39	3	–		10	12 13	20	25	29	30	32	33	35	
DECOMPRESSION STOPS (minutes) at 9 metres									1	1	1	1	2
at 6 metres						1	3	6	9	12	15	18	
SURFACING CODE		B	C	D	E F	G	G	G	G	G	G	G	

DEPTH	ASCENT	No-Stop	Decompression Stop Dives							
42	3	–	9	10	12	21	23	26	28 29 31 32
45	3	–	8	9	10	19	22	24	26 27 28 30
48	3	–		8	9	18	21	23	24 25 26 28
51	3	–			8	17	19	21	22 24 25 26
DECOMPRESSION STOPS (minutes) at 9 metres			1	1	1	2	2	3	
at 6 metres			2	3	6	9	12	15	18
SURFACING CODE		B C D E F	G	G	G	G	G	G	G

TABLE C

Figure 130c

SURFACE INTERVAL TABLE

LAST DIVE CODE	Minutes 15 30 60 90	Hours 2 3 4 6 10 12 14 15 16
C	C	B — A

DEPTH (metres)	ASCENT TIME (mins)	DIVE TIME (minutes) No-Stop Dives				Decompression Stop Dives							
3	(1)	–	∞										
6	(1)	–	359	∞									
9	1	–	49	79	116	182	199	211	220	227	234	241	248
12	1	–	20	31	44	71	83	90	95	100	104	108	112
15	1	–	11	17	24	40	48	54	57	61	64	67	70
18	1	–	7	11	15	27	34	38	40	43	45	47	50
DECOMPRESSION STOP (minutes) at 6 metres						1	3	6	9	12	15	18	21
SURFACING CODE		B	C	D	E F	G	G	G	G	G	G	G	G

DEPTH	ASCENT	No-Stop		Decompression Stop Dives							
21	1	–	7	10	20	26	29	31	33	35	37
24	2	–		8	16	22	25	26	28	29	31
27	2	–			13	18	21	22	24	25	26
30	2	–			11	16	18	19	20	22	23
33	2	–			10	14	16	17	18	19	20
36	2	–			8	12	14	15	16	17	18
39	3	–			8	12	14	15	16	17	18
DECOMPRESSION STOPS (minutes) at 9 metres								1	1	1	1 2
at 6 metres					1	3	6	9	12	15	18
SURFACING CODE		B	C	D E F	G	G	G	G	G	G	G

DEPTH	ASCENT	No-Stop	Decompression Stop Dives						
42	3	–	10	•	13	14	15	16	
45	3	–	9	•	12	•	14	•	15
48	3	–	8	•	12	•	13	14	
51	3	–	8	10	11	12	•	13	
DECOMPRESSION STOPS (minutes) at 9 metres			1	1	1	2	2	3	
at 6 metres			2	3	6	9	12	15	18
SURFACING CODE		B C D E F	G	G	G	G	G	G	G

Figure 130d — TABLE D

SURFACE INTERVAL TABLE

LAST DIVE CODE	Minutes 15 30 60 90	Hours 2 3 4 6 10 12 14 15 16
D	D · C	B · A

DEPTH (metres)	ASCENT TIME (mins)	No-Stop Dives	DIVE TIME (minutes) — Decompression Stop Dives							
3	(1)	∞ 231 –								
6	(1)	– ∞								
9	1	– 8 29	81	96	107	115	122	129	136	143
12	1	– 8	26	33	38	42	45	48	51	54
15	1	–	14	19	23	25	27	28	30	32
18	1	–	9	14	16	18	19	20	22	23
21	1	–	6	10	13	14	15	16	17	18
24	2		–	9	11	12	13	14	15	16
27	2		–	8	10	11	•	12		13
30	2		–	7	9	•	10	11	•	12
33	2			–	8	•	9	•		10
36	2			–	7	8	•	9		
39	3			–	8	•	9			

DECOMPRESSION STOP (minutes) at 6 metres	1	3	6	9	12	15	18	21
SURFACING CODE B C D E F	G	G	G	G	G	G	G	G

42	3		–	8	•	•	9	
45	3			–	8	•	•	9
48	3			–	8			

DECOMPRESSION STOPS (minutes) at 9 metres			1	1	1	1	1
at 6 metres			9	12	15	18	21
SURFACING CODE B C D E F	G	G	G	G	G	G	G

Figure 130e — TABLE E

SURFACE INTERVAL TABLE

LAST DIVE CODE	Minutes 15 30 60 90	Hours 2 3 4 6 10 12 14 15 16
E	E · D · C	B · A

DEPTH (metres)	ASCENT TIME (mins)	No-Stop Dives	DIVE TIME (minutes) — Decompression Stop Dives							
3	(1)	∞ 271 8 –								
6	(1)	– ∞								
9	1	– 9	50	63	73	81	88	94	101	107
12	1	–	14	22	26	28	31	33	36	38
15	1	–	8	13	16	17	19	20	21	23
18	1	–	9	11	12	13	14	15	16	
21	1	–	7	9	10	•	11	12	13	
24	2	–	7	8	9	10	•	11	12	
27	2		–	7	8	•	9	•	10	
30	2		–	7	•	8	•	9		
33	2			–	7	•	8			
36	2			–	7					

DECOMPRESSION STOP (minutes) at 6 metres	1	3	6	9	12	15	18	21
SURFACING CODE B C D E F	G	G	G	G	G	G	G	G

Figure 131 — TABLE G

SURFACE INTERVAL TABLE

LAST DIVE CODE	Minutes 15 30 60 90	Hours 2 3 4 6 10 12 14 15 16
G	G F E D · C	B · A

DEPTH (metres)	ASCENT TIME (mins)	No-Stop Dives	DIVE TIME (minutes) — Decompression Stop Dives					
3	(1)	∞ 332 45 19	7					
6	(1)	∞ 484	81	–				
9	1	–	9	12	16	19	23	27
12	1	–	6	7	8	10		
15	1	–	6					

DECOMPRESSION STOP (minutes) at 6 metres	–	6	9	12	15	18	21
SURFACING CODE B C D E F	G	G	G	G	G	G	G

Figure 132 — TABLE F

SURFACE INTERVAL TABLE

LAST DIVE CODE	Minutes 15 30 60 90	Hours 2 3 4 6 10 12 14 15 16
F	F E · D · C	B · A

DEPTH (metres)	ASCENT TIME (mins)	No-Stop Dives	DIVE TIME (minutes) — Decompression Stop Dives							
3	(1)	∞ 303 25 5	–							
6	(1)	∞ 339	–							
9	1	–	23	33	40	46	52	57	63	69
12	1	–	6	11	14	16	18	20	22	24
15	1	–	7	9	10	11	12	13	14	
18	1		–	6	7	8	9	10		
21	1		–	6	•	7	8			
24	2			–	7	•	8			
27	2			–	7					

DECOMPRESSION STOP (minutes) at 6 metres	1	3	6	9	12	15	18	21
SURFACING CODE B C D E F	G	G	G	G	G	G	G

Figure 133

SURFACE INTERVAL TABLE

LAST DIVE CODE	Minutes 15 30 60 90	Hours 2 3 4 6 10 12 14 15 16
G	G F E D	C B A
F	F E D	C B A
E	E D	C B A
D	D	C B A
C	C	B A
B	B	A
A		A

Using the Tables

Assuming a sea level dive site, with no pressure changes experienced during the last 16 hours, a Current Tissue Code of A can be adopted. This means Table A can be used for dive planning. On Table A, start by looking down the depth column for the depth equivalent to, or next greater than, the planned maximum depth of your dive. The column immediately to the right of the depth column is the ascent column. This gives the time required to ascend at 15 metres per minute to 6 metres, rounded up to the nearest minute.

The dive time section gives a range of times. Choose the time which is equal to, or next greater than, your planned dive time. All dives to the left of the no-stop line will not require any decompression stops during the ascent. Dives to the right of the line require stops as indicated on the decompression stops line, at 6 metres or at 9 and 6 metres. When you have selected your depth and dive time, look down the column to the surfacing code section and note the code indicated.

An Initial Dive

A sea level dive for divers on current tissue code A, to 20 metres. Using Table A, Level 1, look down the depth column until the 21 metre row is found – there is no 20 metre entry, so the next deeper depth is used. It is important that all table interpretations of this nature are made so that the safety margin is increased. The ascent column indicates a minimum of 1 minute should be allowed for ascent from 21 to 6 metres. A range of dive times are then offered, the first group requiring no in-water decompression stops, the second requiring stops varying from 1 minute at 6 metres to 2 minutes at 9 metres followed by 18 minutes at 6 metres. A dive time of 30 minutes is planned, this falls within the 32 minutes entry and will result in a surfacing code of E. If a rectangular dive profile is followed, with most of the dive at the maximum depth of 20 metres, then the ascent should be commenced after 29 minutes, to arrive at the 6 metre ascent check depth with the planned dive time.

On arrival at 6 metres, the actual dive time is checked against the dive plan and a decision made on the final part of the ascent. If the planned time and maximum depth have not been exceeded then the last 6 metres are ascended at the slower rate of 6 metres per minute. If either the time or depth have been exceeded then the rest of the ascent must be conducted according to appropriate contingency plans made before the dive. Note that in this case the chosen 30 minute dive time allows a 2 minute overrun margin in which the divers could still achieve a surfacing code of E and the maximum depth is 1 metre shallower than the table row used. Record carefully the surfacing code and time of all dives, especially if a series of dives are planned.

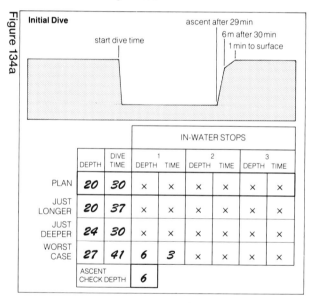

Figure 134a

Initial Dive

start dive time   ascent after 29 min
6 m after 30 min
1 min to surface

| | DEPTH | DIVE TIME | IN-WATER STOPS | | | | | |
| | | | 1 | | 2 | | 3 | |
			DEPTH	TIME	DEPTH	TIME	DEPTH	TIME
PLAN	20	30	x	x	x	x	x	x
JUST LONGER	20	37	x	x	x	x	x	x
JUST DEEPER	24	30	x	x	x	x	x	x
WORST CASE	27	41	6	3	x	x	x	x
ASCENT CHECK DEPTH	6							

Planning a Second Dive

Enter the Level 1 Surface Interval Table from the left-hand column with the surfacing code of the last dive, from the previous example an E. The elapsed time since surfacing is then used to track the current tissue code, in this case 6 hours 15 minutes, which gives a code of B, being in the 4 to 14 hour band of the E row. This means that Table B should be used for a second dive at this time. The plan is for 18 metres maximum depth and Table B is used in the same manner as Table A was for the first example. The 18 metre row also indicates an ascent time of 1 minute and a dive time of 30 minutes is again chosen. Because the dive starts with a raised tissue gas load, the same dive time and a

shallower maximum depth now result in a surfacing code of F, and are much closer to the no-stop border in the table. As the worst case scenario needs a decompression stop at 9 metres, this becomes the ascent check depth for the second dive.

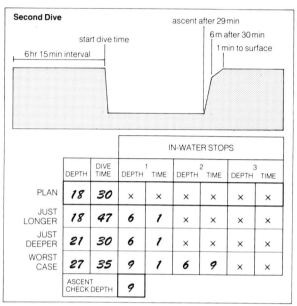

Figure 134b

Second Dive

6 hr 15 min interval   start dive time   ascent after 29 min
6 m after 30 min
1 min to surface

| | DEPTH | DIVE TIME | IN-WATER STOPS | | | | | |
| | | | 1 | | 2 | | 3 | |
			DEPTH	TIME	DEPTH	TIME	DEPTH	TIME
PLAN	18	30	x	x	x	x	x	x
JUST LONGER	18	47	6	1	x	x	x	x
JUST DEEPER	21	30	6	1	x	x	x	x
WORST CASE	27	35	9	1	6	9	x	x
ASCENT CHECK DEPTH	9							

Subsequent Dives

The procedure is exactly the same as that used for the first and second dives. Remember the advice on series of repetitive dives which can cause a gradual build up of gas tissue levels. Keep to sensible levels of daily in-water decompression and take a break after a few days diving.

Decompression Computers

Electronic decompression computers also provide the diver with advice on how to make safe ascents to the surface, avoiding decompression sickness. Most models do this by continuously monitoring elapsed time and pressure, simulating the uptake and subsequent release of gas as the pressure varies. The computers follow a number of different programs, and usually give more conservative results than some of the older tables for single dives.

It is important to remember that the wearing of a decompression computer does not change the diver's physiology or susceptibility to decompression sickness. The computer can provide accurate and reliable depth, time and decompression advice. However, just as with a decompression table, it is up to the diver to interpret that advice sensibly. It is also worth noting that the computer can only accurately monitor the dive profile of the wearer. A dive buddy could follow a significantly different profile and therefore have different decompression requirements.

The general safety information given in this section should be heeded equally by divers using either tables or computers.

The Air Supply

It will have become clear by now that a major factor controlling the length of the dive is the amount of air carried by the diver. A second factor will be the rate at which the diver consumes this air. Both of these factors are variable, but to a large extent predictable. Let us look at the methods used to predict how long our air supply will last or how much air we need for the dive we plan to make.

How Much Air Do We Breathe

The volume of air we breathe in a minute is affected by:

1. The size of our lungs.
2. The degree of effort we are exerting.
3. The depth we are at.
4. Our mental state.
5. Our physical fitness.
6. Our diving experience.

At one end of the scale we have a small, fit, experienced, calm lady diver swimming along gently in shallow water; while at the other end of the scale we have a large, unfit, panicky male diver swimming energetically in deep water.

At rest at the surface, perhaps while you are reading this book, you may be consuming about 6 litres of air per minute. If you get up and walk around, this is likely to double. And if you go for a run, it will probably double again. For general purposes we usually take an average consumption rate for a swimming diver of 25 litres/minute.

The next major factor to be considered is the depth. As we know, the pressure increases by 1 bar for every 10 metres of depth, so our air consumption increases rapidly as we descend.

| Consumption | | | Depth | | |
rate (l/min.)	10 m	20 m	30 m	40 m	50 m
20	40	60	80	100	120
25	50	75	100	125	150
30	60	90	120	150	180

This can be calculated with the simple formula:

Consumption rate × absolute pressure = air consumption per minute

So if we have decided our normal rate is 25 litres/minute and we are diving to 20 metres, our requirement each minute will be

25 litres/minute × 3 bars absolute = 75 litres/minute

We can then determine that if we are planning to spend 20 minutes at this depth we will need

75 litres/minute × 20 minutes = 1500 litres

How Much Air Do We Have?

A diving cylinder has a fixed maximum capacity of air that it can contain. This is a function of the size of the cylinder and the pressure to which it can be charged. These two figures are a feature of the design of the cylinder and the specification under which it is manufactured.

Stamped on the shoulder of a modern cylinder we should find an indication of the cylinder's water capacity or empty volume. This is the volume of air contained by the cylinder when it is at atmospheric pressure, uncharged or empty.

The working pressure will also be stamped on the cylinder, usually expressed in bars, or on some cylinders in pounds per square inch (p.s.i.) (divide by 14.7 to get bars). This working pressure is the maximum pressure to which the cylinder can be charged and therefore controls the potential capacity of the cylinder.

The cylinder's total capacity is calculated as follows:

Water capacity × working pressure = total capacity

To take a popular example,

12 litres × 207 bar = 2484 litres

This calculation assumes that the cylinder has been charged to its maximum working pressure and is still at that pressure. It might, perhaps, have been used already for a dive, in which case it will not contain its full capacity. This is easily checked with a test gauge or by means of the submersible pressure gauge fitted to most regulators. With this we can read the pressure in the cylinder and work out the air available.

Water capacity × gauge pressure = air available

To continue with our first example, we might find the following situation:

12 litres × 120 bar = 1440 litres

At any point during or after the dive it is therefore possible to determine the precise amount of air remaining in the cylinder.

Checking Your Consumption Rate

Since people breathe at different rates, it is worth trying to measure your own rate under controlled conditions. In a swimming pool or an area of protected water, you can swim for a given length of time breathing normally from your aqualung. Ideally, you should be wearing your normal diving equipment so that the effect of drag will be the same as that which you will encounter on a dive. Plan to swim at a steady pace because you are trying to determine your consumption when faced with a possible emergency. Calculate the air in your cylinder before your swim, swim for a fixed time of, say, five or ten minutes, then once more calculate the air remaining in the cylinder. Take the second figure from the first and divide it by the number of minutes you were swimming. The answer is your own personal air consumption figure. Remember to increase it when you are going into colder water or when you are planning to carry out some heavy work or if you know you are less fit than when you carried out the test. Why not do it with a buddy and then you can compare the figures? It may also be interesting to repeat this procedure at least once per season.

How Much Air Do We Need?

We can now bring together the two calculations shown above to help us plan our air needs for specific dives. The usual procedure is, first, to consider the dive we plan to make, calculate the air required for it, then check to see that the cylinder we plan to use will contain sufficient air.

Let us take the example of a dive on a site known to be 27 metres deep. The BSAC '88 Decompression Tables indicate that we can dive to this depth for 24 minutes without the need for stage decompression. How much air will we require? We are assuming a consumption rate equivalent to 25 litres/minute.

25 litres/minute × 3·7 bar × 24 minutes = 2220 litres

This calculation shows that if we have a cylinder of this capacity then we can expect to draw our last breath just as we start to ascend from the bottom. This clearly is not acceptable, so it is normal practice to have a reserve of air to allow for any contingencies, plus air for the ascent. To calculate the air needed for the ascent we consider this as another little dive at half the maximum depth and with a duration based on swimming up at 15 metres per minute, rounded up to whole minutes:

25 litres/minute × 2·35 bar × 3 minutes = 176 litres

So far we need 2220 litres + 176 litres = 2396 litres. To calculate our reserve we will usually plan to return with 25 per cent of our air left in the cylinder. This covers unplanned increases in exertion, due perhaps to having to swim farther or against a current, or delays in leaving the surface, difficulties in the descent or other unforeseen circumstances. So to add the reserve we multiply the air required by 1.25 in our example this gives

2396 × 1.25   2995 litres

We have a cylinder available which has a water capacity of 12 litres and a maximum working pressure of 232 bars. This would give us

12 litres × 232 bars = 2784 litres

This is not enough for the planned dive. We have two options; to reduce the planned duration of the dive or to use a bigger cylinder.

In the first option we can calculate the effective reduction in duration as follows:

$$\frac{\text{Air available}}{\text{Air required}} \times \text{planned dive time} = \text{new dive time}$$

$$\frac{2784}{2995} \times 24 \text{ minutes} = 22 \text{ minutes}$$

To stay within the limitations of our cylinder we will have to amend our dive plan to 22 minutes at 27 metres.

To exercise the second option, we are looking for the cylinder capacity which fits our dive plan air requirement of 2995 litres. This is found as follows

$$\frac{\text{Required capacity}}{\text{Available capacity}} \times \text{available cylinder size} = \text{required cylinder size}$$

$$\frac{2995}{2784} \times 12 \text{ litres} = 12.9 \text{ litres}$$

Thus to carry out a dive of 24 minutes at 27 metres we need a cylinder with a capacity of at least 12.9 litres. In practice this would probably be a cylinder of 15 litres capacity, or a twin set in which each cylinder was at least 7.5 litres capacity. This formula assumes that the working pleasure remains the same for the two cylinder sets.

The Reserve Supply

We have already mentioned the principle behind the reserve supply, but it is worth describing the other ways of measuring this. Some sets, particularly those in use on the Continent and in commercial work, are fitted with a reserve mechanism which warns the diver when the air supply has reached a given pressure level. A restrictor reduces the flow of air to the regulator and this is sensed by the diver. The reserve mechanism must then be operated by the diver to release the air remaining in the cylinder. This type of reserve typically operates at around 30 bar on a single cylinder but bears no relationship to the capacity of the cylinder or its normal working pressure. It will therefore operate at 13–15 per cent of cylinder capacity and this usually indicates the need for an immediate return to the surface except on the very shallowest of dives. In the case of a diver using a 12-litre cylinder, it would give insufficient air for an ascent from 50 metres.

Most submersible pressure gauges highlight the area indicating 0–50 bar cylinder pressure and this provides a better rule of thumb than the 30-bar mechanical reserve, which can still have a role as a final warning. But, most importantly, remember in your dive planning to calculate the amount of air which you plan to hold in reserve and

Figure 135 Cylinder pressure gauge with the 50 bar 'reserve' sector clearly marked

translate it into gauge pressure so that you can read it on your gauge.

Deeper dives will require more air in reserve than shallow dives. Cave divers always plan to surface with a third of their air intact. For dives deeper than 25 metres it is best to plan a reserve of 25 per cent or 500 litres, whichever is greater. For dives at less than 10 metres, 10 per cent or 100 litres minimum should suffice.

If you are planning a dive requiring decompression stops, then remember to allow for the air to be breathed during these stops.

Figure 136
Mechanical reserve warns the diver when cylinder pressure falls to 30 bar

ASCENT AIR REQUIREMENT

Consumption rate (l/min.)	Depth of dive				
	10 m	20 m	30 m	40 m	50 m
20	30	80	100	180	280
25	38	100	125	225	350
30	45	120	150	270	420
40	60	160	200	360	560

Ascent rate of 15 metres/minute assumed.

CYLINDER CAPACITIES

Water capacity (litres)	Working pressure (bars)	Total capacity (litres)	Equivalent in cubic feet
5	200	1000	35·33
7	207	1449	51·20
7	232	1624	57·39
9	207	1863	65·83
10	207	2070	73·14
10	232	2320	81·98
12	207	2484	87·77
12	232	2784	98·37
15	207	3105	109·72
15	232	3480	122·97

Air Supply Calculations

Example 1

We are planning a dive to 30 metres. We have 12-litre cylinders which can only be charged to 200 bars by the boat's compressor. How long a dive can we expect?

Our cylinders will have 12 litres × 200 bar = 2400 litres total capacity. If we assume a rate of 25 litres/minute, we know that we will need 203 litres for the ascent, which is safely covered by taking our reserve figure of 25 per cent of the total, or 600 litres. This will leave us 2400 litres – 600 litres = 1800 litres air available for the dive. At a depth of 30 metres the ambient pressure is 4 bar. So we can work out our requirement as follows:

$$\text{Consumption rate at depth} = \text{surface rate} \times \text{ambient pressure}$$
$$= 25 \text{ litres} \times 4 \text{ bars}$$
$$= 100 \text{ litres/minute}$$

$$\text{Dive duration} = \frac{\text{air available}}{\text{consumption rate at depth}}$$
$$= \frac{1800 \text{ litres}}{100 \text{ litres}}$$
$$= 18 \text{ minutes}$$

Example 2

We plan to dive to 20 metres for 46 minutes. How big a cylinder do we need?

We will assume a consumption rate of 25 litres/minute. Therefore, our planned requirement is found by the following:

$$\text{Ambient pressure} \times \text{duration} \times \text{consumption rate} = \text{total requirement}$$

3 bar × 46 minutes × 25 litres/minute = 3450 litres

We should then add the reserve:

3450 × 1·33 = 4588·5 litres

If we assume a charging pressure of 200 bars, then we will need a set of

$$\frac{4588·5}{200 \text{ bar}} = 22·94 \text{ litres water capacity}$$

This will probably be in the form of a twin 12-litre set.

Alternatively, we might be using higher pressure cylinders, in which case we would find:

$$\frac{4588·5}{232 \text{ bar}} = 19·78 \text{ litres}$$

This will probably be in the form of a twin 10-litre set.

Dive Leadership

In order to ensure that diving is carried out with the maximum of safety and with the minimum of fuss, it is controlled at two levels. The first level is that of the actual group of divers who dive together and they are under the direction and control of a dive leader. The second level is that of the whole diving party, which can comprise many diving groups, all controlled by the dive marshal, who, in many areas of the world, may also be called the dive master.

Dive Leader

The dive leader is the person in charge of a small group of divers who dive together. The group may consist of the dive leader and only one other diver or there may be several divers in the group.

The dive leader is normally the most experienced diver in the group and it is his duty to take control of the dive and make decisions on behalf of the other divers. Having ascertained the degree of experience of each member of the group and having, where appropriate, paired them off, the responsibilities of the dive leader from then on can easily be summarized by remembering the mnemonic 'SEEDS'.

S – Safety
E – Equipment
E – Exercise
D – Discipline
S – Signals

If the dive leader uses this *aide-mémoire* both above and below the water, he will make sure that he does not miss anything vital. Prior to entering the water, he will check each of the above items in the pre-dive brief.
Safety
This will cover such information as reminding beginners about ear clearing and mask squeeze on descent,

Figure 137   The dive leader's briefing

breathing out during the ascent, the importance of correct buoyancy control and the action to be taken if separated. Any specific problems such as shipping fairways, tidal streams, dangerous rocks or wreckage should also be covered.
Equipment
The dive leader will ensure that every item of diving equipment is correctly assembled and in working order. He will further ensure that the members of the party are familiar with the operation of their own and their buddy's equipment. He will outline the correct use of any ancillary equipment such as buddy lines, surface marker buoys, ground lines, etc.
Exercise
This will be a straightforward outline of the dive procedure:
1. The method of entering the water.
2. The mode of descent.
3. The dive plan once submerged.
4. The procedure for surfacing at the termination of the dive.
5. Explanation of any specific drills or tasks.
Discipline
The dive leader will aim to ensure that each diver knows what to do and how to do it.
1. The order of entering the water.
2. The assembly prior to submerging.
3. The need to keep together during the descent, the dive and the ascent.
4. The details for exiting from the water.
Signals
All divers should have a full knowledge of the signals that might be used during the dive. A reminder of emergency signals should also be given. After the briefing session, the dive leader's next task is to get his diving group into, and under, the water. Once submerged, he can still use SEEDS to remind him of his responsibilities and procedures.
Safety
He will ensure that ears are being cleared during the descent and will keep the party close together at this time. On reaching the bottom, he will check that everyone is OK. During the dive, he will again check that the divers are OK. He will check cylinder pressure gauges from time to time to monitor air consumption. He will look for potential hazards and shepherd his divers clear of them. He will make the decision to terminate the dive early if conditions dictate that this is appropriate.
Equipment
The dive leader will satisfy himself that the divers are competently handling their own equipment – adjusting buoyancy, mask clearing, etc. He will offer help if he thinks that help is needed. He will ensure that surface marker buoys, buddy lines, ground lines, etc., are correctly deployed.
Exercise
He will ensure that the purpose of the dive is carried out safely and sensibly. He will try to ensure that each

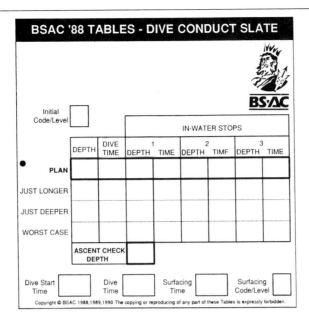

Figure 138 Typical dive record log

member of the group has a useful and satisfactory dive.

Discipline

The dive leader will tactfully ensure that each diver positions himself correctly at each stage of the dive. He will be watchful of the diver who may wander away from direct contact with the group.

Signals

The routine exchange of signals can help overcome the nervousness of the beginner, because he then knows that the dive leader is looking after him and keeping an eye on him. The way in which a diver reacts to routine signals will give the experienced dive leader a useful guide to his state of mind. On the return to the surface and the exit from it, the dive leader will help his partners to de-kit. He will then debrief them about the dive and about their performance during the dive.

Dive Marshal

The dive marshal is the person in overall charge of all the groups of divers as well as being responsible for making all the arrangements for the diving activities. He needs to be an experienced diver and a responsible person, able to plan ahead and anticipate possible problems. In a normal club situation, the dive marshal will be in charge of the diving, which takes place over a single day or possibly a weekend.

He will commence his planning for the dives well in advance of the actual date, following the dive planning checklist.

1. Select suitable sites for the type of diving to be undertaken (e.g. training drills, training dives, wreck dives, etc.)
2. Produce a list of all divers who will be taking part.
3. With the help of the diving officer, select the various diving groups and allocate dive leaders to them.

4. Make sure that every diver has the full details and a timetable of the diving.
5. Make sure that any collective equipment (boat, engine, compressor, etc.) will arrive at the dive site in good time and in good order.
6. Establish the location of the nearest compressor if a portable one is not being used.
7. Check the tides, currents and weather and update his information continuously since, in the event of adverse conditions, he may need to change the diving arrangements or even cancel the dives completely.
8. Delegate as much of the detailed work as possible, otherwise it will be very difficult for him to enjoy a dive himself.

Once at the dive site, the dive marshal will brief all the divers taking part. He will outline specific jobs such as boat handlers, compressor operators, lookouts, surface cover, etc. He will also outline the broad dive plan and the order of diving. Where appropriate, he will ensure that the coastguard is aware of the area and time of the diving for the dive party. He will already have noted the location and methods of contacting the safety services (ambulance, doctor, recompression chamber, coastguard). He should also try to ensure that all divers follow the Diving Code and that minimum disturbance is caused to members of the general public.

At the end of the day's diving, the dive marshal will ensure that all the gear is collected and that any boats are correctly cleaned and stowed. He will check that the dive site is left clean and tidy. He will remember to thank anyone who has helped towards the success of the activities. Not the least of the dive marshal's responsibilities is to ensure that adequate records of the diving are kept.

Safe Open-Water Diving

The Buddy Diving System

The buddy system is, by definition, a pair of divers operating as a single unit, each being responsible for the other's safety both above and below the water. It is one of the most basic safety precautions in sport diving, based on the premise that it is unlikely that the same problem will occur to both divers at the same time, thus enabling assistance to be given should the need arise.

To be effective, the buddy system needs an agreed plan, good communications and the capability to assist others. Sharing responsibility for each other's safety, coupled with the shared experience of the dive itself, will improve both divers' overall appreciation and enjoyment of the underwater world.

Initial Dives

Following initial pool or sheltered-water training, the novice will be ready for his first open-water dive. Ideally, he should be accompanied by a qualified instructor, preferably one who has been involved with his early training. Alternatively, an experienced diver who has previously demonstrated his responsibility towards the needs of the novice diver might prove suitable.

These early and important dives should be planned to give progressively more experience to the novice. His instructor should choose a safe but interesting site, with good underwater visibility and plenty to see. As confidence and ability grow, the novice will soon become a sport diver, at which time he will be in a position to choose his own diving buddy.

Choosing Your Buddy

Clearly, the choice of dive buddy is of great importance and should be carefully considered long before the dive takes place. The choice of diving companion may well be based on similar interests – for example, underwater photography, wreck diving – or simply an understanding of each other's strengths, weaknesses, likes and dislikes.

Before preparing to dive, a dive leader should be appointed to lead the dive. Normally this is the more experienced of the pair. Even if both divers are of equal experience, it should still be established who is going to lead the dive in order to avoid confusion underwater.

Odd Numbers

There are occasions when more than two divers may be involved in the dive group. This may not be the ideal situation, but, if it is unavoidable, the decision to dive must be based on the diving experience of the individuals concerned.

If the ratio of inexperienced to experienced is exceeded, this could, in anything other than very safe conditions, lead to the risk of separation underwater. The tendency is for no one to assume responsibility for the unpartnered diver, which, in effect, makes him a lone diver. A competent and experienced instructor should be capable of handling more than one novice at a time. He must consider whether the diving conditions and dive site are suitable for this, and also, if more than one novice experiences difficulty at the same time, whether he will be able to assist.

Where visibility permits, the diving party may be increased in number only so long as they can still be properly supervised by the dive leader or instructor. Should the group be uneven in number, then the dive leader should be the one not allocated to a buddy pair.

First Line of Safety

The buddy system is fundamental to diving safety, but it must not be considered as the only contribution to diver

Figure 139   The dive commences when both diving buddies confirm they are ready

safety. Dive planning, physical fitness, diving equipment, surface support and diving knowledge will all play an important role. As the sport diver becomes more adventurous, all of these areas will become more significant to the overall safety of the dive. However, the diver's first line of safety will always be the buddy system, each partner sharing the responsibility for the other's safety. A conscious awareness of his partner's position and actions will enable a diver to be ready to provide support at all times.

The Need for a Plan

All dives should be planned and every effort should be made to stick to the plan. Dive planning has a number of distinctly separate aspects, each of which plays a major role in the overall safety and success of the dive.

Preplanning

In planning any open-water diving, attention should be paid to more than only the actual dives on the day. The selection of the site and the purpose of the dive are decisions which can be made well in advance and both are interrelated. For example, a wreck site presupposes knowledge of its general location, although the purpose of the dive is usually quite obvious. However, the choice of a site for general interest and exploratory diving can be crucial to its success. Selection should be made in the light of all available knowledge from previous dives in the area, other divers' information, local knowledge, reference to charts, tidal information and depth of water.

You must check for the best possible access (permission may be required) since it may prove difficult to transport heavy equipment. Long walks carrying diving equipment are best avoided; if possible select your access point more carefully.

Pre-dive Preparation

Before you leave home check your diving equipment.

Figure 140 Dive leader checks his buddy's equipment

Make sure that all your equipment is serviceable and present – torch charged/new batteries fitted, cylinder charged to its working pressure (a compressor may not be available on site), O-rings in place and serviceable (take a few spare ones just in case). Check your drysuit seals or your wetsuit for cuts and replace or repair as necessary. Packing your dive bag in the order that you will fit your equipment on site is a useful habit – for example, basic equipment first, followed by instruments, lifejacket, wet/drysuit, dive regulator and lifejacket cylinder. A useful addition to your kit is a small bag to keep your ancillary diving equipment together and accessible. Do not put your weight belt in your dive bag; instead carry this separately as, apart from the possible damage to other equipment, it makes the dive bag too heavy to carry.

Finally, if a boat dive is planned, do not forget some creature comforts such as windproof clothing, flask of soup, etc.

Dive Planning

Do not enter the water without first planning the dive. Several influencing factors which will always need to be considered before diving are:

The amount of air available for the dive

The depth of the dive

The point at which a safe reserve of air has been reached, which will signal the end of the dive if there are no other limiting factors

Your whereabouts relative to the surface party or point of exit

The prevailing sea/weather conditions

Never dive unless somebody else knows your plan.

Figure 141 Maintain buddy contact underwater

The Dive Plan

Once underwater, stay together and maintain the same position relative to each other. If a change of direction is made, make sure that your buddy understands and follows the new course. Should you become separated from your dive buddy, spend only a short time (30 seconds at the most) trying to make contact, then surface, and wait until your buddy surfaces. On the surface, regroup while the dive leader decides whether to continue or abort the dive.

Preparing to Dive

On-Site Preparation

Before kitting up, a general briefing should take place in which the diving pairs and dive leaders are established. The overall plan for the dive and its timing should be discussed in detail so that everyone understands what is to be done, how, why and where, etc. If you rush to get your equipment on and miss the briefing you may find you are not diving in the first group but in the second, which could mean sitting around in all your gear on a hot day!

Figure 142   Briefing the diving party

Kitting Up

The order or sequence for kitting up will vary, depending on the equipment that you use, but it is well worth developing a routine:

1. Charge and fit the adjustable-buoyancy lifejacket cylinder.
2. Fit the regulator to the cylinder valve, making sure it is the right way up.
3. Turn the air on slowly and check the cylinder contents.
4. Check the regulator is functioning correctly by taking one or two breaths.
5. Turn the air off, check the submersible pressure gauge for a drop in pressure, check the first and second stages of your regulator for leaks, then turn on the air again.
6. Put on the diving suit.
7. Fit the lifejacket.
8. Fit any ancillary equipment.
9. Put on the aqualung with assistance.
10. Fit the weight belt and check that if released it will fall free.
11. Mask, fins, snorkel and gloves are the last items to be fitted prior to entering the water.

Neutral Buoyancy

It is important that divers are correctly weighted for the dive. Neutral buoyancy is essential for safety and comfort. The definition of neutral buoyancy is: when you inhale fully you rise, when you exhale fully you sink, and when you breathe normally you stay virtually where you are.

Figure 143   Each diver helps his buddy kit up

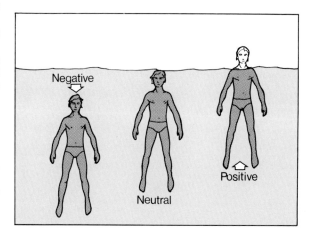

Figure 144   A negatively buoyant diver sinks even after complete inhalation

A neutrally buoyant diver rises on inhalation and sinks on exhalation

A positively buoyant diver floats even after exhalation

Briefings

Prior to diving, a diver-to-diver briefing should take place. This is normally given by the dive leader or instructor. The mnemonic for remembering what this briefing should cover is SEEDS (see p. 118).

Safety – breathe normally/avoid over-exertion/ear clearing/underwater hazards.

Exercise – the purpose of the dive – pleasure/exploration/wreck, etc.

Equipment – check air contents/lifejacket/suit inflation/instruments/quick releases/buoyancy, etc.

Discipline – the position each diver is to maintain during the dive/specific duties/actions if separated, etc.

Signals – signals to be used, including 'specials' for particular tasks.

Figure 145   Checking signals during a pre-dive briefing

Buddy Checks

Checking your buddy's equipment immediately prior to diving is probably the last opportunity visually to appraise your partner's equipment and restate any last-minute instructions relative to the conduct of the dive. The novice diver may well be preoccupied with the coming dive and this, combined with the lack of dive practice and familiarity with his equipment, puts the responsibility for making sure all the equipment is fitted correctly and instructions are understood on the instructor/dive leader.

1. Check fitness to dive.
2. Check the air supply is fully turned on.
3. Check the pressure gauge to make sure there is sufficient air for the dive.
4. Check direct feeds to suit and/or lifejacket are correctly connected.
5. Check harness, weight belt and lifejacket straps are not fouling any other equipment.
6. Check that depth gauge and watch are in place.
7. Check that mask, fins, snorkel and diving knife are fitted correctly.
8. Check that you are familiar with each other's inflation and venting systems to drysuit and lifejacket.
9. Check the signals to be used and that they are understood.
10. Check the actions to be taken in the event of separation.

Fit to Dive? → Air Supply Turned On? → Pressure Gauge Reading Full? → Harness, Lifejacket, Weight Belt, Straps? → Instruments Fitted? → Mask, Fins, Snorkel, Knife Attached? → System Check? → Signals Understood? → Dive Plan, Emergency Actions Understood? → Dive

Figure 146   The pre-dive check

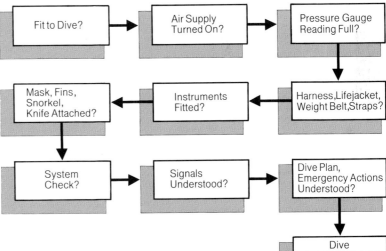

Figure 147   Checking the layout of a dive buddy's equipment

Entry to the Water

Rocky-Beach Entry

Dives from a rocky beach can provide some of the more interesting and diverse underwater terrain. Unlike sandy beaches, there is usually better underwater visibility and more marine life. However, clambering over rocks which are slippery and covered in barnacles while wearing full diving gear can be quite hazardous. Approach this type of entry with care. When planning an entry it is important to be familiar with the effects that tidal changes may have on the access and the ease of entry and exit. High tide may change an easy entry point into an area of strong surge and wave action. Low water could mean a drop-off which is too high to reach the water from or, worse, to get back out.

Entry Method

Use hard-soled boots rather than bootees. They will give a better grip on wet rocks. Carry as little as possible. Keep the hands free to steady yourself and make additional trips for the rest of your equipment if necessary. Choose a solid rock to sit on or lean against while putting on your fins and mask. Unless the water is clear and deep, jumping in should be avoided. It is better to sit down and then edge forward in a seated position until your legs are in the water. Time your entry so you hit the water at the top of the swell or wave, push forward, fin hard and allow the backwash to carry you away from the rocks.

Exit Method

Time the exit so that the wave or swell is at its highest, since this should lift you onto the rocks. If you miscalculate, hold on and wait for the next wave, which will lift you farther up. Avoid using gullies or channels as exits since tidal surge is greater in these confined areas. It should be noted that a diver will lose buoyancy in heavy foam; this should be avoided if at all possible.

Figure 149   When entering from a rocky shore, avoid jumping. It is preferable to enter from a sitting position

Forward-Roll Entry

This type of entry enables the diver to enter the water without needing to hold the mask and mouthpiece in place, leaving his hands free to carry a camera or other equipment.

Stride Entry

The straightforward stride entry requires the diver to hold his mask and regulator in place with one hand while holding down the cylinder harness with the other. The latter should prevent the cylinder being pushed upwards and into the diver's head.

Before entering the water the diver must ensure that there is a sufficient depth of water with no underwater obstructions.

Figure 148   A forward roll and a stride entry

Entry through Surf

In many parts of the world divers will need to enter the water through surf. Most waves and currents are far stronger than a diver and this type of entry should always be approached with considerable caution. When a wave approaches a shoreline, the bottom of the wave slows down more than the top. This causes the wave to be unstable, with the faster-moving top falling over or breaking. Divers should note that a wave has a great deal more energy at the top than it has at the bottom.

Entry Method

If the conditions are favourable, choose an area free from obstructions, rocks, etc. Avoid carrying cameras, which might get lost or damaged. In tropical waters, wear protective clothing and gloves to avoid cutting yourself on coral. Partially inflate your lifejacket to maintain positive buoyancy and, with mask, fins and regulator in place, lean forward to present the smallest surface area to the oncoming waves (an angle of about 45 degrees). As the wave approaches, lower your centre of gravity even farther, lean into the wave and allow the undertow to take you out. As soon as the depth permits, start finning away from the entry area. Once clear, you will probably need to rest and regain your composure before commencing the dive.

Exit Method

Before entering the surf area, check for the best approach. Having done so, move quickly and the moment you can stand up, do so. If this is not possible, shuffle up the beach, allowing the breakers to push you forward and keeping your hands in front of you to fend off obstructions. Hold on to the bottom during the undertow and remember to stay away from the highest part of the wave. If the conditions are very rough, do not dive.

Entry from an Inflatable Boat

Normally, an entry from an inflatable boat is made from a sitting position, by rolling backwards into the water. Because inflatables afford little room, standing up and walking around is not practicable and the process of kitting up usually takes place in a sitting position and in a fairly confined area.

Entry Method

With all of your equipment checked and in place, ensure your fins are free from obstruction and the water behind is clear of obstruction. Keeping your legs together, edge farther over the inflatable tube (without falling in prematurely), hold mask and regulator in place with one hand and roll over backwards in a tucked position.

Exit Method

Keep a firm hold on the boat and pass in any hand-held items. Then, using one hand, release and pass in the weight belt. Disconnect any direct feeds and slacken the cylinder harness straps. Release the harness waist strap and then slip your free arm through the shoulder strap and allow the harness to remain on the arm which is still holding the boat. The cylinder can then be lifted in and stowed by the boat crew. Using your fins and the boat's hand line, propel yourself upwards and into the boat. Keep the mask in place on your face until safely in the boat.

Figure 151 A backward roll from an inflatable boat

Entry from a Large Boat

Diving from large boats presents conditions which are less cramped than inflatables. Entry is usually made by stepping off the deck and entering the water feet first. From heights greater than 1–2 metres, do not look down as you enter, since this could dislodge the mask on impact. Leaving the water is usually via a ladder (fins off), removing your set once on board. In heavier swells it may be necessary to return to the large boat via the covering inflatable. If you attempt to enter the large boat direct from a heavy swell, take the very greatest care not to be struck by the boarding ladder as the vessel rolls with the waves.

Figure 150 A stride entry from the gunwhale of a large boat

Beach Entry

Walk to the water's edge carrying your mask and fins and with the rest of your diving equipment fitted. This will help to prevent sand, pebbles or other foreign matter from getting into the diving equipment.

At the water's edge put on your fins (using your buddy for support), then your mask and then put your regulator in your mouth. With fins fitted, it is easier to walk backwards, checking from time to time for submerged rocks and obstructions; as soon as you are deep enough, start finning.

Although ideal for entries, sandy beaches which are subjected to a lot of tidal movement are seldom interesting for diving because of the poor underwater visibility. Try to head for reefs or rocky outcrops which may make your dive more interesting.

Figure 152 Use your buddy diver for support when fitting fins

The Buddy System Underwater

Descending

Descending into the underwater world can be one of the most exciting experiences for any diver. In tropical waters, with good visibility, the coral and marine life can be seen from the surface and there can be few experiences to equal an effortless descent towards these underwater gardens. Good visibility is not only restricted to the tropics, however, and some tropical areas may experience very poor visibility. Around the British Isles and in most temperate zones, clear water can be found. But the factors controlling this are more complicated and are discussed on page 230. Remote headlands, fjords and flooded quarries can provide the diver with good clear-water diving.

Divers soon discover that water clarity and visibility play a very great part in the overall enjoyment of the dive. Clear water usually means a good dive, while dark and murky water means that greater care needs to be exercised, especially while descending. More dives are aborted in the first few minutes than at any other time. Usually the reasons are ear trouble, buoyancy problems, apprehension or diver separation. These factors are often exacerbated by poor visibility.

Make sure that when the signal to dive is given, your buddy is in fact ready and not engaged in last-minute tasks such as unwinding the surface marker line, adjusting his mask or dumping air from his lifejacket.

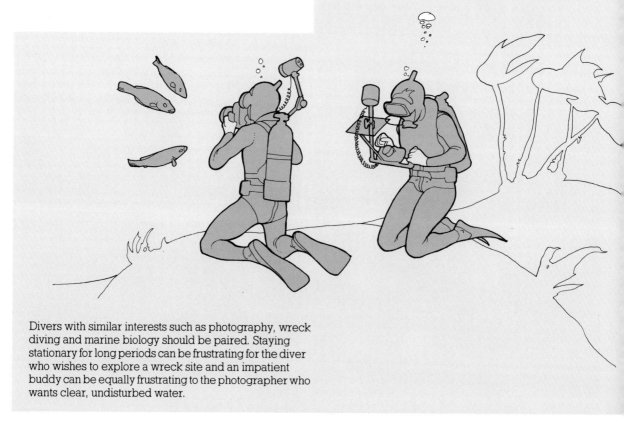

Divers with similar interests such as photography, wreck diving and marine biology should be paired. Staying stationary for long periods can be frustrating for the diver who wishes to explore a wreck site and an impatient buddy can be equally frustrating to the photographer who wants clear, undisturbed water.

Figure 153

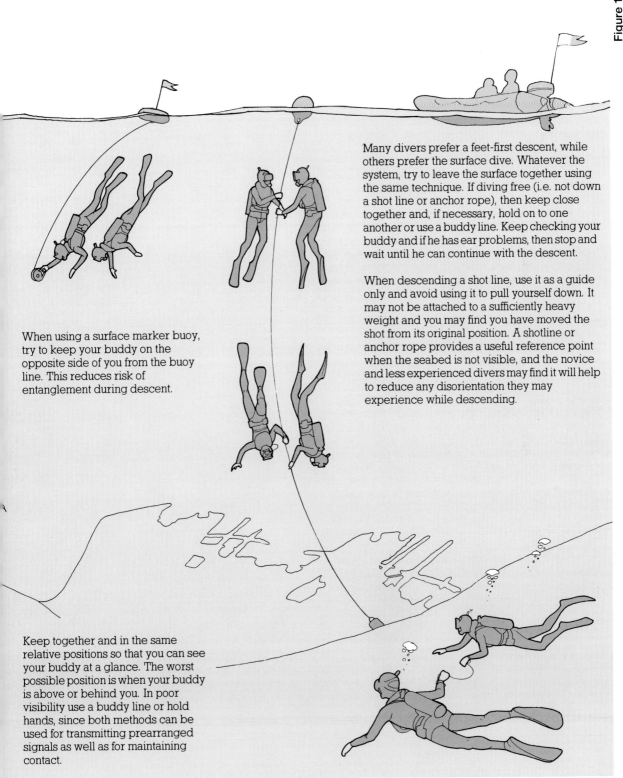

Many divers prefer a feet-first descent, while others prefer the surface dive. Whatever the system, try to leave the surface together using the same technique. If diving free (i.e. not down a shot line or anchor rope), then keep close together and, if necessary, hold on to one another or use a buddy line. Keep checking your buddy and if he has ear problems, then stop and wait until he can continue with the descent.

When descending a shot line, use it as a guide only and avoid using it to pull yourself down. It may not be attached to a sufficiently heavy weight and you may find you have moved the shot from its original position. A shotline or anchor rope provides a useful reference point when the seabed is not visible, and the novice and less experienced divers may find it will help to reduce any disorientation they may experience while descending.

When using a surface marker buoy, try to keep your buddy on the opposite side of you from the buoy line. This reduces risk of entanglement during descent.

Keep together and in the same relative positions so that you can see your buddy at a glance. The worst possible position is when your buddy is above or behind you. In poor visibility use a buddy line or hold hands, since both methods can be used for transmitting prearranged signals as well as for maintaining contact.

Normal Ascents

The decision to ascend is normally made when the cylinder pressure has fallen to a quarter of its full capacity. It is important to have a sufficient reserve of air to regain the surface safely. However, as is explained elsewhere in this manual, a quarter reserve may not be enough if deeper dives, involving decompression, are being made. There are also other reasons for terminating the dive. In particular, the adherence to a prearranged time, to check your whereabouts in relation to the boat and surface cover, cold and fatigue or simply just an uninteresting dive site are all good enough reasons for termination.

Normal Ascent Procedure

1. The 'go up' signal must be exchanged with your dive buddy or group.
2. If you have been using your lifejacket/drysuit for buoyancy adjustment during the dive, do not immediately dump this air but use the buoyancy to assist you in the early stages of the ascent. As your ascent rate increases, control the dumping of air so that you do not exceed the rate of ascent of the small exhaust bubbles. Alternatively, dump the air buoyancy and fin upwards, although, depending on depth, you may have to fin quite strongly to overcome the initial negative buoyancy and gain upward momentum.
3. During the ascent, face your buddy and check his rate of ascent. The correct rate of ascent is 15 metres/ minute up to 6 metres with the final ascent to the surface taking 1 minute. This procedure allows the divers to take control of their ascent at the 6 metre-level and thus ensure a proper passage through this important pressure change. Remember to breathe normally at all times.
4. As you approach the surface, carefully check your rate of ascent. Look up and watch out for surface obstacles. In poor visibility, hold one hand above your head. In this case use your other hand to hold onto your buddy.
5. Immediately on surfacing, turn a complete circle in case a boat should be approaching. Be ready to take evasive action by diving again if necessary. Exchange the OK signal with your buddy and 'keep close together. Leave your regulator and mask in place. If you feel tired, inflate your lifejacket and rest. Signal OK or otherwise to surface/boat cover. Any other form of waving or no signal or response whatsoever will be considered an emergency requiring immediate assistance.

Figure 154

Emergency Ascents

Figure 155

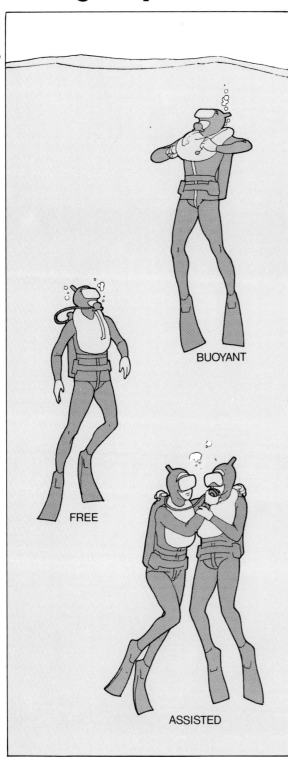

BUOYANT

FREE

ASSISTED

Emergencies very often occur through poor dive practice. Running out of air is the most common. Usually this is not as a result of an equipment malfunction, such as regulator failure, but because the diver has miscalculated his air requirements or failed to check his cylinder contents during the dive.

Anything other than a normal ascent is an emergency ascent. All emergency ascents carry an element or risk, although some are more risky than others. The degree of risk will largely depend upon the training and experience of the diver. If an emergency occurs underwater, an element of excitement, panic or fear is bound to be felt, and under these conditions a person will react correctly only if he is able to perform emergency procedures automatically and almost without thinking. This is where the value of proper training becomes apparent.

Exceeding the normal ascent rate in a state of panic or missing planned decompression stops can expose the diver to possible pressure damage and decompression sickness.

Assisted Ascents

Assisted ascents are a means by which a diver whose air supply has failed or run out is assisted to the surface by his buddy utilising the buddy's air supply. This can be accomplished by one of two means, either by utilising an additional second stage fitted to the buddy's equipment (the octopus rig) or by sharing the buddy's regulator second stage (the shared regulator). Both ascents require that your buddy is in close proximity and that you can attract his attention quickly.

The Octopus Rig Ascent

The simplest and most reliable means of performing an assisted ascent is for the distressed diver to use his buddy's octopus rig. This can take the form of an extra second stage fitted to a low pressure port on the first stage of the regulator, a completely separate regulator fitted to an additional cylinder outlet or even a separate regulator and 'pony' cylinder to give a totally independent system.

Once the distressed diver has given the 'I am out of air' signal, the assisting diver closes to him as quickly as possible, removing the octopus rig from its stowage position and holding it ready for the distressed diver's use. The purge button of the octopus rig should be kept clear so that the distressed diver can use it, should he wish, to clear the octopus mouthpiece of water. The distressed diver then breathes normally from the octopus rig.

Once a steady breathing rhythm has been established, an ascent at the normal rate is performed with both divers maintaining a secure hold on each other and breathing naturally throughout.

The Shared Regulator Ascent

In this technique the assisting diver's regulator second stage is shared. The principle of the technique is that each diver takes two breaths in turn passing the one regulator second stage back and forth between them. Initially the distressed diver may need to take more than two breaths until he has regained his composure. Once a steady rhythm is established the ascent is commenced with each diver ensuring that, while not breathing from the regulator, he is gently exhaling to offset the expansion of air in his lungs. It is essential that the assisting diver remains in control of the air supply and that both divers maintain a close secure hold on each other. This is clearly a more complex procedure and it is explained in more detail in the Progressive Training Skills section of this manual (see p.68).

Controlled Buoyant Ascents

Most types of lifejackets and drysuits are fitted with direct feeds and/or a separate air cylinder which can bring a diver to the surface in an emergency. It must be emphasized, however, that a fully inflated lifejacket/ drysuit (or both) will bring a diver up at an unacceptable rate with a consequent risk of air embolism or explosive decompression.

In an emergency, a drysuited diver may have air within his suit and not in his lifejacket. Should he then inflate his lifejacket, he may be unable to vent both suit and lifejacket during the ascent. It is important that, if either system has been used to gain neutral buoyancy, the same system should continue to be used throughout the ascent.

If using a drysuit with only a standard-size inflation cylinder and no direct feed (e.g. old Navy pattern), it may not be possible to gain enough buoyancy to make a buoyant ascent. In this case a direct feed would need to be fitted to the drysuit or an adjustable-buoyancy lifejacket should be used. For the wetsuited or drysuited diver it is important to familiarize himself with the inflating and venting systems of the lifejacket or drysuit. All adjustable-buoyancy lifejackets and many drysuits are equipped with overpressure valves which automatically blow off when fully inflated. Many have a manual override to enable the diver to dump air should the rate of ascent get out of control. Some drysuits, however, can only be bled through the wrist or neck seals.

The Sequence of Actions

1. Open the tap of your lifejacket air cylinder or press your direct feed (a compressed air cylinder will inflate the jacket more quickly than a direct feed system).
2. As the ascent commences, close the tap or stop pressing the direct feed.
3. Lean your head back, breathe out, watch for the surface.
4. Controlled venting of the lifejacket or drysuit should be carefully employed during the ascent. Be very sure, however, not to vent to the extent that you lose buoyancy and start to descend again.

Free Ascents

Another way of regaining the surface quickly in an emergency is by means of a free ascent. This emergency method is a controlled finning ascent and is dependent on calm, controlled technique for its success.

When the diver finds himself without air he fins steadily upwards. If he finds this difficult, he should jettison his weight belt. The feeling of air starvation may well diminish slightly if he holds his breath *briefly* until the residual air in his lungs expands with the fall in the surrounding pressure. He may be able to get another breath from the regulator for the very same reason.

The diver should then remove the second stage and begin to exhale gently and continually through pursed lips as he ascends. The rate of finning should be slowed as he gains buoyancy and he should try not to overtake his exhaled bubbles.

Most divers feel comfortable during this type of ascent and there is normally a need to breathe out, rather than in. Enough partial pressure of oxygen exists and carbon dioxide will be exhaled as quickly as it is released from the blood stream, preventing any chance of carbon dioxide build-up. The inexperienced diver has most to fear from panic and overexertion, both of which may use up precious oxygen.

As the surface approaches the diver must take the precaution of breathing out faster to avoid serious pressure damage through overexpanision of the lungs which the more rapid changes in pressure might produce. After any type of emergency ascent, the diver should be carefully observed for any signs or symptoms of pressure damage or decompression sickness.

Figure 156   The safest way to the surface is always along the shotline

Coping with Surface Difficulties

Long surface swims to and from a dive site can cause problems, the most common being exhaustion and anxiety. Both these conditions can lead to panic if they are not recognized and controlled.

During a long surface swim, the most common cause of exhaustion is physical exertion which, in turn, leads to an increase in respiration. With the need to breathe more deeply and more rapidly, the diver may be unable to obtain an adequate volume of air from his regulator or snorkel to sustain his increased breathing rate. In this situation the diver should stop swimming and gain positive buoyancy by inflating the lifejacket. Then he should try to relax and concentrate on getting his breathing rate under control; ideally, it should be deep and slow.

In order to increase his air supply, the diver may remove his second stage and his mask. In doing so, there is a risk of water being inhaled inadvertently, thereby adding to his difficulties.

Although physical exertion is a major cause of exhaustion, it is not the only one. Cold, lack of physical fitness and mental fatigue are factors which individually or collectively are potential problems.

Anxiety, imaginary or otherwise, can lead to an increased breathing rate and lack of control in open water. It can manifest itself in a number of ways, such as the feeling of apprehension at being a long way from the shore or knowing that he has to make the return journey after a dive when he may be cold and fatigued. The apparent lack of headway against a rip current, river estuary or tidal stream can lead to the feeling of 'I am not going to make it'. Inability to see the shore due to the surface conditions and distance also makes the diver feel uncertain about his ability to cope with the situation. With good training and diving fitness many of these problems can be overcome. However, the diver should guard against putting himself into situations which are beyond his capabilities. If the diver finds himself exhausted, apprehensive or near to panic, he should stop and assess the situation before reacting.

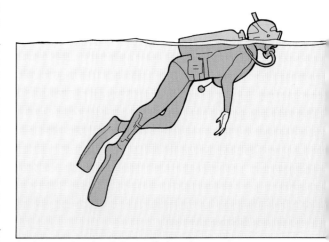

Surface swimming is less efficient than underwater swimming due to the resistance of the equipment in the surface conditions. In addition, the fin cycle is more effective underwater, so the distance he can travel is greater – a point the diver should note should he need to return on the surface.

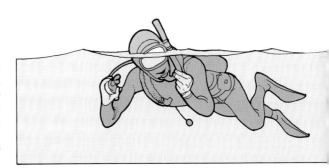

After a dive you may use your snorkel to conserve your cylinder air. Make the exchange from the regulator to the snorkel with your face submerged to avoid the possibility of swallowing water.

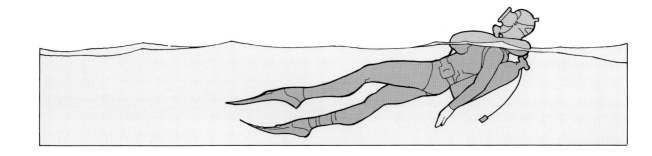

Figure 157

If you find you are becoming exhausted, inflate your lifejacket, stop finning and lie on your back. Try to relax and regain control of your breathing.

On the surface or underwater do not set a pace which is too fast for your buddy or group to keep up. This could lead to exhaustion or separation, since not all divers fin at the same rate.

Use your compass to navigate back to the shore or boat.

Below left
When long surface swims are unavoidable, use your lifejacket for buoyancy. Finning on your back is more comfortable and less tiring than in the face-down position.

Right
In a rip current or tidal stream where progress back to the shore or boat is impossible, inflate your lifejacket and conserve energy. Do not exhaust yourself trying to fin against the moving water, but sit tight and wait. The tidal stream may run parallel to the shore, slackening when it reaches a bay. This could give you the opportunity to swim in. Better still, use a boat for surface cover and wait for it to pick you up.

After surfacing, should you find yourself alone on the surface, try to remain calm. Your buddy may well have surfaced but may be out of sight in the trough of a wave. Use your whistle to attract his attention, swim towards him and regroup.

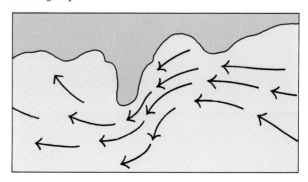

Progressive Open-Water Skills

Diving skills which have been learned in the swimming pool or sheltered training area have to be practised in open water. Even the most experienced divers never stop learning. New techniques in diver safety and personal skills need continual and regular practice if the diver is to maintain a reasonable level of competency in the open water.

Few divers begin their training in open water; most acquire their basic skills in the swimming pool, where their instruction will include the progressive use of full diving equipment before moving to open water. The swimming pool is not open water and it is important to relearn these skills in the underwater environment as the conditions of visibility, temperature, depth and movement of water cannot be simulated in the swimming pool.

Different conditions and sites will widen your experience and appreciation. Make sure that you gain new skills with each of your early dives.

NAVIGATION

1. Simple exercises on dry land using the compass.

2. Surface swimming to a buoy. Counting fin strokes or using the watch to judge distance.

MASK CLEARING

1. In shallow water with full equipment, remove and clear the mask.

2. In progressively deeper water, repeat the mask clearing exercise.

ASSISTED ASCENTS

1. Practising the correct position and sequence in shallow water.

2. Sharing in a static position in shallow water.

CONTROLLED BUOYANT RESCUE

1. In 10 m, using an A- frame (to simulate a diver), control the venting and inflation of the lifejacket/drysuit.

2. Using a shotline, the instructor controls the ascent of the rescue.

Figure 158

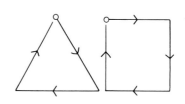

3. Taking a reciprocal bearing back to the starting point.

4. Simple underwater navigation to a buoy and return.

5. More complex use of the compass: squares, rectangles and triangles.

3. Clearing the mask while continuing to fin.

4. Clearing the mask without the regulator in place.

5. Finning underwater without a mask.

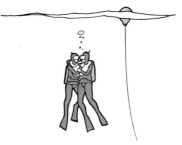

3. Sharing on the move in a horizontal position.

4. Sharing vertically from 10 metres, acting as distressed diver then as the assisting diver.

5. Using an octopus rig.

3. Maintaining positive buoyancy and administering expired-air resuscitation.

4. Towing a distressed diver using the extended-arm method.

5. Landing a distressed diver followed by the actions for aftercare.

Natural Underwater Navigation

Finding your way underwater with any reasonable degree of success is dependent on observation of a number of natural conditions. Reduced light or poor visibility will influence a diver's sense of direction. But by far the greatest influence is the diver's inability to orientate himself in the three-dimensional environment. With no points for reference, poor visibility and the lack of gravitational forces, the diver may even be unable to determine up from down.

The diver is largely dependent on his sense of vision underwater; lighter water above indicates the position of the surface, but remove this and he can soon become lost. The diver may even dive deeper, thinking he is surfacing. Loss of horizontal direction can result in the diver finning around in circles. This problem is not confined to dark or murky water since it can be experienced in very clear, deep water. In midwater, where the bottom and surface are out of sight, the diver may feel that he is surrounded by a sphere of blue water. This is caused by light reflected from the bottom; there is no difference in light intensity to indicate the surface.

With experience, the diver can overcome some of these midwater problems. In clear water the direction of movement of the exhaust bubbles will indicate the surface. Another sure indicator of vertical direction is the depth gauge, even a slight movement of the needle will indicate direction. However, in very poor visibility it may not be possible to use these visual indicators.

Before diving you should fix a reference point in your mind; if the bottom is out of sight, then use a fixed reference point such as the shotline or anchor rope by noting its direction and position. Try to arrive on the bottom with a good sense of position and direction firmly established in your mind.

Figure 159a

Figure 159b

Figure 159c

Figure 159d

Figure 159a Sand ripples generally run parallel to the shore

Figure 159b When neither the surface nor the bottom are visible the divers are 'in the blue'

Figure 159c Note any identifiable landmarks underwater

Figure 159d Navigation is made more difficult by low visibility caused by suspended matter or stirred up bottom sediment

A Simple Square

The diver swims for ten fin strokes from a known position, then turns right at an angle of 90 degrees, fins for a further ten fin strokes, turns right again, swims ten fin strokes, finally makes another right turn and, in ten more fin strokes, he should arrive back at his starting point.

Figure 160

Using Natural Features

Once on the bottom, take a few moments to look around and try to pick out natural features such as rocks or coral. These can be used as fixed reference points. Having chosen a suitable mark, fin towards it, looking behind occasionally to check your point of departure and to ensure that you will be able to recognize it on your return. On arrival at the first reference point choose another one and so on. Remember to note any turns made, and at each turn reorientate yourself with the starting point.

It is important to check your depth. The seabed generally slopes upwards towards the shore, but not always. The natural contours between the rock and sand interface, gullies, ridges and drop-offs are also good underwater guides to direction.

Picking out natural features on flat, sandy or muddy bottoms can be much more difficult. Sand ripples caused by wave action are usually constant in direction and generally run parallel to the shoreline, with the lip of the ripple pointing towards the shore.

Sunlight filtering through shallow water and shadows cast by rocks can indicate the angle of the sun's rays, but neither are totally reliable.

The movement of water, whether by waves, tides or swell, will assist you provided that you know your initial direction. Kelp and loose particles will bend or flow in the direction of the tidal stream; if the direction of this is known, it can give the diver a rough indication of direction of travel, but check whether the tidal stream or current will turn during the dive.

Leaving a trail stirred up by finning close to the bottom on the outward journey may assist the return. This system can only be used in fairly still water, otherwise the trail will quickly be dispersed.

Two factors often overlooked in underwater navigation are time and depth. By using a watch, a diver can time himself from feature to feature, or note the time spent following a ridge or reef, etc. The depth gauge can be used to check the depth at which the dive started and at various other notable positions. This information can assist the diver in making his return trip.

Successful navigation underwater is a matter of experience and practice. A few simple exercises will improve a diver's ability to judge distance and direction.

Figure 161 While swimming along the bottom, try to memorize notable features which can be followed on the return trip. Keep your buddy close by your side

Compass Navigation

Effective underwater navigation using a magnetic compass is an important skill which all divers can master with a little practice. Used correctly, the compass can greatly increase underwater safety.

A diver typically uses his compass to navigate to objects whose bearing he has already taken and set on his compass before diving. He observes an object on the surface, sets the compass, descends and fins towards the object. The object might be an area of interest or the boat at the end of a dive.

Using the Compass

To sight the compass correctly, point the lubber line at the object you wish to reach. The lubber line is normally shown as an arrow in the centre of the compass body and indicates the proposed direction of travel. This is the line that the diver must maintain if he is to stay on the correct heading. He must remember to keep his body in line with the compass lubber line and try to imagine that his body is an extension of that line. If the diver is at an angle to the lubber line, he will end up well off target although the compass heading is correct.

To maintain the correct attitude in relation to body and lubber line, the diver has several methods available to him. With a wrist-mounted compass, place the hand of the arm on which you are wearing your compass on the elbow of your other arm, then hold the compass at eye level, keeping it horizontal. A second method is to mount the compass on a diving console or on a flat slate, where the lubber line can be extended for greater accuracy. An even better solution is to wear the compass on a lanyard and hold it in front with both hands, again remembering to sight over the compass and avoid looking down on it.

The compass scale represents 360 degrees of a circle. The scale is often marked every 5 degrees and numbered every 30 degrees. Compass types are described in terms of the relationship between the scale and the bezel. On type I the scale is mounted on the bezel and runs clockwise (the numbers increase in a clockwise direction). Type II, where the scale is located in the compass body and does not rotate, has the scale running counter-clockwise (the numbers increase in an anticlockwise direction).

To set the first type of compass, sight the destination or target along the lubber line and then rotate the bezel until the arrow point is aligned with the north arrow on the floating compass card, then swim the desired course keeping the 'north' arrow point of the compass card aligned with the arrow point on the bezel. To set the second type of compass, rotate the bezel until the north-seeking needle is bracketed between the two parallel lines. This angle between the magnetic needle and the lubber line must be maintained if the diver is to stay on course.

Figure 162a
Diving compass type I
Markings are on a movable bezel

Figure 162b   Type II
Markings are on the compass body

A Square Pattern
The sides must be equal in distance or time.

A Triangular Pattern
Make sure you turn through 120 degrees and not 60 degrees.

Performance with a compass can be improved by practising on dry land.

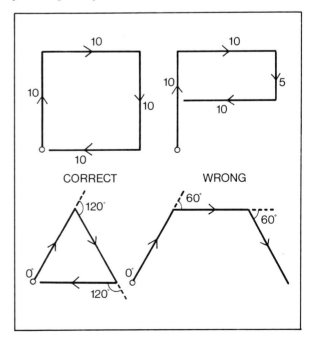

Figure 163

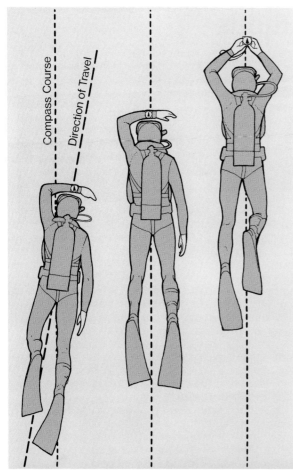

Reciprocal Bearings

A reciprocal bearing is the exact opposite to the direction you are heading (it usually indicates the heading to return to your point of departure), thus the angular difference is 180 degrees. On the first type of compass this is simply where the back end of the lubber line intersects the scale. The second type of compass usually has a notch mark 180 degrees from the two parallel lines; the bezel is rotated 180 degrees to set up the reciprocal for the return leg of the dive. To avoid confusion it is good practice to write down your initial heading and reciprocal bearings on a diver's slate.

Compasses are attracted to ferrous metals (iron, steel). Thus the presence of steel cylinders, watches and dive knives will tend to affect the magnetic needle; some depth gauges, electronic instruments and photographic exposure meters, flashguns and outboard motors will affect it as well. It is best to keep clear of any ferrous items when taking a reading.

The compass will only provide a diver with direction. What is still required is a measure of the distance travelled along a given line. For this, the diver needs a means of judging distance. For example, if a diver takes a bearing on a boat moored in the bay, he may fin right under the boat and surface well past it, because he is unable to judge the distance. With practice a diver should be able to calculate how long it will take him to fin a given distance. One technique is to fin a known distance, counting the number of fin strokes, or to use a diving watch. This will be accurate so long as the diver's speed through the water is fairly constant and is not affected by changing water conditions.

Figure 164 The divers' direction of travel must be in line with the compass course, easiest if compass is hand-held

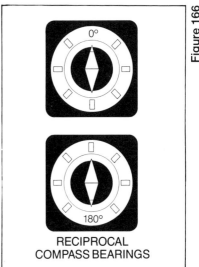

RECIPROCAL
COMPASS BEARINGS

Figure 166

Figure 165 For best results hold the compass in the hand in line with direction of travel

Underwater Search Methods

Underwater Searching

Divers are sometimes called upon to carry out underwater searches and recovery operations by other waters users, such as fishermen who have lost their lobsterpots or boat owners whose outboard motors have fallen off.

Underwater searches are not difficult, requiring little more than average diving ability, good planning, common sense, and, above all, patience and perseverance. Seldom is an underwater search satisfactorily concluded in a short time. If the area of search is large and the object sought is small, a thorough search can take many hours of diving. For an underwater search to be effective, the area to be searched must be narrowed down, and the search technique must be the one most likely to succeed under the circumstances. The divers must know exactly what they are searching for. The areas searched and still to be searched must be distinguished and therefore it is vital that everything is plotted on a chart. The limits of each search-sweep must be fixed by position-fixing methods (see p. 145) and the whole operation carefully planned, conducted and controlled.

The Area to be Searched

All too often a person approaches divers requesting them to look for his lost outboard engine and claims to know exactly where it is lying. All too often the claim is wrong. Only if accurate marks were taken at the moment of loss can such a position be expected to prove correct. At best, such claimed positions are a good starting point.

Among the factors to be considered when narrowing down the search area are:

1. The nature of the object lost. Is it heavy enough to sink immediately and not be moved by the tide or current? Is it something which would drift along with the tide before settling on the seabed? Is it big or small?
2. Which way was the tide/current running at the moment of loss? The loser may not know, but if he can tell you the approximate time of loss, you can check charts and tide tables to see which way it is likely to have drifted.
3. The most likely position of the object. This will be based on the statement of the position given to you, but subject to 1 and 2 above.

Swimline Search

A light baseline, weighted at intervals, is run out at speed from a fast boat following a distinct bearing which can be plotted on a chart. This baseline can be up to thousands of metres in length and is weighted and buoyed at each end. Thus, by horizontal sextant angles the exact position of the line can be plotted on a chart. The baseline is laid out at speed to keep it straight and tight. If desired, a series of parallel baselines can be laid out when a large area is to be searched.

A group of divers, up to twenty if they are versed in the skills of this search method, all wearing similar-sized aqualungs (this is important), descend to the baseline, taking with them a swimline whose length will depend on the number of divers and the underwater visibility. The

divers pay out the swimline at right angles to the baseline on each side of it so that there are an equal number of divers on each side of the swimline controller, who is in the middle, over the baseline. The distance between each diver is such that there is an overlap with adjacent divers' range of visibility.

All divers hold the swimline in both hands. Once the swimline is deployed at right angles to the baseline the controller gives a 'two bells' signal with both hands to start the swim. Each diver repeats the signal to acknowledge it and to pass it on to the next diver. So the swimline (let us say it is 50 metres long with ten divers at 5-metre intervals) proceeds forward, the controller holding station over the baseline. Each diver scans the seabed and if one spots anything which is of interest – scattered wreckage, for instance – he stops the line by giving a 'one bell' signal with both hands, which is the stop signal. Again all divers receive, acknowledge and pass on the stop signal. The sighting is investigated and marked. When ready to go on again, the go signal is given and the swimline proceeds.

When the divers run low on air an agreed signal is given to instruct the divers to close to the baseline and ascend. The controller marks with his surface-marker buoy the point on the baseline which the group has reached. The next party of divers will commence their swimline search from this point or, ideally, from a point a few metres farther back, to give an overlap.

Once the whole distance of the baseline has been covered, the procedure is repeated on the next parallel baseline. The distance between baselines should allow an overlap on the sides of the areas searched. Failure to overlap means that some areas will not be searched – a search *must* be 100 per cent.

There are variations on the swimline search method described here. For example, the controller could be on the end of a swimline while the diver at the other end lays another baseline. On reaching the end of the first baseline, the whole group wheels round and goes back on the newly laid baseline, with the diver who laid it now acting as controller. Other variations use the principle on a smaller scale – for searching up and down reef faces or sweeping along rivers or canals.

A Grid Search

Divers are deployed along a swimline, which is wound onto a reel and secured inside the boat. The search area will have been marked out previously by jackstays suitably weighted and buoyed.

A Grid Search System

The swimline search may be exploited in several ways: touch, dragline, snagline or vision. The important point is to adjust the distance between the divers to suit the prevailing visibility.

The grid search is a very effective way of searching large areas, but requires quite a lot of rope, line, etc., several divers and plenty of practice. The method can be

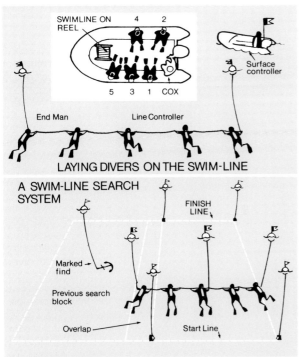

LAYING DIVERS ON THE SWIM-LINE

A SWIM-LINE SEARCH SYSTEM

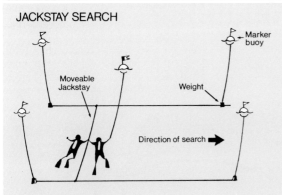

JACKSTAY SEARCH

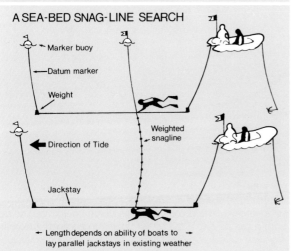

A SEA-BED SNAG-LINE SEARCH

used when searching for relatively small items in a large area.

Jackstay Search

To some extent the grid search has superseded the jackstay search in open water, since the latter requires many more ropes laid on the seabed. For a detailed search of a small area, however, the jackstay search has much to commend it.

The area to be searched is marked off by placing a shotline in each corner and linking the corners with a perimeter of ground ropes. (A shotline is a weighted rope adequately buoyed at the surface and used as a datum line for ascent and descent, as a datum or centre for a search or as a means of controlling ascent during decompression. The weight on the bottom should not be less than 15 kg and the float should have a buoyancy of not less than 50 kg.)

The searching divers can swim along a jackstay – a single rope which is laid between opposite ends of the square/rectangle area to be searched and which can be moved along after each search sweep – or they can follow a compass heading from end to end. On reaching the perimeter rope they move across by a distance which is governed by the underwater visibility, turn round and then swim back.

If a jackstay search is carried out on a flat seabed to look for a large object, a snagline search may also be successful.

Permanent grids are sometimes set up on sites where major investigation and excavations are taking place. Archaeological wreck sites are a good example. As finds are uncovered, their position can quickly be fixed and related to previous finds. The grid does not have to be on the seabed; often it is easier to have it above the seabed, but in visible range of it. Light chain can be used as a jackstay line when searching on undulating seabed.

When searching a rocky seabed or in heavy weed, a jackstay search is more effective. Divers must proceed carefully and methodically to ensure that nothing is missed.

Searches for very small items are obviously the most difficult. Jackstay (or circular searches on a flat seabed) are the best.

An Open-Water Jackstay Search

This is for the meticulous search of a specific area which might have many obstructions. The divers swim in the same direction along the movable jackstay, moving each end to a position twice the visibility distance from the previous one at the end of each run.

A Seabed Snagline Search

This is an effective method where the seabed is flat and clear of obstructions. The two boats lay both jackstays simultaneously and haul them taut after anchoring.

Figure 167

Circular Searches

Circular Searches are the simplest and most widely used of all search patterns. They are generally used for searching large areas of water which have poor visibility and no tidal streams.

All that is needed is a shotline placed in the centre of the area to be searched. A distance line is snap-hooked onto the shotline just above the sinker weight and the divers swim in a circle, keeping the distance line tight. They use a conspicuous object to mark the start of each circular sweep and, on returning to it, move in/out by a distance governed by visibility (allowing some overlap), replace their marker and go around again. It does not take long to search the area of the entire circle and it does not really matter whether they radiate outwards from the shotline or inwards from the end of the distance line.

The number of sweeps necessary will depend upon the visibility and the size of the target object. If a diver lets out 2 metres on the distance line following the completion of each sweep, he will effectively cover the search area even in poor visibility.

An alternative to the use of a marker to indicate the completion of a sweep is to use a reference line from the shotline to the outside circumference of the circle.

Rope drag prevents effective circular searches if the distance or sweepline is longer than about 30 metres (this is true of almost all search patterns). The sweepline can also be used as a snagline. Semicircular sweep searches, made in exactly the same way, can be used when searching off a wall or river/canal bank.

The centre of each circular sweep should be plotted and care taken when covering an area with several circular sweeps to allow sufficient overlap. Remember, compared with squares, circles do not overlap very well!

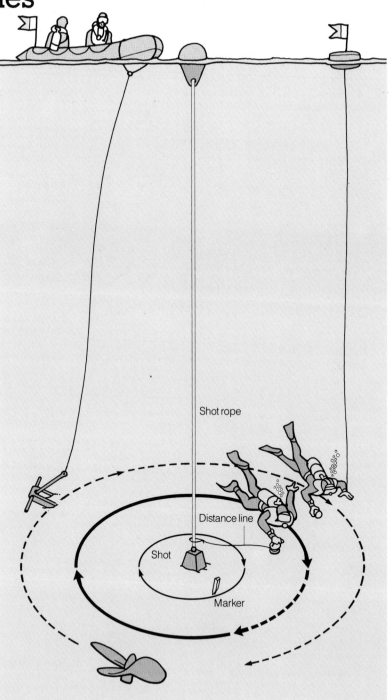

Figure 168   Circular search
This is the simplest method of seabed search where the approximate position of the object is known. The diver keeps his distance line taut as he swims around the shot rope, paying it out to twice arm's reach after every circuit.

Compass Searches

A watch and compass can be used to swim square courses. Square courses of this sort can be extended or altered into a 'square spiral' or overlapping squares, thereby covering a large area of seabed.

The proposed compass course, distances and directions should be preplotted, and the start of each search pattern buoyed so that it can be fixed by sextant angles or compass bearings and plotted on the survey chart.

Figure 169 Practising a circular search

Figure 170

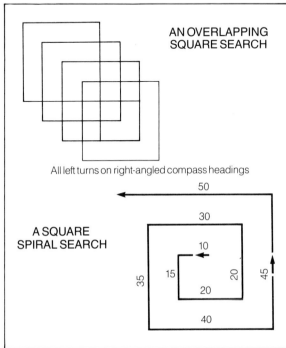

AN OVERLAPPING SQUARE SEARCH

All left turns on right-angled compass headings

A SQUARE SPIRAL SEARCH

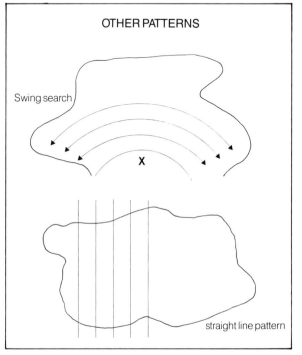

OTHER PATTERNS

Swing search

straight line pattern

Simple Underwater Work

Underwater work requires good organization and teamwork and offers a challenge to divers who are no longer interested in diving for diving's sake. It ranges from simple collecting tasks to involvement in large-scale lifting or salvage projects.

Measuring Underwater Visibility

An interesting and useful task for the newly qualified diver is an exercise to determine the underwater visibility, by first estimating distance and then measuring it, in order to compare both readings. Items needed for this task are a tape measure, a torch, and a slate and pencil for each diver.

The best type of measuring tape is a plastic surveyor's tape on a spool. If this is not possible Figure 171a shows a partly homemade alternative which works well. You will need a length of cloth surveying tape up to 100 metres in length graduated in centimetres and metres or a fine rope marked at metre intervals with a knot, coloured tape or waterproof ink. The torch is used for signalling, while the slate is needed to record distances.

The task is best conducted over a range of depths, so the ideal site is a sloping rockface where the depth increases quite rapidly. Our measurements are to be taken at 5-metre depth intervals, so we need to fix a maximum depth and descend to this depth. There are two distinct advantages to working from deep to shallow water. First, the divers know what their maximum depth is and the timing of the dive can be controlled without running out of dive time. Secondly, if you start shallow and work deeper, the sediment stirred up has a tendency to roll down the slope and the visibility on the deeper sites becomes obscured.

You may wish to employ a movable, vertical shotline as a datum point. In this case you will need to build into your plan the routine to move your shotline. As you will be operating in water of differing depths you will need a 'compensating' shotline system. This uses a smaller weight on the surface end of the line, which is then looped and suspended through the surface buoy. As the depth decreases the line is automatically drawn taut.

Diver A is stationed at the shotline with his slate. Diver B takes the end of the tape and swims across the slope with the other slate. Diver A unreels the tape until both divers can just see each other, when a predetermined torch signal marks the point at which readings should be taken. Diver A writes down the actual distance, while Diver B writes his estimate of the distance. Then they ascend to the next depth position, where the whole process is repeated. If time permits the process can be repeated with the divers' roles reversed.

Figure 171a

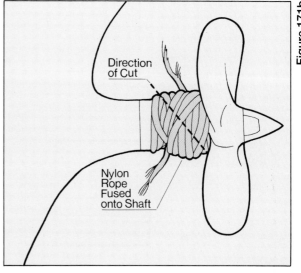

Figure 171b

Figure 171a Measuring tape is best stored on a simple reel

Figure 171b To remove line which is fouling a propshaft, make a diagonal cut

Direction of Cut

Nylon Rope Fused onto Shaft

Recovery

Fishermen sometimes lose lobsterpots or other equipment and to co-operate with them can improve fishermen–diver relationships. Two divers will be needed. The pot marker buoy and line will be the ideal shotline. The rope itself may have become entangled around an obstruction and be very easy to untangle. One diver should do the untangling while the other keeps careful watch in case the untangler becomes trapped. If the lobsterpots themselves are jammed, either in wreckage or in rocks, work your way along the bottom line and when you have released as many as possible give the signal for them to be hauled to the surface.

Fish netting on a wreck is a hazard, especially in low visibility, and a useful task is to form a net-removal detail if the site is a popular one with divers. It is essential that pairs of divers work in close proximity and use suitable cutting devices. The average diving knife is very ineffective against netting and some form of shears or a sharp dinghy knife without a pointed tip is required. Netting is most easily cut if it is under tension and a good technique is to employ small lifting bags to lift the upper parts of the net and keep it taut. Each pair of divers can then systematically work their way along, cutting free as much net as possible. As the last pieces are cut away, the lifting bags ensure that it is removed from the wreck.

Fishermen may ask amateur divers to clear an obstruction from their propeller. If you do this for reward or money you are effectively working as a professional diver and are subject to strict Health and Safety Executive regulations. If you decide to help on the basis of genuine expenses, you need to be prepared for what might be in store. If something is stuck around the propeller shaft, it

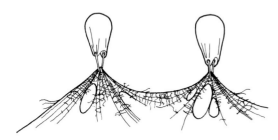

Figure 173   Tension netting with lifting bags

could be a discarded polythene bag or more likely a length of nylon rope. If the latter, it is likely to have been there some time and the heat of friction will have fused it into a solid block around the shaft. In this situation the sawing edge of your diving kife is most effective. Failing this a junior hacksaw or a loose hacksaw blade with tape wrapped round it to form a handle is an effective tool. Figure 171b shows a fouled propeller shaft and also the suggested cutting line. Once you have cut through the mass of rope it can be peeled off in one piece. Ensure you attempt this type of work only in calm water, otherwise you will have the full mass of the boat hitting you on the head on every wave. If necessary, ask the skipper to motor to a sheltered location before you attempt the task.

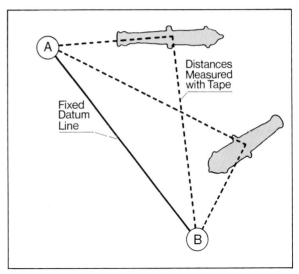

Figure 172   Fixing position by triangulation

Simple Triangulation

Simple surveying and measuring underwater is within the capability of most amateur divers. If you have decided to lift an object from the seabed, it is likely you will want to measure it in order to calculate its weight. Using an underwater slate and a suitable tape measure, work in pairs systematically around the object with the diver who is not recording being responsible for the loose or 'zero' end of the tape. Make a reconnaissance dive to get a good idea of the shape of the object, then prepare a diagram so that only the dimensions need be added.

If a survey of a site is to be undertaken, pre-planning is essential and you may wish to undertake a simple triangulation. In order to do this you need to fix at least one datum line. Figure 172 shows the geometrical basis of a triangulation survey which works on the principle that the position of any object may be fixed by measuring the distance to it from either end of the datum line. A survey of this type is best conducted on a relatively flat site with a lack of weed growth. The length of the datum line will depend on prevailing visibility conditions and you may decide to subdivide your datum line in order to operate in a range of visibility conditions. It is essential you have a pre-prepared recording slate for each measurement so you have only to insert figures as you measure. Once ashore, a scaled-down plan of the site can be made, using the measurements you have taken on the dive.

You may wish to extend your survey by laying down a metre quadrant grid on the bottom, if the site has many small objects. Fine line of negative buoyancy is ideal and should be carried on suitable reels or frames. You may decide to carry a rigid metre square and move it along a fixed datum line as an easier method of conducting a detailed survey. This must be of negative buoyancy for effective use. In all underwater work remember the five Ps principle:

Proper planning prevents poor performance

Lifting

The use of compressed air for lifting heavy objects was pioneered by Cox and Danks in Scapa Flow during the 1920s. Vessels as large as 26,000-ton battleships were raised using the natural buoyancy of the upturned ships after the holes had been plugged and they had been filled with air. Prior to this nearly all ocean salvage had relied on mechanical methods.

The principle of lifting by air is very simple. One litre of water has a mass of 1 kg, so if you displace 1 litre of water with air you will have gained 1 kg of positive buoyancy. An object weighing 50 kg will thus require 50 litres of air at ambient pressure to lift it. Boyle's Law controls how much free air you will need at the operating depth. A 60-kg object will require 60 litres of free air at the surface (1 bar), but will require 240 litres of free air at 30 metres (4 bars). A lifting bag completely full of air and capable of lifting a 60-kg object would lose 180 litres of surplus air by the time it had reached the surface from 30 metres (240 litres − 60 litres = 180 litres). For this reason a lifting bag requires an open bottom to allow air to escape or must be fitted with a pressure relief valve capable of discharging the surplus air.

Figure 174 shows a typical lifting bag. Lifting capacities vary from a few kilogrammes for a diver's personal lifting bag, which may be carried on every dive, to several thousand kilogrammes for commercial salvage operations. The shape of the bag is important since it is necessary to reduce the risk of air spillage to a minimum and to lift the object as close as possible to the surface. In many lifting operations the ascent is very rapid and sudden deceleration as the surface is reached often leads to swinging and collapse if the wrong-shaped lifting bag is used. On the larger bags it is important to have a deflation valve, but this is not essential for small bags, which can be physically toppled in order to vent the air. A valve, however, is the only way of achieving a controlled deflation.

Whereas smaller objects can be raised by fastening a lifting bag directly to the object, many larger objects require the use of wire strops to be positioned in order to achieve a balanced lift. Lifting bags are fastened to the strops by means of shackles; several lifting bags may be used.

Having roughly calculated the weight of the object to be raised, it is better to use several smaller lifting bags rather than one big one. Using several bags allows a greater degree of control and it may be vital to have a controlled ascent on the final lift.

Let us assume the object will require 1000 kg (1000 litres of air) in order to lift it. You have the choice between four lifting bags capable of 250 kg each or a single large one capable of 1000 kg. When you actually lift the object you may find that it becomes neutrally buoyant with 800 kg of lift. With the large lifting bag there is a danger that you will not be able to control the ascent once it starts to move. The air inside will rapidly expand to fill the spare 200 kg capacity and, unless you have a good valve and a good

technique for adjustment, an uncontrolled lift may occur. With the four smaller bags you will be able fully to inflate three of them to capacity without the object moving. The fourth bag will be your adjustment bag, allowing you to feed enough air into it to control the initial neutral buoyancy and with a valve finely to control the ascent.

Figure 175 shows an acceptable configuration for using four small bags for the example quoted above. It is important for the adjustment bag to be located on the fulcrum of the lift so that an imbalance is not created. It may be that you will have to lower the object to the bottom in

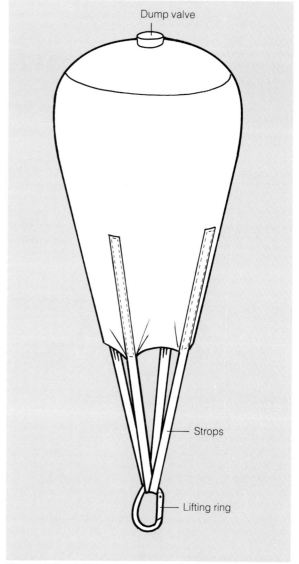

Figure 174 A lifting bag is open at the bottom to allow easy inflation and has a dump valve at the top for deflation and control of ascent

order to reposition one or more of the bags before attempting the full lift.

Successful lifting projects will give divers experience in underwater searching, buoy laying, boat handling and compressor operation as well as the skills involved in filling lifting bags and controlling their ascent.

One word about the nature of the object you wish to recover. Ensure that it is legal to do so and that, once raised, it is not going to be left to rust on some beach.

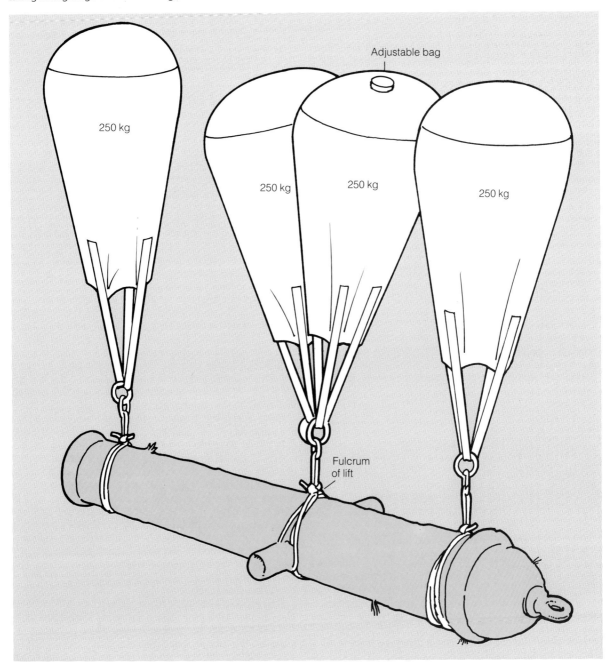

Figure 175

First Aid

Accidents Involving Divers

There are many different accidents which may befall a diver. Some of them are unique to the diving environment but many are just as likely to occur elsewhere. This section deals with general first aid for those accidents which are not strictly diving accidents, although they may well occur in diving-related activities. Those accidents specifically related to diving, e.g. decompression sickness, burst lung, are fully dealt with elsewhere in this manual.

It is not possible to cover more than just the basic elements of first aid. For a comprehensive coverage of the subject the reader is referred to the joint *First Aid Manual* of the St John Ambulance, the St Andrew's Ambulance Association and the British Red Cross Society (Dorling Kindersley, 1982).

Objectives of First Aid

There are three basic objectives of first aid:
1. To preserve life.
2. To prevent the condition worsening.
3. To promote recovery.

The task of the first-aider is to do the minimum necessary, with whatever facilities are at hand, to achieve the above objectives until such time as the casualty can be delivered into the care of more qualified medical aid. The temptation to do more than the necessary minimum must be resisted, as must any well-intentioned, unqualified intervention. This may make any subsequent medical treatment more difficult.

The Priorities of First Aid

In the event of an accident, the first action of a first-aider must be to make an assessment of the situation and decide upon a reasoned course of action. For a minor cut this assessment will be simple and straightforward, but for a major accident the following list of priorities should be followed:

> **safety**
> **basic life support**
> **major bleeding**
> **shock**
> **other conditions**
> **medical treatment**

Safety
Where the casualty is in a dangerous situation, immediate steps must be taken either to eliminate the danger or to remove the casualty from the danger. This may be necessary as much for the safety of the first-aider as for the casualty. This procedure must be carried out as expeditiously as possible in order that first-aid treatment may begin at the earliest opportunity. In certain circumstances it will be necessary, because of life-threatening conditions, to begin first aid before the casualty is fully removed from danger; for example, resuscitation can be given to a non-breathing diver as

soon as he is recovered to the surface; it need not wait until the diver is completely removed from the water.
Basic Life Support
Basic life support is the maintenance of the casualty's respiration and circulation, which are both functions essential to keeping the casualty alive. The treatment of these conditions by expired-air resuscitation (EAR) and external chest compression (ECC) takes priority over *all* other conditions. Because these techniques are of such importance the resuscitation section of this manual is devoted entirely to them.
Major Bleeding
While not an immediate threat to life, if major bleeding remains unchecked, it will very quickly become one. When blood loss approaches one-third of the total blood volume of the body (about 2 litres in the average adult), the remaining blood becomes insufficient to maintain adequate circulation. Therefore, prompt action is required if the casualty's life is not to be put at risk. For this reason the treatment of major bleeding takes second place only to the requirement for basic life support.

The technique used to control major bleeding is to reduce the rate of blood loss so that clotting, which naturally occurs when blood comes into contact with the air, can take place to seal the wound. This is normally achieved by direct pressure on the wound, but in circumstances where this is not possible – e.g. an open fracture – indirect pressure is used.

The first essential is to expose the wound to obtain clear access to it. Pressure can then be applied directly onto the wound using the finger or palm. If the wound is large, apply pressure to either side to squeeze the wound closed. It will be necessary to sustain the pressure for up to fifteen minutes in order to allow clotting to occur. If possible, elevate the site of the injury above the level of the heart. A dressing of sufficient size to extend beyond the area of the wound should be applied and firmly bandaged in place. If this is unsuccessful in controlling the bleeding, apply a further dressing over the top of the first one, but do not remove the first dressing.

Only if direct pressure is unsuccessful in controlling the bleeding or if it is not possible to apply direct pressure should indirect pressure be used. This technique requires pressure to be applied to the artery supplying the wound area at a suitable point where the artery passes across a bone close to the surface of the skin (a pressure point). By compressing the artery against the bone the blood flow to the wound is restricted. Because of the drastic reduction of blood flow to the affected area this method should only be used as a last resort and should not be maintained for more than fifteen minutes.

There are two sites where pressure points can be used. The brachial artery runs along the inside of the upper arm and pressure can be applied to compress it against the bone of the upper arm. The femoral artery can be compressed in the groin where it passes across the pelvis and into the upper leg.

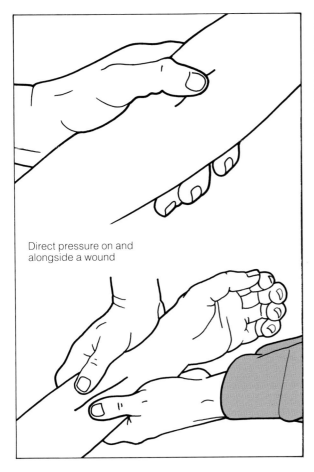

Direct pressure on and alongside a wound

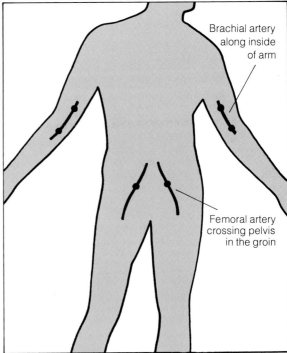

Brachial artery along inside of arm

Femoral artery crossing pelvis in the groin

Figure 176b The main pressure points of the body

Figure 176a Reduce blood loss by applying direct pressure on or immediately alongside the wound

If clean sterile dressings are not available, use whatever is to hand to dress the wound – improvise! Even if what is available is not particularly clean, an infection in the wound is of little consequence if a life is saved.

Shock

Shock is a condition brought about by the loss of body fluid and is present to a greater or lesser extent in all injuries. It can be an extremely serious condition and can even be fatal. The loss of body fluid may be caused by a variety of conditions such as blood loss due to severe bleeding or blistering due to burns. Severe emotional distress can induce a similar state.

The symptoms of shock will gradually become more severe as the casualty's condition deteriorates:

> The casualty feels weak and faint and is generally anxious.
> He feels thirsty.
> He becomes pale with cold clammy sweating.
> His breathing becomes shallow and rapid.
> He may yawn and gasp a lot.
> His pulse rate initially increases but later becomes weak and possibly irregular.
> He may become unconscious.

The treatment for shock consists of reassuring the casualty, making him as comfortable as possible and treating any injuries that may have been sustained. The casualty should be laid down, preferably with the head kept low, and covered to keep him warm – do not apply direct heat, e.g. a hot-water bottle, as this is counterproductive. Do not give the casualty anything to drink but monitor his condition closely and, if he lapses into unconsciousness, place him in the recovery position.

Other Conditions

There are many injuries that a person may sustain which do not directly threaten life; some may even be trivial. Some of these injuries, however, can be very traumatic and will require treatment, not just for the immediate comfort of the casualty but because if they are left untreated they may cause a deterioration of the casualty's condition to the point where life is threatened.

Broken Bones The skeleton exists to provide a basic framework to support the body and to protect the vital organs. Although it is very strong, if sufficient force is applied the bones can be fractured or cracked and the joints can be dislocated, usually resulting in a lot of pain. Because of the proximity of major blood vessels to certain bones, fractures may be complicated further by severe bleeding.

A broken or cracked bone may exhibit some, or all, of the following symptoms:

> Pain around the site of the injury.
> Tenderness to gentle pressure applied to the site of the injury.
> Normal movement of the affected part may be painful or impossible.
> Bruising or swelling of the affected area.
> Deformity or displacement of the affected area.
> Shock.

If an injury to the bone is suspected, the object of first aid is to immobilize and support the site of the injury. This should be done in whatever position the injury occurs and no attempt should be made to move the casualty until this is done unless some life-threatening circumstance dictates otherwise.

In order to immobilize the injury some form of splinting will be required, and some form of padding to support the injury. Splints can be improvised from a variety of items such as paddles, broomhandles or even uninjured parts of the casualty's body. Padding can be improvised from any fabric. Any bandages or bindings should be firm enough to prevent movement but should not be so tight that they cause pain or interfere with the circulation.

Burns and Scalds Burns and scalds not only cause direct damage to the casualty's skin but also reduce the skin's ability to fight infection. The action required of the first-aider is, therefore, to reduce the effects of the heat and also to guard against further infection of the affected area.

Minor burns and scalds are best dealt with by flooding the affected area with cold water. In order for the benefit to reach the underlying tissues, this should be maintained for about ten minutes. A clean sterile dressing should then be applied to protect the area. Lotions, creams or adhesive dressings should not be used. Blisters which form serve to protect the underlying damaged skin and should not be burst deliberately.

Major burns and scalds require a similar treatment, although flooding the affected area with cold water may be impractical. Because of the loss of body fluid to the blistering, shock is a major consideration when treating severe burns and scalds.

Due to the skin's resistance to infection being reduced by the injury, any dressings used must be clean.

Minor Cuts and Grazes Because the rate of blood loss through a minor cut or graze is low, clotting quickly occurs and prevents further blood loss. The wound should be washed gently and a dressing applied to keep it clean. An adhesive dressing is usually the most convenient to use, although the adhesive is usually ineffective in a wet environment if the skin cannot be dried completely before application.

Cramps Cramps are painful contractions of muscles which occur with little warning and are brought about by exercise, lack of salt or body fluids and chilling. The condition is treated by stretching the affected muscle and massaging it until the spasm relaxes and the pain is relieved.

Medical Treatment
At the earliest opportunity arrangements should be made for the casualty to be transported to qualified medical aid, usually by ambulance to hospital. Any handling of the casualty needed to lift them into the transport should be done as gently as possible in order to avoid any further pain or to aggravate his condition. If it is necessary to wait for the transport to arrive, ensure that the casualty is kept as comfortable as possible and is adequately covered to prevent him getting cold. Reassure the casualty throughout and closely monitor his condition for any deterioration or for the appearance of any condition which may take time to develop.

The Recovery Position
The recovery position is a stable position in which an unconscious casualty can be placed and which will ensure an adequate airway and also that any vomit can drain from the casualty's mouth. The positioning of the casualty's limbs ensures that he remains in a threequarters prone position, even with the motion of a small boat. Initial treatment of the casualty often requires that he is laid on his back and then, subsequently, rolled into the recovery position. It is important that while doing this the first-aider provides adequate protection for the casualty's head. Once in the recovery position, the casualty should continue to be monitored for any change in his condition.

Figure 177 The recovery position

First-Aid Kits

First-aid kits need to be designed for the conditions under which they are likely to be used. The larger the group to be catered for and the more remote the situation, the more comprehensive the first-aid kit that is required.

The most basic first-aid kit is one which is suitable for use in a small open boat and which must suffice to return the casualty to shore for more comprehensive assistance. Because of the environment, the kit should be housed in a suitable waterproof container and should contain two large sterile dressings, two triangular bandages, a rescue blanket or large (2 × 1 metre) polythene bag and several safety pins.

Where a larger number of people are involved, e.g. the shore base area for small-boat operations or on a large diving boat, a more suitable selection of items would be:

All of these should be contained in a sturdy, weatherproof container. The preference should be for dressings of the larger sizes since a large dressing can be used on a small wound but a small dressing is of little use on a large wound. Where possible, all the items should be in individual sealed packs so that unused items remain sterile.

The most comprehensive first-aid kit in the world is of no use if no one knows how to use it. This section has scratched only the very surface of the subject of first aid and readers seeking a more thorough knowledge would be well advised to attend a recognized course of instruction in first aid such as those run by the St John Ambulance, the St Andrew's Ambulance Association or the British Red Cross Society.

first-aid instructions
six each of small medium and large standard dressings
large pack of assorted adhesive dressings
three or four large triangular bandages
ten assorted safety pins
three 50-mm roller bandages

50-mm crepe bandage
roll of 25-mm-wide zinc oxide plaster
pair of scissors
pair of tweezers
pack of sterile cotton wool
rescue blanket or large polythene bag

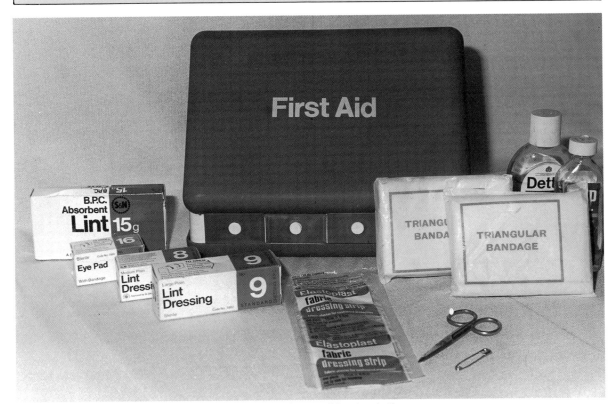

Figure 178   A first-aid kit suitable for carrying aboard a small boat or in the car

Expired-Air Resuscitation

Expired-air resuscitation (EAR) is a simple and efficient means of ventilating the lungs of a person who has stopped breathing. The technique can be performed by people with little training and in almost any circumstances. This latter characteristic makes it especially suited to the diving situation because it can be applied in the water.

Oxygen comprises approximately 21 per cent of the air inhaled into the lungs and approximately 16 per cent of the air exhaled, the balance of 5 per cent being used by the body. Exhaled air, therefore, contains more than sufficient oxygen to support life. By using the exhalations of a rescuer to inflate the lungs of a casualty who has stopped breathing, and the elastic recoil of the muscles of the casualty's chest to deflate the lungs, adequate ventilation can be produced.

Experience has shown that the success of EAR is directly dependent upon two fundamental principles:

> Commence EAR at the earliest opportunity – seconds count!
> Ensure that the casualty's airway is clear and remains so.
>
> Symptoms of Respiratory Arrest
> The casualty is not breathing and the chest is not moving.
> The casualty has a pale appearance with a slight bluish tinge, particularly around the lips and nail beds.

EAR on Land

On land the rescuer generally has the benefit of a stable base on which to work with unhindered access to the casualty. These conditions, however, are not crucial to successful EAR so long as the requirements of a clear airway and adequate seal can be met.

Clear Airway

Before commencing EAR, open the casualty's mouth wide and ensure that there are no foreign bodies or fluid in the mouth or throat. Loose-fitting dentures should be removed but well-fitted dentures can be left in place. Position the casualty's head as shown in the diagram – this prevents the tongue from obstructing the airway. Loosen any tight garments or equipment around the casualty's neck or chest.

Forming a Seal over the Casualty's Airway

The casualty's lungs can be inflated either via the casualty's mouth (mouth-to-mouth resuscitation) or via the nose (mouth-to-nose resuscitation) as shown in the diagrams opposite.

For mouth-to-mouth resuscitation the rescuer uses one hand to pinch the nostrils to seal off the nose and the other hand to grip the point of the jaw and exert a gentle pressure in the direction shown. This opens the mouth and ensures that the tongue clears the airway. The rescuer's mouth is then sealed around the casualty's mouth.

For mouth-to-nose resuscitation one hand is used to

steady the casualty's head in the correct position and the other hand applies pressure to the point of the chin to seal the mouth closed. The rescuer's mouth is then sealed around the casualty's nose.

In both techniques the precise configuration of the hands and fingers is unimportant. What is important is that the hands are kept clear of the windpipe and that the opening which is not being used to ventilate the casualty's lungs is properly sealed off.

If a very small child is the casualty, the rescuer's mouth should form a seal over both the child's mouth and nose.

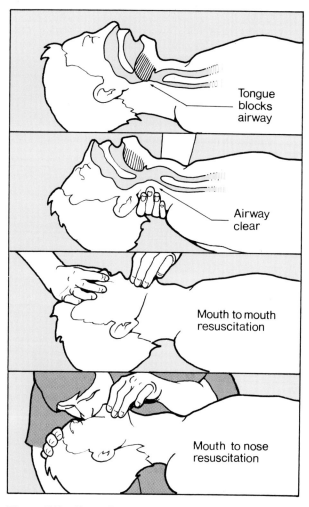

Tongue blocks airway

Airway clear

Mouth to mouth resuscitation

Mouth to nose resuscitation

Figure 179 Extending the casualty's neck is essential if the airway is to be kept clear. Be sure to seal the opening not being used

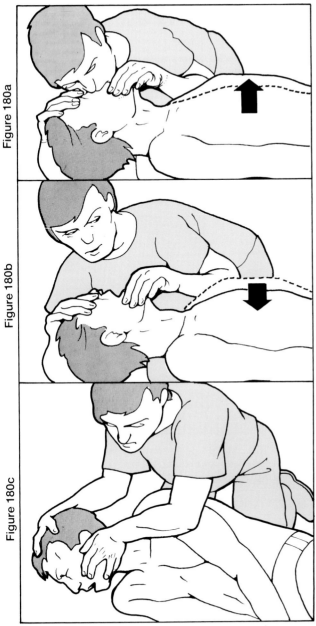

Figure 180a Check that the casualty's chest rises as an indication of effective ventilation

Figure 180b Move your mouth until you see the casualty's chest fall

Figure 180c Should the casualty vomit, turn him over and clear the mouth before recommencing EAR

Performing EAR on Land

Position the casualty's head correctly as described above. This will be most easily accomplished if the casualty is laid flat on his back with the shoulderblades slightly raised, but do not waste time repositioning the casualty if the requirements for a clear airway and a mouth or nose seal can be met – remember, seconds count!

Take a breath and seal your mouth over the casualty's mouth or nose as appropriate. Blow into the casualty's lungs, looking along the casualty's chest to check that it rises as an indication of effective inflation.

Remove your mouth from the casualty's mouth or nose, turning your head slightly to watch the casualty's chest fall and to listen to the sound of his exhalation.

Give two or three full lung inflations, then settle down to a rate of approximately twelve to sixteen breaths per minute. The precise rate of inflations is not critical, the important point being that the rescuer gives effective inflations. This can be judged by monitoring the rise and fall of the casualty's chest and the sound of his exhalations.

After a short period of effective EAR there should be a general improvement in the appearance of the casualty. Once the casualty recommences attempts to breathe, initially match the rate of EAR to assist the casualty until such time as he can continue to breathe unassisted. Once this has happened, continue to monitor the casualty as it is not unknown for breathing to stop again and EAR to be needed once more.

Should the casualty show no apparent signs of recovery, do not give up. Recovery has occurred after considerable periods of EAR. Should you be unfortunate enough to be presented with this situation, you should continue your efforts until either another qualified person takes over, a doctor assumes responsibility for the casualty, or until you are too exhausted to continue.

Action Should the Casualty Vomit

During treatment by the rescuer, experience has shown that up to half of all casualties will vomit. This action may not necessarily occur obviously, as it would with a conscious subject. It may only become apparent by the casualty's exhalations becoming noisy due to the pooling of vomit at the back of the throat. This condition must be dealt with quickly and effectively and it is for this reason that listening to the exhalations of the casualty is important. Continued EAR risks forcing vomit into the windpipe, from where it will be impossible for the rescuer to remove it, with the consequent prejudice to the effectiveness of the EAR.

Should any indications occur that the casualty has vomited, quickly turn him onto his side facing away from you, remembering to protect his head in the process.

Quickly remove all traces of vomit from the casualty's mouth and throat, if necessary using your fingers to do so. When clear, reposition the casualty on his back, visually check that the mouth and throat really are clear, reposition the head and continue the EAR. As this action will of necessity require an interruption to the EAR it should be performed as quickly as possible commensurate with ensuring a clear airway.

Expired-Air Resuscitation in the Water

In-water EAR follows exactly the same principles as apply on land but is complicated by the lack of a firm base for both rescuer and subject, the need to support the casualty at the surface, and the encumbrance of the equipment worn by both the casualty and the rescuer. The techniques used on land, therefore, require modifying to accommodate the changed conditions.

Since it is impossible to perform EAR underwater, the first essential of in-water EAR is to ensure that the casualty remains on the surface. The first priority, therefore, is to inflate the casualty's lifejacket followed by commencement of EAR.

Clear Airway

So that a proper neck extension can be achieved, the lifejacket should not be totally inflated but only to an extent that the stole behind the neck can be squeezed flat. Remove the casualty's mask and mouthpiece and remove your own mouthpiece. It will be of benefit to retain your own mask unless its size prevents you from making an effective seal over the casualty's nose.

By gripping the point of the casualty's chin with one hand and levering against the shoulder with the elbow, as shown in the diagram, the neck can be extended to the required position by the use of only one hand. Just as on land, it is essential that the leverage is against the point of the chin and not against the windpipe.

Forming a Seal over the Casualty's Airway

For in-water EAR there is only one practical method of forming a seal over the casualty's airway and that is the mouth-to-nose method. Extending the airway by the arm-lever method also seals the casualty's mouth, preparing him for mouth-to-nose EAR.

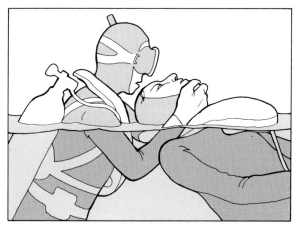

Figure 181   Hold the casualty's chin and place the forearm against his shoulder and use leverage to extend his airway

Performing EAR in the Water

Extend the casualty's neck as described above and place your free hand underneath the casualty's far shoulder. By pushing upwards with this hand the casualty will be made to roll towards you, bringing his nose close to your mouth without the need for you to raise yourself in the water by finning.

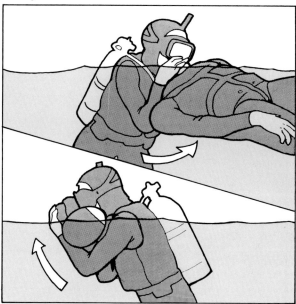

Figure 182   Make a good seal over the casualty's mouth for effective ventilation. This is made easier by rolling the casualty towards you

As the casualty rolls, allow the arm providing the neck extension to move with the casualty by folding the elbow across your chest. Take a breath in and as the casualty's nose approaches your mouth, seal your mouth over his nose and inflate his lungs. On completion of the inflation release the seal and allow the casualty to roll back to the normal floating position.

At the commencement of EAR, inflate the casualty's lungs fully two or three times and thereafter give EAR as frequently as is practical, bearing in mind the requirement not to tire yourself out. As a guide, you should aim for about ten inflations per minute, but remember that fewer effective inflations are worth far more than many ineffective ones.

Once commenced, it is EAR that keeps the casualty alive and all other considerations become subservient to maintaining it. Attracting attention, towing the casualty (if necessary) and removing him from the water must all be phased to minimize interference to the EAR. Only do that which is absolutely essential.

External Chest Compression

External chest compression (ECC) is a method by which a rescuer can induce blood circulation in a casualty who has suffered cardiac arrest. Such a misfortune may be due to a variety of circumstances either directly, such as a heart attack or electric shock, or indirectly as the knock-on effect of some other condition such as respiratory failure.

Symptoms of Cardiac Arrest

While all the symptoms of respiratory failure will also be present, the only reliable indication of cardiac arrest is the lack of a pulse. This can be checked most effectively by finding the carotid pulse alongside the windpipe, a couple of finger widths below the jawbone.

Check Carotid Artery for pulse

There are other points on the body where normally a pulse can be felt, but they can be difficult to locate, either because of their location (e.g. groin) or because of their susceptibility to external influences (e.g. wrist). The pulse should be sought for very carefully as the pulse of a drowning casualty may be very weak, and whereas ECC can be effective in restoring a hearbeat to a failed heart, it can also stop a healthy heart. For this reason ECC should *never* be practised on a live subject.

Performing ECC

Induced circulation is brought about by causing the casualty's heart to be compressed between his breastbone and his spine. This forces blood out of the heart and around the body. The relaxation of the pressure allows the heart to expand back to its resting state, drawing in more blood which is, in turn, expelled by the next compression.

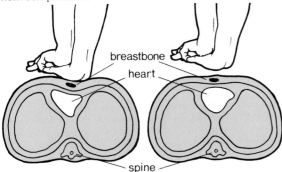

breastbone
heart
spine

Figure 184   Hand position for ECC

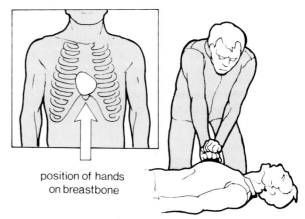

position of hands on breastbone

Figure 185   The position for ECC

To be effective the pressure must be applied to the casualty's chest in the correct position and with the casualty laid face up on a hard surface. You should kneel alongside the casualty and place the heel of one hand on the centre of the lower half of the breastbone, the other hand being placed on top and the fingers being clear of the ribs.

Keeping your arms straight, rock forward to apply weight, in a jerking motion, to the chest of the casualty and with sufficient force to displace the breastbone downwards by 4–5 centimetres for the average adult casualty. You should then release the pressure by rocking backwards. This motion should be repeated at a rate of approximately eighty times per minute. For child casualties the displacement of the breastbone should be proportionally less and for infants the application of finger pressure will be sufficient, although at a somewhat higher rate.

To combine this technique with EAR it is necessary that, after the initial two full inflations of the lungs, a sequence of fifteen cycles of ECC followed by two breaths of EAR be adopted. While EAR is given, the casualty's pulse should be rechecked to determine whether the heart has started beating of its own accord. When this happens cease ECC – do *not* try to assist the heart – and continue with EAR alone as long as remains necessary. Periodically recheck the pulse to monitor the heart.

While the techniques of simultaneous EAR and ECC can be applied by one rescuer, they are extremely tiring. Where possible the task should be shared by two rescuers synchronizing their efforts – one giving EAR and checking the pulse and one giving ECC. This allows a more natural integration of the rates of EAR and ECC than one rescuer alone can achieve. A sequence of one breath of EAR to five cycles of ECC should be adopted after the initial two quick breaths of EAR. To achieve the best synchronization, the inflation of the lung should be timed to coincide with the relaxation of the casualty's chest after the fifth compression.

Diver Rescue

The circumstances under which a diver may be required to perform a rescue vary markedly from one incident to the next. With all aspects of rescue, there are many ways in which a successful outcome can be achieved, depending upon the particular circumstances pertaining at the time. The following sections are not, therefore, intended to be taken as specific instructions, but to offer guidance which can be adapted to suit the particular circumstances.

Incident Prevention

In the diving environment, a train of seemingly minor occurrences can, if not countered, quickly lead to a major incident, with consequent risk to the divers involved. Prevention is better than cure, so before considering what actions are necessary to rescue divers involved in a major incident, let us first consider what can be done either to minimize the risk of an incident occurring or to anticipate the occurrence and prevent a minor incident from becoming a major one.

Training

Diving involves subjecting ourselves to an alien environment. To do this safely requires that the participants are fully trained in the necessary techniques and fully understand the limitations imposed upon them by this environment. Inadequate or incomplete training, therefore, increases the risks to which the divers are subjected. Many of the skills learned during initial training concern the actions to be taken in various emergencies. For many divers, these skills, once mastered in initial training, are not used again unless they are, at some time, involved in an emergency. The diver is then faced with needing to use a skill with which, through lack of practice, he has become unfamiliar and he may no longer be able to cope. The situation, therefore, becomes aggravated rather than alleviated. Regular practising of these skills will ensure that the diver will be able to perform them whenever circumstances require.

Fitness

By its very nature diving requires a reasonable standard of fitness. If this is not maintained the diver can quickly become exhausted and hence a potential risk to himself and his buddy. A physically fit diver may also become temporarily unfit due to the effects of illness, seasickness or the 'morning after' and should not dive until fully recovered.

Figure 186 EAR must be commenced at the very first possible moment immediately on surfacing

Equipment

Badly maintained equipment is a potential source of serious trouble. Underwater your life depends, quite literally, on the correct and reliable functioning of your equipment, so ensure that it is regularly maintained.

There is now a vast variety of types of equipment available. The pre-dive buddy check is, therefore, extremely important because your buddy's equipment may be quite different from your own, and 30 metres down, in an emergency situation, is not the place to try to figure out how your buddy's equipment works.

The Buddy System

The buddy system is a key element in diving safety, but it will only work if the divers are not only in sight of each other but also at such a distance that they can reach each other in time to be of assistance if an emergency occurs. This holds true not only while submerged but also when at the surface, both before and after the dive.

Dive Planning

Dive planning entails not only deciding where and when to dive but also ensuring that the experience of the divers is suitable for the conditions that they will encounter. It should also ensure that any diver whose experience is inadequate is partnered by someone suitably experienced to look after them.

For individual pairs of divers, dive planning means deciding what they are going to do underwater and then sticking to that plan so that there is no confusion.

Stress

Stress is an insidious factor which contributes to a large proportion of diving incidents. It can be physical (e.g. strong tidal streams) or psychological (e.g. poor visibility) and may range from a general uneasiness to blind panic. The symptoms of a build-up of stress may be manifested in a number of ways, but often the individual's ego forces him to try to disguise the symptoms since he does not want to appear to have chickened out. Careful monitoring of your buddy's behaviour both before and during the dive, particularly if he is inexperienced, may allow you to anticipate a problem and to take corrective action before an incident has a chance to develop.

Symptoms which might indicate that a diver is suffering from stress include the following:

> **nervousness**
> **rapid breathing**
> **erratic and unco-ordinated movements**
> **preoccupation with a trivial problem**
> **problems with buoyancy control**
> **no response to signals**
> **wide, staring eyes**
> **vigorous treading of water**

Figure 187   For best results, two rescuers are needed to resuscitate the casualty, alternating between EAR and ECC

The best way to deal with an incident is to prevent it from happening in the first place. Whereas it will never be possible completely to eliminate incidents, taking account of the above factors should enable us to minimize the likelihood of one occurring.

Approaching the Casualty

In the majority of circumstances in which a diver rescue takes place, both the casualty and rescuer will already be in the water and hence some form of swimming rescue will be required. Reaching rescues, throwing buoyant aids and using boats to reach the casualty are all possible alternatives if an incident occurs on the surface, but the buddy system is the only form of assistance which is available underwater.

A rescuer may be faced with a casualty who is either conscious or unconscious. Being passive, the unconscious casualty is the more straightforward one to deal with and the following sections describe just how to deal with such a casualty.

The conscious·casualty, particularly when in a panic, poses a more serious threat to the safety of the rescuer. The most important person in a rescue is the rescuer, and on no account should a rescuer approach a panicking casualty. The casualty should be monitored from a safe distance until either he calms down or he becomes sufficiently incapacitated to pose no further threat and the rescuer can safely be of assistance. Intervention at an earlier point is likely to result in two casualties needing rescue instead of one.

Even with a cooperative casualty, any assistance should be given from behind and in such a way that, should the casualty subsequently panic, the rescuer can quickly distance himself from the casualty's reach.

Recovering the Casualty to the Surface

Buoyant Lift

The recovery to the surface of a diver who has become incapacitated at depth is most easily accomplished by using the buoyancy that can be provided by the casualty's equipment. This requires the minimum of physical effort by the rescuer, who thus arrives at the surface more able to provide further assistance to the casualty. The precise technique will depend on the layout and operation of the casualty's equipment, but the broad principles will be common to all.

In order to maintain control of the ascent the rescuer needs to have access to all the relevant controls of both the casualty's and his own equipment. This will usually dictate that the rescuer is face to face with the casualty.

Buoyancy for the lift is provided by controlled inflation of either the casualty's adjustable-buoyancy lifejacket/buoyancy compensator or, if worn, the casualty's drysuit. The buoyancies of both the rescuer and the casualty are controlled during the ascent to keep the casualty more positively buoyant than the rescuer. This ensures that, should a separation occur during the ascent, the casualty would continue to the surface, albeit uncontrolled, and not sink.

The casualty is grasped in such a way that a positive contact is maintained throughout and so that the inflation and deflation controls can be operated with a minimum of hand movements.

For an adjustable-buoyancy lifejacket, one hand can grasp the front of the stole or a suitable piece of harness and the other hand can grasp the inflator. Lifejackets which have combined inflation/deflation facilities on the mouthpiece tube allow total control to be achieved with one hand, considerably simplifying the operation. Inflation can either be from a direct feed or from an emergency air cylinder. Being a lower-pressure supply, the direct feed is the more controllable of the two and can usually be operated with one hand. The air cylinder gives a much more rapid supply and often requires two hands to manipulate.

Drysuits which are used for sport diving normally have a direct feed for inflation. The direct-feed inflation valve can also double as a positive point of contact, leaving the free hand to control the venting of the suit. Venting of the suit is achieved either by manipulation of the suit exhaust valve or by raising the casualty's arm to vent air at the wrist seal. This latter technique is particularly useful if the rescuer is also wearing a drysuit which is vented via the wrist, since it allows one action to control the buoyancies of both the casualty and the rescuer.

Some drysuits and adjustable-buoyancy lifejackets are fitted with automatic exhaust valves which relieve the rescuer of some of the venting responsibility. These valves should not be totally relied upon to control the ascent because they control only the amount of air in the buoyancy device (lifejacket or drysuit) and do not control any change in buoyancy due to expansion of the suit material.

To perform a buoyant lift the rescuer establishes a positive contact with the casualty and starts to inflate the casualty's buoyancy device. As the casualty starts to rise, inflation is ceased and preparation made to vent air from the device. The rescuer monitors the rate of ascent, either by watching his depth gauge or by watching the bubbles out to one side of the casualty. When a normal rate of ascent is achieved, air is gently vented to control the rate of ascent. This is more easily done as a series of short 'blips' of air rather than by trying to achieve a slow, continuous bleed. Should too much air be vented and the ascent stop or even reverse, the buoyancy device is reinflated until the ascent is re-established.

As the surface is approached, the air in the buoyancy device expands more rapidly and more frequent venting of air will be required to maintain the constant rate of ascent. Slowing of the rate of ascent can also be helped if the rescuer spreads his legs and fins to create the maximum amount of drag.

Once the surface is reached the casualty's adjustable-buoyancy lifejacket is substantially inflated (although not totally – see resuscitation, p. 154) to ensure that he is safely secured there. It is important that this is done using the lifejacket and not the drysuit as, should expired-air resuscitation need to be given, the drysuit may deflate via the neck seal when the casualty's neck is extended.

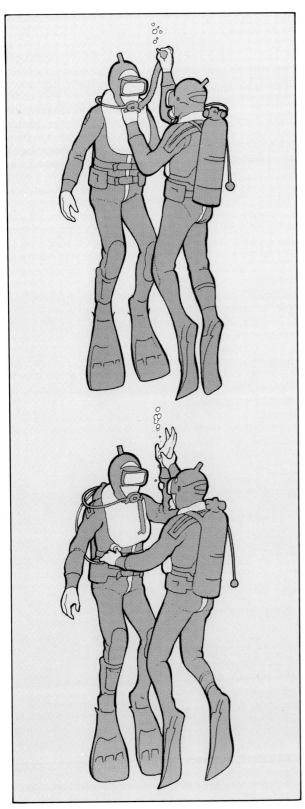

Alternative Methods of Lift

Should the casualty's buoyancy device provide insufficient buoyancy because of a malfunction or due to a depleted air supply, an alternative method of lifting the casualty must be found. There are three options open to the rescuer.

1. Achieve positive buoyancy for the casualty by ditching his weight belt. Depending on the amount of weight carried, this will have a greater or lesser effect, but, once ascending, the rescuer will be able to do little to control the rate of ascent.

2. Use the rescuer's buoyancy to lift the casualty. The rescuer will need to ensure that he does not become separated from the casualty during the ascent because the casualty will probably be lost from view by the time the rescuer has arrested his ensuing rapid, buoyant ascent. Greater security of the casualty might be achieved by the rescuer wrapping his legs around the casualty.

3. Swim the casualty to the surface. This will be very strenuous for the rescuer and, if performed from any depth, the rescuer may well be in need of assistance himself by the time the surface is reached.

The choice of method or combination of methods will depend on how negatively buoyant the casualty is, how much weight is available to be jettisoned and what the depth of water is.

Rescues, by their very nature, always have to be performed in a stressful situation. The easier the technique, both in terms of retaining control of the situation and in terms of physical effort, the more likely a successful outcome. The buoyant lift is an effective way of achieving this, but, as with any technique, requires regular practice if the maximum competence is to be maintained.

Figure 188   If the casualty is wearing a wetsuit, make positive contact and control ascent by inflating or venting the casualty's ABLJ *(top)*.
If the casualty is wearing a drysuit, then venting may be possible or necessary via a wrist seal or wrist-mounted valve. Otherwise locate and operate the dump valve. The other hand will be required for inflation via the suit inflator

Tow Techniques

Is a Tow Necessary?

Towing a casualty is a very strenuous exercise, particularly when it has to be combined with expired-air resuscitation. If there is a practical alternative to a tow, then the rescuer should stay put and summon the assistance to him. For example, a cover boat could motor to the incident far more easily than the rescuer could tow the casualty to the cover boat. When expired-air resuscitation is involved, this allows the rescuer to concentrate on the resuscitation and removes the compromises necessary to combine it with a tow.

Lifejackets

The inflation of the casualty's lifejacket relieves the rescuer of the necessity to support him. If the casualty has been raised from depth, this should be the first priority on reaching the surface in order to ensure that the casualty remains there.

If the casualty is conscious, a full inflation of the lifejacket, giving the maximum buoyancy, will be of most reassurance to him. For an unconscious casualty the lifejacket should not be fully inflated, but should retain sufficient 'give' to prevent the stole behind the neck from interfering with providing an adequate neck extension. This will be necessary to provide a clear airway not only if expired-air resuscitation is required, but also if the casualty is breathing but unconscious.

Drysuits, if worn, should not be used to provide surface buoyancy. The large amount of air introduced into the suit can, with certain types of neck seal, cause a constriction around the casualty's neck. This will, at best, predispose the casualty to panic and, at worst, can be sufficient to interfere with a conscious casualty's breathing. Where expired-air resuscitation is necessary, there is also a high risk that the necessary neck extension will cause some, if not all, of the air to escape via the neck seal, thus losing buoyancy.

The rescuer's lifejacket should, if possible, remain deflated. For rescues involving a long tow, the extra buoyancy provided can be more than offset by the extra drag of the inflated jacket. The added bulk is also an encumbrance to the handling of the casualty. This is particularly true where expired-air resuscitation is concerned. Should the rescuer feel in need of added buoyancy, inflation of the lifejacket should be the minimum necessary. Preferably this should be limited to inflation of the stole around the neck, but not sufficient to inflate the stole in front of the rescuer's chest, where it will cause most interference.

Ditching Equipment

If you are faced with a long tow, very serious consideration should be given to ditching heavy and bulky equipment. Rescue attempts have, in the past, resulted in rescuers becoming so fatigued due to not ditching their equipment that they themselves have needed rescuing. Equipment can be replaced but a person's life cannot.

Where the rescuer is wearing buoyant protective clothing, it may be of benefit for him to retain his weight belt. This will help to keep his legs low in the water and aid finning.

Technique

A conscious casualty should be towed from behind by the rescuer gripping a convenient item of the casualty's equipment such as a lifejacket strap. This will provide a positive contact with the casualty. Should the casualty suddenly panic, it can quickly be released to enable the rescuer to get clear of the casualty's grasp.

With an unconscious casualty, whether breathing or not, a tow will be required which will provide an adequate neck extension to ensure a clear airway. This can be provided by a tow which grips the casualty's chin. In a choppy sea this, on its own, will not give a positive hold and the rescuer's other hand, placed under the casualty's neck or shoulderblades, will provide the necessary security. If expired-air resuscitation is required, this method of tow will enable the procedure to be carried out with the minimum of hand movement.

To combine expired-air resuscitation with towing, some compromise has to be accepted. While static, expired-air resuscitation is performed as often as is practical, as a guide, a nominal ten breaths per minute. When towing this has to be reduced to avoid overtaxing the rescuer. A rhythm of two breaths of expired-air resuscitation every 15 seconds is recommended as a reasonable compromise. Remember, however, that it is the resuscitation which is keeping the casualty alive and this must take precedence

Figure 189a A conscious casualty can be towed by gripping a convenient part of his equipment

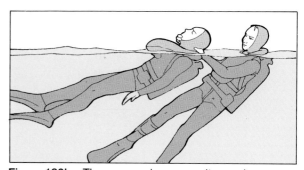

Figure 189b The unconscious casualty needs an adequate neck extension during the tow. This will require two hands

over the tow.

The least effort is required when towing if the drag of the casualty is taken along the length of the towing arm(s). This is achieved when the casualty is directly behind the rescuer. Towing to one side is a waste of much-needed energy.

With the casualty behind the rescuer, it is possible that the casualty's body or equipment may interfere with the rescuer's finning action. In order to avoid this interference, the rescuer should turn his body slightly so that his legs move under and across the casualty rather than directly up and down.

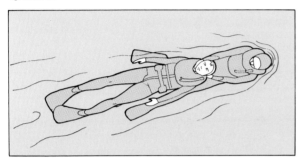

Figure 189c The rescuer should fin to either side or below the casualty for greatest effect

Pace

Towing, especially when combined with expired-air resuscitation, is a very strenuous activity. The rescuer must, therefore, adjust his pace so that he does not overtax himself. If the rescuer overreacts to the urgency of the situation – which is, after all, a not unnatural reaction – he risks not only becoming ineffective as a rescuer, but also becoming a danger to himself.

It is also essential that the rescuer paces his actions to his thoughts. In stressful situations people will often rush into action in ways which are counterproductive. A few seconds' thought might enable far more to be achieved with far less effort. Therefore, when performing a rescue, don't let your actions get ahead of your brain.

Removing the Casualty from the Water

The Conscious Casualty

The conscious casualty is rarely completely incapable and can often contribute towards the effort of removing himself from the water. The rescuer must, however, remain in firm control of the casualty as, particularly with a casualty who is in an agitated mental state, this contribution may be counterproductive.

For a rescue into a boat, the casualty should be encouraged to secure himself to the boat by holding on to a grabhandle, ladder or other suitable point. The rescuer can then remove the casualty's heavy equipment or fins to make it easier to get him into the boat. Once the heavy equipment has been removed, partially deflating the casualty's lifejacket to reduce its bulk will make it easier for him to climb into the boat.

In a small boat such as an inflatable the boat handler or the divers already in the boat can assist the casualty from

above while the rescuer can assist from the water.

With a large rolling boat, it may not be advisable to approach the boat too closely until the casualty is completely ready to be recovered inboard. The approach should then be timed to coincide with the boat's motion and further assistance should be provided from onboard. The rescuer should not provide assistance from directly behind the casualty as, should the boat roll heavily or the casualty slip back into the water, he could be struck by the casualty and injured.

Figure 189d The conscious casualty will usually require assistance to leave the water. Both rescuer and boat crew should assist

Assisting the casualty to land on a shelving shore is more straightforward. The rescuer should assist him to stand up, particularly if he is still wearing any heavy equipment, and to maintain his balance against any wave action until clear of the water.

The Unconscious Casualty

Removing an unconscious casualty from the water will obviously require much more effort than for a conscious casualty. The rescuer should, therefore, enlist as much assistance as possible from other divers, boat handlers or anyone else who is to hand.

For recovery into a small boat, the boat handler should secure the casualty alongside or, if necessary, take over expired-air resuscitation, while the rescuer removes the casualty's heavy equipment and partially deflates his lifejacket. The rescuer will find this easier if he has retained his mask and can see underwater to remove the equipment. With the boat handler pulling from above and the rescuer pushing from below, the casualty can then be recovered into the boat.

To recover the casualty into a large boat, the same procedure can be used but may need to be modified, depending upon the boat's freeboard. With a high freeboard it may be necessary for an assistant to enter the water and secure the casualty alongside or to take over expired-air resuscitation. Because of the greater height involved, recovering the casualty into the boat may require the use of ropes to lift him. These may be passed in a loop under the casualty's armpits or two ropes may be used to parbuckle the casualty into the boat. Deflation of the casualty's lifejacket will reduce his bulk, but great care must be taken to protect his head.

The actual recovery of the casualty into the boat will, of necessity, mean a break in any expired-air resuscitation being administered. This should be done as quickly as possible so that there is the minimum interruption before resuscitation is resumed.

To land a casualty up a shelving beach, his heavy equipment should be removed, if it has not already been ditched, while there is still enough water for the subject to float supported by his lifejacket. The casualty can then be dragged bodily backwards up the shore until clear of the water, where he can be laid flat in safety. If it is necessary to cross a line of heavy surf to reach the shore, all heavy equipment, both the casualty's and the rescuer's, should be removed before reaching the surf. The area of surf should then be crossed and the casualty dragged clear as quickly as possible.

Figure 190a The rescuer will need to remove the equipment of an unconscious casualty before attempting entry into a boat

Figure 190b The boat crew must play the major part in recovering the casualty into the boat, assisted by the rescuer

Figure 190c The rescuer should remove the casualty's heavy equipment and his own fins for a beach recovery

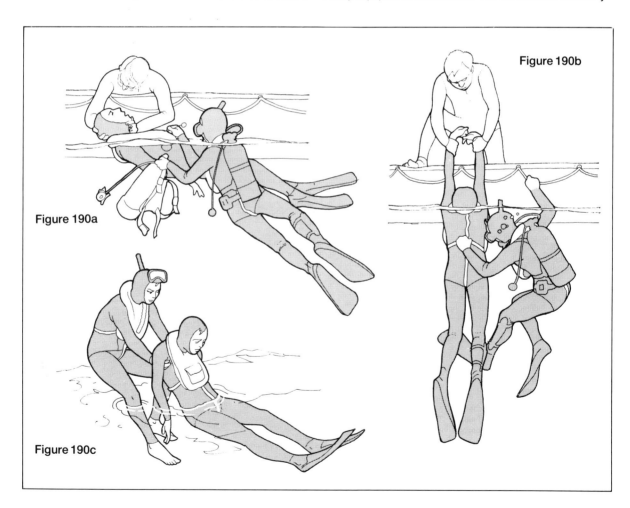

Figure 190b

Figure 190a

Figure 190c

Oxygen Treatment

The administration of oxygen as a means of first aid to a diver suffering from decompression sickness or burst lung can be of significant benefit to the casualty's condition. The effectiveness of resuscitation being applied to a non-breathing casualty can also be improved if oxygen can be introduced into the procedure. This section outlines the use of oxygen treatment under these circumstances as a means of supplementing the treatments detailed elsewhere in this manual.

The Equipment

There is a large variety of oxygen treatment equipment available, most of which is unsuitable for use in the field to treat diving casualties. The following paragraphs describe suitable equipment and the facilities it provides.

Cylinders

Cylinders are available in a range of standard sizes, each size being identified by a letter. The most practical cylinders for use in a portable unit are 'D' size, which, depending upon the material from which they are constructed, have a capacity of from 360 to 415 litres. In the UK all cylinders are colour-coded black with a white neck. Elsewhere in the world other colour codings may apply; for instance, in the USA oxygen cylinders are green overall.

   The portable sizes of oxygen cylinders are fitted with pillar valves, while some larger sizes may have different types of connections. Connection to the pillar valve is by a three-pin register fitting secured by an A-clamp.

Regulator

The regulator attaches to the cylinder by the A-clamp. It acts as a reduction valve, reducing the oxygen pressure to a level suitable for delivery to the mask. For use in a diving

Figure 191a An oxygen cylinder valve showing pin index system

incident, ideally the regulator should provide both of the following outlets:

1. An outlet suitable for connection to a mask fitted with a demand valve.
2. An outlet capable of delivering 10 litres/minute to a constant-flow mask.

The Mask

Masks should cover both the mouth and nose (i.e. oro-nasal masks) and preferably should be of transparent material to allow the casualty's airway to be monitored more easily. For most diving casualties, a mask fitted with a demand valve will be preferable, not just for economy of oxygen use, but also because it will deliver 100 per cent pure oxygen to the casualty. Constant-flow masks are not only more wasteful of oxygen but also deliver a lower concentration of oxygen to the casualty.

   The most useful type of constant-flow mask in the event of a diving incident is known as the pocket mask. This will provide an oxygen concentration to a breathing casualty of approximately 50 per cent and has the added advantage, as will be described later, that it can be used to enhance expired-air resuscitation being performed on a non-breathing casualty.

   Some masks fitted with demand valves have a facility for inflating the casualty's lungs by positive pressure. Due to the risk of damage to the casualty's lungs or stomach, the use of this type of mask is not recommended.

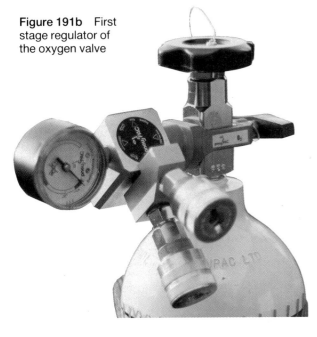

Figure 191b First stage regulator of the oxygen valve

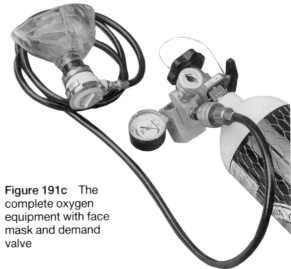

Figure 191c The complete oxygen equipment with face mask and demand valve

164

Administering Oxygen to a Breathing Casualty
The maximum benefit is derived when oxygen treatment is started as early as possible. With the limited supply of oxygen available in the portable cylinders, it is more effective to allow the casualty to use up all the oxygen from the beginning, rather than to try to extend the time over which oxygen is available by periods of breathing oxygen separated by periods of breathing air.

The majority of casualties who will benefit from oxygen treatment will be breathing normally. These will be divers who are suffering from decompression sickness or burst lung. The most suitable equipment to use for this treatment is the mask fitted with a demand valve. The benefits of a constant-flow mask are, however, worthwhile if there is no alternative.

At the earliest opportunity oxygen should be administered via an oro-nasal demand mask and the casualty laid flat on his back. Keep the casualty still and closely monitor his condition.

As soon as possible, the casualty should be evacuated to medical care. Where the casualty's condition is suspected to be decompression sickness, his diving partner should be treated as a potential casualty and should accompany him. If subsequently the partner shows symptoms, he should also be given oxygen via a separate mask, accepting that the supply will be used up faster. If only one mask is available, the first casualty should remain breathing from it.

Oxygen Enhanced Expired-Air Resuscitation
The pocket mask can be used as an aid to expired-air resuscitation with or without the addition of oxygen. The casualty is laid flat on his back with his head tilted back to extend his airway as for normal expired-air resuscitation.

From behind the casualty's head, the rescuer places the pocket mask over the casualty's mouth and nose. He holds it in position by placing one hand on either side of the mask, with the ends of the fingers hooked under the sides of the casualty's jawbones (*not* around the windpipe). The rescuer can then inflate the casualty's lungs by sealing his mouth around the mask outlet and blowing into the mask, and hence into the casualty's lungs. As the rescuer

Figure 192a   Using the pocket mask to administer EAR

removes his mouth from the mask outlet, the casualty is able to exhale.

Apart from the use of the mask to form the seal on the casualty's face, all other aspects are as for normal expired-air resuscitation.

To introduce oxygen into the procedure, the technique is exactly the same as above, except that the pocket mask is connected, via its oxygen inlet, to a 10 litre/minute supply of oxygen. As the rescuer blows into the mask, the oxygen content of his exhalation is supplemented by the oxygen being delivered directly into the mask, thus increasing the concentration of oxygen in the air entering the casualty's lungs.

The material of the mask slides easily over wet skin and under such conditions can be difficult to hold in place. A small towel, kept with the equipment, will enable the rescuer's hands and the casualty's face to be dried, thus avoiding this problem.

Rescue Management

It is extremely rare for a diving accident to occur in a situation where there is no assistance available. Rescue management is the means of making the most effective use of the assistance which can be provided either by other divers or by the emergency services.

For the experienced diver, rescue management begins long before an incident occurs. Dive planning can do much to avoid potential trouble spots such as rough water and excessive currents, and a thorough knowledge of how to contact the emergency services will ensure that there is no time lost should they be needed. During the dive an experienced boat handler will position the cover boat where it can best cover the divers. For instance, if there are many other water users about, the cover boat may need to be positioned between the divers and other boats. Alternatively, an inflatable boat, patrolling upwind of its divers, will still be able to drift towards them to recover them should its engine fail, whereas if downwind it would be driven away from them.

Should an incident occur, while the casualty's immediate rescuer is taking the necessary actions to preserve his life, other divers in the vicinity can do much to render assistance. This assistance must, however, be co-ordinated to ensure that it does not become counterproductive, no matter how well intentioned it is. Control of the assistance must be assumed by the most suitably qualified diver present, such as the dive marshal, boat handler or an experienced diver.

As soon as it becomes apparent that an incident is taking place, a rapid assessment of the situation should be made. This assessment should follow the priorities of first aid given earlier (p. 148) and an appropriate course of action decided upon.

Calm but positive instructions should then be given to the other divers present. These instructions will depend upon the number and capabilities of the divers and the nature of the incident. Generally the more experienced divers will be required to assist by performing such tasks as taking over expired-air resuscitation or removing the casualty's equipment. Even the newest novice can contribute something useful, such as telephoning for the emergency services, fetching a first-aid kit or preventing crowds of onlookers from getting in the way. Allocation of tasks should be carried out quickly and clearly so that all concerned know exactly what they are expected to do and so that there is no confusion.

When the emergency services arrive, they should be made fully aware of any relevant information concerning the incident. If the casualty is to be transported to a hospital, a recompression chamber or some other medical facility, he should be accompanied by another diver fully conversant with the incident. In the case of a decompression accident, the casualty's partner should also accompany him to the recompression facility.

The essence of rescue management is to make the most efficient use of the resources available at the time of the incident. Under no circumstances should the emergency services administer Entonox to a casualty suffering from a decompression incident. In such circumstances the casualty's partner should also accompany him to the re-compression facility.

Figure 192b Oxygen enhanced EAR

Charts

A chart is the sailor's map, but unlike a map which is used for finding your way around on land, a chart deals with the sea and coastal regions. Charts display a great deal of information, some of which is not necessarily of use to divers.

Charts covering a large area of the earth's surface in little detail are called 'small-scale' charts; those covering a small area in much greater detail are called 'large-scale'. Generally speaking, the larger the scale the more detailed will be the information displayed – which is ideal for divers and dive planning.

British Admiralty charts may be obtained through any Admiralty chart agent. However, before buying your chart consult the *Admiralty Catalogue*. There is a smaller version of this publication – the *Home Waters Catalogue* (NP 109) – for the UK coast. In both publications the pages illustrate sections of the coastline superimposed with rectangles of varying size. These represent the chart's coverage and include the chart number, which should be quoted when ordering. Small rectangles indicate greater detail and larger scale. In addition to Admiralty charts, there are others which the diver may find more suitable for his purpose. These include the Stamfords and Imray series, which are published for yachtsmen and include tidal and local pilotage information.

The Cardinal Points

The earth can be regarded as a sphere. The direction in which the earth rotates is called 'east', where heavenly bodies, like the sun, appear to rise. The opposite direction to this is called 'west', where the sun sets. The earth rotates on its axis, whose extremities are known as the north and south poles. If we divide the earth in half by an imaginary line, this line is known as the equator, and we can express our position as being north or south of the equator. Similarly, if we divide the earth through the poles by a straight line, called a meridian, we can express our position as being east or west of it.

Latitude and Longitude

Meridians of Longitude
The division of east and west is by international agreement, the Greenwich meridian running through Greenwich, London (0 degrees longitude). The horizontal position of a place is its angular distance from the Greenwich meridian, measured from the centre of the earth. This is called its longitude, starting from 0 degrees at the Greenwich meridian to 180 degrees either east or west to the opposite side of the globe.

Parallels of Latitude
The vertical distance of a place is its angular distance from the equator, measured from the centre of the earth. This is called its latitude, starting from 0 degrees at the equator to 90 degrees either north or south at the poles.

Degrees and Minutes
Each degree is divided into 60 units, called 'minutes', and each minute is further divided into 60 seconds, but for practical purposes tenths are used.

The Nautical or Sea Mile
One minute of a degree of latitude, measured along a meridian, is by definition a nautical mile in length (1852 metres). It means the accuracy of such a position can be

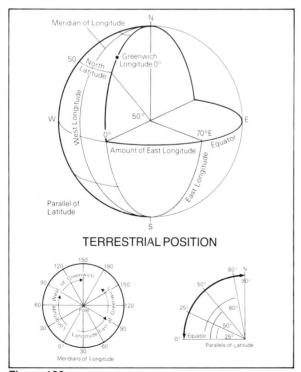

Figure 193

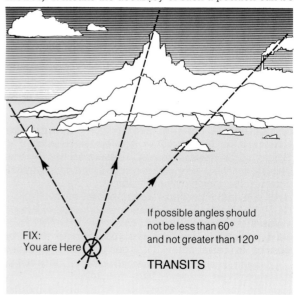

Figure 194

specified to 185·2 metres (1/10 of 1852 metres).

Latitude is displayed along the sides of a chart and can also be used for measuring distance since 1 minute (1') is 1 nautical mile.

Longitude is displayed along the top and bottom of a chart and is only used for plotting longitude. Since the meridians converge towards the poles, the linear distance is reduced. For this reason longitude scales are never used to measure distance.

The Compass Rose
The compass rose appears at least once on every chart and, in the case of large areas, it may be printed twice, usually in an area of sea with little navigational detail.

The rose consists of an outer circle graduated at 1-degree intervals from 0 degrees to 360 degrees and an inner circle which is offset for magnetic variation but is really only of use for the year printed on the axis. The compass rose can be used to obtain true courses and bearings.

Courses and Bearings
If we draw a straight line on the chart from one position to another, i.e. from harbour entrance to a known wreck site, the direction or course can be obtained from the compass rose. In order to read off the direction, you need to transfer the direction from your drawn line to the compass rose using a pair of parallel rulers. Placing the parallel rulers on the drawn line, carefully 'step off' until one edge passes through the centre dot of the rose; this will give you two readings on the rose, 180 degrees apart. One is from the harbour to the site and the other from the site back to the harbour. The secret in deciding which to use is to assume your start position as the rose centre and then travel to the graduated scale in the appropriate direction to get the course.

The course or bearing obtained in this way is a true course/bearing and does not allow for magnetic variation and deviation – so beware of using this information directly with a hand-bearing compass or diving compass.

Selected Chart Symbols
To interpret chart symbols it is essential to obtain a copy of Chart 5011, the *Symbols and Abbreviations* booklet. Although most symbols are self-explanatory, this booklet will give you far more information. Chart symbols can provide the diver with valuable information on the foreshore, rocks, seabed, dangers and wrecks.

Transits
Having found a good dive site you will need to fix its position. In coastal waters this is generally done by taking transits (a position line established by noting the coincidence of two visible permanent landmarks), but remember charts are not printed for divers and as such may not have conspicuous objects printed on them. Choose objects which a ship's navigator would use. Do not use buoys for transits as they move!

Tidal Stream Data
Tidal stream information can be obtained from a chart of the dive area or from a tidal atlas, which usually covers a much larger area and is therefore of only general use.

Tidal Stream Diamonds
Tidal diamonds are small magenta diamonds, containing a letter, printed on charts indicating where tidal streams have been recorded. The letter corresponds to a table of data often found near the title of the chart.

The table displays the tidal streams for six hours before and after high water at some local standard port. The reliability of the information drops rapidly from the plotted position. To determine the expected direction and speed for a drift dive, you first need to find the interval between high water (at the standard port) and the actual dive time.

The table is entered with this known interval and a line of data can be read. The 'dirn' is the actual direction in which a diver will drift, while the speed of the drift will depend on whether there are spring (Sp) or neap (Np) tides that day. If your interval falls in between two of the tabulated hours, simply find the average. Accurate calculations are not generally needed since you are only using this information as a general guide for dive planning.

Tidal-Stream Atlases
There are several sources of tidal stream atlases, the main authority being the Admiralty. Each atlas gives information for a stretch of coastline or area of sea (e.g. the Irish Sea). The Admiralty publishes a booklet for each area covered, giving it a reference number, whereas other sources usually supply a collection of smaller charts covering many areas.

The presentation of the information is the same no matter what the source may be. The direction of the tidal stream is shown by arrows, which point in the direction of the flow. The speed of the stream is printed in tenths of a knot, both for springs and neaps. A typical example may show 07,12 between the arrows, indicating 0·7 knots during neaps and 1·2 knots for springs. The speed of the stream is often further emphasized by bold printing.

The flow of water around the coast is continually changing direction and speed during its duration. The tidal-stream atlas must cover six hours before high water through to six hours after high water and this is done by printing a page for each of the thirteen hours.

Tides and Tidal Streams

Causes of Tides

The periodic vertical movement of the sea level is caused by the combined effect of centrifugal force and gravitational attraction between the earth and the moon and to a lesser extent the earth and the sun.

Although several heavenly bodies apply gravitational pulls on the earth's oceans, it is the sun and moon that have the most influence. These two bodies cause an envelope of water to form an egg shape. This egg-shaped envelope is virtually stationary and the earth spinning inside gives an observer on its surface the impression that the water level rises over a six-hour duration and then falls over a similar time.

For the sea level to fall from high water to low water and return to high water again (one cycle) takes twelve hours. Such a tide is known as a 'semi-diurnal' tide. There are areas of the world, such as the Pacific, where this cycle takes twenty-four hours. In these cases the tides are called 'diurnal' tides.

The sun, the moon and the earth all change their relative positions in their orbits, but since the moon is nearer to the earth, its movement is more significant and the main changes occur in about a twenty-eight-day cycle (a lunar month).

Spring and Neap Tides

The effects of the sun and moon on the earth's tides are as follows:
1. When the moon is directly between the sun and the earth, the combined gravitational pull of the moon and the sun is strongest and we get the highest high waters and the lowest low waters. The change in level between high water and low water (range) is the maximum – these are known as spring tides.

2. A similar effect occurs when the moon is on the far side of the earth from the sun, but still in a straight line. This is also known as a spring tide.
3. When the moon is at right angles to the earth/sun axis, we get the least range between high and low waters – known as neap tides.

The sea level continually changes, on an hourly basis, due to the earth revolving inside its egg-shaped envelope of water. The range of this rise and fall changes on approximately a seven-day-cycle because the moon is orbiting the earth every twenty-eight days.

Careful observation of the moon's shape in the sky (phase) can help the diver estimate what tides to expect; however, do check with the tide tables.

Tidal Patterns

The land masses of the earth distort this simple tidal pattern as they divide the water into oceans, seas and basins of varying depth, width and shape.

Whether an ocean's coastline experiences a twenty-four-hour diurnal tide or a twelve-hour semi-diurnal tide depends on which body (the sun or the moon) is the dominating force. Shallow seas and basins such as the North Sea and the English Channel have the further complication of reduced depth.

Use of Tide Tables

Tide tables give the predicted times of high water and low water, and the range of each tide, on every day of the year. For standard ports (various places around the coast), the times are extracted directly, but care should be taken to add one hour during the April–October period, since printed times are always in Greenwich Mean Time (GMT) but we use British Summer Time (BST) during that period.

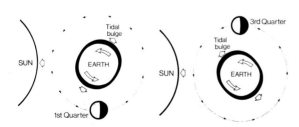

EFFECT OF SUN AND MOON ON THE TIDES

Figure 195

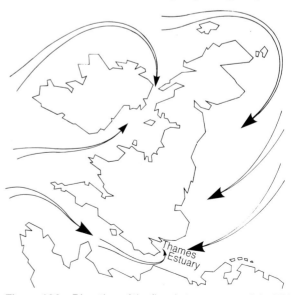

Figure 196   Direction of the flood stream around the UK

Times of high water can also be used to find slack-water time as this is given relative to high water (e.g. 1 hour 20 minutes before high water at Plymouth).

The comparison of high-water height and low-water height gives the range of the tide. To determine whether to expect spring or neap tides on the day, simply compare the range of the day with a few ranges from the same month at the same port. Some tables print the average range for springs and neaps to help make this decision simpler.

Terms and Definitions

Chart datum (CD)   The level below which the tide never or rarely falls.

Height of tide   The height of the sea surface above chart datum at any given instant.

High water (HW)   The highest level reached by the sea surface during any one cycle.

Low water (LW)   The lowest level reached by the sea surface during any one cycle.

Predicted range of the tide   The difference in height between successive high water and low water for one particular cycle.

Spring tides   Those tides of maximum range occurring about twice a month, at or near new or full moon.

Neap tides   Those tides of minimum range occurring about twice a month, at or near the first and last quarters of the moon.

Equinoctial springs   Greater than average spring tides occur near the equinoxes (March and September), at new and full moon.

Mean high water springs (MHWS)   The average height of high water at spring tides throughout the year.

Mean low water springs (MLWS)   The average height of low water at spring tides throughout the year.

Mean high water neaps (MHWN)   The average height of high water at neap tides throughout the year.

Mean low water neaps (MLWN)   The average height of low water at neap tides throughout the year.

Highest astronomical tide (HAT) and lowest astronomical tide (LAT)   These are the highest and lowest predictable tides under average meteorological conditions.

The datums of mean high water springs (MHWS) and chart datum (CD) are used to measure heights of land objects and seabed levels respectively.

Knowing the height of conspicuous landmarks can be very useful for position fixing and site location. If the seabed is below the chart datum, which is usually the case, the distance is known as a 'charted depth' and will be shown on the chart in metres and tenths (e.g. 5_8 means 5·8 metres). There are occasions when the seabed rises above the chart datum, in which case the distance is a 'drying height'. To distinguish this from a charted depth a line is drawn underneath the figures (e.g. $\underline{4_2}$ means 4·2 metres above chart datum).

> **Diving depth of water = height of tide + charted depth.**
> **Diving depth of water = height of tide − drying height.**

Using Tide Tables

Rule of Twelfths

A convenient although not completely accurate method of calculating the depth of water at any state of tide is the Rule of Twelfths.

A tide may be expected to rise or fall, as appropriate, for approximately:
  1/12th of its range in the first sixth of its duration
  2/12ths of its range in the second sixth of its duration
  3/12ths of its range in the third sixth of its duration
  3/12ths of its range in the fourth sixth of its duration
  2/12ths of its range in the fifth sixth of its duration
  1/12th of its range in the final sixth of its duration

Procedure

1. Determine time of high and low water and height of high and low water from the tide tables.
2. Apply BST/GMT conversions as appropriate.
3. Calculate range (height of high water minus height of low water).
4. Calculate duration (time between two successive tides, i.e. low water to next high water or vice versa).
5. Apply corrections, from the standard port to which the tide table refers, to that of the chart, for both range and duration if necessary.
6. Apply the difference between slack water and high/low water from tidal-stream information on the chart to give the time of slack water in terms of BST/GMT.
7. By the Rule of Twelfths, determine the depth of water at slack (or required time) by adding the resultant portion of the tidal range to the charted depth and the height of low water/high water above/below chart datum.

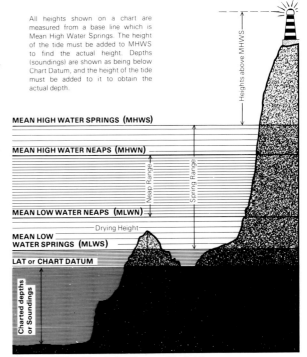

All heights shown on a chart are measured from a base line which is Mean High Water Springs. The height of the tide must be added to MHWS to find the actual height. Depths (soundings) are shown as being below Chart Datum, and the height of the tide must be added to it to obtain the actual depth.

Figure 197   Chart depths and heights

Small Boats 1

Types of Small Boat

Diving can take place from virtually any craft provided that getting back on board is easy and safe. The ease of re-entry depends on the freeboard of the boat – the distance from the water to the top of the sides of the boat. The safety depends on stability – in other words, whether the boarding diver will cause the vessel to heel dangerously.

What type of small boat is best for general diving? There is no absolute answer, although some guidelines can be set out. The choice lies between the inflatable (with either inflatable keel, wood-stiffened keel, or rigid hulled) and the fibreglass dory. Other vessels, such as ex-Army assault craft, fibreglass speedboats and small dinghies, are not as suitable due to their reduced seaworthiness.

Most diving groups opt for the inflatable because of its seaworthiness. It has a shallow draft, tremendous buoyancy (supplied by the large tubes) even when swamped, and is extremely stable. The low freeboard allows easy access to the water and minimum effort on re-entry. With a powerful engine an inflatable is a high-speed planing craft capable of carrying a full diving team and their equipment. The best compromise between portability and seaworthiness is a 4–5-metre model fitted with a 40–50-h.p. outboard motor. The seaworthiness of the rigid-hulled inflatable also warrants consideration, although it is more difficult to launch. The ideal is a 6-metre inflatable with a rigid fibreglass hull, fitted with twin 50-h.p. outboards. Regrettably, such a vessel is beyond the pockets of most divers!

Although there are many very easy and convenient launch sites for boats transported on boat trailers, there are other sites where the launch spot leaves much to be desired; there are also a number of very awkward spots indeed. The fact that a normal inflatable can, if necessary, be broken down into a number of loads and then reassembled at the water's edge is an advantage, although less than might initially be imagined.

The dory is also quite popular. It is equally good at planing and is built in fibreglass. The larger sizes can be fitted with a small cabin for shelter. Dories are too heavy to launch without a trailer and this limits potential launching sites.

A good design can be very stable with buoyancy being supplied by a double skin and often built-in tanks, doubling as seats, along its length.

Figure 198 An inflatable diving boat

Figure 199 An inflatable boat with a rigid hull

Figure 200 A dory style fibre glass boat

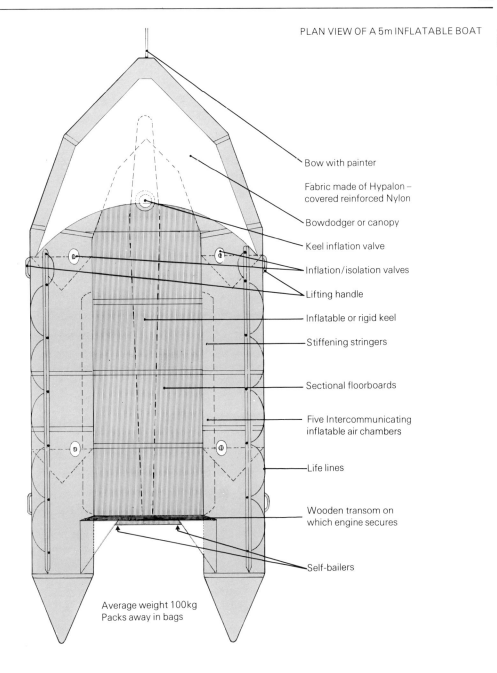

Figure 201

PLAN VIEW OF A 5m INFLATABLE BOAT

Bow with painter

Fabric made of Hypalon – covered reinforced Nylon

Bowdodger or canopy

Keel inflation valve

Inflation/isolation valves

Lifting handle

Inflatable or rigid keel

Stiffening stringers

Sectional floorboards

Five Intercommunicating inflatable air chambers

Life lines

Wooden transom on which engine secures

Self-bailers

Average weight 100kg
Packs away in bags

SIDE VIEW OF A 5m INFLATABLE

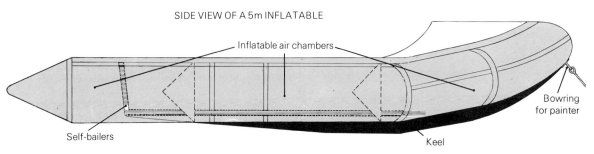

Inflatable air chambers

Self-bailers

Keel

Bowring for painter

Outboard Engines

Most small diving boats are powered by an outboard engine. These are very powerful for their physical size and they are quite reliable when correctly maintained.

A small inflatable carrying four kitted divers requires at least a 25-h.p. engine to plane, otherwise a small motor of perhaps 5 h.p. is adequate for displacement speeds. For larger craft carrying more divers and equipment over longer distances in bigger seas, the engine must be increased in size to between 40 h.p. and as much as 125 h.p. Too much power can be wasted on a small boat and can even be dangerous, particularly in relatively inexperienced hands.

Engine layouts vary somewhat, but starting is usually by a pullcord at the top of the engine. Most engines are fitted with a manually controlled choke for starting. All but the smallest outboard engines require a separate fuel supply from a remote tank via a flexible hose. Throttle control and steering is provided by the tiller arm, while gears are usually controlled by a separate lever on the side of the engine. An emergency-stop button is essential, although its position depends on the make of engine.

Larger engines are normally bolted permanently to the transom of the boat. They are usually fitted with remote throttle control, steering, electric starting and sometimes engine tilting.

Outboard Engine Fuel Supply

Outboard motors are usually two-stroke engines running on a fuel of petrol with two-stroke oil mixed in a ratio of anything between 1:10 and 1:100. You must use the correct mix for your engine.

Some high-powered outboards use a separate oil tank and inject oil to vary the oil–fuel ratio according to the engine loading.

Some fuel tank filler caps have an air bleed valve incorporated to allow air to enter the tank to replace the fuel as it is used. Do not forget to open it when running the engine!

Fuel tanks can be located out of the way under the bows. The fuel line is vulnerable to sharp edges or heavy weights, which can respectively cut the line or restrict the fuel flow. Both of these events usually stop the engine. A spare fuel line is a wise (if unusual) precaution.

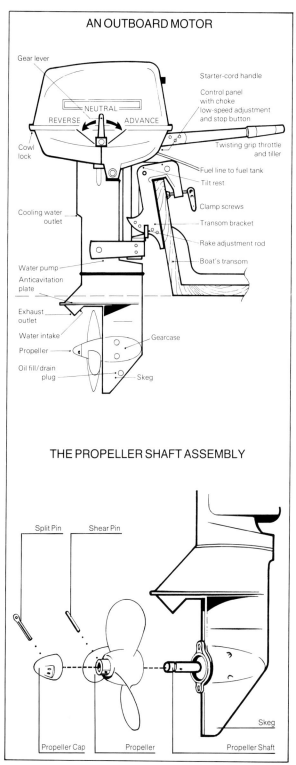

Figure 202

AN OUTBOARD MOTOR

THE PROPELLER SHAFT ASSEMBLY

Boat Trim

This is controlled by two factors – the engine tilt angle and the weight distribution in the boat.

For a boat to plane correctly the tilt angle must be just right. This is normally adjusted by moving a large pin behind the engine transom mount from one set of holes to another. If the tilt angle is too great, the boat's bow points upwards and the stern digs in. If the tilt angle is too small then the bow digs in and the stern tends to rise.

If all the load in the boat is near the stern then the stern will tend to dig in. Conversely, all the weight in the bows will cause the stern to rise. In extreme cases this can allow the propeller to draw air down and cavitate. This is manifested by engine racing and loss of power.

The weight in a boat is best distributed fairly evenly, with perhaps a slight bias towards the stern. This varies from boat to boat, so some trial and error is required. Indeed, with a boat that is somewhat underpowered, it may be necessary to move weight forward to get it planing initially.

Figure 203

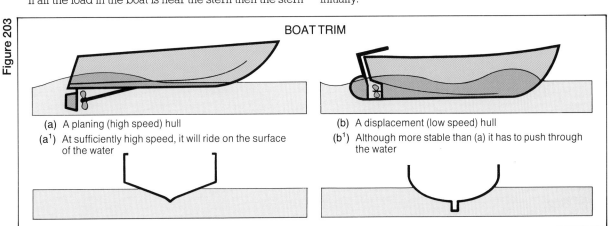

BOAT TRIM

(a) A planing (high speed) hull

(a¹) At sufficiently high speed, it will ride on the surface of the water

(b) A displacement (low speed) hull

(b¹) Although more stable than (a) it has to push through the water

Figure 204

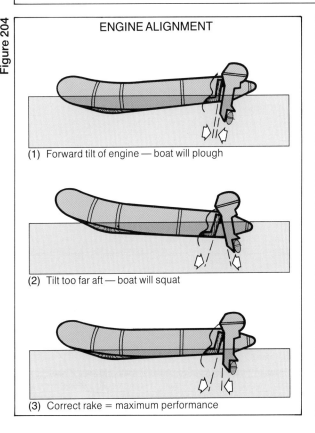

ENGINE ALIGNMENT

(1) Forward tilt of engine — boat will plough

(2) Tilt too far aft — boat will squat

(3) Correct rake = maximum performance

Figure 205

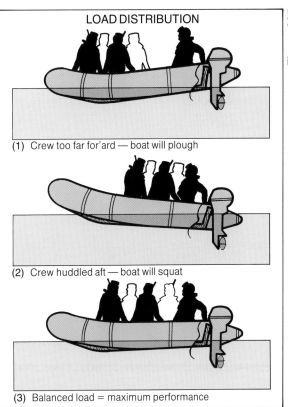

LOAD DISTRIBUTION

(1) Crew too far for'ard — boat will plough

(2) Crew huddled aft — boat will squat

(3) Balanced load = maximum performance

Boating Equipment

The equipment you carry in your boat should be beyond reproach, as you should give yourself every chance of successful boating.

Your list of standard boat equipment plus one or two items (e.g. spare engine) for particularly ambitious trips should include:

In Boat
4 paddles
pump
baler
bilge pump (80 litres/minute)
5 kg CQR anchor + 3-metre chain
5 kg folding anchor + 3-metre chain
anchor warp (150 metres of 10-mm rope)
sea anchor
assorted additional lengths of rope and cord on
storage frame
3 buoys
rigid diving flag on pole
charts (photocopy sealed in clear foil)
decompression table (glued to transom)
hot drinks
spare fuel tank (25 litres)
further spare fuel (on occasions)
spare 4-h.p. engine (on bracket)

In Tool Box
Spares: plugs, shear pins, split pins, propeller nut,
propeller, starter cord, fuel line, valve inserts for
inflatable, valve covers, floorboard bolts, etc.
Repair materials: plugs for hull, hull patches, glue/
emery paper, insulating tape, heavy copper wire,
WD40, etc.
Tools: plug spanner, pliers, screwdrivers,
adjustable wrench, etc. (all tools on lanyards), dry
rags

In Sealed Emergency Box
flares – 4 parachute, 4 hand, 4 smoke
4 diver recall signals (weighted)
whistle
torch
compass
emergency food – glucose tablets, chocolate,
raisins, toffee bars
tins of water
self-heating soup cans
space blankets
first-aid kit (including sea sickness tablets)
coins for telephone
large-denomination note for fuel purchase

It is not intended that these lists are comprehensive. Although trips should never be planned on the basis that rescue is at hand, it is likely that in most parts of Britain you will be fairly quickly noticed and the rescue services notified. This is not always the case in some of the remoter parts of Scotland, where the rescue facilities are either spread very thinly or else almost non-existent.

Rope

Ropes can be made of either natural or synthetic fibres. Natural-fibre ropes (such as cotton, hemp and coir) soak up water and usually sink, which is often an advantage, but they are also slow-drying and are subject to mildew and rotting. Synthetic ropes are mainly made from nylon, Terylene or polypropylene. Nylon is the strongest for a given size of rope. Most of these synthetic ropes float, resist rot, oils, acids and bleaching agents.

The Lay of a Rope
Both types of rope can be either hawser-laid or cable-laid, indicating that the three strands are twisted left-handed or right-handed respectively. Synthetic ropes may have an extra centre core to keep their shape.

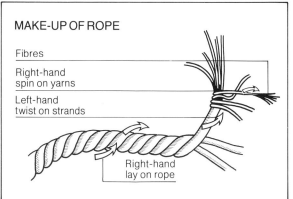

MAKE-UP OF ROPE

Fibres

Right-hand
spin on yarns

Left-hand
twist on strands

Right-hand
lay on rope

Figure 206

Rope Sizes
Rope sizes are quoted as the diameter in millimetres, measured to the outer edges of the strands. In addition to possessing adequate strength, ropes used in diving should be large enough to be easily handled. An ideal size is about 10–12 mm for use when diving from small boats.

Rope Stowage
Ropes in diving boats appear to be a sure recipe for time-consuming tangles unless they are methodically handled and stowed. Coil a rope if you can, otherwise keep ropes stowed in a box or bag until they are needed. They should then run out freely and untangled. Note that a neat coil of rope will not pay out freely unless it is first 'flaked down' onto a clear area. Very long lengths of rope (e.g. for large searches) can be best controlled if they are reeled off and on a suitable drum.

Care of Rope
A rope should be coiled in the hand, not round an elbow, as this is conducive to twists. Finish off the coil by putting three round turns at the end nearest your hand and thread the last half-metre through the top end of the loop.

Figure 207

COILING AND STOWING A ROPE

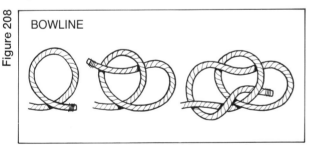

Ropes with frayed ends should not be used. The ends of synthethic ropes should be cut and sealed with a hot knife blade.

Do not allow ropes to come into contact with oil or petrol as these can weaken the rope in addition to making it unpleasant to handle. Do not stand on rope as this can easily damage the rope, especially if there are sharp edges under the pile of rope.

Knots

It is not true that the more you tie up a rope the stronger the knot becomes. A simple and appropriate knot is much more effective. There are about four thousand known knots, but a very few will suffice for most purposes in diving.

The bowline is a secure, permanent knot used to form a loop in the end of a rope. The short end can be 'stopped' for extra security by lashing it to the main rope with twine or by threading it through one of the strands of the main rope.

Figure 208

BOWLINE

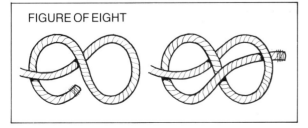

A figure-of-eight knot is useful for preventing the end of a small rope from accidentally running through a check or deck lead.

FIGURE OF EIGHT

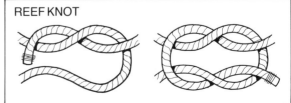

A sheet bend is the best general knot for joining two ropes. If the ropes are of different thicknesses, the 'bight' is put in the thicker rope and the thinner rope is used for the 'looping'. An extra turn can be used to form a double sheet bend which is more secure, although no stronger.

SHEET BEND AND DOUBLE SHEET BEND

A round turn and two half-hitches can be used to secure a rope to fixtures such as a bollard. If the first half-hitch is passed under itself, the knot becomes a fisherman's bend (or anchor bend); this is self-tightening and is used to secure lines to anchors, etc.

ROUND TURN AND 2 HALF-HITCHES   FISHERMAN'S BEND

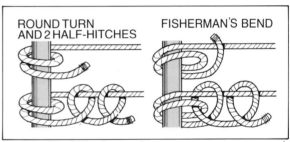

A clovehitch can be used to secure a rope to a round spar or bollard. It is not a very secure knot unless the short end is 'stopped'.

CLOVE HITCH

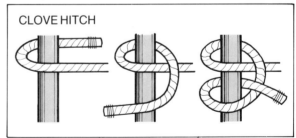

A reef knot is used to secure two ends of an equally sized rope together. It can unfasten if not kept under tension and must not be used as other than a binding knot.

REEF KNOT

Handling Small Boats

Trailing

Most boats are transported to the sea aboard boat trailers. These should be robust and have heavy-duty wheels and suspension if they are to be used on anything other than short journeys along good roads.

You must comply with the law relating to trailing regarding loadings, lights, sharp projections and speeds. Load the trailer so that it is about 25 kg nose-heavy; secure items transported inside the boat. It is best not to use the boat as a baggage trailer. Cover the propeller with something substantial, such as a heavy plastic bucket.

Launching

Launching a boat should be carried out with intelligence and prior planning. The exact technique will depend on the size and weight of the craft and on the shoreline features. These can vary from manhandling the boat over very broken ground to launching from a smooth slipway.

Most diving boats are now launched from trailers, and a simple, methodical procedure should be employed.
1. Ensure the boat is ready for the sea. Fully inflate inflatable tubes. Check fuel, and fuel control lines, anchor and other boat equipment, safety and emergency equipment.
2. Untie the boat from the trailer.
3. Wheel the trailer into sea until the vessel floats off.
4. Two people should hold the bow into any waves to avoid broaching.
5. Pull the trailer out and take above the high-water line. Park it sensibly.
6. The rest of the party should load equipment under the supervision of the cox.
7. The cox places equipment where required.
8. The cox starts the engine, the diving party gets aboard and the boat journey commences.

Loading

To put large amounts of diving equipment in an inflatable obviously requires a certain amount of organization. The toolbox and emergency box (both empty flare boxes) go under the spray deck, together with a large plastic basket taking the anchor systems and other odds and ends. This is stowed so that it is quickly available in an emergency. It is useful for each of the four divers to be given a 25-litre, square plastic container with cutaway sides for their gear; these are lashed across the boat immediately aft of the spray deck. Next come the cylinders (perhaps two sets per diver for longer trips), lashed down behind the gear drums, followed by the weight belts. Finally come the four divers, two fuel tanks, plus a container for cameras and sensitive equipment. This layout of divers and equipment works well, especially on longer boat journeys.

The maximum load that a small craft is designed to carry is specified by the manufacturer. This maximum is for still-water conditions. In sea conditions, the maximum load should be reduced, and in heavier conditions the loading will have to be substantially reduced.

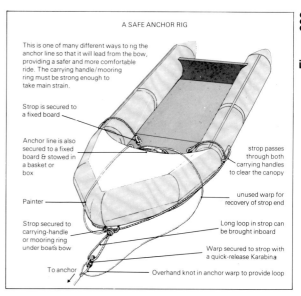

A SAFE ANCHOR RIG

This is one of many different ways to rig the anchor line so that it will lead from the bow, providing a safer and more comfortable ride. The carrying handle/mooring ring must be strong enough to take main strain.

Strop is secured to a fixed board

Anchor line is also secured to a fixed board & stowed in a basket or box

Painter

Strop secured to carrying-handle or mooring ring under boat's bow

To anchor

strop passes through both carrying handles to clear the canopy

unused warp for recovery of strop end

Long loop in strop can be brought inboard

Warp secured to strop with a quick-release Karabina

Overhand knot in anchor warp to provide loop

Figure 209

The Coxswain

The cox is in total command of the craft and is responsible at all times for its safety and the safety of the passengers. He must be a good seaman with appropriate experience of small boat handling.

He must be fully aware at all times of:

> **conditions within the boat**
> **events around the craft**
> **engine and gear settings**
> **potential problems and likely solutions**
> **weather and sea state**

Handling inflatables

Most inflatables used for diving are capable of reaching planing speeds when adequately powered. Their handling characteristics must be learned thoroughly before attempting to operate them alongside divers in the water. The final approach to divers will be as a displacement vessel so the low-speed handling must also be understood.

Small boats powered by outboard engines are steered by directing the propeller thrust in the direction that you want the boat's head to turn. This gives great manoeuvrability at low speeds with low engine throttle positions. Going forward, the turning point is about one-third of the boat's length from the bow, giving a fairly large turning circle. In reverse, the pivot point is around the engine itself, so the boat can be turned in its own length.

At high speeds, small boats will bounce badly in even quite small waves. There is a danger of bouncing both people and equipment out of the boat. Speed must be reduced before this happens, although, for reasons of economy and time, it is best to plane whenever the conditions allow. The best tactic is to use all the engine power to get the boat onto the plane and then to reduce the throttle position until the boat is at the minimum planing speed, as this is most comfortable for the passengers and most economical on fuel.

When planing, the boat is skimming over the water and sharp turns are not possible. The boat slides sideways in turns, the amount of slip being governed by the degree of 'V' in the hull design.

It is not enough merely to cut the engine when you wish to stop rapidly in an emergency when travelling at speed, as the stern wave and the boat's momentum will wash the boat forward quite some distance. A crash stop can be achieved by cutting the throttle setting rapidly while simultaneously pushing the tiller fully in one direction. This causes the boat to go sideways and to stop in a few feet.

It is most important to learn and practise all aspects of small-boat handling. A boat-handling course is the most effective way of achieving this.

Anchoring*

There is much to be said for not anchoring a diving support craft if it is operating singly and much to be said for anchoring the main support craft if there are two or more boats. Generally, it is best practice to have one vessel covering the divers quite closely, and this point is more fully discussed in the section on diving techniques (p. 188).

If you are going to anchor, then it should be done properly:

1. Have a suitable type and weight of anchor attached to an appropriate line (or warp). The warp should consist of about 3 metres of chain with a suitable length of 10–12-mm rope attached.
2. Feed the anchor warp into a bucket or other suitable container. Pass the inboard end of the line through a small hole in the bottom of the container.
3. Attach a quite large (50-cm) buoy to this end, so that the whole anchor system can be immediately jettisoned in emergency, then recovered later.
4. Anchor by lowering the anchor to the seabed and very slowly running the boat downwind or downtide to lay the warp out along the seabed as it is payed out.
5. Pay out line to a length about two or three times the depth in which you are anchoring. Increase this length in rough conditions or in strong tidal streams, although

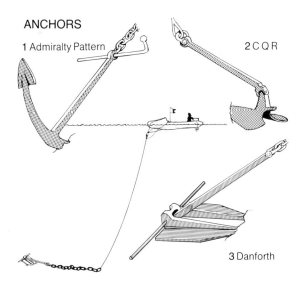

ANCHORS

1 Admiralty Pattern

2 C Q R

3 Danforth

Figure 210 Different types of anchor are used in different conditions. For small boats it is always advisable to attach about 3 metres of chain to the anchor to improve its performance

you will probably only anchor in such conditions in an emergency.

6. If you decide to anchor in a substantial depth, such as 50 metres, the anchor warp may be best organized as a series of 20–30-metre sections, fastened together with snaplinks or double sheet bends.
7. Check that the anchor is holding you in the desired position.
8. Lift (weigh) the anchor by motoring very slowly forward as a crewman pulls in the line. When the line is vertical the anchor should lift off the bottom; if it is stuck, it is sometimes possible to motor past this position and attempt a pull from the other direction. Failing this, either a *pair* of divers with spare bottom time can retrieve the anchor or it will have to be abandoned.
9. Pay the line into the container as it comes aboard. Stow the anchor itself securely.

A sea anchor consists of a length of line with a bucket or fabric drogue attached. It is streamed out over the bows to reduce the drift of the boat in a wind and to keep the bows into the sea after an engine failure.

---

*Boathandling and seamanship are covered in greater detail in a companion volume entitled *Seamanship for Divers*.

Weather

Before diving it is obviously important to listen to the weather and shipping forecasts and carefully evaluate them. Wipe-clean pads are handy for recording forecast details. When following the weather it is useful to have a small pocket aneroid barometer and a yachtsman's anemometer; both of these can be obtained relatively cheaply. Take the advice of fishermen and other locals, although a group of experienced divers in a well-kitted inflatable is a substantially more seaworthy combination than some of the small boats used by inshore fishermen.

Even in moderate weather it is recommended that it is wise to exercise too much caution. Turning back or not starting out when conditions are doubtful do not require the judgement born of years of experience.

Fuel Usage

Boating distances can sometimes be substantial; thus you must plan your fuel accordingly. If you work on the formula of half a litre of fuel per horsepower per hour, you will only slightly overestimate the fuel consumption of modern outboards on full throttle. It is also useful to know how long your outboard will run on full throttle on a full tank of fuel as this gives an idea of operating range. It is imperative to remember that sea conditions may allow you to plane to a site, but may prevent you from doing so on the return trip. Running off-the-plane as a displacement craft will use at least four times as much fuel as on-the-plane for the same

distance. Faulty plugs and badly adjusted outboards also use more fuel.

Planing

There are very many sites in British waters that can only be realistically reached by a planing vessel. Such a craft will also sometimes allow you to beat bad weather home. Ensure that your boat, when fully loaded, has a reserve of power to enable you to plane whenever sea conditions allow. This increases the safety of the excursion generally and also allows the divers to spend less time on boat journeys which are therefore less chilling and not so tiring.

Handling in Rough Seas

The preparation of both boats and personnel must be more thorough when you intend to operate in heavier seas. The equipment used should be of heavier duty and must be fully comprehensive. The crew will have to be more experienced to be effective.

When planing into strong winds there is a significant chance that a lightly loaded inflatable will be flipped right over. There should always be more than one person aboard and the extra people should sit well forward as ballast.

When travelling slowly with a following sea there is always a chance of pooping, i.e. having a wave catch up the boat and swamp it over the transom. Thus a robust boat should not have a low, cutout transom to accommodate the

Figure 211   An inflatable boat can operate at high speeds when properly equipped

outboard engine. Either use a false transom or a long-shaft motor.

The direction and strength of the wind and how long it has been blowing largely determine what can reasonably be tackled in a small boat. It is not possible to quote categorically what is or is not feasible – so much depends upon the boatman and crew, the type of craft and what shelter there is from islands and headlands. As a general indication, a wind of Force 4 or 5 will usually make life uncomfortable in a small boat, especially if the coast is very exposed and the wind has been blowing for some time. Furthermore, the effects of wind and tide working against each other should never be underestimated. Conversely, an offshore wind gives apparently excellent and enticing sea conditions, but beware an engine failure.

When caught in difficult sea conditions, it is often possible to take a longer route back, using the shelter of islands, headlands or planing along the wave troughs to avoid a more time- and fuel-consuming displacement journey. In many conditions you will find the need for a second 25-litre tank of fuel, occasionally more. Having the extra fuel in an outboard tank, although expensive, is far superior to petrol-can-and-funnel transfers.

Remote Areas

At exposed sites the use of two boats operating together is sound sense. For the vast bulk of dives the second boat is a good insurance against breakdowns in quiet areas. In the bigger seas experienced on exposed coasts it is prudent to plan for a slightly smaller load than normal. Reducing the load too far obviously brings the danger of lifting in the wind, whereas too great a load causes continual shipping of water in some seas. For a 4–5-metre inflatable a maximum of four divers with equipment is prudent, whereas in more sheltered waters it might be possible to have six divers in such a craft. Two inflatables of such a size, each with three divers and a boathandler, are a very versatile combination. At many sites, this allows one boat to be anchored, while the other acts as a pick-up and cover craft. In remoter parts it is prudent to have a portable VHF radiotransmitter aboard.

When operating well away from normal bases it is advisable to take many more spare parts, along with the tools and knowledge to use them. The boats and engines should be in tip-top condition before being taken to remote areas. The back-up required is greater and should certainly include two-way radios. It is most desirable to operate vessels in groups of at least two.

Figure 212 A portable VHF radio can be essential when operating in remote areas

Weather and the Diver

The subject which friends can be guaranteed to talk about when they meet is the weather. The reason why it seems so important to people living in the British Isles is its unpredictability. In many other parts of the world one can predict the weather more certainly. In these areas, dive planning, with regard to the weather, is a relatively easy task.

Weather in the British Isles can often play havoc with carefully laid plans and only the foolhardy would attempt to carry on in very poor conditions.

The question remains, however, just what constitutes poor weather and how do we predict it? The aim of this section is to outline those aspects of the weather which are likely to affect our dive plans, how we are able to find out accurate forecasts for the area where we are diving and how we can predict the order of weather events from simple observations. Those aspects of the weather which particularly concern divers can be listed simply as: wind, sea fog and poor surface visibility because of low cloud and rain.

By far the most important feature and the one which makes or breaks a dive plan is the strength and direction of the wind. It is recommended that small boats should not be launched when the wind strength reaches Force 4 or above on the Beaufort Scale (see Appendix 4, p. 249). This scale is a useful guide to wind strength using observations of the behaviour of the waves. Force 4 on the Beaufort Scale is listed as: 'Moderate breeze, 11 to 16 knots. Waves are longer; many white horses.' Such a wind strength, if one is diving in a fully exposed site, would be quite difficult from a small boat. It may be that the selected site is in the shelter of land and in such cases, provided the journey there and back is possible in safety, diving may proceed.

It is very important that you take into account the direction of the wind in relation to your chosen dive site. Waves are generated by the wind and the wave action is transmitted through the upper layers of water. The distance that a wave travels is known as its 'fetch' and the greater the fetch the bigger the wave. The most common or prevailing wind direction in the British Isles is southwesterly and it is therefore obvious that a southwesterly (remember that a wind direction is always given as the direction it blows from) wind Force 4 will have a much greater effect off the west coast of the country than it will have off the east coast. The waves have had the whole width of the ocean to generate height and strength.

Sea fog is a real problem to divers because it is difficult to predict and often descends unexpectedly and very quickly. Unless you are able to get a quick compass fix on land or some other suitable datum point, you can feel very isolated and can get lost very easily. If there are divers in the water and they are not using surface marker buoys, the situation can be quite dangerous. Fog is merely cloud at ground (sea) level and is the result of condensation of warm air as it meets a relatively cold surface. Advection fog, the correct name for sea fog, occurs when a warm airstream meets a relatively cool sea surface. This is especially a problem in the North Sea in the summer, when we get a warm southeasterly airstream from the European Continent. Inland we experience hot, settled weather, but what starts out as a hot day by the coast can end with visibility of just a few metres and diving discomfort. Sea fog is obviously something to worry about if we live in areas where warm air and cool seas meet.

Low cloud and poor surface visibility occur when we have periods of precipitation (the name which covers rain, drizzle, snow, etc.) and these are much easier to predict. Periods of rain are usually associated with strong winds and often combine to give poor diving conditions.

Weather Variables

Changeable weather is due to the distribution of land and sea and the warm and cold air that this distribution brings about. What you should remember is that warm and cold air do not mix when they meet. The line where they meet is called a 'front'.

Air pressure is defined as the weight of a column of air pressing on the earth's surface and the average air pressure acting at sea level is 1013 millibars (slightly more than one bar), but there are variations and the air pressure is then said to be high or low.

To explain this we need to refer back to warm and cold air. One of the properties of air is that when it is warmed it rises and when it is cooled it sinks. If the average pressure is 1 bar, then air which rises exerts less than the average pressure on the earth's surface and it is said to be low pressure. Conversely, air which sinks exerts more than the average pressure and is said to be high pressure. Where there is a pressure imbalance the high-pressure air will always move towards the low-pressure air in an attempt to equalize. When this happens we get a wind and the greater the pressure difference the stronger will be the wind.

To add a further complication to the picture, as warm air rises it cools and as it cools the water vapour in it condenses to give clouds and, eventually, rain. Warm air may be forced to rise over a range of mountains (this explains why highland areas receive more precipitation than lowland areas) or more commonly when it meets an area of cooler air.

Figure 213 shows the significant position that the British Isles occupies in the world climatic scene and helps explain why we have such variable weather. The British Isles lie on the dividing line between the cold air masses from the polar regions and the warm air masses from the tropics. The line where they meet is known as the 'polar front', seen as the black line with waves on the map. Warm air from the south drives wedges into the cold air from the north over the Atlantic Ocean and this battle gives rise to a depression, our most common weather phenomenon in the British Isles.

Figure 214 shows a typical depression, as seen on a weather map with the various features labelled. In the British Isles the whole mass moves southwest to northeast

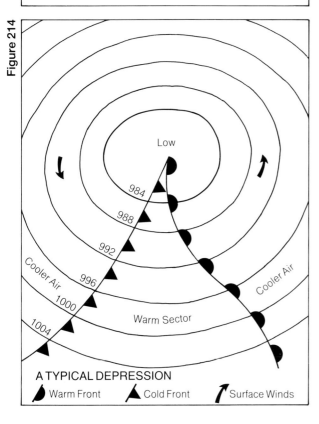

Figure 213

Polar Air

Polar Front

Tropical Air

BATTLE OF AIR MASSES

Figure 214

Low

984
988
992
996
1000
1004

Cooler Air

Cooler Air

Warm Sector

A TYPICAL DEPRESSION

🌢 Warm Front   ▲ Cold Front   🏴 Surface Winds

and gives us a reasonably predictable sequence of weather as it passes. Because it is reasonably predictable, it is useful to divers when planning dives. Basically, a depression is a wedge of warm air that is sandwiched between two areas of colder air. Depressions are born in the Atlantic Ocean; referring back to Figure 213, you have to imagine wedges of warm air driving into areas of cold air. The warm air does not mix, but rises over the cold air to give a warm front. At the same time cold air at the rear squeezes the warm air sandwich to produce a cold front. As the air rises on the warm front, clouds form, and as the front passes over the country, a period of rain usually occurs lasting between five and twelve hours. There follows a drier period as the warm air passes until the cold front with its heavy showers and cooler winds crosses to announce the end of this particular depression.

Figure 215 shows a cross-section through a typical depression. Note the sequence of clouds along the warm front.

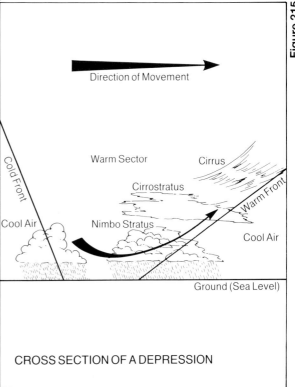

Figure 215

Direction of Movement

Cold Front

Warm Sector

Cirrus

Cirrostratus

Warm Front

Cool Air

Nimbo Stratus

Cool Air

Ground (Sea Level)

CROSS SECTION OF A DEPRESSION

Figure 216 shows the main types of cloud and how to recognize them. As a warm front approaches, the first signs are the high, wispy white cirrus clouds as they are driven along by the high-velocity jet stream of the upper atmosphere. Gradually the sky becomes covered in high cirrostratus cloud and the sun takes on a water halo. The cloud base becomes lower and greyer until the grey nimbostratus rain clouds bring their predictable load. Large anvil-shaped cumulonimbus clouds are often the sign of an approaching cold front with heavy showers,

182

Figure 216

a Cirrus clouds

b Cirrostratus clouds

c Fair weather cumulus clouds

d 'Anvil' cumulus clouds

together with an increase in wind strength, particularly as each shower approaches.

Divers can obtain more information from studying a typical depression on a weather map (Figure 214). First of all you will notice that the word 'Low' appears at the centre of the system. The lines which connect all places of equal barometric pressure are called 'isobars'. The closer together the isobars, the greater the pressure gradient and the stronger the wind. The other interesting fact is that the surface winds in a depression affecting the British Isles always blow anticlockwise so that, as a depression approaches, the wind will be southeasterly, then

southerly, southwesterly, westerly, and finally, as the cold front approaches, northwesterly. An intense depression has isobars very close together; this means very strong winds and rain and should almost definitely rule out diving. Warm fronts without colds fronts and cold fronts without warm fronts are also quite common and never produce settled conditions.

Areas of high pressure, or anticyclones, are the opposite to depressions and usually give days, even weeks, of settled and fairly predictable weather. Figure 217 shows a typical anticyclone. Note that the word 'High' appears at its centre and the fact that the pressure builds up towards the centre. This is the opposite to what happens in a depression. Notice also the isobars are a long way apart, a sign of light winds. What wind there is has a clockwise direction in the northern hemisphere and this is the opposite to what happens in a depression. In the British Isles anticyclones produce hot, dry spells in summer and frequently cold clear days with severe night frosts in winter. They are, however, the conditions when fog frequently forms because of lack of dispersing wind. In summer especially beware of sea fogs, as mentioned earlier in this section. A much shorter-lived weather phenomenon is a ridge of high pressure, which is often squeezed between two depressions. This gives a day or two of fine weather and light winds between the more unsettled conditions associated with a depression.

British Weather

Fortunately, weather information for the British Isles is easy to acquire and is usually accurate. The media are the easiest of the available resources. One of the best sources is the television weather forecast which follows each news bulletin. This uses easy-to-understand symbols and gives an accurate forecast for up to twenty-four hours ahead. Recent techniques use satellite photographs and predicted weather sequences. Wind direction and strength are predicted, as is any precipitation, etc. The weather forecast for farmers, usually broadcast at Sunday lunchtime, gives an outlook for the week, but remember that the longer the prediction the less accurate it may be. Radio weather news also follows news bulletins, but often

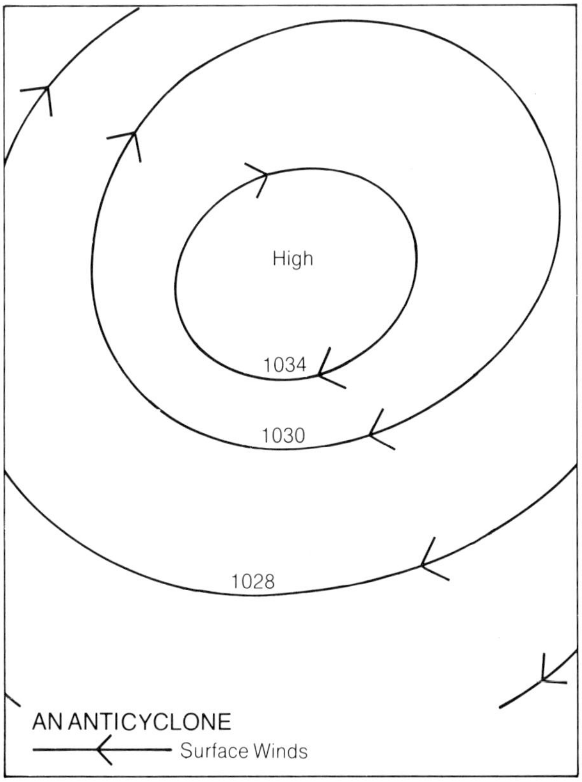

these are more general and of less use. Daily newspapers often carry a daily synoptic weather map which gives a reasonable area forecast covering the whole country, again for twenty-four hours. The shipping forecast on Radio 4 long wave at 0033, 0555, 1355 and 1750 hours gives pressure readings, wind strength and surface visibility conditions for each sea area, together with a more general forecast. Remember, however, that sea areas are very big and what is happening in one part of it may not occur in another. What is predicted for the open-sea areas does not necessarily apply to the coastal strip, where the majority of diving takes place. The coastguard carries a current weather forecast for his area which is updated every six hours. He can also advise on sea state and surface visibility. The meteorological office 'Marinecall' service provides up-to-date forecasts for the British Isles which is divided into 15 regions. A pocket-sized information card is available with all relevant telephone numbers. Contact Telephone Information Services Ltd on 01-236 3500 for details. RAF stations always have a meteorological centre on site and will often be happy to supply you with an area forecast. On site the harbourmaster's office usually has an up-to-date forecast for the area and this can be useful when diving from a port.

It is very important to use your own observations in dive planning. Watch for any signs that wind strength is increasing or that ominous clouds are on the way. This should guide you in your plan and, when on site, perhaps lead to an aborted dive and escape to the nearest shelter. Lighthouse keepers can sometimes be contacted by phone to ascertain local weather and sea conditions.

Some Weather Types around the World

In many parts of the world there is a more predictable climate and this ensures more accurate dive planning as far as the weather is concerned. The Mediterranean Sea, for example, is blessed with anticyclonic high pressure between April and October, with clear skies and sun being the general pattern. Temperatures climb rapidly in the summer to the upper 30 degrees Celsius and even higher in the eastern Mediterranean. The winter period sees more unsettled weather with thunderstorms being common, especially over northern coastal regions. Winds, however, are very unpredictable and can be exceptionally strong. Many divers who visit the Mediterranean coast of France will be familiar with the Mistral which howls down the Rhône valley, often blowing to Force 9 on the Beaufort Scale. Many Mediterranean dive-boat operators consider waves of half a metre too high and so winds can be quite a problem. The Caribbean and the Far East often have hurricanes and typhoons respectively at various times of the year and it is as well to avoid these seasons. The Red Sea should be avoided at the height of the northern hemisphere's summer because of the oppressive heat, while the west coast of the USA, especially California, has a very pleasant Mediterranean-type climate. The Great Barrier Reef off the Queensland coast of Australia provides excellent diving possibilities, but the region is subject to strong trade winds and occasional severe tropical storms.

Figure 217

AN ANTICYCLONE
←——— Surface Winds

Fresh-water Diving

Fresh-water Systems

Fresh-water diving is often overlooked in those parts of the world where the sea is readily accessible. However, diving in fresh water can be a very worthwhile experience, especially if you take the care to locate good sites.

Rivers can yield splendid diving. Short, fast-flowing rivers with rocky beds can have deep pools with excellent visibility during the periods cf reduced water flow in the early summer. Larger rivers tend to carry sediment and, consequently, the visibility can be poor. The world's major rivers will virtually always be full of sediment. Rivers in Britain rarely exceed 2–3 metres in depth, except in pools and gorges. The deepest British river pools are about 15 metres in depth.

For most divers fresh-water diving is synonymous with lake diving. Lakes can vary from small ponds to major inland seas. In Britain, the lakes and lochs are quite small, although they have some intriguing features. Below 6 metres, most British lakes consist of featureless, silty bottoms, although occasionally there are underwater cliffs and silt-covered rocky slopes. Lake depths in Britain are usually between 15 and 75 metres, although in Scotland they are much deeper, with the deepest being Loch Morar at 310 metres.

Flooded gravel pits and reservoirs are very useful for training. Canals can be very choked with debris but can often be the home of interesting small forms of life. Cave diving is usually undertaken in fresh water but is a very specialized technique requiring special training which is not offered by the BSAC.

Locating good fresh-water sites takes some care. There are very few lakes or rivers for which charts are published, although steep contours on land maps can often indicate where a lake will have a steep, rocky slope. Geological maps may indicate areas where gorges or pools might have formed. Sometimes there is useful information to be gleaned from publications intended for fishermen or canoeists.

Geological Formations

The geological formations found in fresh-water diving can be one of the main attractions. Caves have already been mentioned. They must not be dived without comprehensive training. River chasms are fascinating places to explore with an aqualung. Be very careful not to be swept under underwater overhangs or into gorges or other places from which you cannot escape.

Many rivers flow through a series of deep pools and in Britain these can occasionally reach 15 metres in depth and are often the home of fish. They can yield splendid diving, but remember not to antagonize any fishermen who may be fishing the pool that you wish to dive.

Pools and gorges are often formed in places that are geologically interesting. The water may have cut the riverbed along the line of a geological weakness or, sometimes, may have cut across a dyke of intrusive rock. Such features are usually very rewarding to explore.

Waterfalls occur on many rivers and often have a deep pool at their base. It is possible to swim right under the waterfall in times of low water flow. Rarely does the force of the falling water reach farther than about 1 metre underwater in British rivers. In spate, such pools and waterfalls are extremely inhospitable and should not be dived. Take care when swimming or snorkelling down rivers that you do not inadvertently get swept over a large waterfall!

Most of the features discussed above are best found in rivers. However, lakes can also provide unusual geology in the form of steep or even vertical rock walls. These are usually found in lakes or lochs that have been formed by the flooding of a glacial valley, the ice having previously cut steep sidewalls. In the UK there are walls that run vertically to depths of at least 80 metres in some Scottish lochs. There are obvious dangers for trainees and relatively inexperienced persons diving at such sites; even for experienced divers these sites can be quite challenging.

Figure 218   Rivers can sometimes offer exceptional visibility

Life in Fresh Water

Fish life can be one of the factors that makes fresh-water diving worthwhile. Salmon can often be seen in rivers and there are few experiences to compare with diving in the centre of a river pool surrounded by perhaps a hundred large salmon. Trout are often seen, although they do not have the majesty of the salmon. Eels can be very common in rivers in summertime and they can range from very small fish right up to those as thick as a man's arm, the latter being somewhat disconcerting in low visibility. Rivers may also contain the colourful perch, whereas the predatory pike is more a fish of the lakes. A large pike is a formidable fish, but there is no record of one ever attacking a diver.

Fresh water contains lots of other life. Fresh-water crayfish are not often seen, although they are not uncommon in British rivers. Frogs, toads and newts can be seen in small expanses of fresh water.

It is worth bearing in mind that some bodies of fresh water can be polluted with corrosive industrial chemicals or with disease-bearing organisms. Common sense will be a good guide to not diving in such places. Failing that, ask the local diving clubs and/or health officials.

The Law and Access

Most rivers and lakes are owned by someone or, at least, the access to the water is owned by someone. You must have their permission before diving. On some rivers, the right to fish is jealously guarded and divers will not be welcome. Do not dive without checking whether permission is needed.

Fresh Water around the World

In the centre of continental land masses, fresh-water diving can assume considerable importance. European divers often dive in lakes and rivers, whereas in Britain these are mainly used for training. In the USA there is much diving carried out in the flooded fresh-water caverns of Florida. There is also a lot of diving to explore old shipwrecks in the Great Lakes, along with many smaller bodies of fresh water and rivers throughout the middle of the country. Africa has a lot of fresh water in some localities. Divers regularly dive in fresh water in Zambia, and photographers have filmed both crocodile and hippopotamus underwater. In Australia there is a lot of diving in flooded caverns, although this exceeds what the average sports diver should attempt.

Figure 219   A fresh-water eel

Fresh-Water Diving Techniques

Diving Conditions

Diving in normal fresh water is generally straightforward. There are no tides and virtually no currents in most lakes (although this is not the case in large inland seas). Lakes present an enclosed body of water and surface marker buoys are not usually needed except for training purposes or if other water users are present.

Fresh water is less dense than salt water. Consequently our buoyancy will be reduced, typically by about 2–3 kg. If you previously dived in sea water, weight belts should be adjusted before diving in fresh water.

The visibility of fresh water is largely controlled by the catchment area for the water in the system. Rivers very often carry large amounts of sediment (and always do after heavy rain) and, on occasions, this reduces the visibility in the river to zero. It also reduces visibility in the lakes into which the rivers run and causes the bottoms to be covered in a layer of silt. If the river or lake is fed by water that has drained from peaty areas or heathland, then the water will often be yellow, or even brown, in colour. This will quickly reduce the visibility. In fact, fresh-water visibility can vary from zero, through 2–3 metres, to well over 30 metres on occasions.

Fresh water is often gloomy and the lack of life contributes to this feeling, as do the substantial dark depths. However, the shallows of most lakes are often clear, bright and pleasant.

Be careful not to stir the bottom unnecessarily with your fins. A small mud trail can be useful for finding your way back to your place of entry but heavy trails of silt will reduce the visibility to zero. This can easily jeopardize the safety of trainee divers when they attempt to increase their depth experience.

The bottom of all large areas of fresh water is at a temperature of 4° Celsius. Most divers consider this to be cold. In general terms, the temperature of fresh water will be cooler than the sea, and this coldness adds to the seriousness of the dives.

Some lakes lie at altitude, so the appropriate corrections should be made to the measured depth for calculating decompression or no-stop dives (see pp. 112–113).

Lakes and manmade areas of fresh water are frequently used for training, with drills such as underwater search methods being popular. The greater degree of control and the less changeable conditions make fresh-water sites particularly useful for practising such techniques.

Sometimes, during the wintertime, divers are tempted to carry out dives under the ice of frozen-over lakes and rivers. These tend to be mainly fresh water. There are several dangers in diving under ice, not the least of which are getting lost and running out of air. The specialist techniques employed in under-ice diving are discussed in detail in the *BSAC Manual of Advanced Diving*. If you are a trainee or novice diver do not attempt to dive under ice.

Figure 220 Preparing to dive at an inland site

Moving-Water Techniques

Lake diving is relatively easy, but this is not always the case with river diving. Slow-flowing rivers and large river pools are usually quite safe, but fast-flowing rivers present a number of problems.

Shallow, rocky areas of the river only present dangers if there is substantial water flow and if the diver cannot avoid being swept over the boulders. In these circumstances, mouthpieces may be lost or limbs damaged. Take care to keep clear if in doubt.

In fast-flowing rivers it might not be possible to reach the side immediately adjacent to the dive site. This is not normally a great problem since usually it is possible to reach the side and get out farther downriver when the rapid-flowing section has been passed.

There can be a good deal of turbulence in certain parts of very fast rivers. In the UK this is not a problem for the properly equipped and trained diver. There are much bigger rivers overseas, however, and it is certainly possible to get into very serious difficulties in some of the big turbulent eddies and 'stopper' waves.

When water is sufficiently agitated to form foam there is another danger. The amount of foam displaced by the diver is not enough to provide adequate buoyancy and the diver will consequently sink. This is not a real danger in streams and small rivers, but requires attention in larger rivers.

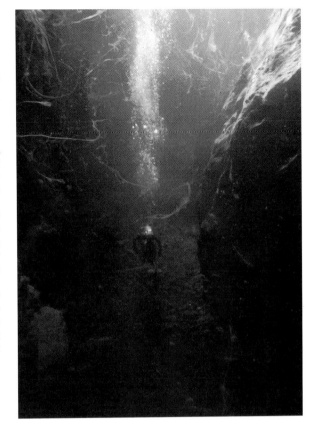

Figure 221 Rivers often have many obstacles but can present interesting diving

Figure 222 Moving with the flow of water is exciting as long as the flow is not too strong

Diving from Small Boats

Why is it that virtually all experienced divers prefer to dive from boats rather than the shore? Quite simply, there is better diving to be found farther offshore. This diving is often somewhat deeper and the visibility is frequently better. It is much more pleasant to slip into the sea from a boat than scramble into the water over the shore wearing full diving equipment. Usually it is less tiring to fin to the site from a boat than from the shore.

If the boat can be left at a safe place between dives, only the cylinders have to be transported after the dive. This can often be achieved when operating from one place at a time by arranging a permanent mooring in a sheltered spot, although this may invalidate some small-boat insurance policies.

The usual approach used when operating from small boats is that the dive takes place in two waves. This is especially valuable when two or more boats are operating as a team. The diving is organized so that the first wave dives, leaving enough experienced people at the surface to man the base and cover boats. When the first wave has completed its dive and been safely picked up, the second wave kits up and dives, while the first-wave people take the roles of surface-cover party.

All of this organization presumes the presence and direction of a leader. Usually the cox of the boat will fulfil this role. Often he is also the group leader and will direct the diving as well.

Boating Techniques

Most techniques are covered on pp. 176–7, but it is worth mentioning a few points here.

Launching the boat will take pre-planning, especially in less than ideal conditions. The need for everyone to be ready at the same time and to work as a team is paramount. The boat should be held bows to the sea while the loading process takes place. If the launch is through surf then teamwork is even more essential. It may even be necessary to launch the boat itself and anchor it beyond the surf zone, then swim individual pieces of diving equipment out to it.

When under way, you should remain seated and hold on to the grablines if conditions are at all rough.

On arrival at the dive site, it is best, with one boat, to keep it mobile during the dive. By not anchoring, the boat is ready to assist divers immediately.

When working with two boats, one is usually employed as a base. It is anchored by clipping it to a buoy, which in turn is clipped to the appropriate number of 50-metre and 25-metre lengths of warp leading to the anchor; this allows rapid casting loose if this becomes necessary. The boats have a reinforcing rope passed through the painter attachment point and then under the boat to points on the transom; the painter is additionally strengthened by a rope passing through the carrying handles and attached to the floorboards.

After the dive, the boat must be landed and, again, it is necessary to work as a team. With rough surf, it may be necessary to swim all the heavy gear ashore before bringing the boat through. Face the vessel into the waves when it is shallow enough for people to enter the water and hold the boat. Teamwork soon moves the mound of equipment back to the vehicles and trailers, provided everyone pulls their weight.

One point to beware of with beach recovery sites is the state of the tide. This will be different for the launching and recovery! If the beach is steeply sloping, it is usually easiest to launch at low tide and recover at high tide. This is not always possible, but the principle ought to be borne in mind.

Boat Diving Techniques

There is limited space available in normal small boats for equipment and for kitting up of divers. Consequently, for short boat journeys, it is often convenient for the divers to kit up fully ashore before entering the diving boat. For longer trips, however, this may be inconvenient. Stow diving gear in the boat in the reverse order to which it is wanted, i.e. first-wave divers' gear in last. Each diver should sit in a different area of the boat and then be assisted to kit up efficiently by divers from the second wave.

In sheltered conditions, when one boat is anchored as a base, breathing sets may be hung in the water around the boat, thus creating more space when moored. Divers then kit up in everything but their aqualung before entering the water and fitting it.

The dive buddies then ensure that all their equipment is fitted correctly. Entry into the water is usually accomplished by means of a backward roll. The diver sits on the edge of the boat and ensures that none of his hoses are caught and that he will not flip any loose equipment into the water with his fins. He then rolls backwards into the water, with one hand over his mask and regulator mouthpiece and the other holding his aqualung harness at his side. Both buddies should surface and check all is well before descending together.

Cover procedures for the boat are quite simple. Having raised the diving flag, the boat should follow the divers' surface marker buoys or bubbles, keeping a few metres clear, until the divers surface and signal that they are OK. At that stage, the boat should move to the divers and pick them up.

As the boat approaches the divers from downwind, they should swim about 5 metres apart. The boat then gently moves between them and puts the motor out of gear. The divers swim to the side of the boat and catch hold of the grablines. They remove and pass to the divers in the boat first their weight belts and then their aqualungs, not forgetting to disconnect any direct feeds and/or inflation hoses first. The persons stowing this heavy gear should be careful not to damage any delicate equipment, such as cameras, in the process.

Once relieved of this weight, it is straightforward to enter the boat by holding onto the grabline, bobbing down in the water, then finning hard upwards while pulling on the grabline. While you are still lying on the side of the boat it is often helpful if another diver removes your fins. Quickly enter the boat and stow your gear, as other divers will be anxious to enter the water in their turn. After a quick debriefing with the group leader, the time for swopping experiences with your buddy is after the second wave has started its dive.

If the boat is too high to enter in this way, a boarding ladder can be used. In its absence, it is possible to climb over the transom by using the outboard cavitation plate as a foothold. Make sure the engine is stopped.

Seasickness is not usually a problem in small boats when they are underway. However, the rolling of a moored boat in a swell may well induce sickness in some divers. A seasick diver is inefficient and loses interest in co-operating with his group. If you are prone to seasickness, consider using an antidote. Several should be tried, but beware of the side effect of drowsiness adding to nitrogen narcosis while diving. For many divers, a relatively new preparation – Stugeron – seems best in this respect.

The cooling effects of a strong wind, flying spray and diving should be remembered, so hot drinks and waterproof anoraks are recommended. When using a wetsuit, a nylon boilersuit worn under all the diving gear can be first class for increasing cold resistance.

Conclusion
Before setting out on any boat trip, leave your route, destination and estimated time of return with your shore party; frequently they can monitor your progress through binoculars from a headland. With a pair of portable VHF radios much more effective contact can be kept, and the hot meal made ready for your return! The coastguard should be informed of your departure and your subsequent return.

Boat diving is very rewarding indeed. With a little forethought it is easy to render it much more enjoyable by anticipating events and paying attention to all the minor details that make it a more efficient operation. One way of discovering some of these tricks, and also learning how to handle boats generally, is to attend a boat handling course.

Figure 223a Launching an inflatable boat on a slip

Figure 223b Covering a pair of divers

Figure 223c Recovering the divers

Figure 223d Beaching an inflatable boat

Diving from Larger Vessels

The reason for the growing popularity of diving from larger vessels is not hard to find. It is usually more comfortable and convenient. In some ways it can be likened to living in a hotel and jumping out of the window for an excellent dive, followed by climbing back in and immediately stowing the gear, showering and being warm and comfortable again. These vessels provide a hassle-free means of diving amidst pleasant, like-minded company.

Larger vessels usually have reasonably sophisticated navigational capabilities, such as radar and a Decca navigator. These allow offshore sites, such as wrecks and shoals, to be pinpointed more easily.

It is normal for such vessels to provide inflatable boats as tenders and a supply of compressed air from a compressor. Many of them also have aqualung cylinders, diving weights and other equipment. This type of vessel, in spite of its cost, is thus ideal for the majority of more adventurous diving.

Charter Vessels

The range offered by these vessels can be hundreds of miles and many remote sites can only be reached safely in such boats. Diving safety, especially on deeper dives, is substantially increased by having a large platform from which to operate.

It is more natural and also more cost effective to explore dive sites from the sea. Diving trips aboard large vessels are naturally sea-based rather than land-based like car-and-inflatable dive trips. A week spent aboard such a vessel is a most effective way of achieving many big dives in a few days.

There are a number of hirers operating in British waters, though some of these are of a temporary nature. In Britain, the trend has been to convert old fishing vessels, although a few custombuilt vessels are now appearing. These should be much more convenient, because their features are customized to divers' requirements. There are charter vessels available for hire in most parts of the world where diving is popular. Some of these can be quite luxurious.

When booking these vessels, it is imperative to check

Figure 224 A group of divers return to harbour on a charter vessel after a day's diving

up in advance how far the skipper will take you (get written acceptance of your plans, subject to weather), what his attitude (and the attitude of the cook/crew) is to heavy weather and remote places, and what duties (if any) are expected of you. Experience of hiring the same vessel in two different seasons shows that the skipper and his team can make or break an expedition, and no amount of wrangling afterwards can redeem a lost holiday.

A second way to achieve the freedom of more distant areas is to hire a self-sail motor-sailer or cruiser. If you are a competent sailor, and if you can convince the hirer of this, then you have the capacity to sail and dive wherever you feel the weather conditions will allow. The space on such vessels is limited, and you should check how the hirer feels about loading his vessel with diving gear. Obviously, however, these vessels do not usually have the robustness and range of the larger charter vessels.

There exists yet another solution, perhaps best of all, and that is to form a syndicate of divers and buy and convert a secondhand fishing boat. The plan could then be to take turns running it during the summer months. Some diving groups have tackled this successfully, although the costs can be very high.

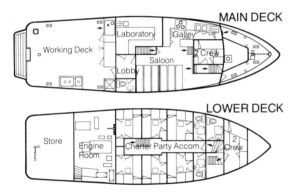

Figure 225 Plan of suitable charter vessel

The Charter Vessel in Action
It is futile to pretend that larger boats do not roll in the heavy seas experienced in offshore waters. Seasickness can be a problem, especially in the first couple of days of a vacation. It is best treated with one of the modern remedies that appear to cause less drowsiness. Test the effects of such a drug before using it while diving.

One of the experiences welcomed by most divers is helping with the running of the vessel. This allows them to gain experience in a wide range of skills from navigation to helming, although anchor watches rapidly become less than popular!

Diving from a Charter Vessel
Equipment is best stowed in bags or bins, and these should be well secured in anticipation of heavy weather. There is a lot more space on a charter vessel in which

divers can kit up. Nevertheless, tidiness is still important otherwise the whole deck space becomes cluttered with diving gear and underwater photography equipment.

The skipper's knowledge of divers' abilities is very important. Some are divers themselves, or have worked with divers, and have an excellent approach. Others have little conception of how powerless a diver can be when up against the might of the ocean. It should be clearly pointed out to such skippers that divers usually want to be dropped within a few metres of their dive site, that they only move at speeds below about 1 knot, that they cannot catch a boat being blown by a moderate or strong wind, that they can see very little from their eye height of a few centimetres when at the surface, and generally that they desire to be picked up smartly when they are exposed to a significant swell. They are also not very tolerant of a boatman who is not competent at handling his vessel or who appears to want to play games with it.

Time is at a premium on these vessels, as they move from dive site to dive site. It is advisable to have all the first-wave divers in an advanced state of readiness as the site is approached. Consequently, people should begin preparing for the dive and kitting up in good time. Meanwhile the second wave will handle the cover boat and generally assist the first wave. On their return, the roles are reversed.

Entry into the water is usually by means of a forward jump from the gunwale. Jump firmly into the water and, immediately you hit it, fin slightly away from the side of the boat to allow following divers a clear entry. The vessel should have its engine out of gear, but it is still worthwhile moving away to avoid making contact with a rolling vessel.

Exit from the water onto larger vessels is usually accomplished by entering a tender first, then transferring divers and equipment to the parent vessel. This is best achieved by having the large vessel make a lee for the tender; then the divers should work as a team rapidly to transfer the equipment back to the main vessel. With smaller charter vessels, and sometimes with larger ones in calm seas, it is possible to enter the vessel directly from the water by means of a diving ladder. This should extend at least 1 metre underwater, ideally 2, to allow for the roll of the vessel. Ideally it should stand at least one-third of a metre away from the side of the vessel and have a central spine with steps either side so that a diver can readily climb it with his aqualung and fins on. Do not underestimate the difficulty of attempting to leave the water by such a ladder if the vessel is rolling and the ladder less than ideal in its design.

After the dive, the tender is best secured in davits or brought aboard before travelling to the next site. Many tenders have been lost while being towed.

Smartness in timing and running the first dive of the day will usually mean that a second, distant, site can be reached in time to dive in good daylight, while the divers are complying with decompression table rules and losing nitrogen from their bodies.

Night Diving

To those who have never been on a night dive, the obvious question is 'Why bother?' Well, the answer lies in the fact that many underwater animals which hide during the day come out to feed at night and can be easily spotted in a diver's torch beam. Many of the species of crustaceans and molluscs use the night hours in this way, and some of their predators, such as conger eels, follow suit. By day, many of these species can only be seen at the back of holes or under rocks, but by night they can be found in open spaces.

Figure 226 A parrot fish asleep in its protective mucous cocoon

Although visibility under the water is obviously restricted by the darkness, this situation should not be confused with low-visibility situations caused by particles suspended in the water. At night, the clarity of the water is often very good, and this sensation is heightened owing to the fact that the diver's horizon is restricted to the penetration of his torch beam. This causes the diver to concentrate on the objects that his beam of light shines upon. Sites dived at night often seem to have a lot more life than when dived during the day. In reality this is not so, but during the day the diver's horizon is wider and he may not spot all that is there.

A trick worth remembering is that, because of the inability of low-angle sunlight to penetrate the water surface, the seabed becomes darkened (and nightlife becomes active) before it is fully dark at the surface. The clever night diver uses this fact to aid surface recovery by the cover party after his 'night' dive.

Even a complete night dive is seldom totally dark. If the diver switches off his torch, he will be surprised at the amount of light there is. Reflected sunlight from the moon and starlight are major sources, but once the diver's eyes have become accustomed to the dark he may see the water apparently glowing, and when he moves in the water the disturbance causes a display of phosphorescence. This is caused by phosphorescent plankton giving off a glow when they are disturbed.

The use of a torch allows the diver to see easily under the water and, because the light source is close to the objects on which it is shone, the full spectrum of light is available to illuminate them. This means that instead of the usual blue-green look seen in daylight, the bright colours that actually exist are revealed to the diver. Plants and animals that look black by daylight are suddenly shown to be coloured in scarlets and purples. The same effect is, of course, available to photographers using artificial light and can lead to a rewarding pastime.

The night dive therefore provides an experience in which the senses are sharpened, the animals are more obvious and the natural colours are fully restored by the torch light which the diver carries.

Night-Diving Techniques

Night diving can provide a rewarding experience but, to be done safely, it must be properly organized. All the standard rules of diving must apply and, in addition, there are several other things that must be in place before the dive marshal can be satisfied that everything will go according to plan.

The major additional problem to the night diver and to those responsible for his safety is the increased difficulty in communication, both between the divers and between the divers and the surface party. These problems demand separate consideration.

Communication between the divers can be maintained if both the divers carry a torch and shine the torch light on their hands as they use the normal diving signals. It is a good idea to draw the buddy's attention to the signal before it is made otherwise he may not notice it. Care should be taken not to shine your torch in your buddy's eyes since this spoils his night vision for some time. Buddy lines can be used on night dives, but usually the water clarity will be sufficiently good that they are not required. With a little care and practice, the diver should be able to keep visual track of his buddy by watching for his torch beam. If either torch fails during the course of the dive, it is a wise precaution to terminate the dive and to return to the surface, unless a spare is carried.

Communication from the divers to the cover party, whether they are in a boat or on the shore, is more difficult. Torches can again be used and the recommended lamp signals should be followed. Divers should avoid flashing their torches around on the surface, unless they are trying to signal, to avoid confusing the surface party. In sheltered and calm conditions (which are recommended for night diving), voice communication on the surface is fairly effective, although direction is hard to judge.

In order that the divers have a means of identifying where the cover party is, it is a good idea to place a light on the beach or raised up in a boat which the divers can easily see when they surface. The light on the beach could be sensibly replaced by the light of a barbecue bonfire, which then serves two purposes.

The selection of a site for a night dive should be such

that there are as many natural marks as possible which show the extent of the site and help prevent divers from becoming lost. A sheltered bay or cove provides an ideal place for a night dive, especially for those for whom it is a first-time experience. Other natural formations such as a cliff wall provide a very good guide on which to navigate out and back. The site should ideally not be too deep, since it is foolish to expose the divers to the rigours of deep diving on top of coping with darkness. Underwater incidents are much more difficult to deal with in the dark, so minimize the risk and keep it shallow. A site with a maximum depth of 10–15 metres is ideal.

There is a great deal to commend the use of a familiar daytime site for a first night dive. It may even be worth laying a weighted guideline on the bottom so that the divers are aided in their navigation.

An artificial reef under the water, such as a shallow wreck, also provides a good site for a night dive. It is easily approached and left by means of a buoyed shotline with which divers can easily maintain contact while underwater.

If divers wish to dive at night on a site with a more open aspect or with a moderate tidal stream flowing, then clearly they need to be covered by a boat. There are two main techniques for the boat to keep in contact with the divers. Both involve the use of surface marker buoys. It is possible for the boat to tether to the divers' buoy and

follow the divers around. The engine should not be used for this, as it would obviously endanger the divers when they surfaced. Consequently, the cover party must be prepared to row, otherwise the boat will impose a tremendous drag on the divers. The second technique is to mount a suitable light beacon on the surface marker buoy which the cover boat then follows at a safe distance. In either case, the boat should not attempt to cover more than one pair of divers at a time.

It is important when night diving that dive marshalling procedures are at a premium and that everyone is accounted for, both when entering and leaving the water. The marshal should ensure that everyone knows and understands signalling and emergency procedures before they get in the water.

If divers become separated from their cover party at night, it is highly likely that they will not be found until it gets light, by which time they could be in poor condition. For this reason, it is good practice for divers to carry personal flares when night diving. Thus, in the event of separation or other emergency, they can draw attention to themselves.

When carried out safely, night diving can be very well worth the effort involved.

Figure 227 A powerful underwater lamp lights up the nocturnal scene

Low-Visibility Diving

Low visibility is the reality for much of the diving that takes place in coastal and inland waters in Britain and northern Europe. There are many reasons why the visibility is restricted. Some of these are seasonal and others depend on the location.

In addition to visibility, there are other factors which reduce the diver's ability to see and communicate underwater. Darkness is an obvious example, but even highly overcast conditions can make a significant difference to underwater visibility. Artificial situations such as the interior of a wreck can also reduce the diver's ability to see. It is particularly important to avoid stirred-up sediment on dives since this will quickly reduce visibility, even in areas of quite good visibility.

Reasons for Diving in Water of Low Visibility

Many professional divers have no choice in the matter. The work which they have been employed to undertake may occur in waters which have naturally low visibility or the act of working itself may cause a disturbance which reduces visibility. Sport divers, however, have a choice as to where they dive and it is not so obvious why they should wish to dive in these conditions.

Many of the wrecks which attract divers lie on stretches of the coast where one or more of the conditions mentioned above are prevalent. If you want to dive such wrecks, then you need to train to cope with the conditions.

Marine archaeology is another area of sport diving which is likely to require diving in poor, if not zero, visibility conditions. In this case, most of the cause is likely to be the diver himself as he disturbs the bottom or uses an air lift to clear an area.

Other activities on the bottom, such as searches, are likely to cause similar problems. Grovelling for old bottles in shallow lakes with your arms deep in mud or searching for marine organisms that live in the bottom will tend to reduce visibility.

Since divers wish to take part in these activities in spite of the conditions, it has been necessary to develop diving techniques that allow them to be carried out in safety.

Techniques for Low-Visibility Diving

The major problem that low visibility causes to the diver is that it reduces his ability to communicate with his buddy and, unless steps are taken to compensate for this, both the diver and his buddy are put at increased risk.

In good visibility the diver and his buddy can swim up to several metres apart if they wish and still maintain good contact and communication. As visibility is reduced, maintaining contact between the divers becomes an increasing problem. With visibility of above 5 metres there should be no problem for the divers. At 2–5 metres, divers with good technique and good discipline should be able to maintain contact even when free swimming, although the use of a buddy line will make the task easier. Below 2 metres a buddy line is certainly necessary and below 1 metre a single diver operating on a lifeline to the surface may be more appropriate.

For free-swimming divers, there are a number of techniques which will help to reduce disturbance of the bottom, and hence increase visibility. The first is to master the art of buoyancy control so that the diver can move along above the bottom. Secondly, avoid using legs and fins for propulsion as this causes severe bottom disturbance. Pull yourself along using hands and arms. Boulders, kelp stipes, etc., make good pulling points. Keeping your fins still also has the advantage that your buddy, following close behind and trying to maintain contact, is less likely to have his mask dislodged by them.

Descents and ascents need especial care in low-visibility water. Many divers descend feet first to avoid banging into an unknown bottom with their head. Surfacing is usually performed cautiously, with a hand above the head, to avoid bumping into surface objects such as jetties or moored boats.

Loss of confidence is also a major problem in low visibility, especially for the inexperienced diver. In this sort of situation, a buddy line is highly recommended. Even for experienced divers the buddy line can be a valuable tool as it gives the freedom to go out of sight of each other yet still remain in contact. Communication between divers using the buddy line should be by the standard signals discussed on pp. 64–5.

The use of a buddy line between the divers in no way conflicts with the use of a line to the surface and a surface marker buoy. The two lines serve quite distinct roles. The first allows constant communication between the diving pair. The second keeps the surface party in contact with the divers.

There is a temptation to simplify matters and dispense with the buddy line by allowing the second diver to hold on to the surface marker buoy line some distance away from the diver with the reel. This method suffers from the fact that a diver holding onto the line makes the surface marker buoy even more difficult to control, and the natural tugging of the buoy on the line makes it very difficult for either diver to know whether messages are being sent or not.

Navigation while using a buddy line can be much more difficult. It is very easy for the leading diver to be drawn off course by a constant pull on the buddy line from his partner. In low visibility it is very difficult to realize that this is happening. The effect on navigation is exactly the same as that of a tidal stream side on to the divers and needs to be allowed for or guarded against.

Buddy lines have limited application for low-visibility diving in confined spaces or where there are obstructions on the bottom. Divers should carry a knife in case of inextricable entanglement, but in using it contact with buddy and surface will be lost. In these conditions other techniques may be more appropriate.

Roped-Diver Operation

For diving in very low visibility (of less than 1 metre) it is more appropriate to consider replacing free diving pairs with a diver secured by a lifeline to the surface and tended by another experienced diver.

This technique avoids the likelihood of divers getting in each other's way or displacing equipment, especially if a task of work is to be performed. The disadvantage of the technique is, of course, that any equipment failure, such as a regulator malfunction, is less easily dealt with if there is no buddy close at hand. This means that the link to the surface tender is vital. The tender should be an experienced diver who understands the problems faced by the roped diver. As a back-up to the diver, a fully kitted stand-by diver should be ready to enter the water and assist the roped diver should this become necessary.

The line itself needs to be of reasonable thickness. If it is too thin or too thick it is very difficult for the divers to handle. It should also be capable of taking the weight of a fully kitted diver. An 8–10 mm rope with a breaking strain of around 450 kg is appropriate. The length required may depend somewhat on the circumstances of the dive, but care should be taken not to let the rope get too long. About 30 metres is a manageable length. Any longer, and the likelihood of tangling or snagging increases. It is a good idea to mark the line in a suitable way at, say, 5-metre intervals, so that the tender can keep an easy check on how much line is out.

The line must be securely tied to the roped diver. The rope should be passed round the body under all equipment. The diver should be able to jettison tank, weight belt, etc., without having to remove the rope. The rope should be secured by a bowline and the knot made where the diver has access to it. The other end of the line should be in the hands of the tender, but he should tie the free end to an appropriate object (e.g. tree, boat, etc.) so that if it is jerked from his hands it is not lost.

Both diver and tender must know and recognize the standard signals, the communication procedures and what to do if messages are not properly received and understood. It is good practice for the diver and tender to rehearse the signals together before the diver enters the water.

The tender should be prepared to give all his attention to the diver while he is in the water. If he is not paying attention, he may miss some signals. The tender should ensure that the line is kept free of obstructions and that signals are passed quickly. Care should be taken to ensure that the line does not become tangled. Coiling and uncoiling the line as it comes in and out is good practice. The line should be neither too tight nor too slack. In the first case, the diver's progress will be impeded, while in the second, signals are difficult to transmit.

The tender must be prepared to react to any obvious difficulty or if signals remain unanswered or confused. The

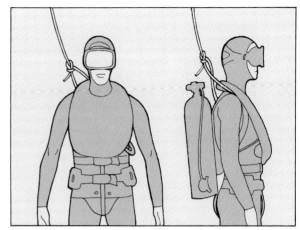

Figure 228 The rope must be attached to the diver underneath his main equipment and fastened with a secure knot, usually a bowline

best action is to mobilize the stand-by diver, who will go down the lifeline of the diver in trouble, but secured by his own line and tender. Trying to haul a diver to the surface on his lifeline may only compound the situation if the line is caught on an obstruction.

The tender should remember that the safety and comfort of the diver is his responsibility. It is bad practice to change tenders while the diver is down as signals may be lost or the diver be otherwise confused by the change.

From the diver's viewpoint, patience is the keyword. He must be prepared to wait until the line is right and the appropriate signals given before proceeding. Swimming against a taut line will only exhaust the diver. Similarly, if he returns faster than the line is recovered, he may miss a vital signal. If he should become entangled in the line, it is imperative he remains calm and then quietly sorts it out.

The stand-by diver should be fully kitted-up, and ready to enter the water before the diver actually enters the water himself. The stand-by needs to be prepared to act quickly in an emergency situation by going down the line and getting to the distressed diver quickly. A stand-by cylinder of air is a good idea in case it takes time to get a trapped diver clear of an obstruction.

In very low visibility small problems can be magnified. Claustrophobia can develop and the panic threshold can be lowered. It is important that in these situations the diver remains calm and gets himself out of his problem by slow, premeditated actions. A knife is essential, and a torch is a very good idea. If both hands are required for a task of work, the torch (or torches) can be mounted on a light plastic helmet which can be worn by the diver.

Drift Diving

Why?

Why should we wish to dive in tidal streams? In some cases it is a matter of necessity, as our desired site may lie in tidal waters. Many wrecks were lost for the very reason that they were caught in a strong tidal stream and swept onto rocks. In many other cases, however, it is a matter of choice. Moderate to strong tidal streams will tend to keep an area free of sediment and generally make for more interesting sites. A gentle tidal flow will even keep a fixed site, such as a wreck, free of the stirred-up sediment from other divers.

Added to this, where tidal movement is substantial, the very movement of the water brings suspended organisms as food for larger life forms, the food web is stimulated and life in these areas is generally very prolific. The final reason is simply that drift diving, when carried out safely, is a very pleasant and exhilarating experience since much ground can be covered with little effort.

We are now considering a situation directly opposite to normal diving, where we usually try to dive at slack water. Now we may be looking for tidal streams or not looking to avoid them, so we must consult the charts, tide tables and tidal-stream atlases to find out when to get an acceptable strength of tidal stream.

In passing, we should note a point of terminology. A tidal stream is a movement of water caused by the tides. A current is a movement of water caused by any other factors, such as ocean circulation, wind drift or river flow.

Operating in Moderate Tidal Streams

We shall define a moderate tidal stream as one having a speed of up to 2 knots. When we plan to enter significant tidal streams, there are several factors that must be taken into account. Most importantly, we must now always think in terms of movement and not of a static position. If you do nothing at all on a drift dive you will steadily move along the bottom, so this must be regarded as the norm. This orientation of attitude is the key to successful drift diving.

We must ensure that we have adequate surface cover. Normally this will take the form of an inflatable boat, although in some long, narrow straits it is possible to shore dive in tidal streams and still regain the shore. The best way to maintain contact is to have the divers marked with a surface marker buoy, which can easily be followed by the boat.

Surface marker buoys are almost always essential when drift diving. Make sure the buoy and its reel are of good quality. The reel must be convenient to use – that means it should be fast and easy to reel in and out. There should be enough line (at least twice the intended depth) and the line should be thin to minimize drag on the water (25 kg breaking strain braided fishing line is ideal). The buoy should be large enough to be visible (the inflatable ones have a distinct convenience) to the cover boat from a reasonable distance and should have a buoyancy of 10–20 kg (or even more in offshore conditions).

Be careful to enter the water together with your buddy, otherwise you may become separated. The best way to do this is to enter the water holding onto a grabline at the side of the boat, then assemble at a prearranged point, dive together, and stay together throughout the dive.

It is very important to keep together while underwater. To do this it is necessary to operate as a team by arranging a plan and sticking to it. You must also realize that holding onto a rock while your buddy drifts on is the equivalent of your finning away hard in still water.

Try to avoid being swept into eddies or behind rocks or into gullies (i.e. into stationary water) while your buddy is still in the tidal stream. You will separate in, literally, a very few seconds in these circumstances. Once you are separated by a distance greater than visibility, you will be very lucky to re-establish contact, so take the appropriate care.

If by any chance you do become separated, you should look around for a few seconds to attempt to locate your buddy. Look both for your buddy and also just above the bottom for the slightly lighter colour of your partner's bubble stream. If you see nothing, drift on for a few more seconds and, if you still see nothing, you must make for the surface alone. Be very careful to maintain an upward direction throughout your solo ascent.

Responsibility of Cover Boats

The team in the cover boat must keep the divers' surface marker buoy in sight at all times. The best way to do this is to circle it continuously, so that contact is maintained, especially in rougher seas. As it is difficult to follow more than one surface marker buoy at a time, there should only be one diving pair in the water at any time, unless very similar dive plans have been intentionally organized in advance.

The cover party must be aware of the danger of the possible presence of surface overfalls that could prevent them following the surface marker buoy. In such a case the dive plan should be modified in advance. If divers do get to the other side of heavy overfalls, then the cover boat should first see if it can go around the broken water. If not, it will have to attempt to pass through the overfalls – this can be hair-raising, although large inflatable boats are very seaworthy craft and can take much rougher seas than might be imagined.

Remember that the divers will expect to find the cover boat close by when they surface. In most circumstances the absence of the cover boat could considerably embarrass the divers. For this reason a sound boat with a reliable engine should always be employed.

Surface Separation

There is a further danger of separation – separation on the surface due to mist or poor visibility. This can cause buddies to become separated from each other or from the cover boat. It may also cause the cover boat to lose the parent vessel. It is important, therefore, that you only attempt drift dives in conditions of good visibility or, at the most, very light mist, unless you are totally sure of your position. It is also possible for divers to lose sight of the cover boat in a very heavy swell and such conditions are best avoided when drift diving.

While the divers and the cover boat should never become separated, the fact remains that this sometimes happens. At such times it is extremely useful (and reassuring) to be able to attract the attention of the cover boat. It may be possible to do this with a whistle, although these are difficult to blow effectively when they are full of water and your lips are cold. Alternatively, some divers carry a small orange flag wrapped around a collapsible mast. This can be extended to about 2 metres and then waved to attract the attention of the cover party.

The most effective way of attracting attention is to ignite a flare. Waterproof flares are available with an orange smoke at one end and a red flare at the other, and some lifejackets are provided with pockets in which to carry them. This, of course, is an extreme measure and may also alert other water users and watchers, so only use it when really necessary. If you do fire a flare, it is best to use the orange smoke in daylight hours. Hold the flare downwind and fire it positively. If you find yourself in a position in which you consider that a flare is required, make sure that you use your flare to maximum advantage – in other words, fire it when you think it has the best chance of being seen.

If the divers and the cover boat become separated, it is imperative that a sensible procedure is followed in attempting to re-establish contact. The cover vessel should patrol downstream in the direction that the tidal stream is flowing. Note that even a strong wind has only a little effect on divers floating on the surface, even if they have their lifejackets fully inflated. There may even be some merit in dropping a reference buoy if the cover boat is well offshore – at least you then have a reference point for your search. You should have worked out in advance the strengths and the directions of the tidal streams at different times of your dive, partly in anticipation of this possibility.

If you are one of the pair of divers who are separated from your cover boat, then you are in an invidious position. Remain together (fasten a buddy line between each other) and conserve your air in case you subsequently have to make a difficult exit through heavily foaming breakers. If you are within reach of the shore then you can attempt to reach it – many have! Do not remain tied together during an attempt to get out on a very rough shoreline. It is advisable to retain your weight belt unless buoyancy is a problem, in which case you should jettison it without delay. In some circumstances, it even may be prudent to jettison your cylinders. If reaching shore is not possible, then remain calm and make yourself as noticeable as possible with whistles, flags and even flares.

From the seriousness of the procedures just described it should be very apparent that you must not become separated from your cover party, so take the precautions to dive sensibly and with prior planning.

Figure 229 The cover boat keeps the divers' surface marker buoys in sight at all times and marks their presence by flying the divers' 'A' flag

Deep Diving

For the purposes of restricting this discussion the assumption has been made that no person reading this book for the first time is contemplating diving beyond 40 metres. The *BSAC Manual of Advanced Diving* treats deep diving in more detail and includes a detailed discussion of diving demanding stage decompression.

Deep diving is a most emotive subject in diving circles. Some divers rather foolishly consider that the maximum depth that a diver has attained is a measure of his competence. A safe dive to a depth greater than that previously visited will add to the diver's experience, but its value is not proportional to the depth reached. Of course, for many diving is an adventurous sport and one way of achieving that adventure is to dive deep. For others, who wish to experience as much of the ocean as possible, to penetrate deeply is to explore a little more of the wonderful underwater realm.

However, deep diving is accompanied by extra dangers and the BSAC recognizes the need for clear, sound advice for potential deep divers, but advice that is tempered by the need for caution.

It is difficult to define a deep dive. For a novice, any dive over about 15 metres is deep, whereas for an experienced diver 30 metres is not tremendously deep. However, 30 metres is a good point to set as the limit beyond which all diving should be regarded as deep. The comments offered here apply especially to diving in British waters. In warmer and clearer waters some of the difficulties are somewhat overstated, although most of them still apply.

The Increased Risks of Deep Diving

There are increased risks involved in deep diving and these must be clearly understood.

> The risk of serious decompression sickness increases with the rapid decrease in permitted bottom time when the diver is deeper than 30 metres.
>
> Poor light, often poorer visibility, increased cold, unfamiliarity with the surroundings are all factors that can contribute to the higher risk of the diver being affected by nitrogen narcosis.
>
> Nitrogen narcosis means that careful monitoring of depth, bottom time and air consumption is made less certain just when more care is actually necessary.
>
> For many divers there is a psychological fear of deepness and darkness. This problem can exacerbate nitrogen narcosis as well as contribute to other problems.
>
> Air consumption is increased not only by depth but also by the cold, by anxiety and by the heavier exertion of diving and breathing at depth.
>
> Loss of buoyancy at depth can cause considerable problems for all divers. The use of buoyancy compensation devices such as drysuits, adjustable-buoyancy lifejackets and buoyancy compensators, is essential on these dives.
>
> Diver rescue poses a problem at any time but the above factors compound a rescue from depth. In addition, the sheer physical distance to the surface complicates any rescue.
>
> The limited availability of emergency services in the event of an in-water accident or a post-dive decompression problem complicates a potential deep-diving incident.

Having evaluated deep diving carefully, why should a person wish to expose himself to these risks? Some divers wish to explore new sites, particularly to investigate specific wrecks or examine marine life. Other divers wish to dive deep to increase their personal experience and performance and to further their sense of enjoyment and adventure.

Categories of Deep Diving

It is useful to categorize deep dives by depth bands.

30–40 metres

Increased care and experience is required for most dives. Nervous and unskilled divers should think carefully before entering this region. It is important to consider that dives below 30 metres are not for everyone, no matter how long they have been diving. Even very experienced divers need to be more aware, taking into consideration not only their own ability, but also that of their buddy.

40–50 metres

This is the kind of diving that should only be undertaken by a small proportion of sport divers. Many divers do not wish to undertake these dives, nor are they competent to do so. To dive to these depths in safety, you must be very experienced, dive-fit, and demand the right conditions and back-ups.

50 metres +

The BSAC strongly recommends that dives in excess of 50 metres should not be undertaken by sport divers. Diving in this region, especially in British waters, requires a very high degree of competence, aptitude and experience and must be considered the domain of a very few.

The above comments apply particularly to most British waters. When the water is warm and/or clear, some of the deep diving constraints are reduced, thus allowing somewhat greater depths to be attained in many parts of the world.

Personal Equipment

The diver must be thoroughly familiar with his personal equipment. He needs to be able to put his hand on his direct-feed inflator, say, without hesitation. Many problems on deep dives are caused by divers using unfamiliar equipment acquired just for this dive, thus causing problems with buoyancy and ill-fitting harnesses, etc. Design your system for deep diving and know how to use it.

Air Supply

A totally adequate air supply is essential for deep diving. The majority of incidents are caused by an inadequate supply of air, often resulting in too rapid ascents. It is an excellent idea to plan to end the dive with a reserve of about one-third of your air remaining. This air can also be useful on the surface when there is a swell.

It would be unwise to recommend cylinder capacities for deep diving as air consumption varies for each individual and is also dependent on the underwater activity pursued. Calculation and provision of sufficient air is the responsibility of the divers, dive leaders and group leader.

The quality and reliability of the regulator is also extremely important. An unbalanced regulator with poor inhalation and exhalation resistance will result in an increase in air consumption. A regulator which is of good quality and is reliable will give considerable confidence to its user in addition to its ease of use.

Although running out of air on a deep dive is a rare occurrence, it can be a most frightening experience. Regulator failure is very rare, but, nevertheless, some thought must be given to alternative air supplies. These could be an octopus regulator (i.e. one with two second stages), a complete second regulator mounted on an independent manifold, or a small (pony) cylinder mounted on the main cylinder and fitted with an independent regulator. Some divers even fit two full-size cylinders on their back as a twin, but each is fitted with a separate regulator and no manifold is fitted.

Buoyancy

Buoyancy loss need not be a problem with the use of direct-feed inflators. However, it is important that divers are aware of buoyancy loss and compensate during their descent rather than waiting until the target depth and maximum negative buoyancy is reached. The total buoyancy loss can be as great as 6–9 kg at a depth of 30 metres when wearing a thick wetsuit.

A direct-feed inflator on the adjustable-buoyancy lifejacket is essential for dives over 30 metres when wearing a wetsuit. However, in the absence of an inflator it is necessary to use the air cylinder on the lifejacket to compensate for buoyancy loss. Oral inflation by removing the regulator mouthpiece at depth with the subsequent dangers connected with nitrogen narcosis (dropping or fumbling the regulator) present too great a risk.

When using the cylinder in this manner, divers must be conscious that the air in the lifejacket should not be dumped until the ascent is under way. Divers should also know the correct method of controlled buoyant ascent. This involves slowly venting air on ascent to achieve a normal rate of ascent, and not dumping all the air at depth, which will result in negative buoyancy.

A drysuit gives much better and safer control over buoyancy at depth than a wetsuit. All modern drysuits are fitted with direct-feed inflators. To prevent the suit squeezing, it is necessary to bleed air into the suit as the diver descends, so the question of negative buoyancy does not really arise. Of course, the full buoyancy of the lifejacket is still available should an emergency arise. For this reason, plus its greater insulation properties at depth, the drysuit finds favour amongst most divers who regularly dive deep.

Instruments and Accessories

It is vital that depth and time are accurately recorded on every dive. On deep dives the inaccurate recording of times and depths has led to many decompression and other incidents. Consequently, instruments must be regularly checked for accuracy and have bold, luminous faces. At depth, with the problems of narcosis and poor light conditions, they must be clearly readable.

The use of a bottom timer, which automatically switches on and records bottom time (provided you initially set it), and a depth gauge with a maximum depth recording needle has much to commend it. Further developments in decompression computer technology have made these computers the ultimate solution to deep diving instrumentation.

A powerful, reliable torch can transform an uneasy dive in poor visibility to one in which the objective may be seen, explored and enjoyed in relative ease. It also provides the buddy divers with a means of location and identification in the gloom.

A decompression table slate is essential on these types of dives for reference during the dive, although they should not be used for dive planning during the dive. Do not try to memorize dive times for different depths. Instead, write out the figures for the planned dive on a separate slate.

Deep-Diving Procedures

Boat Support

It should be readily apparent that deep diving requires considerable organization and equipment and, therefore, the amount of support required is much higher than for normal diving. Deep diving is certainly easier to conduct if carried out from the more spacious platform of a charter vessel rather than a small, cramped inflatable. The larger vessel is usually equipped with an echo sounder, position-fixing equipment, radio and ample deck space on which to organize the equipment.

It is important that the skipper is fully briefed before diving operations begin and that, in turn, he briefs the divers concerning his way of operating. Ensure that you have clearly informed the skipper of the abilities and limitations of divers in the water.

For deep diving on wrecks and rock features, it is essential that sites are pinpointed accurately and divers put on the site rather than near it! Ensure that a shotline or anchor warp leads the divers to the intended site by accurate position fixing, then check the depth with the echo sounder.

A spacious inflatable can provide a platform for deep-diving operations. It will probably require a somewhat higher degree of pre-planning and thought to achieve the same level of comfort and safety when compared with

Figure 230 For deep diving, a shotline is used to mark the dive site and spare sets are attached to it at decompression stop levels. In low visibility the divers use a line and reel to maintain contact with the shotline

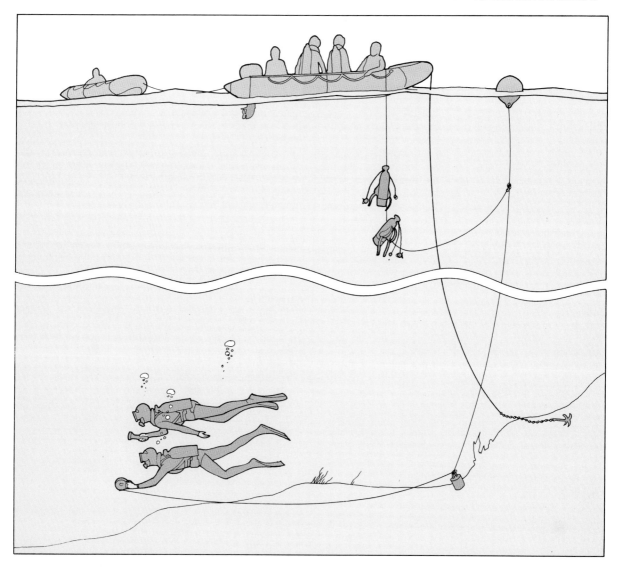

charter vessels. The use of both echo sounder and radio is recommended. Two inflatables, operating as a team, provide a good, safe platform in most conditions.

Buddy Diving Procedure

Individual preparations should be fastidious, yet relaxed. Personal diving equipment should be checked thoroughly. The dive leader and his buddy must plan their particular dive to fit into the overall diving plan with particular emphasis on time, air consumption, routes to and from the datum point, and any special responsibilities related to the overall plan. Each diver must familiarize himself with his buddy's equipment – inflation and deflation systems, releases and alternative air supplies.

Entry into the water should be at the group leader's instruction. After checking each other at the surface, watches are zeroed and the descent commences with both divers leaving the surface *together*. Avoid wasting valuable bottom time with too slow a descent. Maintain neutral buoyancy at intervals during the descent. Throughout the descent, position yourself so you can monitor your buddy's progress (i.e. face to face) and use the shotline hand over hand. Always maintain the same position on the shotline as this helps overcome any feeling of disorientation and, in the event of nitrogen narcosis, is very reassuring.

At the target depth, check each other again. Be decisive – if the actual depth is significantly deeper than planned and if you lack the experience and planning to go deeper, then the dive should be abandoned. At the target depth, continue to monitor your depth, time and air carefully and check with your buddy at frequent intervals throughout the dive. Make sure when a change of direction is made that your buddy is aware of this and follows the new route. Monitor yourself and your buddy for signs of narcosis. If these become severe, you should attract your buddy's attention, give a clear signal to abort the dive and return to the surface.

Remember that deep diving is about being safe. Move deliberately and carefully and be observant of your surroundings, especially their fascinations and potential hazards. Avoid stirring up silt, as you will probably want to return to the shotline along the same route.

Always allow enough time to relocate the shotline and be conscious of disorientation in reduced visibility. Tiredness and cold can make the return seem longer than the outward leg, so plan to arrive at the shotline with a little time to spare before the planned ascent.

At the 6m level, check your dive time and maximum depth with your buddy prior to ascending. Careful timing at significant depths is not always easy and is consequently prone to error. Try to avoid taking the bottom time to its final limit. Ascend at a rate of 15 metres/minute and remember that if you ascend more slowly you are adding to your bottom time. Air used for buoyancy compensation during the dive should not be vented off prior to the ascent but, instead, should be used to give very slight positive buoyancy by progressive venting during the ascent.

At the surface, the back-up team should assist you into the support craft. De-kit precisely, stowing your equipment as you do. Have a careful debriefing with your buddy and make your report to the group leader.

Conclusion

Some of the added risks and dangers of deep diving have been identified here. Remember that these increase in proportion to the depth. However, with the above points in mind, deep diving in the 30–40-metre region can be enjoyed, but only by those divers with sufficient experience and knowledge to do so.

Deep diving is a challenging area of our sport, but one that requires a high practical level of expertise.

Figure 231   Divers return to decompress on a decompression bar after a deep dive

Adventurous Diving

Adventurous diving is difficult to define. It is not solely advanced diving, although this enters the equation. It is not just diving which involves an increased risk factor for its own sake. It is not merely exploratory diving, although, again, this is an important facet. It need not happen exclusively on expeditions, although these usually contain adventurous diving in good measure. It is a combination of these things, and more.

Adventurous diving is more easily understood if we go back to the roots of sport diving, when people dived just for the fun of it. Every dive was an adventure into the unknown. Training, while recognized as very important, was certainly only seen as a means to an end. The outward-looking urge was what drove the more enlightened of our predecessors onwards to greater achievement.

Adventurous diving may entail diving well offshore, in deep water and in substantial tidal streams, in the very places that most divers have, in the past, avoided. In fact, remoteness is one of the key attractions. It means applying the attitudes of the pioneers of diving to our modern levels of attainment.

The justification for adventurous diving is not hard to find. It is, in essence, an attempt to satisfy man's outward urge – his desire to 'boldly go where no man has gone before'. All adventure sports embrace this attitude in good measure.

Sport diving is an adventure sport. It can and, indeed, must take its place alongside the other great outdoor adventure sports of mountaineering, speleology, ocean sailing, flying, etc.

What are its rewards? Essentially, the pleasures are those of exploration of both the environment and of our own selves. Furthermore, the greatest reward is that of achieving the 'ocean experience'. This is the desire to see and experience the ocean in all its moods. To see the small creatures of the reefs and also dive with the great oceanic sea mammals. To explore rock formations, such as tunnels and pinnacles, and to dive onto ocean shoals. To dive deep, not for its own sake, but because one wants to see as much of the ocean as possible.

The ocean experience is exceedingly difficult to put into words. It is perhaps best expressed as the desire to be at one with all aspects of the ocean and to overcome the limitations placed upon us by human physiology and our rather puny and ill-adapted physique. The rewards can be those of being first to see some new sight or observe some novel life form.

Many divers consider that we must explore our ocean realm more fully. As divers, this is surely our right and, indeed, our responsibility.

Figure 232   Adventure lies in exploring man-made reefs such as this substantial wreck or (figure 233) beautiful coral walls descending to the ocean floor

Figure 233

Shipwrecks

Wreck diving is the *raison d'être* for many experienced divers. For them, there is nothing quite to compare with the excitement of the descent to a 'virgin' wreck. Most divers, as they progress through their training, have the desire to explore wrecks, not just for their intrinsic interest but also for the rich life they hold.

The concentration of wrecks varies around the world. Any area of sea or waterway where there has been extensive shipping or where modern wars have been fought will be rich in wrecks. Hazardous coasts with isolated dangers that intrude into the shipping lanes or fishing grounds will also have a history of wrecks. The coasts of the British Isles qualify on all these counts and are especially rich in wrecks. Other parts of the world are famous for ancient wrecks, especially the Mediterranean or the coral-encrusted areas of the Caribbean. Some of these hold archaeological artefacts of enormous scientific and historical significance. Others have attracted a more adventurous group of excavators who are concerned basically with the market value of the hidden relics.

Ownership

Every wreck is owned by somebody. This is usually the owner at the time of the sinking, the state (for very old wrecks), an insurance company, a salvage firm or perhaps an enterprising diving club. With the exception of designated historic wrecks or recognized war graves, both of which are usually protected by government regulations, you may dive any wreck in the open sea. However, those in harbours, anchorages and fairways are often subject to local byelaws and the control of an appropriate local official.

What you must *not* do is to tamper with a wreck belonging to someone else or to remove items from it unless you have the owner's permission. This extends to those small trophies and souvenirs beloved of so many divers.

Causes of Shipwrecks

Vessels are wrecked for a great number of reasons. The foremost of these is bad weather, such as high winds, rough seas or fog. All of these can cause a master to lose either his way or control of his vessel. In bygone days, before the advent of navigational aids such as radar, sailing vessels were much more at the mercy of the weather than nowadays and many vessels were lost because of this.

Hazards to navigation, such as reefs and small islands, have often led to ships being lost. Many have run aground and have been subsequently refloated. Others have not been so fortunate and have become a total loss. The human errors of masters, navigators and helmsmen have been responsible for the loss of vessels down the years.

Vessels have also been lost because they became disabled, due to power failure, steering faults, dismasting, etc., and have drifted out of control onto some hazard.

Collisions have been the cause of many shipping losses.

The sheer volume of shipping in small, concentrated areas such as harbours, estuaries and narrow straits had led to many collisions and losses because of lack of sea room or manoeuvrability.

In times of war many ships go to the bottom due to mines, torpedoes, aircraft, gunfire or other methods. The end result is the same – a desperate human tragedy at the time and, years later, another splendid wreck for divers to explore.

Wartime Wrecks

Many of the wrecks around the European coasts are the result of hostilities in the two world wars. Having been badly damaged at the time of their loss, many of them are now in danger of collapse. Due care should, therefore, be exercised on these war losses, and, indeed, on all old wrecks. Large numbers of wartime wrecks contain live ammunition such as shells and mines. These can be very dangerous and certainly must not be tampered with, nor should any attempt be made to recover them.

Wrecks in Fresh Water

We should not assume that all wrecks are in the sea. Some wreckings have occurred in fresh-water lakes and waterways. Most of what has been said still applies. In addition, one should remember that these wrecks can often be rather deep and in rather poor visibility. This is frequently offset by the superior state of preservation in which they may be found and the quite different atmosphere which surrounds them.

Life on Wrecks

Wrecks in the sea provide an ideal place for the colonization of marine life. A wreck on a muddy bottom will become an oasis for encrusting marine life. Any wreck that projects off a flat bottom into a tidal stream will also provide a solid substrate on which filter-feeding life can grow. Fish, in particular, are attracted to the shelter provided by wrecks.

Some fish life can be a slight danger to the unwary diver. Conger eels live in dark holes and, not surprisingly, resent being prodded with diving knives. In warmer waters, moray eels also inhabit wreck crevices. Although not naturally aggressive, both types can inflict an unpleasant bite if provoked sufficiently.

The depth at which a wreck lies governs the types of marine life to be found there. Shallow wrecks in temperate waters are usually covered with a profuse growth of weed. In warm waters, coral growths can quite quickly mask a wreck and will eventually hide it completely.

Condition of Shipwrecks

The quality of a wreck dive is dependent on a number of factors such as visibility, underwater conditions, diving support, experience of the divers and, of course, the condition of the wreck itself.

The wreck's condition can depend on its age, its

exposure to wave and tidal action, and its depth. The material used to build the ship controls how the vessel will degrade. Wooden vessels will break up quite easily and will also be attacked by some sea life. Iron vessels will rust, of course, although when the iron corrodes it may do so preferentially by acting as an anode and help to preserve the brass and copper fittings.

If the wreck has been commercially salvaged or dispersed with explosives to prevent it becoming a shipping hazard then it may hardly be recognizable.

It should be possible from research to judge the condition of a wreck before visiting the site itself, by taking into account the above factors.

Best Type of Wrecks for Diving

This largely depends on what your personal aspirations are and naturally these will also reflect your standard of training. Obviously, the ease of access will also have a considerable bearing. Most divers consider that a substantially intact wreck in an accessible site, i.e. a depth of about 20–30 metres of clear warm water, is the ideal. Unfortunately, these are in rather short supply!

A wreck represents a time capsule for its period in history. For nautical archaeologists and for many enthusiastic amateur divers this can be very important, irrespective of the condition of the vessel.

Equally, a gold-carrying wreck, smashed up on a beach, will probably be of much more interest to would-be treasure hunters than to divers, who prefer an intact 50-metre-long vessel in 25 metres of water.

Vessels lost by collision can often yield the best wreck diving because they have usually been lost in the deeper water of a shipping lane, often in enclosed and relatively shallow coastal water. Those wrecks that remain will generally be in deeper water as wrecks in shallow channels will either have already been salvaged or dispersed In addition, these wrecks can often be traced through local archives, as described below.

An undiscovered wreck is the dream of most divers. The thrill of being first down, with the ever-present lure of 'hidden-treasure', is probably the force motivating most enthusiastic wreck divers.

Locating Wrecks

Locating wrecks which are not well known can provide divers with a great challenge. We should distinguish between two different problems – locating an exact position on the seabed where a wreck is definitely known to be and finding a wreck whose position is known only approximately or, in the case of ancient wrecks, not known at all.

How we go about locating a position on a stretch of water depends on the environment of that water. Thus, if the position is well out to sea, out of sight of land, we have no option but to use some electronic means of position location. If off a plain, flat, featureless coast, we again have problems, and electronic position fixing is once more important. When operating off mountainous or other well-featured coasts, it is usually quite easy to find at least two good transits (see p. 167), although describing these so that another person can use them may be quite difficult. Estuaries usually provide easy conditions for the location of transits, as do small areas of fresh water.

Figure 234   Divers explore the flattened wreck of the Balboa in Georgetown harbour in Grand Cayman

Wreck Diving

Equipment

In addition to the diving equipment used for normal diving, there are several items that can be very useful in wreck diving. The first of these is a small, very sharp knife for cutting fishing line and nets. A powerful torch allows detailed examination of all those intriguing nooks and crannies with which most wrecks abound. A protective helmet has obvious uses in enclosed spaces, and those that allow the attachment of head torches are particularly useful.

A powerful torch is also good for locating your buddy in low visibility. In good visibility a high-power lamp will allow you to work slightly apart and still know where your buddy is.

Protective gloves are worthwhile even in warm waters – sharp metal plays havoc with hands or neoprene mittens. Many keen wreck divers wear a nylon overall over their suit to protect it. This is worthwhile, but you must ensure that the suit is close fitting and has no loose parts that can snag on projections or sections which can trap pockets of air.

Some divers go wreck diving with large numbers of tools clipped to themselves. These are then employed to detach and recover souvenirs, such as portholes, from the wrecks. Unless you own the wreck or have the owner's full permission, this practice is illegal. If vigorously pursued it has the danger of bringing divers into disrepute as looters.

Slack Water

If the wreck lies in an area subject to tidal streams, it is generally best to dive at slack water. In strong tidal streams or in poor visibility this is usually essential. The exception is when a number of dive pairs are diving on a small wreck; the presence of a slight tidal stream can help by sweeping away the suspended matter stirred up by the previous dive pairs.

Securing to the Wreck

If the wreck is not buoyed on your arrival, whatever method you use to locate it, you will ultimately be best advised to drag a grapnel or anchor into the wreck and buoy the line. The first pair onto the wreck should tie the grapnel line onto a piece of wreckage. This is released by the final pair of divers, usually at the beginning of their dive.

If you have more than one diving boat, the best way of diving a wreck is to anchor one boat directly to the wreck, while the other boat covers the dive pairs. With only one boat it is better to buoy the wreck and leave the boat free for cover purposes.

If the wreck is permanently buoyed with a strong line, then it is more usual for the dive boat to tie onto the marker buoy.

On deep wrecks it may be advisable to arrange a shotline that is vertical, or nearly so, in order that the descent and ascent are as short as possible. Stage decompression can be undertaken on the shotline.

The Descent

Descend the anchor line or buoyline hand over hand, periodically checking your buddy as you go. Many divers experience some apprehension at the beginning of a long descent to an unseen wreck. The sight of the wreck usually removes this feeling. In low visibility, it is advisable to descend the last piece of shotline in a feet-first position. The last few metres of rope can be marked with a different colour to indicate that you have nearly reached the wreck.

If the shotline is vertical, it is easy to become disoriented during the descent. Try to avoid this by observing natural phenomena such as the direction of the tidal stream or the angle of sunlight. Failing these, a compass can be employed. It is useful to know the orientation of the wreck in order to relate your dive pattern to the wreck layout, and to report to later divers. However, the effects of a large mass of iron on the compass can be significant.

In poor visibility or on very broken wrecks with wreckage scattered everywhere, it can be difficult to retain your orientation. Locating the shotline for your ascent can then prevent problems.

Movement on Wrecks

Most wrecks contain silt and mud, so you should fin just above the bottom to avoid stirring up too much sediment. When there is a tidal stream running, it is excellent practice to move to the lee of the wreck or into its holds, out of the tidal flow. The water movement is then only a problem when you briefly move from one sheltered area to another or when you round the extremities of the wreck.

Do not forget to explore the seabed around a large wreck, because many unusual items may have fallen off. Masts lying on the seabed are usually worth a look, with interesting fittings to examine, often with lots of encrustations growing on them.

You must be rather cautious in your movements because wrecks contain a number of hazards. There are almost always many sharp edges and projections – these can easily damage hands and suits. In addition, large sections of wreckage which appear quite solid and substantial can be delicately poised and could damage a diver if disturbed. Many wrecks are fished heavily by sport fishermen and consequently there is much lost fishing tackle with numerous sharp hooks just waiting to snag the unwary. Monofilament nylon fishing line is virtually invisible underwater and can easily entangle the diver. Wrecks often also snag the nets of commercial fishermen and these can pose quite a danger to the incautious diver, especially in low visibility. Obviously, a sharp knife that is easily accessible is essential for all wreck diving.

A further caution concerns diving on fairly deep wrecks. The apprehension felt by many divers in these circumstances can significantly increase the effects of nitrogen narcosis. You should watch for this in both yourself and your buddy. While on the subject of deep wreck diving, some wreck dives will need stage decompression, which requires special techniques and precautions.

The Ascent

It is important that you leave sufficient time towards the end of your dive to relocate the shotline; on deep wrecks this may be imperative. If the visibility is good and the wreck in good, recognizable condition, then this relocation is relatively easy, although later divers may still have difficulty due to sediment stirred up by earlier divers. On broken wrecks and/or in low visibility it can be exceedingly difficult and the use of a distance line from the bottom of the shotline may be well advisable. An excellent procedure is to fasten a flashing electronic beacon to the bottom of the shotline on your descent. This will be visible over a long distance and even in poor visibility can be seen for several metres.

Try to locate the shotline with a minute or two of dive time still remaining. Ascend the line, hand over hand, frequently checking your buddy. On deeper dives, there should be a spare aqualung (fitted with an octopus regulator) fastened to the shotline at 9 metres.

Penetration

Some divers will want to penetrate into the inside of a wreck. The surface is then no longer directly accessible and the dangers inherent in this should be clearly understood. Stirred-up sediment or collapsing structures can very easily prevent your return to the entrance. If you must go inside a wreck, then you must be attached to a lifeline tended by your buddy, who should remain outside the wreck. You *must* be appropriately trained, experienced and equipped for this type of diving.

Penetrating a large wreck is an advanced diving procedure and is dealt with fully in the *BSAC Manual of Advanced Diving*.

Figure 235   A shotline is dropped on the wreck so that divers can descend directly, explore the wreck and return to make their ascent by the shotline

Cliff Diving

Cliff diving is one of the most exhilarating types of scenic diving and is actively pursued by many divers. In warmer climates the term 'wall diving' is used to describe this type of dive. The rewards are great, provided that a few hazards are kept in mind.

Types of Cliff

The best types of cliff diving take place on vertical or overhanging rock faces. Sometimes the term is also applied to very steep boulder slopes and to mixed slopes of mud, sand, boulders and rocks.

The only really important distinction with steep rock cliffs is whether the bottom of the cliff is within the range of air-breathing divers or whether it lies deeper, beyond the reach of sport divers. This has a considerable bearing on the safety aspects of the diving.

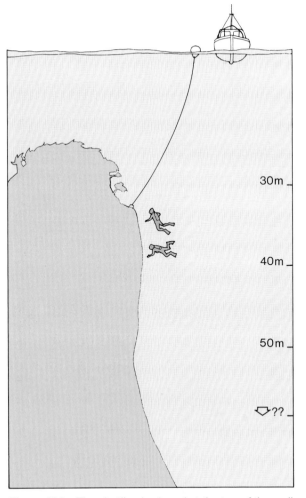

30m

40m

50m

▽??

Figure 236   The shotline is placed at the top of the wall and the divers descend the wall taking care to maintain neutral buoyancy

Cliff Diving

Many divers find that 'sky diving' down a huge, vertical cliff by using buoyancy control is a most exhilarating experience. It is possible to undertake a 'big' dive with little physical effort. Additionally, the encrusting marine life is very often profuse and is set out in such a way as to make its observation and photography both easy and enjoyable.

There are, however, a number of extra dangers which are associated with diving on walls. These essentially derive from the fact that there is no bottom directly under the diver. This means that there is a danger of sinking to greater depths than planned or even beyond the reach of potential rescuers. On some walls you appear to be hovering over a black pit and many divers find this psychologically disconcerting.

Some cliffs also lie near strong tidal streams and there can be vertical eddies running down the wall. In addition, in poor visibility it is fairly easy to become disoriented and to lose sight of the wall, leaving you with a mid-water ascent. All these factors add together to suggest that you should delay this sort of wall diving until you are a relatively experienced diver.

A variety of precautions should be taken when cliff diving. The divers should be experienced, and in diving trim. They should not be of a particularly nervous disposition. The divers' buoyancy must be well adjusted and they must be particularly careful not to be overweighted. The use of a drysuit is recommended for most cliff diving because of the precise control of buoyancy that it allows. Torches are useful, especially if the cliff is dark and/or deep or if it faces north and is consequently in shadow for most of the day. Buddy lines are occasionally useful, the more so in poor visibility. Surface marker buoys are not normally used, unless there is a significant tidal stream and the plan is to drift along the face. A shotline down the cliff can be a useful guide. If the cliff does not start at the surface, it is extremely good practice to have a shotline leading to the edge of the wall if you plan a deep exploration. This, of course, will have to be positioned by members of the back-up dive team.

Control your buoyancy finely or descend and ascend the cliff in an upright position. Try to avoid stirring up sediment off the wall and having to descend and ascend in your own cloud of gloom. Be ever cautious about the danger of sinking too deep.

Figure 237   The life on vertical faces can be profuse but changes will be observed at different depth levels

Figure 237

Ocean Diving

Diving well offshore, apparently in the middle of the ocean, is a sensation that many divers deny themselves. Such diving allows you to become more at one with the sea by enabling you to experience more of what the oceans have to offer.

Ocean Diving

Ocean diving, by definition, takes place well offshore. The comments on shoal diving are largely applicable here too. The dive sites may well be difficult to locate and electronic navigational techniques together with echo sounding will usually be required.

Rescue from a potential incident may well be substantially delayed, if it comes at all! This implies that the divers should be competent and experienced. They must evolve an agreed dive plan and stick to it. There will be no shore for the divers to aim for if in difficulty and so they must work as a team with the cover boats.

In normal conditions there is no reason why separation of the divers and the cover party should occur. However, the consequences of such separation could be dire and, therefore, great care should be exercised. The use of surface marker buoys is mandatory. The location devices and techniques discussed in the drift diving section are relevant and should be consulted (pp. 196–7).

Tides at offshore sites are generally slight, although tidal streams and even ocean currents *can* be troublesome to divers in the water.

A swell is almost always present at ocean sites and can be deceptively large, since there are few reference points against which comparisons can be made. The puny abilities of a diver can be quickly exceeded by even a moderate swell. The effects of a swell are most noticeable in shallow areas near the tops of shoals and these comments should be heeded (pp. 212–213).

One of the exciting possibilities of ocean diving is that of seeing large, oceanic animals such as sharks and whales. You are now entering their environment and anything may happen!

So far we have assumed that you will be diving on the seabed. However, when attempting to dive with ocean creatures you may choose to enter the water where the bottom is hundreds or even thousands of metres deep. The hazard should be obvious – that of becoming disoriented and sinking to dangerous depths. The lack of reference points increases this possibility and, therefore, great care should be exercised in depth keeping. Such diving should not be attempted unless the divers are very experienced.

The Importance of Cover Boats in Shoal and Ocean Diving

When diving at offshore sites the dive should be viewed as a team effort between the divers and their cover party. The divers *must* be locatable as they are totally dependent on the cover boat to pick them up after their dive. Consequently, neither the boat nor the divers should do anything unplanned. Both should stick to the prearranged plan.

To aid this location the divers must use a surface marker buoy or perhaps a delayed surface marker buoy. They should carry whistles and flags mounted on extendable masts. A personal flare can be worth its weight in gold in the event of separation. These techniques and equipment are discussed more fully in the section on drift diving and this should be consulted (see pp. 196–7).

The boat used for covering the divers should be in sound condition and must be fitted with a reliable engine. The cox should be levelheaded and experienced in handling small boats and should also be knowledgeable about local tidal streams. Usually, the cover boat will be operating from a parent vessel and it is helpful if the two are in radio contact. In a swell, divers on the surface can sometimes be seen from the greater height of the parent vessel when they may be invisible from the cover boat.

Figure 238   Ocean diving offers the opportunity to observe large animals such as this basking shark

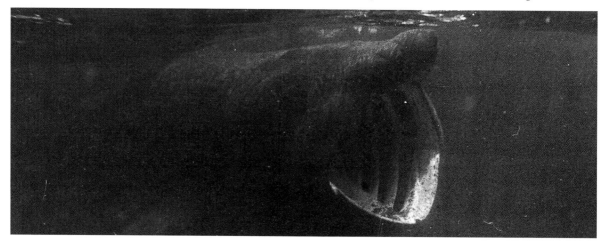

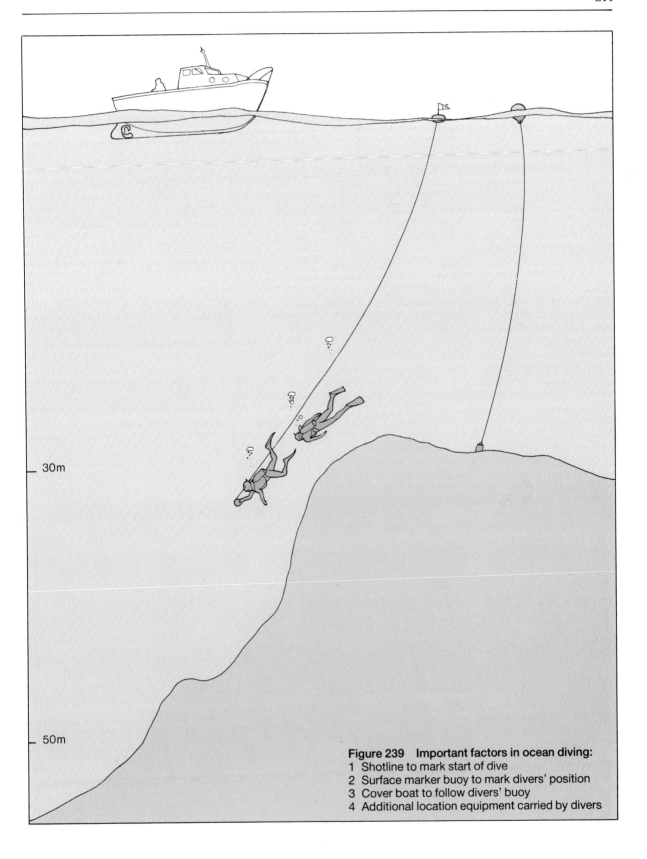

Figure 239   Important factors in ocean diving:
1 Shotline to mark start of dive
2 Surface marker buoy to mark divers' position
3 Cover boat to follow divers' buoy
4 Additional location equipment carried by divers

30m

50m

Shoal Diving

A submarine shoal is an area of the seabed that is shallower than the surrounding area. Usually these shoals are well offshore, although this is not always the case. Diving on such shoals is a great experience because you have the sensation of exploring an underwater island.

One of the main attractions of shoal diving is that such places act as oases for marine life. The best shoals are those composed of hard rock which protrude some distance from a sandy seabed. These provide a substrate on which marine life will settle. Often there will be large shoals of pelagic fish near such shoals, and frequently the tops of the shoals have large individual specimens of solitary fish. There is also the possibility of seeing some of the large midocean wanderers.

Although strictly not a diving matter, the location of shoals can be somewhat difficult. For inshore shoals, transits from the shore may be necessary, although it may be possible to detect shallow shoals by looking for weed or breaking waves. However, for offshore shoals, electronic means have to be employed and this should be successful with large shoals. Small shoals well offshore can be very difficult to locate and repeated runs with an echo sounder may be required.

Once a shoal is located it should be marked with a shotline. This should have a heavy weight (perhaps 25 kg) connected by a heavy line (of about 10 mm diameter) to a substantial buoy (say 50–100 kg buoyancy). This shotline will act as a reference for both the divers as they descend and ascend, and also for the surface party.

It is most essential that surface marker buoys are employed on all shoal dives. Care must be taken to ensure that the buoy line does not entangle the shotline – if there is any tidal stream then the buoy line can be trailed slightly downtide. The delayed surface marker buoy technique can be very effective for stage decompression if there is little or no tidal stream and if the surface visibility is good.

One of the novel aspects of diving on a reasonably deep shoal is that the descent has to be made through midwater, with no visual reference other than, perhaps, the rope of a shotline. Once out of site of the surface and the seabed, the diver appears to be surrounded by a sphere of blue water. This is referred to as being 'in the blue' and can be somewhat disconcerting. It is caused by light being reflected from a light-coloured bottom so that all directions appear equally bright. It mainly occurs in tropical water, in Britain the greener water leads to the expression 'in the murk'. In this case the water colour usually becomes darker with depth, thus hinting at the direction of greater depth. However, deep blue water is encountered in the clear, offshore waters of the northwest of Britain.

Many shoals have substantial depths nearby, so great caution must be exercised not to venture too deep, especially if there is a tidal stream running or when visibility is good. An extra safety margin of bottom time should be allowed as most shoals are some distance from shore and any potential rescue would, therefore, take longer.

An increasing swell can rapidly put shoal diving out of sensible reach. It becomes very difficult to stay near the top of a shallow shoal in a big swell. It is also very uncomfortable and somewhat difficult to attempt to carry out stage decompression stops on a shotline, although a lazy shot or a delayed surface marker buoy largely circumvents the problems of depth variation and water turbulence.

Figure 240 A school of fish on a shallow shoal in tropical waters

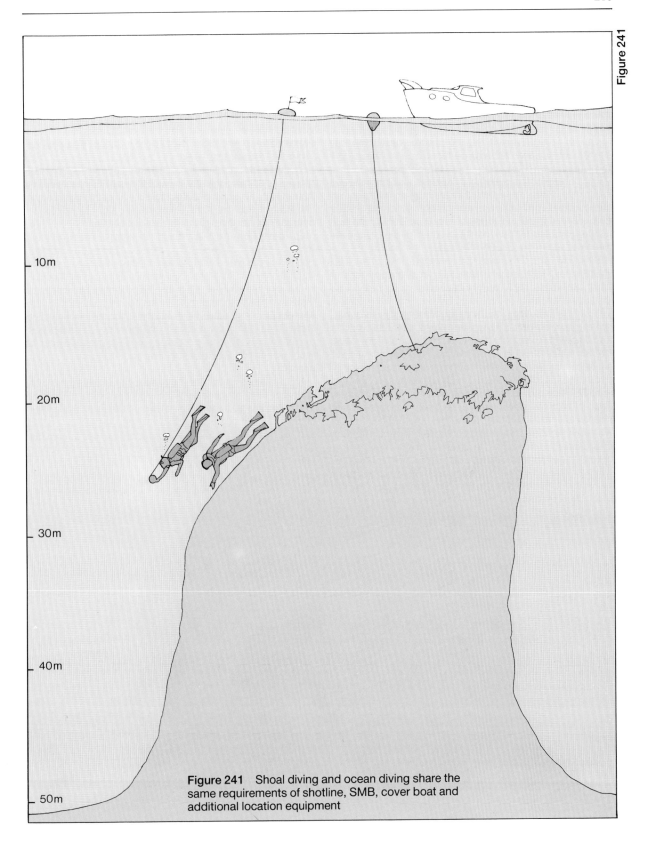

Figure 241

10m

20m

30m

40m

50m

Figure 241 Shoal diving and ocean diving share the same requirements of shotline, SMB, cover boat and additional location equipment

Cold-Water Diving

General Cold-Water Diving

By the term 'cold-water diving' we mean diving in the latitudes of the world where the water temperature is sufficiently cold to necessitate the wearing of some form of diving suit to protect the diver from the cold. This statement covers much of the globe, and certainly includes Britain and northern Europe for the whole of any year.

In much of this geographical area, the wearing of a suit will provide sufficient safeguard, and therefore we need only concern ourselves with diving techniques for waters where the temperature drops below about 10°C. In Britain and central Europe these are the winter diving conditions in the sea. If we go to higher latitudes, the conditions are likely to last for much longer periods of the year. It is also worth noting that, even in summer, the temperature of many bodies of fresh water, including rivers, may still remain very low.

It is obvious that body temperature drops when exposed to cold water. How much it drops will depend on how well you have protected your body. It may not be so obvious to the diver that body temperature will continue to fall once out of the water until the body can be fully rewarmed. This fall can be even more rapid than the drop in body temperature in the water and, if it is not arrested quickly, hypothermia can set in. Thus, the diver is at greatest risk from the time he finishes his dive and leaves the water until he has changed back into warm clothes again. Long periods sitting in open boats in a cold breeze can only exacerbate the situation.

Much of the data on which these observations are based has come from monitoring divers' performances while diving in Antarctica.

The situation is made worse by repeat dives, especially if the diver has not been able fully to rewarm between the dives. The rate of temperature drop is likely to be higher on a second or subsequent dive, and again the amount by which the body temperature drops will depend on water temperature, dive time, surface interval, surface chilling factors and body insulation.

A diver in these circumstances is not always the best judge of just how cold he is becoming. This indicates the need, in these situations, for rigorous dive marshalling in order to ensure that divers do not accidentally overexpose themselves in or out of the water.

In the water the body must, therefore, be protected from cold temperatures. The choice is between a wetsuit and a drysuit. A good-fitting wetsuit can be quite adequate for even very cold water conditions. Divers in Antarctica regularly dive using 10 mm thick neoprene wetsuits. However, for general cold-water diving, including the seemingly inevitable messing about on the surface that this entails, many sport divers choose a drysuit. The type of drysuit is not too important, provided that the diver is wearing adequate thermal insulation of one form or another.

Once out of the water, however, the situation is quite different. The properties that make wetsuits work under the water to keep the diver warm act against him on the surface. The thin layer of water trapped between the suit and the body soon chills and conducts heat away from the body. The prime requirement for a wetsuited diver

Figure 242   Divers prepare for an ice dive by cutting a hole in the ice

before, and especially after, a dive is to wear a windproof garment.

The drysuited diver has a similar problem. Partial inflation of the drysuit with air while in a boat can help the situation, since this serves as an extra layer of insulation between the suit and the body, thereby reducing the chilling effect.

The colder the water and air temperatures, the stronger the chilling effect of the wind and the more insulation the body needs. The extremities of the body are great conductors of heat. Divers should protect exposed heads and hands and woollen garments such as balaclavas and mittens are most effective. Full facial protection may be necessary on occasions and neoprene face protectors have been developed to meet this need.

Diving under Sheet Ice

Diving under sheet ice is a specialized and potentially risky form of diving. However, if it is carried out correctly it offers some unusual challenges to the sport diver.

Sheet ice can occur either on fresh water or, in constantly cold climes, on the sea. Once the water has frozen over, the wind cannot disturb the mass of water and any sediment tends to settle and visibility may become significantly better than normal for the area. Even in very cold water, life exists, and with good visibility this can be enjoyed by the sport diver. The additional technical challenge of diving under ice can be a stimulus in itself. Whatever the challenge, the dive must be carried out safely and diving under ice demands special techniques.

Of course, by going under the ice, divers cut out one very important escape route from difficulties – the swim to the surface and fresh air. Thus, problems which can be resolved simply on a normal dive can assume more serious proportions under ice. The freezing of a regulator in cold conditions is an example of a problem which can be catastrophic unless proper safeguards are taken.

Never dive under ice without a safety line, which should be securely tied to the diver and to his tender on the surface. With this precaution, there is a chance of a diver being rescued.

Before the dive it is necessary to cut a hole in the ice to allow divers access to the water, so take adequate tools to cut the ice. You will not cut 10–12 cm thick ice with a diving knife! An ice axe is ideal, but other tools can be improvised. The hole should be large enough to admit two divers at the same time.

If you are cutting a hole in the middle of an ice field, make sure that the ice can take the weight of your party and all the gear before you start cutting holes. Having to rescue the surface party will not get your dive off to a good start!

It may be a good idea to mark the hole under the water with something bright (e.g. a flashing strobe beacon) which the divers can spot easily and which will help them locate the exit.

Because of the high risk if a diver gets lost under ice, the emphasis should be on making sure that he does not. Divers should dive in pairs, each attached by a separate lifeline to a suitably experienced tender on the surface.

One lifeline with a buddy line to the second diver is not an acceptable alternative. A broken lifeline will then lose two divers. The normal rules of roped-diving conduct should be followed as described on page 195. A stand-by diver should be ready on the surface with a lifeline twice as long as that used by the divers. In the event of a lost diver he can then attempt a search.

Care should be taken to ensure that lifelines are securely attached to the divers (with a bowline knot round the chest, under all other equipment). Only two divers should dive from one hole at any time, and any other holes should be far enough away so that lines cannot become tangled.

It is normal diving practice for buddies to look after each other. Under ice this task is even more critical. The dive should be abandoned if there is any malfunction of equipment. If a diver becomes detached from his line, his buddy must bring him back. If he becomes lost in spite of this safeguard, the buddy should return and the stand-by diver should enter the water. The best technique for finding a diver lost under ice is for the stand-by diver to go to the extremity of his line and carry out a circular sweep. By doing this he should with luck snag the lost diver, who can then return along the line to safety. If the first attempt fails, the sweep should be repeated on the bottom.

In addition to these diving procedures, the diver should pay special attention to his gear. Environmentally protected first stages of diving regulators, octopus regulators and pony tanks with a separate regulator have all a part to play.

Figure 243   A diver and a Weddel seal under pack ice

Dangerous Tropical Marine Animals

In comparison with temperate waters, tropical seas are alive with creatures which can bite, sting, devour or otherwise injure the unwary diver. While it is not possible to cover the full range of these potential risks, some of the commoner dangers will be mentioned.

Figure 244b

Figure 244a

The barracuda has an appearance and reputation almost as great as that of the shark. It is usually seen in groups of up to several hundreds. A speared fish or a bleeding diver might attract a barracuda, but they do tend to regard divers with an apparently baleful eye. In murky water they sometimes strike at shiny objects which they may have mistaken for dying fish, so do not draw your knife casually.

Figure 244c

Moray eels are common residents of most reefs and are usually docile and retiring. However, they should not be provoked as they can strike very much faster than a diver can react and they have very sharp and powerful jaws. The bite can easily become infected.

Everyone's favourite nasty sea creature is the shark. However, most species of shark are extremely unlikely to attack a diver, although all should be treated with respect. The occasional shark encountered on a dive will usually ignore a diver on the bottom, but may take more interest in a snorkeller or swimmer splashing on the surface or a diver returning to the surface. A shark which becomes interested may circle before approaching and would normally bump a potential victim, as this is the way in which they 'taste' if the object is edible. A violent punch on the nose or eyes of an attacking shark may dissuade it from pressing further attacks. However, avoidance is the most sensible precaution.

If sharks are known to be present in a particular area which is important to the diving project, 'bang sticks' can be employed by a designated shark guard. A bang stick consists of a rod, tipped with a 12-bore shotgun cartridge, which will explode when pushed against an attacking shark. These weapons should be used with considerable caution, because a wounded shark can be even more dangerous. Of the fatalities which occur, many result from attacks by the great white shark (made famous by the film *Jaws*), which has a worldwide distribution but appears to be most common in the waters around southeast Australia and off California.

Figure 244d

Sea snakes are common in some parts of the world, and especially in the tropical Pacific Ocean and off northern Australia. Although extremely poisonous, they are not aggressive and do not have large jaws or fangs. As with every other potentially dangerous creature, they should not be provoked.

Figure 244e

Figure 244h

There are several types of fish with very painful, and sometimes deadly, stings. The lionfish displays long, feathery fins in brilliant colours; it should not be approached closely or touched as a number of the dorsal fins contain venom. The stonefish is perhaps the most deadly tropical fish that can be encountered. It is perfectly camouflaged and this is a very good reason for not touching anything on the bottom. Various scorpionfish exist and all can give unpleasant or dangerous stings from their spines. Stingrays are common in all tropical waters; they burrow in sandy bottoms and their sting can cause extreme pain or even death.

The spines of tropical sea urchins can be poisonous. If knelt on or stood on, they can puncture the skin and leave painful wounds that often turn septic.

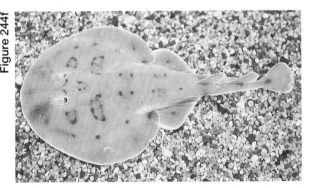

Figure 244f

Figure 244i

Electric or torpedo rays are capable of giving a severe electric shock which can paralyse a man. Fortunately, they are rarely encountered by divers.

Figure 244g

A very innocent, small, but poisonous resident of the Australian reefs is the blue-ringed octopus. The adult octopus is often picked up by divers and snorkellers, who believe that it must be safe as it is so small. It is deadly.

Coral tends to be sharp and can cause unpleasant cuts, but, in addition, fire coral can cause extremely nasty stings and weals to the careless diver who brushes an arm or a leg against it. It is tan in colour with a white edging, and is easily spotted after the initial identification has been made. Jellyfish, starfish, cone shells and many other seemingly innocuous marine inhabitants can cause unpleasant injuries. So the simple rule for diving in tropical waters must be to touch nothing. Local knowledge should always be tapped for details of dangerous creatures in a particular area.

Treatments of injuries caused by the above creatures vary greatly. Open wounds should be cleaned with fresh water and coral cuts respond well to antibiotic powder. Some poisons, e.g. from a stonefish, break down rapidly with heat, so the first-aid treatment is to immerse the damaged area in very hot water. Stonefish antivenom serum is available and should be carried in remote areas. If a diver is bitten or stung by any marine creature about which there is any doubt, prompt medical advice should be sought.

In general, if diving in remote tropical areas, you should carry a comprehensive first-aid kit together with one of the texts that details dangerous marine life and how to treat its effects.

Diving in the Tropics

Why?

Diving in the tropics is very attractive due to the warm water and pleasant sunny conditions. There are several different underwater environments in tropical waters, but by far the most popular with divers is the coral reef. The good underwater visibility, variety of corals and colourful fish life explain why many divers travel to distant parts of the world in order to dive on coral reefs.

General Cautions

The most significant difference experienced when diving in the tropics, in comparison with diving in temperate UK waters, is that the conditions underwater are very often easier and pleasanter. This is a direct result of a mean sea-water temperature in the range of 26–29°C, which is warmer than many swimming pools.

The increased water temperature is mirrored on land by not only much hotter air temperatures, but by considerably stronger sunlight. For the pale-skinned North European there is a considerable risk of sunburn or sunstroke unless adequate precautions are taken. A hat should be worn at all times and exposure of the skin to direct sunlight should be severely restricted at first. It is important to ensure that any suntan oil, cream or lotion is a barrier against ultraviolet radiation and not just an exotic moisturizer. The real danger from the sun comes during the middle of the day, as the morning and evening sunlight is much more gentle.

Extreme sunlight can have a dramatically detrimental effect on diving equipment and consequently all cylinders, rubber items and photographic equipment should be kept in the shade at all times.

On the whole, tropical weather is much more predictable than a temperate climate and as such offers less of a hindrance to diving. However, in the monsoon season changes can be sudden and extreme. It cannot be stressed too strongly that local information must be obtained regarding onshore or offshore winds and the likelihood of sudden changes. The most severe tropical storms – typhoons and hurricanes – tend to announce themselves well out to sea and plenty of warning is given and should be heeded.

Coral Reefs

The majority of tropical diving is carried out on the coral reefs which encircle most tropical shores. Coral reefs are formed by colonizing polyps which continually secrete calcareous skeletons. Within these coral-creating animals live single-celled algae, which, as with all plants, need sunlight to live. As a result, coral reefs only flourish in warm, sunlit conditions.

The coral reef grows from the shallow (30–60 metres) seabed towards the surface. On reaching the surface, some of the coral on the crest dies off as it is exposed to air. This semi-submerged crest allows a lagoon to form to the shoreward side, while the reef continues to grow to seaward. This is a much simplified description of reef construction; local conditions can vary to produce a great variety of reef forms.

The lagoon behind a fringing reef may be shallow and offer good snorkelling in 2–10 metres over a mainly sandy bottom, as conditions within the lagoon tend to be inimical to coral growth. Lagoons which are many miles across may be formed behind a large barrier reef.

The reef crest forms a platform which may vary greatly in width; this can be a dangerous place to dive, for it is often shallow, rough and always extremely sharp. However, the reef crest may be totally exposed at low water and it may then be possible to walk about on it (wearing shoes).

It can be dangerous to be caught to seaward of a reef in rough conditions while in the water or a small boat. The crest can usually be crossed through gaps and channels of varying size. However, the diver should not rely on these as a method of reaching the calm lagoon as there will almost certainly be a fierce surge to seaward. All diving to seaward of the reef crest should be done with boat cover.

The fore reef, to seaward of the crest, is of most interest to the diver and it is here that the greatest clarity can be found (up to 70 metres). Visibility within the lagoon may often be reduced by fresh-water run-off. The greatest variety of fish, coral and other life is usually found on the fore reef. The reef itself often offers spectacular deep diving on drop-offs, which can lead to 2000 metres or more.

Diving in the Tropics

The image of the bikini-clad tropical diver may be a little misleading as the very nature of all coral reefs necessitates some form of protective clothing. While the water is generally very warm, prolonged submersion in any but the warmest of waters can result in considerable chillling. Therefore, it is recommended that at least a 4 mm wetsuit jacket be worn. In addition, the razor-sharp coral can produce cuts which rapidly go septic in tropical conditions. A pair of tough jeans or trousers and thin neoprene or other gloves are the usual solution. British divers tend to be familiar with diving on a relatively safe, smooth bottom and readily settle on it. However, reef diving almost precludes direct physical contact with the coral, and this can take a little getting used to.

One habit well worth developing is to enter the water from the shore by shuffling the feet, rather than taking strides. This should prevent you from standing on the spines of any poisonous fish by nudging them out of your path.

The greater clarity and warmth of tropical waters can easily lure the unwary northern diver into overstaying his intended bottom time. There is little perceptible change in water colour in the initial 40–50 metres of tropical water and, in addition, the added confidence and comfort generally result in a more economical use of air. Unless care is taken to check depth gauge, watch and decompression tables frequently, it is very easy to go too

Figure 245a

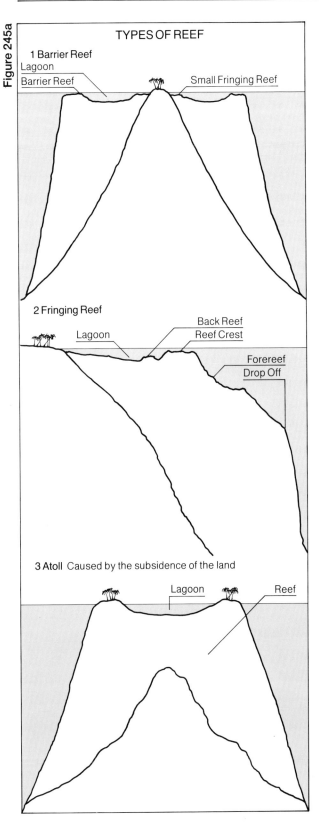

TYPES OF REEF

1 Barrier Reef

Lagoon

Barrier Reef — Small Fringing Reef

2 Fringing Reef

Lagoon — Back Reef — Reef Crest

Forereef — Drop Off

3 Atoll Caused by the subsidence of the land

Lagoon — Reef

deep for too long. As very many tropical dives are carried out on the vertical wall of the fore reef, precise dive organization and leadership, along with careful weighting, are prerequisites for safe diving. The black depths of northern wall diving are rarely apparent in tropical diving and awareness of depth is an important skill to develop at an early stage.

Many British divers visiting the tropics dive with unfamiliar, hired equipment, and often with buddies of different nationalities who may well have come through different training systems. It is important to make yourself familiar with the equipment, and check that signals and emergency procedures are understood and that safety standards are upheld.

In addition to the spectacular coral reefs, any wrecks in tropical waters offer superb diving. There are a number of sites around the world where large numbers of Second World War wrecks are found in some profusion. Coral encrusts the wreckage very quickly and adds dramatically to the basic lines of the shipbuilder.

Night-time shows off the coral reef at its best, with most of the individual polyps open and feeding and many larger creatures, such as octopus and turtle, active. These creatures are often dazzled by lights and are thus easily approached. Full protective clothing is even more essential at night, as unseen dangers, such as jellyfish, can cause painful or even fatal injuries.

Summary

Protect yourself against the sun. Never dive without a watch, depth gauge and suitable protective clothing. Beware of diving too deep for too long.

Be careful of waveswept coral and do not swim to seaward of a reef crest unless you are absolutely sure you can get back.

Do not touch or pick up anything unless you are sure of what it is.

Do not provoke any marine creature. It may well bite back.

Do not swim or dive with a bleeding cut. It can only attract unwelcome visitors.

Figure 245b   A coral coastline (Red Sea)

Diving Schools

Novice Diver

Most sport diving is done as a recreational activity and, as such, is pursued in the diver's leisure time. This means that holidays are frequently used to practise the sport. The traditional path followed by most British divers is to acquire the necessary skills and knowledge by joining a diving club with regular evening and weekend training sessions before undertaking a diving holiday. However, especially in warmer climes, a different path is the norm. This involves part or all of a holiday being spent at a diving school, very often learning to dive from start to finish in the sea. This is a relatively quick way to obtain diver training. Equipment can usually be hired from the school and all the necessary facilities are readily available. Gradually this type of training is becoming more common in Britain. Fairly intensive instruction is provided and quite rapid progress is possible. Although this method may be more expensive, it often suits people who are unable to fit into a club training schedule. Frequently, having learned to dive in a diving school, a diver may then join a local club in order to pursue the sport further and to gain wider experience.

Most diving schools are resort-based and usually offer a trial dive to tempt the beginner. This is either in a swimming pool or a sheltered sea site on a one-to-one ratio with an experienced instructor. The first dive is little more than a short trip underwater to give a degree of acclimatization to the equipment and environment. Normally, people trying the sport in this way will have to give an assurance as to their medical fitness. They will not be expected to have any high degree of swimming ability. It follows that the instructor will not be expecting any high degree of watermanship from such clients.

Following a handheld introduction to the underwater world the prospective diver is offered some sort of training course. This may be to the national standards of the country concerned or to BSAC standards if the school is BSAC-approved. Any introductory course will normally include mask and mouthpiece clearing and air sharing and will be accompanied by appropriate theory instruction. At some stage in the training course both theory and practical tests will be attempted and some form of certification awarded on successful completion of the course.

British Sub-Aqua Club recognized schools, both within Britain and abroad, usually offer two levels of instruction. The basic level is that of Novice Diver, normally a one-week course, which does not require BSAC membership. This is very much an introduction to the sport. Sport Diver level requires BSAC membership and a medical examination, but provides a deeper insight to the sport combined with varied diving experience in open water. These two courses correspond to the CMAS international standards of One- and Two-Star Diver respectively. Other qualifications may be offered, particularly by schools abroad, so anyone planning to use such training as a start to diving with a British club would be wise to consult BSAC headquarters on the equivalence that a particular qualification might have.

Learning to dive in warm, clear waters can be a most rewarding introduction to the sport and far more interesting than a long-term study of the tiles of the local swimming pool! If a recognized training course is followed successfully, much of the normal branch or club training programme may be short-circuited.

Figure 246   A flat top dive boat popular in the Caribbean

Experienced Diver

In many foreign diving areas visitors may have no option but to dive with the local diving school. This may be a result of legislation or because of a monopoly of facilities such as air or cylinders. It may be that worthwhile diving can only be reached in boats run by the diving school. Any or all of these factors may be the reason for experienced divers having to dive with a diving school, possibly for the first time if their training was with a club or a BSAC branch.

To get best value for money in these circumstances the school must be convinced of the diver's ability as quickly as possible. Qualification record books and CMAS cards play a part, but very often logbooks showing recent diving history have an equal role. Medical certificates and cylinder test certificates may also be needed. BSAC headquarters have a wealth of information to assist divers planning trips abroad.

Certificates and logbooks have a value, but many diving schools will also make some form of practical assessment for the responsibility it is accepting. This may be a formal test in a swimming pool or in shallow water, or it may be a form of assessment dive on which the diver is carefully and often unobtrusively observed closely. This observation will usually include watching how you kit up,

enter the water and dive, and also the monitoring of air consumption and depth. Do not forget you will also be watched after the dive, so tidy away your equipment and take the opportunity to help other divers. The sooner you demonstrate your ability the sooner you will be taken on the really good dives you are paying for.

By using a diving school, the diver is paying for services usually provided free within a branch or club, whether this be air, training, boat or dive-leading skills. Using a diving school may enable diving to fit into a family holiday. If a diver knows that a diving trip will mean just two hours away from the family who are on the beach, it can be much more acceptable than the equivalent half-day branch dive. It is also quite nice to be able to walk away and leave someone else to refill the cylinders and clean the boat and other equipment, knowing that you have paid for walk-on, walk-off diving!

Besides diving for pleasure many schools will also offer clients the chance to undertake more advanced training courses. These courses may be further diving skills, learning how to teach diving or even aimed at becoming a professional diver. Many courses are designed to give a purpose to diving, such as photography, marine life identification, archaeology or even the use of underwater explosives. Often these courses can provide logbook endorsements.

Diving with a school overseas can be a good way of 'going native'. There is no doubt that the special diver-to-diver relationship which develops between diving buddies can cross national barriers. Often the diving school may organize social events such as barbecues to complement the diving. These events also help non-diving companions and families to enjoy the holiday.

You should expect things to be different from the usual club dive. Adopt an open approach to techniques and habits which may be different from those you are used to; they are usually the best methods for the local situation. Try not to appear to be dogmatic, even if you cannot appreciate the delicacy of an after-dive sea urchin! Do remember that you represent your branch or club and others who follow may be judged by your performance and behaviour.

Figure 247 An instructor helps his pupil with her equipment

Figure 248 Enjoying a dive in tropical waters

Diving Careers

It can be argued that anybody who goes underwater, whether for sport or for a living, must have a special temperament and personality. Professional divers, however, need more than this. They must be healthy and tough, both physically and mentally, in order to work in a hostile and sometimes stressful environment. They must have the intelligence to learn and to cope with the problems of an industry that is becoming more complex and more technical. The professional diver should have the patience to deal with long periods of inactivity, interspersed with bouts of hard work. He should also enjoy the challenges of applying his specialist technical and practical knowledge, sometimes involving complicated equipment and difficult procedures, in an exacting and exciting profession.

In the professional diving world, diving is rarely an end in itself; it is an essential means of transporting a man underwater and returning him safely to the surface. The professional diver not only requires the diving skills necessary to survive underwater, he needs a second specialist set of skills to enable him to complete a task once he has reached the work site.

This is true of any field of professional diving, whether it relates to a commercial saturation diver using an oxyarc cutting torch on a submarine pipeline or a diving archaeologist surveying a historic wreck. The professional diver has to have some other ability to supplement his pure diving skills. With this in mind, the main fields that present opportunities for a diving career can now be investigated.

Commercial Diving

By far the greatest opportunities for a diving career exist in the commercial diving world, where there are numerous companies employing professional divers to work on civil engineering projects and in the offshore industry. These commercial divers are engaged on projects where the work sites can range from canals, rivers, docks and harbours, to the offshore oil and gas production fields.

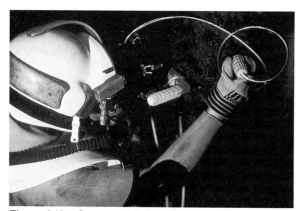

Figure 249   Commercial diver inspecting an undersea structure

Traditionally, commercial divers have been regarded as underwater labourers and, in the past, the tasks they have been called on to do have been comparatively simple, although often strenuous and dangerous. The standard equipment used by these earlier divers was the conventional 'closed helmet' standard diving dress with the breathing air passed down to the diver through an air hose from a pump on the surface. This 'hard hat' diving system was very successful and has been used on many difficult underwater salvage operations. A prime example is the raising of the German battleships scuttled in Scapa Flow at the end of the First World War. Even today, in many parts of the world, 'standard' diving dress is still used by professional divers when working at shallow depths, usually in docks, harbours and inland waterways.

Today's commercial diver finds that he needs at least the same diving skills as his predecessors. The restrictions of the medium in which he is working still exist, as do the problems presented by the physical and physiological effects of being underwater. However, this is where the similarity ends. The modern commercial diver is no longer just an underwater labourer. Recent developments have made it necessary for him to learn many new skills.

The trend to explore and produce oil and gas offshore, at ever-increasing depths, has resulted in the development of very complicated and expensive systems to allow deeper diving. Today's diver, working on a typical offshore installation, has to be fully knowledgeable in a very wide range of subjects, from exotic gas mixtures to the complexities of saturation diving systems.

To train a commercial diver, especially for saturation work, requires long hours of technical study and many practice sessions to familiarize him with the various systems and diving techniques. Further comprehensive training will probably have to be given to equip him with the second set of skills needed to do useful work underwater.

The offshore diver will be required to carry out tasks of an extremely varied nature. The following gives a few examples:

> Inspection of platform structures using non-destructive testing (NDT) techniques to test for cracks in welds, for example, by using ultrasonics. Pipeline repair by replacing damaged lengths of pipe with new sections using hyperbaric welding techniques.
> Installation and maintenance of submarine structures.

It can be seen that this type of work requires commercial divers to be expert in a wide range of technical fields, from construction and maintenance engineering to specialist trades such as NDT and high-quality welding. As underwater tasks become more technically demanding, the trend is for existing specialists and qualified engineers to train as divers. These people probably have the best chance of a successful diving career.

One way to become a commercial diver is to complete an approved commercial diving course and then learn a particular skill, such as the ability to do NDT work. The diver can then subsequently specialize in this type of work for the rest of his diving career.

Nevertheless, people entering the commercial diving world in this way will probably find that their later career options are restricted. Diving is not a lifetime occupation; there are not many commercial divers over the age of forty. Some ex-divers may work as diving supervisors, but without further qualifications most have to move into alternative careers for the remainder of their working lives.

A better, alternative, approach is first to get a good primary qualification, such as a degree or diploma in a branch of engineering, while at the same time continuing to dive or learning to dive with an amateur diving club like the BSAC. Following this education, an approved commercial diving course can be attended before experience is gained working as a diver in the industry. Later on there is every chance of a further career in underwater design and management. People with this background are becoming increasingly valuable as the industry becomes more technically demanding.

Diver Instruction

With sport diving increasing in popularity, there are some opportunities for people to have a full-time career teaching amateur divers. In the UK and abroad, there are BSAC-recognized schools and in many parts of the world there are other professionally run schools teaching sport diving, usually in holiday resorts.

Most national amateur diving clubs or federations have a qualification system which includes instructor gradings. It is possible for a person to obtain one of these grades in the normal course of amateur diver training and then to apply for a full-time job as an instructor in a diving school.

Nevertheless, the career prospects of this kind of occupation must be realistically assessed. Also, the long hours spent underwater, whether in a pool or in the sea and very often at a limited number of dive sites, together with the repetitive teaching necessary to do this work, make the 'glamorous' lifestyle sometimes associated with this activity look rather less attractive.

Scientific and Research Diving

Since the aqualung was made generally available after the Second World War, there has been a fast growth in the field of underwater research. Today there are a large number of people who need to dive to study the subject of their particular interest. These diving scientists work in areas such as underwater archaeology, fisheries research, marine biology, oceanography and diving medicine.

This branch of professional diving represents the extreme case where the divers involved are usually highly qualified in their field of study. Anybody contemplating such a career needs to think very hard about the effort involved in obtaining the required non-diving qualifications. Research divers may not always dive on a regular basis as the work may be seasonal. They quite often need to recruit amateur, and sometimes commercial, divers to help with large projects such as archaeological digs and large-scale surveys.

Figure 250 Checking scientific equipment installed on the seabed in a research project

Special Interests

Shipwrecks

For many divers, one of the greatest thrills is to locate and dive on a virgin wreck. The research which is needed can be likened to a detective story, with evidence being pieced together from many sources until a fairly precise location emerges. The search then switches to the open water, where a number of techniques may be employed to locate the wreck. The excitement caused by the anticipation of the first dive on a major, unknown wreck can be very intense and is only exceeded by that of the post-dive stories and celebrations!

Before the diving itself we have first to research our new wreck. It may be that you have accidentally stumbled on wreckage underwater and you wish to know more about it. Alternatively, you may be looking for a known vessel by researching various sources of information.

Researching shipwrecks can be an intriguing, involved and sometimes tedious business. Time spent piecing the story together and cross-checking the details from various sources of information is hardly ever wasted. It can often lead to the location of an undived old wreck which has, perhaps, been forgotten by history.

Nautical Archaeology

The diver's natural curiosity in shipwrecks often leads to a deeper interest in nautical archaeology. This is mainly the study of ships and shipbuilding since the early civilizations of mankind, although it also extends to the examination of flooded dwellings and other artefacts. Specially trained amateur divers have made a considerable contribution to nautical archaeology in the past. Without them, in fact, many projects would not be economically viable.

Many archaeological remains are accidentally discovered by amateur divers, while others are only located after comprehensive research. It is imperative, in either case, that the subsequent investigation is carried out with care and with due regard for scientific method.

Important sites in Britain can be designated as sites of historic importance under the Protection of Wrecks Act, 1973, and are then legally protected while a full survey and excavation is organized and carried out.

If an amateur diver stumbles across an important find, he should report this to a local nautical archaeologist, who will advise the correct action to take. Usually this will be to report it to the appropriate Nautical Archaeology body.

Having located a promising site, the nautical archaeologist will first carry out a detailed 'predisturbance survey' before he attempts any excavation. The excavation itself is a precise, painstaking process with all details being recorded at every stage. The tools used vary from powerful airlifts to delicate fanning with the diver's hand. Material which has been preserved underwater can rapidly deteriorate in air, so as finds are lifted to the surface, they are conserved using one of a number of specialist techniques. Finally, a full report of the project, complete with plans, drawings and photographs, is prepared and published.

Underwater Orienteering

Underwater orienteering involves precise navigation around a predetermined course and has a small but enthusiastic following, especially in the Nordic countries.

The sport allows its successful participants to demonstrate extreme competence in navigation with instruments. Most divers use a compass, depth gauge and watch attached to a board held in front of them. Some competitors use a small propeller to measure the distance travelled, while others achieve this by counting fin beats. Some divers, especially from Scandinavia, use much more sophisticated instrumentation.

British championships in underwater orienteering are held periodically, although these have not taken place for some years.

Figure 251a Many sport divers participated in the archaeology work involved in the excavation of the *Mary Rose*, Henry VIII's flagship. The wreck has since been raised and now resides in its own museum in Portsmouth

Octopush

Octopush is best described as underwater hockey and has become rather popular in Britain recently. It involves teams of opposing players trying to score a 'gull' by pushing a lead disc – the 'squid' – between the opposing team's 'gullposts'. Players use mask, fins and snorkels and carry a wooden 'pusher' to contact the squid. No bodily contact is allowed.

At its simplest, octopush is excellent training for snorkelling activities and is used as such by many diving groups. At the other extreme, there are individuals who regard the game as an end in itself and who, in fact, are not interested in diving, nor have they received any training with aqualungs.

A league is organized in Britain and teams from many branches compete fiercely for supremacy in the league table. Britain also has a national team who travel widely to compete with other countries.

Figure 251b Octopush is fiercely contested at club, national and international level

Underwater Photography

Underwater photography is a most challenging yet rewarding activity for the diver. The ability to record all that goes on in the underwater world can bring back many happy memories which can be savoured long after that special diving holiday.

Success in underwater photography depends upon:

an understanding of the problems
availability of effective equipment
maximizing the underwater conditions
following instructions precisely
patience and perseverance
luck

Figure 252a An amphibious underwater camera, the Nikonos

Problems of Underwater Photography

The first problem is that of the photographer himself being underwater and the fact that he is subject to the stresses of the underwater world. This does not make for relaxed photography. Good dive training and experience are the only solutions to this problem.

Equipment must be protected from the pressurized salt water. It is also usually expensive and can be rather bulky.

Regrettably water absorbs light. In fact, 1 metre of totally clear sea water reduces the ambient light intensity to 42 per cent of its original value. Red light is lost selectively by 10 metres, causing everything to become blue or green, then ultimately grey.

Underwater visibility, at best, approximates to a thick land fog. Yet we attempt to take photographs in such conditions! The only way to make the most of the visibility is to use wide-angled lenses or shoot silhouettes or to work only in close-up.

The suspended matter in the water will also considerably reduce contrast underwater. We can do very little about this.

Figure 252b The Nikonos with supplementary close-up lens and frame fitted

Refraction at the glass/water interface makes things appear nearer (or larger) than they really are, so due allowance must be made when estimating distances for focusing. The use of a curved or domed front port will minimize this effect.

Handling cameras underwater can be difficult. It is best to bolt all the components of the system together so that one-handed operation is possible.

Equipment for Underwater Photography

All equipment designed for underwater use has to be protected from the water and the pressure. This is usually achieved by building a housing to take the equipment, although amphibious equipment is available which has an integral housing which allows it to be taken directly underwater.

The film format is almost always 35 mm, although roll-film cameras are sometimes employed if results of especially high photographic quality are required. There is a much greater range of 35-mm equipment available and it is much more portable and somewhat cheaper than roll-film equipment.

Figure 252c The Nikonos with electronic flashgun

Figure 253 A surface camera and its underwater waterproof housing which allows the use of all the normal controls and the attachment of a flashgun

There are a number of simple underwater photography systems now available, all of which take 35-mm film or smaller. These cameras do not offer the sophistication of more expensive cameras, but they can yield remarkably good results when operated within their limitations.

The Nikonos system of amphibious 35-mm photography equipment is very popular. The camera is internally sealed by a series of O-rings. It is quite robust, simple and relatively easy to use and has proved to be very reliable if well maintained. There is a comprehensive set of accessories available that enables nearly every aspect of underwater photography to be undertaken.

Single-lens reflex cameras (usually 35 mm) can be housed in either plastic or metal cases, the latter being more robust but more expensive. Housed cameras are more versatile than the amphibious Nikonos system, but they are slower to use and much less convenient in arduous conditions. If you are starting from scratch, they are also more expensive.

The best lenses to use are generally those that give as wide an angle of view as possible. The normal underwater wide-angle lens has an angle of view of 94 degrees. The other type of lens that is widely used is the so-called macro lens, which allows close focusing.

Extra lighting is usually supplied by means of an electronic flash. Nowadays this is regarded as virtually essential, although somewhat temperamental! Again, both housed surface units or purpose-built amphibious units are available. The latter are better although more expensive.

Flashguns with the choice of rechargeable or disposable batteries have much to commend them. Recharge facilities must be investigated carefully if NiCad cells are to be employed.

Film in Underwater Photography

Generally a slow (25–64 ASA) film is used for close-ups, whereas a faster (200–400 ASA) film is used for longer shots and views. Occasionally there will be the need to increase speed by two or four times by means of 'push-processing'. In the tropics it is often possible to manage with a medium-speed film (64 ASA) for all types of shots.

Figure 254 Diver using camera with close-up lens

Techniques of Underwater Photography

Photomacrography (photography of subjects at lifesize or a greater magnification) is a heavily exploited technique. Usually an extension tube is fitted to the camera with lighting from a small electronic flash unit arranged at 45 degrees above the lens–subject axis. Focusing is either by a single-lens reflex screen or by a wire frame finder. After exposing and evaluating a test film, photomacrography is usually found to be a most dependable technique.

Close-up photography is very similar in technique to photomacrography except that the magnification is between about one-fifth and lifesize. Either a macro lens or a supplementary lens is used, or a short extension tube can be employed. This is another widely used technique for recording marine life.

Fish photography is in a category of its own. Unless the fish are very large, the technique is effectively one of close-up photography at a larger-subject distance. The standard technique is to employ a lens of longer focal length (typically 80–105 mm).

The photography of divers (and large creatures) is best undertaken with a camera fitted with as wide an angle lens as possible (usually 15–20 mm), with or without flash as appropriate. This technique minimizes the effect of suspended matter between the subject and the camera lens and will, therefore, make for the best resolution and contrast. Photographing large wrecks and underwater views is severely limited by water visibility. The best that can be managed is to use the widest-angle lens available, and perhaps a full-frame or ordinary fisheye lens. Focal lengths of 15 mm or less are appropriate on the 35-mm format.

Handling Cameras Underwater

The technique of handling a camera underwater is made more difficult by adverse surface and water conditions.

Rough water makes operating from boats quite tricky. The fairly robust nature of life aboard charter vessels means that extra care will have to be taken with valuable (and relatively delicate) photographic equipment.

In the hot, dusty conditions of the tropics it is vital to protect the equipment from both the dust and the heat. The heat causes salt water to dry quickly after the camera has been immersed and the resulting salt deposits can be very damaging. Wash the equipment in fresh water after every dip if possible. Do not forget that under these conditions the photographer also needs some shelter and attention to keep going effectively.

In very cold conditions, it is the photographer rather than the equipment that needs special attention. To function effectively the photographer must be comfortable. This involves keeping warm before and after diving and also keeping warm on the dive by the use of effective protective clothing.

Figure 255 With patience the diver can get very close to fish. This shot was taken by the diver in the picture using a wide-angle lens

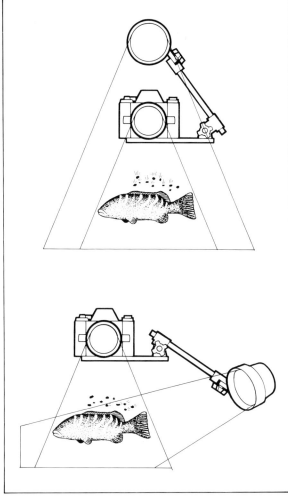

Subjects in Underwater Photography

The selection of subjects for your camera is rather important. Details of colourful marine life are always popular. Shots of divers doing something are much better than photos of your dive buddy grinning into the camera! In good visibility, try to include a foreground with a splash of colour (sparingly lit with a flash) along with an interesting background such as a diver, the hull of the boat or the surface. There is ample scope for creativity underwater.

The efforts involved in thinking about subject selection in your underwater photography are well worthwhile in that you will produce many more memorable photographs. However, ultimately it is only you yourself whom you should aim to please, so if you are satisfied with your results that is justification enough. Remember, beauty is in the eye of the beholder.

Figure 256a Back scatter from suspended particles is limited if the flash is positioned to one side of the camera instead of immediately above

Figure 256b A close-up shot using an extension tube

Figure 256c A wide-angle lens allows the foreground and background to be featured in the picture

Underwater Visibility

The distance that the diver can see underwater is called the visibility and it is one of the main factors controlling the quality of diving. The variables affecting water clarity are somewhat complicated and will be examined in turn.

Underwater Visibility

Pure, midoceanic water can have a visibility of up to 100 metres and polar waters can be even clearer. Coastal waters never match this, since they always carry particles that interfere with water clarity. This particulate matter is both organic and inorganic in origin, and is collectively termed the 'seston'. The seston includes plankton, decaying organic matter, disturbed bottom sediment, mineral particles, industrial and domestic pollution, and matter discharged by rivers.

Plankton consists of minute organisms which live mainly in the top few metres of ocean water. It is of particular interest to divers to know when conditions become ripe for them to proliferate rapidly, create a plankton bloom, and consequently reduce underwater visibility from many metres to as little as 1–2 metres. Plankton levels are low in British waters in winter, although rough seas bring plenty of nutrients to the surface layers of the ocean. In spring, as the sunlight grows stronger, there is a sudden outburst of plant activity (usually in March or April); within a week the phytoplankton will multiply a hundredfold and in a fortnight by a factor of perhaps 10,000. As summer approaches, these numbers are reduced by the exhaustion of food and by the feeding of zooplankton. The zooplankton are consumed, in turn, by small fish, and so on up the food chain. There is a second plankton bloom, usually in September, caused by the autumn storms bringing nutrient-rich deeper waters to the surface while there is still sufficient light to allow the phytoplankton briefly to bloom again.

Underwater visibility is also controlled by factors other

Figure 257 Rivers will usually carry silt to the sea causing poor visibility in the estuary area

than the amount of plankton in the water. Polluted water usually has poor visibility but, fortunately, this is largely restricted to industrial areas. Around busy harbours and coastal towns there is an increased level of pollution, but these are seldom prime dive sites.

The nature of the bottom at the dive site will be one of the factors which determine visibility. A site with a rock/stone bottom is likely to have much better visibility than a site with a loose bottom such as sand or mud. In the latter case, the bottom is prone to disturbance by wave and tidal stream action, particularly if the water is relatively shallow. Any storm action will obviously make this situation worse and, at the same time, any natural debris that had fallen to the bottom gets stirred back up into the water column. Strong tidal streams or currents will have a similar effect.

If you dive on a muddy bottom you will soon appreciate how easily this can be disturbed and how immediate is the effect on the divers' ability to see. Once disturbed, such a site will take many hours to settle again.

As mentioned, storms stir up the bottom sediment and reduce visibility, but this is not such a problem around rocky headlands, although it can be on the more sandy coasts. Storms and strong winds create waves, and these interfere with the light passing through the surface. Light passage is at its best when the surface is calm and the sun is high in the sky. Obviously, very dull days do not help; neither does the low sun of high latitudes, late evenings and wintertime.

The type and temperature of the water is another factor which affects visibility. Areas of sea which are prone to fresh-water run-off from the land may suffer in this respect. The fresh water and salt water tend to remain in separate layers, because of the difference in density, until wave action, or some other disturbance, mixes them up. This results in huge haloclines and turbidity in the water, which can distort, as well as hinder, vision. In the Norwegian fiords, these haloclines have been observed to reach a depth of 30 metres or more. Within the halocline the visibility can be very poor, but below it crystal-clear water can be found.

Fresh-water run-off can bring another problem which significantly affects visibility in the sea, and this stems from the solids which are carried by river water and then dropped as the flow slackens when the fresh water enters the sea. Observed from the air, it is often possible to see huge, brown slicks stretching out into the sea from river mouths, thus marking areas of extremely poor visibility.

Many British rivers are short and do not carry vast quantities of fresh water to the sea. However, after prolonged heavy rain the visibility in the long sea lochs, particularly those with narrow mouths, is very considerably reduced. Visibility is usually better on the flood tide, which brings cleaner oceanic water, than on the ebb tide, which carries away stirred-up shallow water sediments, peaty fresh water, sewage and industrial pollutants.

In general in Britain, visibility of 10 metres can be expected in the summer in most places on the northwest and southwest coasts, and this usually extends to 20 metres around rocky headlands. The east coast visibility is about half these figures. The Channel and southeast waters have rather poor visibility, however. On the rocky Atlantic islands and exposed northwest headlands visibility can reach 30 metres or more. Visibility in estuaries or rivers is often reduced by sediment-rich fresh-water run-off. Near towns, industrial and human pollution reduces visibility. Shallow shores facing the prevailing weather will stir up rapidly if the wind and swell increase. Finally, all the factors affecting plankton blooms can grossly affect underwater visibility.

After heavy rain, sheltered fiords and sea lochs can have visibility down to 30 cm (or even less) on exceptionally bad occasions. Winter visibility is normally 5–10 metres off the southern part of the west coast; visibility for the east coast is again about half this.

In bodies of fresh water, the ground over which the water has flowed will determine its clarity. Slate quarries, for example, are often noted for the clarity of their waters, whereas lakes that have filled from streams that run over peaty moorland are likely to have extremely poor visibility with the water a deep yellow-brown colour. Rivers are only clear at times of reduced water flow. This is usually in early summer, but the possibility of clear water under ice, when most incoming water is frozen, can also be considered by the hardy.

Choosing the Right Weather/Visibility Conditions

Natural conditions vary throughout the year and you will have to pick your holiday time carefully in order to maximize the chances of getting good conditions. The conditions that matter most are for you to decide, depending on your aspirations. The environmental factors that might enter into your deliberations are visibility, air and sea temperature, sunshine and rainfall, wind strength and sea state.

In Britain, the alternatives appear to be either to go in May/June for the long sunny days and accept the poorer visibility, or go in July/August for the better visibility and slightly warmer conditions and accept rather more rain.

Marine Life

Figure 258a

Figure 258b

Figure 258c

Figure 258d

Figure 258e

Figure 258a Tube worm

Figure 258b Organ pipe sponge

Figure 258c Fisheye view of an anemone

Figure 258d Limahians

Figure 258e Nudibranch

Figure 258f

Figure 258g

Figure 258h

Figure 258i

Figure 258j

Figure 258f   Clown fish

Figure 258g   Star fish

Figure 258h   Lobster

Figure 258i   Striped butterfly fish

Figure 258j   Goldsinny wrasse

Marine Biology Projects

Most divers take an interest in the marine life that they see and most have a desire to know a little more about it. It is very satisfying to be familiar with the main groups of marine life and so be able to assign unknown creatures to their appropriate families and finally identify them with one of the many reference books. The photographs on pp. 232–3 should point you in the right general direction.

However, many divers go beyond a simple interest and become absorbed by more detailed studies of marine life, often under the direction of professional leaders. Some of the types of projects undertaken are described below.

Most projects will involve the identification of plants and animals. These skills are quickly learned from a variety of guides. Some professional assistance will be required for the more difficult groups.

Study of a single species is very easy to start with little experience. Marine life such as sea urchins, kelp and crown-of-thorns starfish have been the subjects of such studies.

Area surveys are important in establishing what species are actually present at a given site. Precise observation and recording skills will be required.

Checklists of species can be produced by divers visiting a group of sites in an unrecorded area. This will then allow a baseline to be established for future surveys. Recording the variety of habitats available to marine life at a given site can also be important in determining what life to expect.

Monitoring studies require a clearly defined scientific procedure over a period of time at the same site. Long-term, profound changes in populations and communities can occur from a variety of causes. Repeated detailed documentation allows changes in marine life to be studied over long periods.

Experimental measurements, such as of physiological processes, can be studied, although advance planning and a high calibre of personnel are required.

Collections of specimens can be very valuable for systematic study back home by professionals based in museums or other research institutes. Collections from particular sites, especially rocky, nearshore habitats, have seldom been made. Expert advice should be sought on how to collect and preserve the specimens. Detailed notes of depth, date, habitat and name of recorder should always accompany the specimens.

Photography of specimens in the natural state in their habitats can be invaluable for later study and for comparison with the preserved specimens. Both detailed close-ups of specimens and panoramic views of habitats will be useful.

It is important that a report is written at the end of a project. This should be well organized yet simple, with little embellishment. The report should be lodged with the appropriate expert so that it can be consulted by others in later years.

In all marine biological projects, recognized scientific methods should be followed. This involves systematically designing the experiments, collecting the results and producing the final report. Only if the work is fastidiously completed will it have value to other workers in the same field. In this way, however, a genuine contribution to human knowledge can be made and this is very satisfying to many divers.

Figure 259 Setting up a current meter for use in underwater research

Figure 260   Tagging a pinna shell

Figure 261   Making a photographic record of coral types

Figure 262   Photographing a fine specimen of John Dory

Figure 263a

Figure 263b

Figure 263c

Figure 263d

Figure 263e

Figure 263a   Cone fish

Figure 263b   Conch

Figure 263c   Edible crab

Figure 263d   Sea anemone

Figure 263e   Seal

Observing Marine Life

One of the biggest attractions in diving is the ability to observe the sheer amount and diversity of marine life that abounds in the oceans of our planet. Remembering that 71 per cent of the earth is covered by water, what finer playground could a naturalist demand?

The tropical waters of the world are particularly rich in profuse, colourful marine life. The fish life of coral reefs, and the variety of the corals themselves, comprise one of the most memorable wildlife communities of the seas.

The marine life of temperate waters (such as those that wash Britain's shores) is also most rewarding. The diversity of species cannot match that of tropical waters, but the number of each species probably exceeds that of their tropical counterparts.

A catalogue of such species will be found in a number of guidebooks (e.g. *Hamlyn Guide to the Seashore and Shallow Seas of Britain and Europe* by Campbell, and *Collins Pocket Guide to the Sea Shore* by Barrett and Yonge).

The main groups of marine life in British waters are:

Mammals

Grey seals can be seen, and often accompany divers, at many sites. The common seal also inhabits our waters. Dolphins and whales (including killer whales) are quite frequently sighted.

Fish

Pelagic fish, by their nature, are not often seen by divers; it is mainly the bottom-living fish that are seen while diving. The main fish of note are wrasse (ballan, cuckoo, etc.), dogfish, rays, flatfish, anglerfish, lumpsucker, conger eels, ling, cod, pollack, gobies and blennies. Basking sharks are also common in certain places. You can expect to see the occasional large visitor from deeper waters, and in fact a sunfish has been recorded. No really large sharks have yet been seen, although medium and smaller varieties have been recorded.

Crustaceans

Lobsters are found in the areas with a boulder bottom, and crawfish are frequently found. There are both spider and hermit crabs, and edible and other crabs, some of which grow to a large size. Squat lobsters hide in cracks; Norway lobsters occur in deeper muddy bottoms.

Molluscs

Topshells, limpets and cowries are all common. Octopus and cuttlefish are also frequently to be seen. Seahares and many species of nudibranchs are very common in certain habitats.

Echinoderms

Sea urchins are common (and grow very large) and sea cucumbers are frequently recorded. Starfish are plentiful, with the common, purple, spiny, cushion, sun, feather and brittle stars all to be found.

Worms

Peacock-fan worms are found in sheltered waters and at the back of the deeper sea caves. Serpulid tubeworms are found on many of the rocky surfaces.

Anthozoa

Huge numbers of anemones form colonies which are characteristic in certain areas. Notable are *Sagartia, Bolocera, Cerianthus* (burrowing), *Corynactis* (jewel), *Metridium* (plumrose), *Actinia* (beadlet) and *Urticina* (dahlia). Cup coral (*Carophyllia*) is common, as is soft coral (*Alcyonium*).

Other Encrusting Life

Sponges (especially *Myxilla, Hymeniacidon, Ircinia* and *Halichondria*) are very common; tunicates (especially *Dendrodoa, Clavelina* and *Ciona*) abound. Hydroids (especially *Tubularia*) are well represented, particularly in surge gullies.

Drifting Life

Aurelia, Cyanea and *Rhizostoma* jellyfish are common, as are sea gooseberries and comb jellies. Long strings of salps are also prevalent at the right time of the season. By-the-wind-sailors sometimes occur in large shoals.

The polar oceans of the world also have very abundant marine life, although the variety of species is somewhat limited. The large sea creatures of high latitudes – such as polar bears, walruses, seals, killer and other whales – should provide excitement aplenty for any diver.

Many early divers entered the sport as spearfishermen. Nowadays, most underwater hunting is done with a camera. Many marine life enthusiasts have formed groups whose objective is to protect marine life and preserve it for future generations to enjoy. In Britain, the Marine Conservation Society is in the forefront of this conservation effort.

Only the briefest introduction to marine life can be given here, but many publications can be found which will provide more detailed information.

How to Select Good Dive Sites

Most of us work in towns and cities and the actual time available for our sport is rather limited. Thus, we must make the most of the time we have available. This means carefully picking the best time of the year to maximize our chances of getting good weather and good underwater visibility.

However, there is one factor that is even more important and that is the choosing of the actual dive sites themselves. So how are good sites selected? You should think very carefully and analytically about a number of factors, including seeking out good information by means of research. What are the sources of information?

Sources of Diving Information
It is essential that you research your intended diving area as much as possible. The time and money spent on this are hardly ever wasted.

Diving Guidebooks and Magazines
Many short dive guides are produced from time to time covering specific areas, but most are not readily available. The same applies to magazine articles covering both general areas and detailed wreck sites.

Other Divers
An important source of information is experienced divers and clubs or centres based in the intended area. It is always worthwhile writing to them prior to a diving visit in a new locality. Lists may be available from the club's headquarters.

Nautical Charts
You must also refer to nautical charts for your area. There is no substitute for the information that can be gleaned from a precise examination. Regrettably, however, large-scale charts often do not exist for the areas where divers most need them.

Ordnance Survey Maps
In Britain we are extremely fortunate to have access to a superb range of land maps. The series which are of use to divers are:

> The obsolete 1:63 360 (1-inch) series. This is the only series to show isobaths (submarine contours). These are a valuable guide, since the British Admiralty does not systematically chart the coast on a large scale. Most libraries have complete sets of the 189 sheets covering Britain.
> The 1:50 000 standard map. This series is intended for walking and coastal explorations and you should have the ones covering the areas you intend to visit.
> The 1:25 000 series. This shows good detail and is much better than the 1:50 000, although quite a large number is required if you are visiting a sizeable area.
> The 1:10 000 series. This is superb for minute coastal detail and is very useful for small, intricate pieces of coast where no good chart exists.

Obviously, other countries have their own mapping agencies. The effort spent in acquiring detailed maps is always worthwhile.

Geological Maps
In Britain, the 1:50 000 coastal geological maps can be an unsuspected source of information for divers. If you compare these carefully with the Ordnance Survey maps of the same scale you can gain useful data.

Air Photographs
These are available for many areas of the world. A full set exists for the British coast. Detailed examination of these can yield considerable information about coastal sites.

Admiralty Publications
Many of the British Admiralty publications are very useful to divers and deserve to be much more widely known. It is wise to consult those listed that cover your plans.

The Admiralty *Sailing Directions* (or *Pilots*) describe coastlines and shallow rocks in great detail and are an invaluable source of information, especially on tidal streams. Independent organizations also produce sailing directions for many of the more popular sailing areas of the world.

It is vital to have tide tables and tidal-stream data. The Admiralty tide tables, published annually, are the definitive source of information. The Admiralty also publishes tidal-stream atlases, mainly for British waters.

The Admiralty publishes lists of lights and radio signals. However, similar information, together with tidal data and much other general information, is published in various nautical almanacs.

Using the Information
A close examination of charts reveals depths in general, the sites of underwater shoals and reefs, where isobaths run close together or even disappear into each other, and the location of foul ground. They will also give tidal data in narrows and around headlands.

Large-scale land maps will enable you to find and examine fine coastal detail, especially on rugged headlands. They will also enable you to locate launch spots to suit your boat. Finally, they can be a guide where no detailed chart is produced. They do not give depths (except the obsolete 1-inch series), although the fine detail of coastal features can sometimes give an indication.

The rock type can be determined from geological maps. Where this is soft and the coast is eroding without the presence of strong tidal streams, then the coast will probably be shallow and the bottom covered with sediment. Where the rock is harder, there may well be underwater cliffs, especially if tidal streams are strong. This is also a function of raised beaches and submarine shelves, as these determine depths close to the shore.

Geological maps will also show where dykes run into the sea. If these are softer than the surrounding rock, they will erode to form channels, which often make spectacular dives. Geological faults can also allow selective erosion into channels, gullies and tunnels. Conversely, if the intruded rock in a dyke is hard, then it will form a rocky reef which, on a sediment-covered bottom, will present an oasis for the colonization of life.

The angle at which rocks dip towards the earth can also indicate good dive sites. If the dip is towards the land, then big sea cliffs can be formed, whereas when the dip faces the sea a series of ledged terraces will be formed. Inclined rocks can erode to provide ledges and crevices which marine life will colonize. When rocks which are prone to erosion form the bottom, they may well erode to form overhangs under which solitary fish often make their home.

Specific Factors

Wrecks

The wreck diver will be well aware that wrecks are best preserved in deeper water. Shallow-water wrecks have the unfortunate habit of breaking up. Wooden wrecks break up and disappear faster than metal ones. Usually, all that remains of old wooden wrecks are fragments and artefacts. As a general rule, the bigger, deeper and newer, the better!

However, the time spent on research and the dry search is never wasted. A couple of hours on the surface in an uncomfortable sea is infinitely preferable to committing divers to the water too soon and wasting the day.

Marine Life

Divers interested in marine life will use their own criteria for good dives. For the rest of us it is well to remember that life is richest where there is strong tidal flow because the whole food chain is supported by the plankton drifting past. Various habitats are favoured by different types of marine life, so select your site according to what you wish to observe. Wrecks also provide an excellent artificial reef habitat for life.

Photography

The underwater photographer usually wants good underwater scenery, such as rocks, boulders, cliffs, channels and tunnels. He also wants good life and good wrecks. Then he needs good visibility, just like all the other divers!

Summary

We must differentiate between locating good sites in general and making sure we arrive at the sites when conditions are favourable. The factors discussed above always apply, but there are other factors that are more variable. The main ones are the weather and underwater visibility. Of course, the latter is somewhat controlled by the former.

Finding good sites is not always easy, but these principles may help. As in most things, there is nothing to beat good information, coupled with patience, perseverance and common sense, and all assisted by a generous portion of plain good luck!

Figure 264 An interesting prospective dive site with protected parts and swift tidal currents

British Diving Locations

Figure 265

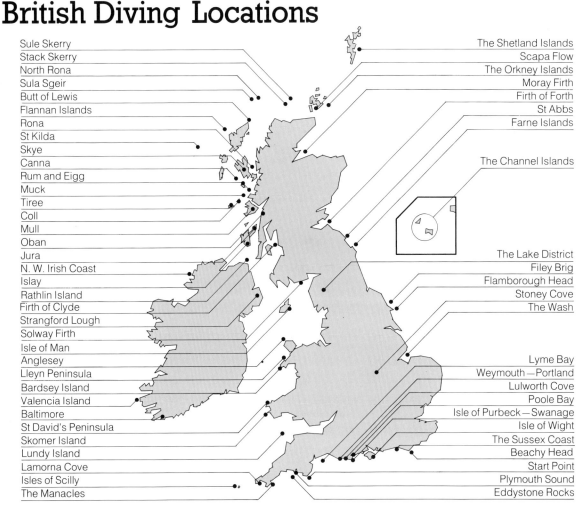

Sule Skerry
Stack Skerry
North Rona
Sula Sgeir
Butt of Lewis
Flannan Islands
Rona
St Kilda
Skye
Canna
Rum and Eigg
Muck
Tiree
Coll
Mull
Oban
Jura
N. W. Irish Coast
Islay
Rathlin Island
Firth of Clyde
Strangford Lough
Solway Firth
Isle of Man
Anglesey
Lleyn Peninsula
Bardsey Island
Valencia Island
Baltimore
St David's Peninsula
Skomer Island
Lundy Island
Lamorna Cove
Isles of Scilly
The Manacles

The Shetland Islands
Scapa Flow
The Orkney Islands
Moray Firth
Firth of Forth
St Abbs
Farne Islands

The Channel Islands

The Lake District
Filey Brig
Flamborough Head
Stoney Cove
The Wash

Lyme Bay
Weymouth—Portland
Lulworth Cove
Poole Bay
Isle of Purbeck—Swanage
Isle of Wight
The Sussex Coast
Beachy Head
Start Point
Plymouth Sound
Eddystone Rocks

Visibility is best at the southwesterly and northwesterly extremities of Britain, and particularly off the western headlands and the outlying rocky islands.

Marine life exhibits the greatest variety in the southwest, although the northwest is almost as good. The life in the North Sea is different and perhaps not generally as prolific.

Area Survey

What follows is a brief summary of diving around the UK, starting in northeast England and circling the coast in an approximately clockwise direction. Only the main areas and diving trends will be picked out and, consequently, many details are omitted.

Lying just off the Northumbrian coast, the Farne Islands provide excellent diving in clear water down rocky walls to depths of about 20 metres. The extremities of the islands experience strong tidal streams, and the outer islets have substantial seal populations. Both these and seabirds can be seen underwater.

The Yorkshire coast is heavily dived by local diving groups, especially at Flamborough Head and Filey Brig. There are several interesting offshore wrecks. The visibility is often rather poor, although it can occasionally be quite good. Generally, the seabed slopes gently out to sea and the whole coast is heavily exposed to easterly and north easterly winds.

The southeast coast from the Wash to the Isle of Wight has been the scene of much maritime activity over the years and this makes this section of particular interest to those interested in wrecks of all ages. The visibility and life can be disappointing at certain times of the year as the coast is relatively shallow.

The south coast west of the Isle of Wight begins to take on a more rugged character and improves as one moves west. The deepwater wrecks in the Channel provide challenging diving for many local diving groups, with Weymouth being a base for much diving activity.

Devon and Dorset have a much more interesting coast for divers, partly because there are many more bays and headlands. The visibility is quite good and the marine life is very varied and there are many wrecks.

There is the challenge of diving at the Eddystone Rocks, 12 miles offshore. Diving facilities are generally quite good and the area has many spots which are popular with divers from all over the country.

Cornwall provides some of the best diving in England. The visibility is usually excellent and marine life profuse. There are large numbers of wrecks at a variety of depths. Tidal streams are strong and there are many dangerous reefs.

The Scilly Isles lie off the coast of Cornwall. Again, excellent visibility is usually experienced. There are many wrecks, but most of these are well broken up because of the relatively shallow depth.

Lundy lies in the Bristol Channel and yields superb diving on life-filled rocky walls. The island is a marine nature reserve.

West Wales has good diving around the rocky headlands and the islands of Skokholm and Skomer. The visibility is often quite good and the marine life is plentiful at all depths. The tidal streams can be significant.

Anglesey and North Wales are popular areas for divers from northern England, as well as North Wales. The Lleyn peninsula also has pleasant diving. The visibility can be disappointing but there are many wrecks. Being an island, Anglesey offers shelter in any weather conditions.

Northwest England has generally poor diving off industrial coasts. The Solway Firth, off the Cumbrian coast, yields disappointing diving.

The Isle of Man has good, varied diving and usually provides a sheltered site. Marine life and tides are much in evidence.

Northern Ireland has superb diving, especially on the west coast. There are many wrecks as well as much marine life and considerable depths. The west coast is heavily exposed to the Atlantic swell and to storms. Tides and visibility can both be of some magnitude.

The greater Clyde Estuary in southwest Scotland is a very popular area among local divers. There are many large, deep wrecks resulting from the heavy surface shipping. The visibility is moderate to poor, with the deep wrecks being very dark. Generally, the marine life is rather poor.

The western seaboard of Scotland has legendary diving amidst clear waters on rocky shoals and cliffs washed by many tidal streams. Most of the coast has the advantage of being well sheltered.

The Inner Hebrides of Islay and Jura provide excellent diving. Islay is rather flat but has a diving centre. It has strong tides and many major wrecks, although many of these are well broken up. The area centred on Oban (in which we include the Inner Hebrides of Mull, Coll and Tiree, together with the major inlet of Loch Linnhe and its associated sea lochs) is extremely popular with divers. The diving is excellent and includes many substantial wrecks, rich marine life, strong tidal streams, good visibility, depths to 50 metres, and good shelter in the event of rough weather. The Hebridean islands of Rum, Eigg, Muck, Canna (the Small Isles) and Skye offer exceptional diving in very clear waters. There are huge submarine walls and a number of big wrecks. Tidal streams can generally be quite strong, very strong in places.

The northwest coast of Scotland gives diving of a very high calibre indeed. Marine life is profuse and visibility excellent.

The clear waters of the Outer Hebrides are well known. The southern end of the Outer Hebrides consists of a long string of small islands which offer memorable diving. The northern tip of Lewis – the Butt of Lewis – has some of the best shallow, scenic diving in UK waters.

Rocky islets lying west and north of the Outer Hebrides – Rockall, St Kilda, Flannan Isles, Sulasgeir, North Rona, Sule Skerry and Stack Skerry – offer, perhaps, Britain's best diving. They are remote and challenging, the visibility is enormous, the marine life profuse and colourful, and the depths can be considerable.

St Kilda demands special mention. Beyond argument, it offers the best scenic diving in North European waters. The visibility and life (both marine and terrestrial) are fabulous! Depths reach beyond 50 metres and the rock scenery, above and below the surface, virtually defies description. The submarine walls, overhangs, archways, tunnels and caves leave nothing to be desired.

The north coast of Scotland has very good scenic diving, running from the cliffs of Cape Wrath to the vast tidal areas of the Pentland Firth.

Orkney offers good diving in clear water, with large numbers of wrecks scattered amongst the northern islands. Tides and depths can be considerable.

Scapa Flow lies at the south of the Orkney Islands and is too good to miss. It is Nirvana for the wreck diver as it contains the highest concentration of shipwrecks in the world! After the First World War the German High Seas Fleet was scuttled here, and seven enormous wrecks remain, along with many others too numerous to mention.

The clear waters of the Shetland Isles are full of life and offer superb diving among cliffs, shoals and tidal streams. These islands have been likened to St Kilda – high praise indeed.

The eastern seaboard of Scotland is somewhat disappointing. Generally, it is muddy, with only moderate to poor visibility, and with depths falling gradually out to sea.

The Firth of Forth has poor visibility but many shipwrecks. It is popular with local divers.

The fresh-water sites in the UK are important to many diving groups. The lakes of England and Wales offer good training facilities, although they are generally rather muddy with often rather poor visibility and little life. Most of the lochs of Scotland are dived infrequently because they are full of very deep, brown, peaty water, but there are some notable exceptions. Flooded gravel pits and reservoirs provide popular training sites in the south of England.

World Diving Locations

Figure 266

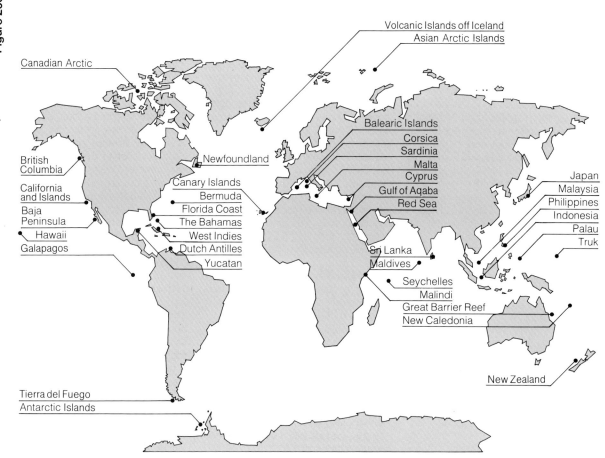

Canadian Arctic

Volcanic Islands off Iceland
Asian Arctic Islands

British Columbia
California and Islands
Baja Peninsula
Hawaii
Galapagos

Newfoundland
Canary Islands
Bermuda
Florida Coast
The Bahamas
West Indies
Dutch Antilles
Yucatan

Balearic Islands
Corsica
Sardinia
Malta
Cyprus
Gulf of Aqaba
Red Sea

Japan
Malaysia
Philippines
Indonesia
Palau
Truk

Sri Lanka
Maldives

Seychelles
Malindi
Great Barrier Reef
New Caledonia

New Zealand

Tierra del Fuego
Antarctic Islands

This can only be a brief glimpse at the many and varied diving locations available to the travelling diver. If any part sounds good to you, then be sure to look for more detailed information in other sources.

International Diving Influences
Sport diving started in the South of France, and the Mediterranean countries still play an important part in world diving.

The British influence on world diving has been very significant and the British Sub-Aqua Club has been at the forefront of developments in diving and training techniques. The way that the BSAC is organized is envied by many overseas divers. About 17 per cent of BSAC members

are overseas and the many overseas branches have spread BSAC influence over large parts of the world.

The American influence on world diving has probably been the most significant factor in recent years and now the American domination of western hemisphere and Pacific diving is almost complete. Diving and training are largely organized through diving stores. There are a number of training agencies, including NAUI, PADI and the YMCA.

Dive Sites Around the World
Diving in Britain has been surveyed on pp. 240–241 and the only areas of international importance are Scapa

Flow, St Kilda and the western seaboard of Scotland.

Scandinavia has much to offer the exploratory diver. The fiord coast of Norway has superb diving in clear and potentially very deep water, although the marine life is rather sparse.

The Norwegian coastline would extend from the north pole to the equator if stretched out! The volcanic islands off south Iceland have splendid diving on deep, submarine shoals with huge numbers of different kinds of fish.

In many ways the Mediterranean has been the cradle of sport diving. The waters are clear and quite warm. The fish life is much depleted, although the life improves in the eastern Mediterranean. Sites range from Spain, southern France and Italy to Greece and North Africa. The islands of Sardinia, Corsica, Malta and Cyprus all have diving centres and better than average diving.

The Red Sea has exceptional diving in clear, warm water and on coral reefs teeming with fish. The area is very popular with British and European divers, as it is the coral reef habitat closest to Western Europe. The area can be covered by visiting Israel for the Gulf of Eilat, Egypt for the southern Sinai peninsula, and Sudan for the western shores of the Red Sea.

Many divers have explored in some detail the myriad islands in the Caribbean Sea. A large number of coral reefs and drop-offs occur and the fish life is profuse, although perhaps not quite so varied as in the Red Sea. There are many diving facilities and charter boats available and most of these are advertised in the American diving magazines.

Florida and its Keys are very popular with American divers. The comments about the Caribbean also apply here. Diving is organized through the local dive stores and centres.

The waters off the northeastern USA are much cooler; wreck diving is very popular among the local divers.

Fresh-water diving and cavern diving are popular in continental USA since many divers live vast distances from the coast.

California and its islands are heavily dived and might be thought of as the home of American diving. The waters are quite warm, becoming very warm in the south. There are many diving facilities. The lagoons of the Baja peninsula in Mexico are the breeding grounds of the grey whale and, consequently, many diving charter vessels visit them.

British Columbia, in western Canada, has an extensive fiord coast and the diving is similar to that of Scotland and Norway.

The Caribbean coast of Central America offers a number of rich diving areas, the best-served being Honduras and the Yucatan peninsula of Mexico.

South America has not been significantly explored by divers. The rugged fiord coast of Tierra del Fuego must have great potential. There is little information on the other coasts of South America.

Antarctica and its islands again have a great potential for exciting diving. Some of the islands have been dived by British Antarctic Survey divers, but vast unexplored tracts remain.

Australia has a great variety of diving, although, in international terms, it is the Great Barrier Reef that is important. This is the greatest natural feature on earth, stretching for 1500 miles along the northeast coast of the continent. The corals and fish life are extremely diverse and the area is the Mecca of diving. There are several diving centres and charter vessels available.

New Zealand diving is not so well known although it is very good. The New Zealand continental shelf is, in fact, as large in area as the mainland USA. The water varies from temperate in the south to subtropical in the north. The marine life, consequently, is very varied. The offshore volcanic islands of the North Island have especially rich undersea communities.

Micronesia, and especially the island of Palau, is very special in diving terms. The diversity of marine life is greater here than anywhere else on our planet. From here, the life gradually diminishes in terms of variety of species, although the actual numbers of individuals increase as the more northern waters are approached.

The Pacific Islands offer superb diving and a great many are unexplored. The coral reefs abound with fish in clear, tropical waters. There is also Truk Lagoon, where the remains of the Japanese Second World War fleet lie.

To the east of the Pacific lie the very special Galapagos Islands. The marine life here is possibly slightly disappointing when compared with the unusual terrestrial life. The diving is curious, amidst volcanic features and in waters created by the mixing of hot and cold currents.

The diving of eastern Asia is virtually unknown in western circles. The great rivers carry down vast amounts of muddy sediment, but away from these there must be good diving. The visibility around Hong Kong is rather disappointing. Japan's rocky shores are explored by many local divers and may have international potential.

The Indian Ocean has splendid diving off East Africa and on the islands of the Maldives and the Seychelles. The fish life of the islands can occasionally be a little disappointing, but the waters are warm and clear. There are diving facilities in all these areas.

Figure 267   Diving a tropical drop-off

Appendix 1: BSAC Diving Qualifications

Qualifications Awarded by the National Snorkellers Club
Snorkeller Award
Not necessarily a member of the club, the holder is usually a youngster. He has successfully completed a BSAC Snorkeller Award Course and is qualified to use basic equipment in the pool only.
Advanced Snorkeller
As above, but in this case he will be a member of the National Snorkellers Club. He will have completed the open-water snorkel Test D and will have logged not less than six open-water snorkel dives.
Snorkel Instructor Certificate
This is awarded to physical education teachers or youth leaders who have passed an examination which allows them to train and examine youngsters for the Snorkeller Award.

National Snorkellers Club Qualifications
On joining a branch of the BSAC as a full member, youngsters who have trained within a branch of the BSAC-NSC should be given the following consideration: holders of the Snorkeller Award should be credited with those parts of training which are recorded in their NSC logbook and may progress immediately to aqualung training so long as all other requirements are met (e.g. age, fitness, etc.).

The NSC Snorkel Instructor Certificate is not a BSAC diving qualification as such, and open-water snorkelling experience is not required. Holders of this standard who wish to become full members of the BSAC should be credited with those parts of the training lectures which apply to Novice Diver and may progress immediately with pool aqualung training.

Qualifications Awarded by BSAC-Recognized Diving Schools
Persons who receive instruction at a BSAC-recognized diving school may obtain the following qualifications.
BSAC Novice Diver Certificate
The Novice Diver certificate is issued by BSAC-recognized diving schools and is identical to the BSAC award of the same name. The holders are not obliged to take out BSAC membership.
BSAC Sports Diver Qualifications
BSAC schools may award Sports Diver qualifications to holders of the Novice Diver certificate who subsequently join the BSAC (general branch or the special branch attached to the diving school) and who complete the necessary qualifying dives and theory test.

Qualifications Awarded at Branch Level
The BSAC system of training is a continuous process which gives a clear path from novice to highly experienced diver. The path has a number of reference points to which current ability and experience can be related. These reference points are the qualifications of Novice Diver, Sports Diver, Dive Leader, Advanced Diver

and First-Class Diver. From time to time, as the sport develops, the test requirements leading to BSAC diving qualifications are reviewed and, after national agreement, adjusted to suit the following definitions:
Novice Diver
A diver who is competent in the safe and correct use of all appropriate open-water aqualung diving equipment in a sheltered-water training area and is ready to gain open-water diving experience in the company of a dive leader or more highly qualified diver/instructor.
Sports Diver (CMAS Two-Star Diver)
A diver who has gained some open-water diving experience and is considered ready to take part in dives partnered by a diver of the same, or higher, grade. A Sports Diver will not have sufficient experience to take a Novice Diver on open-water dives.
Dive Leader
An active, experienced and responsible diver, competent in dive leadership, who may lead others on open-water dives.
Advanced Diver (CMAS Three-Star Diver)
A fully trained and responsible diver who is competent to organize and lead branch diving activities. (Qualifications of Novice Diver, Sports Diver, Dive Leader and Advanced Diver are awarded by the branch committee.)

Nationally Awarded Qualifications
First-Class Diver (CMAS Four-Star Diver)
An Advanced Diver who has attained a higher than average level of knowledge and ability, assessed through nationally conducted examinations and able to utilize divers and diving in order to achieve major tasks or project objectives.

Once awarded, BSAC diving qualifications can only be withdrawn by the National Diving Officer of the club.

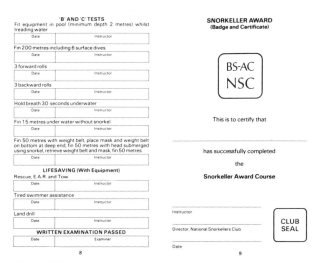

Figure 268

Instructor Qualifications

In addition to these diving qualifications, the following instructor qualifications are also available:

BSAC Club Instructor (CMAS One-Star Instructor)
An Advanced Diver who has attended an Instructor training course and passed a Club Instructor examination. The qualification entitles the holder to take a leading part in the training and testing of members in the pool. He is considered to have a good knowledge of practical and theoretical teaching methods.

BSAC Advanced Instructor (CMAS Two-Star Instructor)
A BSAC Club Instructor who has passed an Advanced Instructor examination. He is considered to have a thorough knowledge of practical and theoretical teaching methods and is capable of instructing members both in the pool and in open water.

BSAC National Instructor (CMAS Three-Star Instructor)
A BSAC Advanced Instructor who has passed a National Instructor examination. This is the highest instructional grade available in the BSAC. The holder is expected to be a completely competent instructor, with a wide experience of diving and an extensive knowledge of practical and theoretical teaching methods. He is most likely to be engaged in training members on a regional or national level.

International Recognition of BSAC Diving Qualifications

Through the World Underwater Federation (CMAS) the BSAC has gained international recognition of its diving and instructional qualifications. These international certificates are particularly useful when diving overseas and can be supplied to members by club headquarters.

The CMAS uses the star rating for each diving grade,

Figure 269a

Figure 269b

and the preceding paragraphs showing the qualifications awarded at branch and national level include the CMAS equivalent for each BSAC grade.

Figure 269c

ADVANCED DIVER QUALIFYING DIVES

10 open water dives to be completed from at least 5 different sites and on at least 5 different dates. Each dive to have a minimum submerged duration of 15 minutes: Total duration of the 10 dives to be not less than 5 hours. Dives should show experience of any 4 of the following:— Night dive/Zero visibility dive/Underwater Search/Recovery operation/Dive to 40 m/Dive with decompression stops/'No clear surface' dive.

Member to read notes on page 4 before recording dives here.

Type of Qualifying Dive	Date	Site	Dive details verified by

CERTIFICATION OF QUALIFYING DIVES

Date

Branch Diving Officer

22

ADVANCED DIVER QUALIFICATION

A fully trained, experienced and responsible diver who is competent to organise and lead Branch diving activities.

This is to certify that

has completed the required training
and is qualified to attend
open water meetings as a

BSAC ADVANCED DIVER

Branch Diving Officer

Branch Secretary

BRANCH STAMP

Date

★ ★ ★

(Equivalent to CMAS Three Star Diver)
Formerly known as BSAC Second Class Diver.

23

Appendix 2: The Diver's Code of Conduct

The British Sub-Aqua Club

More and more people are taking to the water, some for recreation, some to earn their living. This code is designed to ensure that divers do not come into conflict with other water users. It is vital that you observe it at all times.

Before Leaving Home

Contact the nearest British Sub-Aqua Club branch or the dive operator local to the dive site for advice about the local conditions and regulations.

On the Beach, River Bank or Lakeside

1. Obtain permission before diving in a harbour or estuary or in private water. Thank those responsible before you leave. Pay harbour dues.
2. Try to avoid overcrowding one site; consider other people on the beach.
3. Park sensibly. Avoid obstructing narrow approach roads. Keep off verges. Pay parking fees and use proper car parks.
4. Do not spread yourselves and your equipment since you may upset other people. Keep launching ramps and slipways clear.
5. Please keep the peace. Do not operate a compressor within earshot of other people or late at night.
6. Pick up litter. Close gates. Be careful about fires. Avoid any damage to land or crops.
7. Obey special instructions such as National Trust rules, local byelaws and regulations about camping and caravanning.
8. Remember divers in wetsuits are conspicuous and bad behaviour could ban us from beaches.

In and on the Water

1. Mark your diving boats so that your club can be identified easily. Unmarked boats may become suspect.
2. Ask the harbourmaster or local officials where to launch your boat and do as they say. Tell the coastguard or a responsible person where you are going and when you are back.
3. Stay away from buoys, lobsterpots and pot markers. Ask local fishermen where not to dive. Offer to help them recover lost gear.
4. Remember ships have not got brakes, so avoid diving in fairways or areas of heavy surface traffic and observe the *International Regulations for the Prevention of Collisions at Sea.*

5. Always fly the diving flag when diving, but not when on the way to or from the dive site. Never leave a boat unattended.
6. Do not come in to bathing beaches under power. Use any special approach lanes. Do not disturb any seal or bird colonies with your boats. Watch your wash in crowded anchorages.
7. Whenever possible, divers should use a surface marker buoy.

On Conservation

1. Never use a speargun with an aqualung. Never use a speargun in fresh water.
2. Shellfish, such as crabs and lobsters, take several years to grow to maturity; overcollecting in an area soon depletes stocks. Only take mature fish or shellfish and then only what you need for yourself. Never sell your catch or clean it in public or on the beach. Do not display your trophies.
3. Be conservation conscious. Avoid damage to weeds and the seabed. Do not bring up sea fans, corals, starfish or sea urchins – in one moment you can destroy years of growth.
4. Take photographs and notes, not specimens. Shoot with a camera not a speargun – spearfishing makes fish shy of divers. Never spearfish wrasse or other inshore species since once an area is depleted of such fish it may take a long time for them to recolonize.

On Wrecks

1. Do not dive on a designated wreck site. These are indicated on Admiralty charts and marked by buoys or warning notices on the shore nearby.
2. Do not lift anything which appears to be of historical importance.
3. If you do discover a wreck, do not talk about it. Pinpoint the site, do a rough survey and report it to the BSAC Archaeology Adviser and the Council for Nautical Archaeology, who will advise you.
4. If you do not lift anything from the wreck, it is not necessary to report your discovery to the Receiver of Wreck. If you do lift something, you must report it.
5. If your find is important, you may apply for it to be designated a protected site. Then you can build up a well-qualified team with the right credentials and proceed with a systematic survey or excavation under licence without outside interference.

Do not let divers down – keep to the diver's code.

Appendix 3: Trouble at Sea

Search and rescue operations are co-ordinated by HM Coastguard; they can call on the inshore rescue boats and the large seagoing lifeboats of the Royal National Lifeboat Institution (RNLI), other ships, aircraft and helicopters of the Royal Navy and the Royal Air Force and the police and other organizations. *All this is not to be lightly invoked.*

If needing help but not in distress, use the International Flag signal V or the Morse Code signal V (· · · –): 'I require assistance.' To draw attention to the signal, it is permissible to fire a white flare.

The signal W (in Morse · – –) is used when medical assistance is needed.

Recognized Distress Signals
Radio and Morse
The Morse Code SOS (· · · – – – · · ·) made by lamp, radio or sound, and the 'MAYDAY' call by radiotelephone.
International Distress Frequencies
Radio telephone 2182 kHz; Radio Channel 16 VHF (156·8 MHz). Repeat 'MAYDAY' three times, give the name of the vessel and your position. State the nature of the trouble and what action you are taking. A listening watch is maintained by the coastguard on Channel 16 (156·8 MHz) which is also the safety calling frequency for maritime VHF. If, later on, assistance is no longer required, cancel the distress signal.

HM Coastguard Maritime Rescue Centres are on constant watch on VHF Channel 16.

Coastguard call signs give the name of the centre (see map) followed by 'Coastguard' – for example, 'Solent Coastguard'.

Channel 67 is the small-boat safety frequency.

Channels 16 and 67 are your most important radio links – make sure both are included in your radio equipment.

When using VHF Radio, remember:

> To listen out before calling.
> To call the station you need *once*; then, if necessary, call again after a short interval.
> To be brief. Decide what you want to say before going on the air.
> If you or others are in distress, give the following information:
> name and call sign
> position
> nature of distress and assistance needed
> number of crew
> intentions

Pyrotechnic Signals
Inshore, up to 3 miles out, use red handflares and orange smoke signals; in coastal waters use two-star red flares or red parachute rockets; offshore, use red parachute rockets. In coastal or offshore waters, let off the first two signals close together within about two minutes. Keep back at least one red handflare (in darkness, gale or poor visibility) or orange smoke (for daylight in light winds) to

signal your position to approaching rescuers.
Hold flares well away from you and fire downwind.
Other Signals
In small boats, slowly and repeatedly raising and lowering outstretched arms or an article of clothing on an oar.

The flag signal NC or a square flag having above or below it anything resembling a ball.

The continuous sounding of a siren or whistle.
Answering Signals
Answering signals made by lifesaving stations when distress signals are seen are:

> In daylight an orange smoke signal.
> At night three white star rockets are fired at one-minute intervals.

Disposing of Out-of-Date Flares
Never fire out-of-date flares either at sea or on land. Flares deteriorate with age. Time-expired flares can be unpredictable.

Do not use them as fireworks.

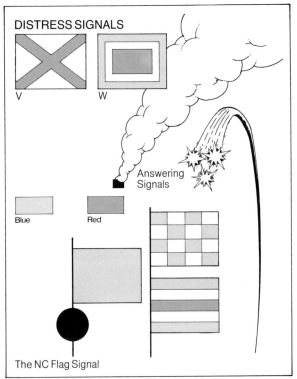

Figure 270 Distress signals

Appendix 4: Safety at Sea

Weather-Wise

An up-to-date weather forecast is essential for divers – bad weather probably causes about 80 per cent of all incidents. So, if you are shore diving or taking a boat out, be sure to get the latest forecast and remember – it is often rougher than it looks from shore!

Details of weather services in the British Isles can be obtained via the press, radio, television and coastal stations. Most local authorities and harbour masters post local forecasts outside their offices. You can get forecasts from the nearest meteorological office or dial the telephone weather service (number in the local telephone directory). You can find out about local sea conditions by telephoning the local coastguard.

Sea and Swell

Sea Waves caused by wind at a given place.

Swell Waves formed by past wind, or wind at a distance.

Short swell The length or distance between each successive wave is small.

Long swell The length or distance between each successive wave is large.

Low swell The height between the lowest and highest part of a wave is small.

Heavy swell The height between the lowest and highest part of a wave is great.

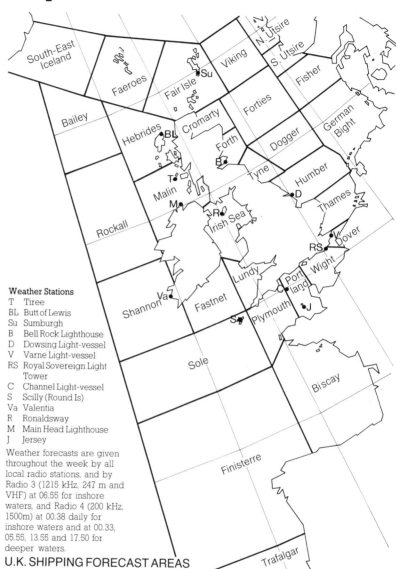

Figure 271

Weather Stations

T   Tiree
BL Butt of Lewis
Su Sumburgh
B   Bell Rock Lighthouse
D   Dowsing Light-vessel
V   Varne Light-vessel
RS Royal Sovereign Light Tower
C   Channel Light-vessel
S   Scilly (Round Is)
Va Valentia
R   Ronaldsway
M   Main Head Lighthouse
J   Jersey

Weather forecasts are given throughout the week by all local radio stations, and by Radio 3 (1215 kHz, 247 m and VHF) at 06.55 for inshore waters, and Radio 4 (200 kHz, 1500m) at 00.38 daily for inshore waters and at 00.33, 05.55, 13.55 and 17.50 for deeper waters.

U.K. SHIPPING FORECAST AREAS

INTERNATIONAL SWELL SCALE	
Code figure	State of the swell in the open sea
0	None
1	Short or average length; low
2	Long
3	Short
4	Average length; moderate height
5	Long
6	Short
7	Average length; heavy
8	Long
9	Confused

FOG AND VISIBILITY SCALE FOR SHIPS AT SEA		
Code number	Description	Definition
0	Dense fog	Objects not visible at 5 m
1	Thick fog	Objects not visible at 200 m
2	Fog	Objects not visible at 400 m
3	Moderate fog	Objects not visible at ½ ml
4	Mist or haze or very poor visibility	Objects not visible at 1 ml
5	Poor visibility	Objects not visible at 2 ml
6	Moderate visibility	Objects not visible at 5 ml
7	Good visibility	Objects not visible at 10 ml
8	Very good visibility	Objects not visible at 30 ml
9	Excellent visibility	Objects visible at more than 30 ml

BEAUFORT WIND SCALE (NUMBERS 1 TO 6 ONLY)

For an effective height of 10 metres above sea level.
* This table is only a rough guide as to what may be expected in the open sea. Small boats may be unsafe in conditions of Force 4 upwards and should *never* venture out to sea above Force 6. In enclosed waters or when near land with an offshore wind, wave heights will be smaller and the waves steeper. Figures in brackets indicate the probable maximum height of waves.

Beaufort number	Descriptive term	Mean wind speed equivalent in knots	Deep sea criterion	Probable mean wave height* in metres
0	Calm	<1	Sea like a mirror	—
1	Light air	1–3	Ripples with the appearance of scales are formed, but without foam crests	0·1 (0·1)
2	Light breeze	4–6	Small wavelets, still short but more pronounced; crests have a glassy appearance and do not break	0·2 (0·3)
3	Gentle breeze	7–10	Large wavelets; crests begin to break; foam of glassy appearance; perhaps scattered white horses	0·6 (1)
4	Moderate breeze	11–16	Small waves, becoming longer; fairly frequent white horses	1 (1·5)
5	Fresh breeze	17–21	Moderate waves, taking a more pronounced long form; many white horses are formed (chance of some spray)	2 (2·5)
6	Strong breeze	22–27	Large waves begin to form; the white foam crests are more extensive everywhere (probably some spray)	3 (4)

WHEN IS IT HIGH TIDE?

Tidal Constants Relative to High Water at London Bridge
Add (+) or subtract (−) to time at London Bridge. The places given in the table are listed anticlockwise, starting from the Thames Estuary.

Place	Hour/minute
Southend	−1.25
Clacton	−2.11
Felixstowe	−2.18
Aldeburgh	−3.23
Lowestoft	−4.26
Great Yarmouth	−4.55
Wells-next-the-Sea	+5.11
Skegness	+4.25
Grimsby	+4.2
Bridlington	+3.11
Scarborough	+2.43
Whitby	+2.19
West Hartlepool	+2.5
Sunderland	+2.0
Alnmouth	+1.22
Berwick-upon-Tweed	+0.55
Dunbar	+0.33
Leith	+0.41
Kirkcaldy	+0.38
Fife Ness	+0.20
Dundee	+1.11
Montrose	+0.30
Aberdeen	−0.20
Fraserburgh	−1.25
Lossiemouth	−2.0
Inverness	−1.38
Dornoch	−1.40
Golspie	−2.14
Wick	−2.28
Thurso	−5.31
Tongue	−6.6
Kylesku	+5.39
Ullapool	+5.29
Portree	+4.59
Plockton	+5.9
Mallaig	+4.26
Tobermory	+4.23
Oban	+4.13
Crinan	+3.33
Greenock	−1.32
Ayr	−1.52
Portpatrick	−2.38
Balcary Point	−2.12
Annan	−2.2
Whitehaven	−2.35
Barrow-in-Furness	−2.46
Morecambe	−2.36
Blackpool	−2.41
Wallasey	−2.37
Llandudno	−3.18
Holyhead	−3.32
Nefyn	−4.30
Barmouth	−5.47
Aberystwyth	−6.12
Cardigan	+5.40
Skomer	+4.28
Tenby	+4.28
Llanelly	+4.32
Swansea	+4.33
Porthcawl	+4.40
Barry	+5.13
Clevedon	+5.18
Burnham-on-Sea	+5.17
Ilfracombe	+4.28
Padstow	+4.8
St Ives	+3.43
Lizard	+3.20
Falmouth	+3.36
Plymouth	+3.54
Salcombe	+4.6
Torquay	+4.39
Lyme Regis	+4.46
Weymouth	+5.5
Swanage	−3.23
Cowes	−2.30
Ventnor	−2.50
Southsea	−2.28
Bognor Regis	−2.28
Brighton	−2.38
Hastings	−2.47
Dover	−2.42
Margate	−2.1
Sheerness	−1.19

(Printed by permission of the Liverpool Observatory and Tidal Institute.)
NB: The times of high water at London Bridge or Dover may be obtained from the newspapers each day and from various almanacs and other publications.

COASTGUARD MARITIME RESCUE CENTRES

Coastguard Rescue Centres and Telephone Numbers

ABERDEEN	0224 592334
Shetland	0595 2976
Pentland	0856 3268
Moray	0779 74278/9
Forth	0333 50666
YARMOUTH	0493 851338
Tyne/Tees	091 257 2691
Humber	0964 650351
DOVER	0304 210008
Thames	025 565518
FALMOUTH	0326 317575
Solent	0705 552100
Portland	0305 820441
Brixham	08045 58292
SWANSEA	0792 366534
Hartland	023 74641
Milford Haven	064 65218
Holyhead	0407 2051
Liverpool	051 931 3341
CLYDE	0475 29988
Ramsey	0624 813255
Belfast	0247 883184
Oban	0631 63720
Stornoway	0851 2013

In an emergency for coastal or sea rescue, dial 999 and ask for 'Coastguard'.

The above list may change from time to time.

Index

254

Photograph Acknowledgements

Thanks are due to the following for allowing the use of copyright photographs:

John Bantin, figures 53a, 54, 64, 103; Geoff Barker, figure 3; Steve Birchall, figure 8d; George Brown, figures 244e, 258a, c, d, f-j, 263c, e; Mike Busuttili, figures 2, 4, 5, 7a-d, 8e, 9a-e, 10c, 79, 112, 113, 114, 133, 156, 223a-d, 229, 231, 234, 255, 256c, 258b, 258e, 263b, 267; Richard Chesher, figure 244h; Dick Clarke, figures 233, 242; Mike Coltman, figure 257; Alan Crooke, figures 103, 246; Walter Deas, figure 244g; Diver Magazine, figures 1 (a Syndication International photograph), 7e; Colin Doeg, figures 238, 251b, c; Bernard Eaton, figure 251a; David George, figure 8f; Laurence Gould, figure 232; L.F. Grannis, figure 13; Jim Greenfield, figures 8c, 263d; J. Hazzard, figures 6, 10a, b; Mike Holbrook, figure 256b; Ken Lucas, figure 244f; John Lythgoe, figure 8a; Christian Petron, figures 8g, 226, 237, 250, 260; Mike Portelly, figure 247; Chris Prior, figure 263a; Gordon Ridley, figures 159b, 218, 219, 220, 221, 222, 264; Carl Roessler, figure 244d; Flip Schulke, figures 11a-c, 248; Peter Scoones, figures 159a, 244b, 262; Seaphot, figures 122, 216, 249; Herwath Voigtmann, figures 244a, b, i; Howard Wagstaff, figure 187; Roy Waller, figure 8b; Warren Williams, figure 259, 261

Illustrations provided by Rico Oldfield, Brian Croxford and David Sisman.

The British Sub-Aqua Club would like to express its appreciation to Twickers World, Club in Eilat, and Aqua-Sport Eilat for their assistance and hospitality while taking the front cover photograph for this manual.